NEW BRITISH DRAMA
IN PERFORMANCE ON THE LONDON STAGE: 1970 TO 1985

NEW BRITISH DRAMA IN PERFORMANCE ON THE LONDON STAGE: 1970 TO 1985

Richard Allen Cave

St. Martin's Press
New York

First published in the United States of America in 1988

Printed in Great Britain

ISBN 0–312–01912–2

Library of Congress Cataloging-in-Publication Data

Cave, Richard Allen
New British drama in performance on the
London stage, 1970 to 1985
Bibliography: p.
Includes index.
1. English drama—20th Century—History and
criticism. 2. Theater—England—London—History—
20th century. I. Title.
PR736.C28   1988   822'.914'09   87–35584

ISBN 0–312–01912–2

For Elizabeth:

*the ideal companion at the theatre
as in all things*

CONTENTS

PREFACE

To attempt a totally exhaustive study of new playwriting in England over a fifteen-year period would have been a gargantuan task and there would scarcely have been room to offer any criticism of substance about each play mentioned. Selection was inevitable: the problem was how to select in a way that would give a clear sense of the spirit of the age, the range and diversity of our contemporary drama. Some parameters I decided on were in a sense arbitrary: that plays discussed in detail had to have been staged professionally in London and be available in print; that only plays for the theatre be studied, even in the case of dramatists like Beckett, Hare or Stoppard, whose works over the period include some notable scripts for television, radio and film. Beyond this I have chosen to approach my subject through a variety of changing perspectives: each of the following chapters is devoted to the work of one or two dramatists who seem over the period to have aimed at and achieved the most original innovations in dramatic form and have in consequence created a distinctive personal style. Two of the playwrights under dicussion — Beckett and Pinter — already had by 1970 established reputations, but began to refine and develop their respective techniques in surprising ways which seem now with hindsight to be natural progressions but which in 1969 could not have been readily anticipated. Noticeably they alone among their contemporaries have effected this process of renewal. (Arden since *The Island of the Mighty* and *The Non-Stop Connolly Show* has turned his attention increasingly to radio. Osborne's output since *West of Suez* has been fitful; and, though in plays like *A Sense of Detachment* and *Watch It Come Down* his characteristic verbal energy was apparent, the searing anguish that once fuelled his great tirades had been reduced in scale to the peevishly vindictive and the substance seemed both dated and thin on observation and feeling, when compared with writing like Hare's *Plenty* or Bond's *The War Plays*. Tragically Wesker has not found a London venue for his large-scale works, like *The Wedding Feast* and *The Merchant*, since the R.S.C. abandoned its production of *The Journalists*; only

intimate plays like *The Friends* and chamber works such as *Caritas*
have been seen and of these only *The Old Ones* broke new ground
stylistically.) A further two of the dramatists in this conspectus —
Storey and Griffiths — flourished in only the early part of our
period as conspicuously dramatists of the seventies: they found a
personal style rapidly and as rapidly explored it seemingly to the
limits of its capacity for expression. The remaining four —
Stoppard, Ayckbourn, Hare and Bond — have over the last fifteen
years come fully into their powers and excitingly have begun to
undergo that process of change and renewal that has made Beckett
and Pinter continuing luminaries in our theatre.

A select band of eight writers, however major their apparent
status, cannot give the full flavour of a period. I have endeavoured
to overcome this deficiency by two methods. Either I have
broadened the discussion of a particular play (as in the chapters
devoted to Pinter, Storey and Griffiths) to include comparisons
with plays on similar themes that are handled in more conventional
formats or which attempt a different kind of technical or structural
innovation. Or, as in the remaining chapters, I have made the
study of the dramatist the focus of a debate about recent
developments in the handling of a particular *genre* or style:
Ayckbourn and Stoppard in the context of a discussion about new
forms of comedy since Joe Orton's death, for example; Hare in
the context of contemporary political drama; Bond of ways of
handling the history play. While this method has achieved the
breadth of scope I was aiming for, I am aware that some dramatists
have eluded detailed mention — John McGrath, Simon Gray and
Christopher Hampton to name but three. Omission is not intended
in any way to disparage their consistently fine achievement.

We live, we are often told, in an age of Directors' Theatre.
Obviously this is true where the traditional repertoire is concerned.
But the situation with new playwriting is different. George Devine
established the Royal Court back in 1956 as a Playwrights' Theatre
first and foremost, though it was also an Actors' Theatre too, since
Devine — himself a fine actor — directed in a way to enhance the
performer's artistry as a vehicle for the dramatist's. Though Devine
died at the start of the period I am discussing, his spirit and his
principles have lived on powerfully at the Court, even,
remarkably, with directors and artistic personnel who were not
directly trained by him. Despite the growth of London venues for
experimental drama — the Bush, the Half Moon, the Donmar
Warehouse, the Pit, the Cottesloe, the Studio at the Hammersmith
Lyric, the Young Vic, the Hampstead Theatre Club — the Royal

Court and its Theatre Upstairs remain the prime exhibition space for new talent: their policy, despite continuing financial crises, is as daring and as confidently sustained as in Devine's days as Artistic Director. The period 1970 to 1985 has seen several dramatists becoming directors of their own work — Beckett, Ayckbourn, Hare, Bond — and creating productions remarkable for their discipline where self-indulgence might have been expected. We have seen the formation of groups — Joint Stock is the most notable — where actors come together with a writer and a director and shape a play through improvisation around a given theme, pooling their creativity and diverse experiences. Several dramatists have found a particular actor's voice or stage personality afford an impulse to write: Beckett for Patrick Magee and Billie Whitelaw; Stoppard for Michael Hordern; Hare for Kate Nelligan; Bond for Yvonne Bryceland; and Pinter, while he denies writing for specific performers, always casts his plays so meticulously that one is left with the impression that he wrote with a particular group of actors in mind (casts in revivals of his work, however good, seem to lack a certain *authenticity* in their roles). I have endeavoured to reflect this close relation between the dramatist and the actor in the period by examining plays in the following chapters from the standpoint of their initial London productions, especially in cases where an actor's particular technique contributed immeasurably to the communication of the play's meaning in performance. I would wish this study to be as much a celebration of the art of the actor as of the dramatist.

There are many who have helped directly or indirectly in the writing of this study, whom I would wish to thank. Three colleagues and friends — Katharine Worth, Jackie Bratton and Inga-Stina Ewbank, with whom I have had the pleasure and privilege of teaching contemporary drama during these years: I have profited richly from their writing and conversation at work and while theatregoing. Winifred Bamforth, formerly of the Extra Mural Department in the University of London, created numerous occasions (in courses of special lectures and on the International Summer School for Graduates, which she ran magnificently for many years) when I could explore in lecture-form material which has subsequently found its way into these chapters. Mrs Foster, the Librarian at the British Theatre Association, has with her characteristic calm efficiency helped me repeatedly with my enquiries about texts, dates, details of casting. Lynne Truss, who has regularly commissioned reviews of plays from me for the Arts Page of the *Times Higher Education Supplement*, kindly agreed to my inclusion here of some of that material in an expanded form.

Lastly my wife, to whom this book is dedicated, has assisted at every stage of its composition, a lively critical presence always. I am profoundly grateful to them all.

Richard Allen Cave

NOTE

Many of the productions discussed in this study, especially those staged at the Royal Court, were photographed superbly by John Haynes. A collection of his work published by Thames and Hudson, *Taking the Stage* (1986), is an invaluable record of new British drama in performance on the London Stage since 1970 and, as such, is a visual counterpart to what is attempted in this series of essays. Rather than re-print here a small part of the wealth of material his book has made accessible, I would encourage the reader to study it alongside this one.

CHAPTER ONE

HAROLD PINTER

With Pinter's last two stage works of the Sixties, *Landscape* and *Silence* (Aldwych, 1969),[1] the prevailing tone of his writing changed: the pervasive sense of threat had gone, the nerviness that gave a slightly hysterical timbre to the laughter his wit provoked had relaxed. The fears and desires that give the characters their particular identities and condition the quality of the relationships they establish together had in former plays largely to be inferred by the audience from the fluctuating patterns of the characters' behaviour. In *Landscape* and *Silence* Pinter began pushing at the frontiers of realism in his work, extending them to encompass a more open statement about the reaches of the mind without losing touch with the characters' social being. When the psyche found expression in earlier plays it was always by indirect means: the gradual intrusion of innuendo into a seemingly flat, often stilted discourse; the obsessional monopolising of the dialogue by one character who indulges in an extended narrative; the retreat by another into a prolonged silence or his emergence from silence into a feverish volubility; a sudden enthusiasm when a character realises how easily a simple domestic object could become an effective weapon; the onset of compulsive, even at times manic, movement, as if a character were possessed. It is the conflict of psychological forces between the characters that controls how the action develops and dictates the pace of the dialogue; and what is seen and heard is a metaphor defining qualities of interior being.

Landscape and *Silence* reverse this structural equation: action is stylised almost to the point of being an emblematic *tableau*, movement in chronological time being arrested, as it were, at a point of significant tension, while the forces of the unconscious that have gone to the shaping of that image are given play and given voice. Even the settings had in performance an obvious symbolic quality that was quite new in Pinter's work: *Landscape* may have presented the familiar Pinter situation of a couple seated at a kitchen table, but John Bury's seemingly realistic design carried one rivetting surreal feature — an immense crack, a kind of chasm,

1

bisected the stage isolating the wife on a promontory-like fragment; the room, the recurring icon in Pinter's plays, established from the opening of his very first, was in every way here being broken up and opened out. *Silence* was set in a void of mirrored surfaces reflecting from multiple perspectives the one image of three figures, so close and yet emotionally so divided, physically so separated yet in the life of the mind such constant presences beside each other. The stage picture was at once beautiful yet formidable because relentless. Pinter's method here seemed to approach closer than ever before to Beckett's, presenting the audience with a startling image which it takes the duration of the play fully to expound and invest with meaning. But whereas Beckett's field of study is man's hunger for metaphysical satisfaction, Pinter's — at least in his recent work — is man's yearning for wholeness and permanence in his emotional being and the traps that the mind can spring against itself to keep it from a state of bliss. In *Landscape* and *Silence*, *Old Times* and *Betrayal*, the characters' sexual identities, their singularity, is defined more by the nature of their losses than their individual achievements and the pervasive mood is now elegaic. Both the one-act plays build up an impression of a wealth of desire in the characters that is overwhelmingly painful because unappeased, being either wholly unexpressed or expressed badly for want of a proper imaginative sympathy within the relationships. Sensitivity, kindliness, care, the characters possess to a degree, but they fail to let these be active principles because their energies are curtailed by a network of fears, inhibitions and prejudices.

Beth's whole being in *Landscape* is centred on a yearning for some transcendent sexual experience and motherhood — "Would you like a baby? I said. Children? Babies? Of our own? Would be nice." [p. 9] — and Duff patiently offers himself to her, but Beth retreats from his rough familiarity into a carefully articulated fantasy about a lover of infinite tenderness whose presence keeps her in a state of perpetual arousal but never forces her to consummation. The unnamed one is at once all-powerful yet totally submissive, so perfect a gentleman that he is no man; and Duff, resentful and hurt, manifests more and more strongly those aggressive aspects of male lust that set him apart from Beth's cherished ideal and foster terrors that compel her to retell her story to herself with ever greater attention to circumstantial detail in order to find calm and control. The more urgent her need for Duff, the more surely the particular nature of that need unmans him; the more desperate his want of Beth's affection and trust, the more keenly he insults her sense of her essential femininity. Desire sets up an antagonism that reduces Beth and Duff to cruel parodies of their fuller selves: he is betrayed into sadistic fury, real or imagined; she into the role of martyred victim. From this standpoint she cannot perceive how Duff is not without generosity of spirit, however gauche its expression; and he cannot appreciate in Beth the profound sensuality that lies behind her prim, spinsterish manner. The full poignance of the situation lies in the fact that the couple we see before us are elderly: Beth's withdrawal into herself has over the years rendered her virtually catatonic (throughout Duff always speaks directly to her, whereas Beth directs her gaze and speech unrelentingly at the audience). He speaks in the present at first with the tale of his day's exploits, but turns increasingly to memories of their past experiences together and crucially to his confession once of his infidelity and her willingness then to forgive him. It is as if he is searching for reasons to explain her lack of response till, mindful of her complete torpor, he speaks openly out of the cumulative weight of his despair uttering his fantasy-desires of treating her brutally like the object she makes him feel himself to be and of battering her into awareness. With an imperturbable composure, Beth speaks always out of an imagined past, a world of lost possibilities made real to fancy, where she is perennially young and virginal. The different threads of their separate narratives interweave, cut across each other, fall in startling juxtapositions and fade into silence. Always the stage picture of the elderly man talking to the ageing woman whose gaze is ever on vacancy stays unchanged: like the lifetime's experience which *Landscape* encapsulates, it can only intensify, never fundamentally develop. A tragic past and the bleakest of futures are contained in the present which is the duration of the performance, so compact and allusive is the structure of the play.

Action is similarly reduced to the narrative that is memory in *Silence* as the three lovers recall their tormented past together and, in remembering, recover all the anguish of that time: Ellen loving Rumsey and being rejected by him; her being loved in her turn by Bates and her rejection of him. How beautifully Pinter shapes the syntax to evoke the dilemma of conscious choice and the nagging of unconscious but instinctive preference: "They turn to move, look round at me to grin. I turn my eyes from one, and from the other to him" [p. 45]! Adolescence, adulthood, old age: the shuttle of memory moves effortlessly back and forth through time weaving the pattern of self-knowledge; but to our eyes and to the eye of the minds of the characters themselves they are caught — whatever age the timbre of their voices may evoke — at that moment when the arbitrariness of desire broke up a long sustained balance of intimacies, forcing them into exile away from each other. The experience of loss, which it costs each of them such an effort of the emotions to recover, is precisely what confirms each of their identities: that is their tragedy. After such awareness of pain, the rest can be but silence. Defeated by the very intensity of their feelings, there is no future for any of them beyond an awareness of merely existing. More than with *Landscape* the play's structure is built out of cyclic repetitions: the events that reveal the essence of the lovers' relationship are told to us through narrative fragments that make up Ellen, Bates and Rumsey's individual monologues — variations in detail between the three accounts help us steadily to grasp the situation and define the characters' contrasting modes of perceiving what happened. All three remain confused about their own and each other's motives and have only the facts of the separation, their own private feelings and an enduring emptiness and inertia to help them resolve the past in their understanding. When all that can be remembered factually about the past has been recalled, the tension slowly winds down; ever briefer fragments from the narratives are reiterated until there is only silence and three unmoving, drained faces as the lights slowly fade.

The remarkable fact about this ending viewed over several performances was its capacity to provoke two quite different interpretations of its significance. Were Ellen, Rumsey and Bates finding, like so many of Beckett's characters, that constant, deliberate recall of the past could in time numb the anguish by familiarising the imagination with the experience to such a degree that memory became a routine and held no fears, that the voice of conscience urging on them the need to recollect could be silenced? At other performances the effect could be quite different from this. As the long monologues dwindled away to brief phrases surfacing out of ever longer periods of silence and the full complement of circumstantial detail in the narratives was steadily lost, the token phrases which remained seemed charged with an intensity of emotional associations so painful that the gathering silence became an increasingly welcome release. It was as if recollection of the past had so sensitised the characters' nerve-ends that the shortest of phrases could set up echoes of association in their minds, flooding each consciousness (and ours) with the weight of suffering cumulatively invested in these memories over the years; from such an ordeal the only release would be the silence of the grave. Either interpretation was psychologically convincing and both were equally poignant. The distinction lay in the quality of the vocal tone assumed by the actors; how they orchestrated their voices in relation to each other; how they corporately paced and so shaped the silences; the degree to which phrases formerly anchored in a narrative context were repeated now with an exact recovery of the vocal line and emotional intensity with which they were first uttered, touched a paler, more etiolated note, or carried a sharper edge of desperation. The three actors are quite isolated from each other by this point in the play within their respective stage areas, so must remain acutely sensitive to each other aurally if they are to work together to create a coherent emotional and psychological structure of meaning. The anguished need of the characters to bridge the distances between them, which is the impulse generating the whole action of the play, exactly complements the predicament of the actors.

The challenge that Pinter sets his performers with this lack of precise definitions at the end of *Silence* is to respond to the situation and the given text as a collaborative improvisation, to see it as offering at once a freedom of possibilities and the discipline of finding together an emotional truth that rings soundly for each of the characters. It is a great test of an actor's sensitivity to the psychological nuances of what he is communicating vocally to an audience, of how meticulous his control is of the pitch, placing and timbre of his voice. The demand is that he use that voice like a virtuoso instrumentalist. Yet it is not simply in asking for a display of technical proficiency that this and more recent works by Pinter are exacting for actors; it is more in the way the plays expose what that proficiency indicates about an actor's powers of judgement and the strength of his creative intelligence. As Peter Hall has observed from his experience of directing most of Pinter's new work for the theatre since *The Homecoming*: "You can't do any of the plays without technique, but technique is not enough. You have to reveal yourself in order to endorse the author".[2] This of course is true of any play making an extensive use of a subtext; but it is particularly taxing for the actor in a play that does not allow him to build a character through a chronological development and that presents a situation rather than an action, choosing in preference to naturalism to distil the essence of a lifetime's experience of a relationship into an allusive poetic structure where space and time are at the dictate of memory or on occasions (and more alarmingly) responsive to wish-fulfilling fantasies. For Pinter what a character senses *might* have been his present state is every bit as indicative of why he is now the man he is as the actual past that shaped his present self. In the flow of consciousness, imagined possibilities and remembered actualities have an equal value; and it is there that, in seeking to define the spiritual quality of the relationships his characters have established together, Pinter has begun to set his plays. The dramatic structure is free-wheeling to accommodate past, present, a likely future and the characters' privately imagined alternatives to these states. Though this kind of structure was to reach perfection in *Old Times*, it was being steadily evolved through *Landscape* and *Silence*. Not since Strindberg has a dramatist set actors quite such a formidable task in achieving a coherent characterization while the action moves, often by highly rapid though always smooth transitions, through many different dimensions of reality, blending dream, memory and life. It need hardly be stated that it requires considerable imagination in an actor as well as technical proficiency to encompass such transitions and make them credible; but what is noticeable about Peter Hall's casting of all three full-length Pinter plays staged by him in the Seventies is his reliance on actors with not only an established reputation but also with a powerful and immediately recognisable stage-personality. It was in working round, through and sometimes against their idiosyncratic stage presences that Hall's casts found that point of coherence on which to focus the multi-dimensional perspectives of character that Pinter conceives: "You have to reveal yourself in order to endorse the author".

Consider Peggy Ashcroft as Beth in *Landscape*. Perhaps her most outstanding gift as an actress is her ability to convey the inner radiance of a character through the warmth and naturally musical cadences of her voice. Of her work in the Sixties one remembers her particularly as a Duchess of Malfi (Aldwych, 1960) who knew such security in her love for her Antonio that she found a passionate joy in the ordeals that prefigured her death as proving the staunchness of her devotion and she found too in death, when it came, so calm a transcendence that the response of her tormentor — "Cover her face; mine eyes *dazzle*" — was wholly apt. There was too her Mrs. Alving in *Ghosts* (Aldwych, 1967), quietly amused by Pastor Manders' tedious scruples, anxieties and platitudes — amused but not contemptuous, her love for the man having matured over the years to a generous affection, a tone that significantly never once coloured her references to her husband. Realising subsequently the extent to which her withholding such affection from Alving had brought tragedy on her household, Ashcroft's Mrs. Alving was stirred to a vision of man's infinite capacity for loving, only for that surprise and joy to be quenched by the knowledge that Oswald, on whom all her new-found enthusiasm was centred, was dying. And there was her Queen Katharine in Shakespeare's *Henry VIII* (Aldwych, 1970-71): fierce in her self-defence because serenely confident in her conscience, knowing that the accusations against her were mere statecraft, and composed in her exile from court, assured of its insignificance beside her access to an inner peace and intimations of a metaphysical bliss (no masque of angels here — the voice alone conjured visions out of the gathering shadows). At the outset of *Landscape*, hearing the dreamy, awed tones of Ashcroft's voice — "I would like to stand by the sea. It is there." [p. 9] — we had all our expectations about her stage-presence aroused. We felt at once the warmth, the charisma; but the stage picture devised by Pinter and Bury posed an immediate challenge to that response, for we were compelled to register how those qualities were completely withdrawn from David Waller's Duff, who, genial and boorish, sat gazing at her across the expanse of table. As Ashcroft handled it, Beth's mood of quiet rapture varied in intensity from a sensual eagerness at the thought of the lover's touch on her skin, through awe at the memory of walking in the morning mist to breathless expectancy at sensing the lover's approach, and jubilation at the recurring phrase, "I am beautiful" [p. 12]. But the modulations were always willed from within, prompted by the story she tells herself, not spontaneous expressions of instinctive feelings. Denied a dramatic situation to justify it and an intimate rapport with her fellow actor in which it might flourish, Ashcroft's charisma seemed increasingly exposed to our view as a fine but conscious technical accomplishment; and that worked as a kind of correlative for Beth's psychological state: in her the impulse to generosity, lacking the object of its choice on which to lavish all attention, has turned inward; the radiance is self-generated and self-regarding, an indulgence. By struggling to preserve what is best in her as an inviolable mystery, Beth has destroyed the power to create in herself and Duff. "Oh my true love I said" [p. 30] are Beth's last words in the play and Ashcroft's voice thrilled with ecstasy; but so complex by that stage of the performance was the web of ironies and psychological tensions that the effect was chilling and pitiful. It was an inspired piece of casting to use so rich a stage personality and voice as Ashcroft's to characterise a consciousness as arid as Beth's, for it achieved a wealth of pathos that another actress might have missed. Ashcroft's Beth was tragic because one sensed throughout the profound resorces of feeling that were lying fallow, the passions trapped in a mechanism of the mind that were being worn down to an effete sentimentality. To quite an unusual degree the very nature and quality of the performance here "endorsed" Pinter's conception. And the same proved true of *Old Times, No Man's Land, Betrayal* and *A Kind of Alaska.*

If Pinter's dramatic method has recently developed affinities with Strindberg's, the most telling dramatic effect in *Old Times* (Aldwych, 1971)[3] owes something of a debt to Ibsen: the shadowy presence of Anna by the window beyond Kate and Deeley, as they call her to mind in anticipation of her arrival in their house as a guest, and then — by a subtle shift in the lighting — her spectacular intrusion into their talk, herself in mid-sentence as she pours forth excitedly her memories of her past life with Kate, brimming over (seemingly) with vitality and confidence. One recalls those powerful, because almost supernatural figures like the Stranger in *The Lady from the Sea* or Hilde Wangel, whose rap at the Masterbuilder's door comes so frighteningly on cue — figures who share some half-forgotten past with one partner of a marriage and return like clinging, predatory ghosts aggravating all the tensions between the wedded couple that they have for some time previously learned how to live with and in some measure suppress. As such they are at once a challenge and a threat, eerie because they seem to embody forces which have lain dormant in the dark reaches of consciousness but which are willed into being by the characters' very dread that they might still exist. Intimacies with the stranger are recalled and promises of a way of life wholly different from that now lived by the three characters, wife, husband and visitor, are invoked in order to highlight the lack or the frustrating of passion in all their present selves; their futures seem in consequence to be living deaths in being wholly committed to the mundane and the routine. The pressures of time and death are felt suddenly quickening the pulse beat, urging the characters to measure the claims of individuality against the achievements of marriage, to attempt an assessment and hazard an awakening. The haunting voice from the past seems a call to the wild and the new, a rediscovery of the self, but, if pursued, may become a lure towards a more complete awareness of death in the spirit. Ellida can exorcise her ghost, when she realises that her present life has greater freedom than living out her obsession with the past would bring her, but Solness is too stricken with guilt about the present to be capable of taking so objective a look at the past, which is a temptation to him precisely because it seems quite uncontaminated by obligations and responsibilities. Solness's choice destroys him because he cannot envisage a future that is genuinely new; he tries to arrest time, reverse its course, recover his youth and be again the man he was; and impetuousness hastens his end.

That similarly is the motive and the fate of Anna and Deeley. Each provokes in the other a need to recover a lost intimacy with Kate; they vie with each other over who can claim the fullest possession of her; neither appears to have a self beyond what their intimacy with Kate confirms and so each dreads being dead to her affections; Kate knows that and cherishes it as a source of strength. Anna and Deeley make a display of their sexual potency yet it is curiously vapid, being so rooted in tales of past conquests; it is Kate who in the way she offers Anna a cigarette, relaxes in a rich yawn after her bath, enjoys the touch of towel, powder and bathrobe against her skin, is truly sensual, because quite unselfconsciously so. Her gestures, her stillness betoken an intense living in and for the moment, an absolute acceptance of herself moving in the flux of time. Anna and Deeley's speech is almost entirely in the past tense, the time they seek to render permanent. That to Kate is like talking about her as if she were dead. When in the closing scene of the play she chooses to talk of the past, it is not out of a desire like theirs to inhabit it as a continuing reality but to mark her complete separation from it, which signifies in its turn a necessary withdrawal of her sympathies from them: "I remember you lying dead"[p. 71]. Her use of the past tense is factual, categorical, precise. The time for rivalry and banter between Anna and Deeley is over; once the past is so fixed, they have no further experience to make the subject of speech and are reduced to Kate's preferred element — silence; then their only expressions are gestures of hopelessness and fatigue, while Kate remains upright, contained, clear-eyed in her gaze out beyond the present to the future. Asked by Anna in the drift of conversation what she does during Deeley's absence on business trips, Kate replies, "Oh, I continue"[p. 39]. In time it proves to be the shrewdest self-appraisal in the play, though at that moment it seems to Anna and Deeley to confirm their view of Kate as rather a cultural vegetable — "You have a wonderful casserole . . . I mean wife. So sorry. A wonderful wife"[p. 20]. Both feel she needs to "take an interest" in life, yet the more her silence compels them to talk of their own interests, the more giddy and frantic their idea of "life" seems; in their hunger for some permanence they exhaust experience — as Deeley says of Sicily where Anna now apparently lives: "I've been there. There's nothing more to see, there's nothing more to investigate, nothing. There's nothing more in Sicily to investigate" [p. 43]. That is why they have to live relentlessly through their memories of the brief period of calm they each once knew with Kate. They in fact denigrate in Kate what they envy, seeking relentlessly to claim possession of her in the hope of mastering the secret of her composure. But to admit to the desire for self-sufficiency is in itself to recognise how far they are from achieving such a state. Anna and Deeley's defeat is ineluctable. Kate inhabits the fact of self-sufficiency and so remains to them a tantalising enigma. Much of the humour of *Old Times* comes from Kate's prosaic undercutting of their play with metaphor:

ANNA: She was always a dreamer.
DEELEY: She likes taking long walks. All that. You know. Raincoat on. Off down the lane, hands deep in pockets. All that kind of thing.
ANNA *turns to look at* KATE.
ANNA: Yes.
DEELEY: Sometimes I take her face in my hands and look at it.
ANNA: Really?
DEELEY: Yes, I look at it, holding it in my hands. Then I kind of let it go, take my hands away, leave it floating.
KATE: My head is quite fixed. I have it on.
DEELEY: (*To* ANNA) It just floats away.
ANNA: She was always a dreamer. [pp. 23-24]

A mystery Kate may be to Anna and Deeley, but she is no mystery to herself.

As with *Landscape* in production, so with *Old Times*: the particular casting put one almost immediately in touch with the emotional and psychological undercurrents that make up the subtext of the play. Vivien Merchant (Anna) had a powerfully erotic stage personality and that was explored through many variations by Pinter: she commanded instant attention with her elegance and poise, because they seemed the product of considerable restraint on a passion that, as the voice intimated, was aching for a more complete expression. Her apparent sophistication was exciting on stage because it carried with it suggestions of danger and unpredictability: the gentility was too conscious a mask. Hers was however the kind of stage-personality that could easily tip over into a camp parody of itself, as she allowed it to do to brilliant comic effect in playing Mrs. Loveit in *The Man of Mode* (Aldwych, 1971) as a desperate virago, struggling to sublimate the lusts that Dorimant had roused in her, her body tense with a fierce will-power that her instincts could all-too-easily cause to relax; and again in playing Madame in Genet's *The Maids* (Greenwich, 1974), where she encompassed the rhetoric of the part with a wide-eyed, girlish vivacity, living through all the emotional exaggerations with unthinking commitment as though extremes of feeling, now tragic, now rapturous, were her natural medium. With less technical control, Miss Merchant's stage-persona was a kind that could easily have hardened into a type, the *femme fatale* of male fantasy, the woman who wills herself to project a personality that is exclusively a response to masculine emotional needs. Interestingly it was just such a steady conversion of her complex erotic persona into a limited stereotype that Pinter examined in *The Homecoming* (Aldwych, 1965) and which made the conclusion of that play so disturbing in its ambiguities: Ruth's victory over her husband's family — becoming in their household the woman they wanted but on her own exclusive terms — was also visibly a defeat because of what, as a conscious choice, it cost her in herself. In her performance as Anna, Miss Merchant kept this hint of camp extravagance, of the conscious playing of a role, beautifully under control but allowed it just sufficient weight so that, beside Kate, she seemed slightly unbelievable; and that kept one meticulously on one's guard against her and her more dogmatic assertions about the truth of the past. This subtle suggestion of unreality created other resonances within the play which we must return to.

Kate, the apparently "perfect" wife and "perfect" friend, was played by Dorothy Tutin, whose stage-presence is quite the antithesis of Vivien Merchant's. Miss Tutin excites attention by the fact of not appearing to demand it in any extrovert way; there is scant element of display in her customary style (though her range is so impressive that she can summon such a quality on occasion as with her Cressida (Stratford and Aldwych, 1960-61), a "daughter of the game" to the very carriage of her backbone). She has a wonderful gift for evoking through the voice the inner lives of the characters she is portraying especially in moments of self-discovery, when the recognition of a capacity for joy or the extent of future suffering seems to take the character by surprise only to become instantly all-consuming. She seems invariably to seize on the possibilities for emotional growth in a particular role; feeling, as she projects it, whatever its tone, has a startling purity and commitment. One remembers from Miss Tutin's past a gallery of unsentimentalised portraits of innocence, her Viola in *Twelfth Night* (Stratford and Aldwych, 1958-60) discovering what it is to love only to dread hazarding its expression and so risk rejection; or her Ophelia (Stratford, 1958) and her Varya in *The Cherry Orchard* (Aldwych, 1961), seeking for ways not to let the fact of rejection destroy an ardour and devotion which have come to be fundamental to their very being. The subtlety of Miss Tutin's technique lies in her so commanding the structure of a part that she can appear moment by moment to live in the flux of emotions and so convey a convincing artlessness. Kate, though the focus of much of the dialogue in *Old Times*, is herself largely silent; yet her few random contributions to the talk show that she is by no means a withdrawn, unthinking presence: the tone is always perfectly judged, the tenor often devastatingly apt. For all Anna and Deeley's banter about her vegetative state, Kate has an alert intelligence within her calm. Miss Tutin's Kate was a woman brooding on silence, relishing it, not like Beth as a means of escape into necessarily private fantasies, but for the greater knowledge and control that it brings her over her social being. Anna has a partial understanding of this quality in Kate, thus directing us to appreciate it: "As you know," she remarks to Deeley, "ripples on the surface indicate a shimmering in depth down through every particle of water, down to the river bed" [p. 37]. Anna's intuition about Kate's habit of mind is sound, but she fails to engage with it imaginatively; it simply strengthens her view of Kate as dreamy, otherworldly. Both Deeley and Anna see her as an innocent in need of their protection — a view which of course flatters their need to dominate and possess her. Kate was indeed, as Tutin played her, an innocent but not the kind who is vulnerable and easily rendered woebegone. Hers was a rarer, stronger kind of innocence: that of a woman so secure in herself that her integrity was absolute and inviolable. It was not simplicity she knew, but serenity. Having tested the strength of her will by diving to the riverbed of her consciousness, Kate has a firm hold on reality and it is noticeable that, when finally she asserts that reality against Anna and Deeley's pretence, she does so in terms not of water, the element they choose to believe is natural to her, but of mud which is to her a source of life and to them an image of death.

Colin Blakely, who played Deeley, has a gift for making commonplace men interesting, encouraging an audience to take a fresh look at characters we might suppose we know through and through because they are average and rather tedious — the kind of role it is so easy and tempting to caricature. If he found hitherto unsuspected subtleties in the part of Torvald in Ibsen's *A Doll's House* (Criterion, 1973), playing opposite Claire Bloom's Nora, it was because he excels at portraying rather stocky men, unimaginative and blundering, whose incipient tendencies towards brutality spring from credible fears of existence; though they lack heroic potential, they are never wanting in pathos. His Torvald was broken by the discovery of a courage in Nora and a will to shape her own destiny that he could never summon up in himself. *Old Times* opens in the middle of what has obviously been a protracted questioning of Kate about Anna; Deeley's curiosity, as Blakely played him, had an insistent, near obsessional tone to it that precisely matched his way of searching through her replies in quest of ambiguities that required clarification. The questions stimulated only more questioning; his curiosity was never appeased, rather knowledge seemed to inspire in him only a greater doubt. Blakely built his whole performance out of this initial image of futile questioning, seeing Deeley as a man so broken by his inability to cope creatively with the insights his curiosity led him to discover that finally he lost all sense of his own identity: "We took a pretty austere look at the women in black. The little old women in black. I wrote the film and directed it. My name is Orson Welles" [p. 42]. If Anna's obsession with the past seemed to be a search for conviction that she once possessed a zest for living which, if recovered, might prolong her youth into middle-age, Deeley's seemed the more desperate quest for any point of emotional certainty in his life, some proof of his worth for another, that might halt the process of disintegration that Anna's intrusion into his life with Kate had exposed and aggravated. Even his talk of his love for Kate seemed a bid for affection exposing his want of trust in its continuance. Desperation possessed his being, making awareness unreal, a nightmare that culminated in what is perhaps the most humiliating experience for a man of his would-be stalwart type — collapse into bitter sobbing. If there was pathos in Blakely's performance, it was because he stressed how the spiritual terror of the man was relentlessly stifling in Deeley that trust in another out of which affection might grow. The very mode he chose of expressing his need prevented the chance of its fulfilment.

When the uncertainties of the first act shape themselves into the nightmare of Act II (the second setting is a virtual replica of the first but with the disposition of the furniture reversed),[4] it is at Deeley's instigation. With Kate absent at her bath, he changes tactics with Anna, abandons the combative stance and begins to talk familiarly of a past attraction to her, of meetings in pubs and at parties, stressing always what he felt was the blatancy of her sex-appeal, her knowingness:

Later we all went to a party. Someone's flat, somewhere in Westbourne Grove. You sat on a very low sofa, I sat opposite and looked up your skirt. Your black stockings were very black because your thighs were so white. That's something that's all over now, of course, isn't it, nothing like the same palpable profit in it now, it's all over. But it was worthwhile then. It was worthwhile that night. I simply sat sipping my light ale and gazed . . . gazed up your skirt. You didn't object, you found my gaze perfectly acceptable.

. . . There was a great argument going on, about China or something, or death, or China *and* death, I can't remember which, but nobody but I had a thigh-kissing view, nobody but you had the thighs which kissed. And here you are. Same woman. Same thighs. [p. 51].

Anna says she has never heard a sadder story, but neither confirms nor denies Deeley's account. It certainly bears out a provocativeness in Anna's appearance, a self-conscious femininity. More confusingly, though, Deeley's tale stresses how Anna seemed to be trying at that time to imitate Kate and how the clothes that kissed her thighs were ones she had either stolen from Kate or worn at Kate's behest. In Deeley's mind the women's identities appear to be dissolving and coalescing. In the previous act Anna told of an experience she once had while living with Kate of seeing a man in their room one night, who appeared to be first welcomed then rejected by Kate, whom she too turned from and left to his tears before he again sought Kate's company and then finally departed. The memory is vague, she says, implying it may be no more than a waking dream; yet would it not, even on those terms, have a kind of truth? Even to think of it gives it a possible existence. Is Deeley now trying to exorcise her disturbing dream, that seems to emblematise his unmanning, by invoking another dream which shows that his potency is the match for her power to captivate? When Kate returns from her bath and with an easy matter-of-factness silences the tensions between Anna and Deeley, it is Anna's dream that Kate seems to compel them all to enact; it marks Deeley's defeat but, like all dreams, it carries significance for the dreamer too, for (as Kate insists) it marks Anna's demise as well; it is as if Anna's will to unman Deeley had killed the woman in herself.

Old Times moves through memory and dream to the purely symbolic (mime, one of the root-forms of theatre, with which the play ends, is wholly apt and eerie here because it is a form of expression that in stylising action is wholly allusive). This allows Pinter to let a wealth of possible meanings resonate in his audience's imagination at the conclusion but in a perfectly controlled, cogent and pertinent way. Is Anna, at once so powerful a presence and yet so unreal, a projection into middle age of the kind of woman Deeley married in Kate but who has now been lost to him (however potently desired) as Kate herself has matured and changed over the years of their marriage, becoming steadily unknown to him because he could not sensitively adapt to her transformations? As he fondly sings to Kate: "Oh! how the ghost of you clings" [p. 29]. Or is Anna perhaps a manifestation of the "sexually forthcoming" woman that Kate knows her husband longs for her to be [p. 73], but which seems to her a travesty of her true self? Does the charged erotic atmosphere of the play intimate possible infidelities in the past or the present, that Kate and Deeley turned or are turning from the perplexities and antagonisms they experience together to an easier sensual rapport with Anna? And is Kate's self-sufficiency in so intimate a context a moral achievement or a defeat? Different performances making for subtle shifts of emphasis would highlight now one character's predicament, now another's, so that a range of narrative and psychological explanations could suggest themselves as defining the situation, each quite probable yet none conclusive, for (like a true symbol) the strength of *Old Times* lies in its comprehensiveness. Pinter contrives through his structure to release his audience's imagination into the sexual consciousness of each of his characters to see how the fundamental forces which condition their particular masculine or feminine identities and give desire in them its individual quality will erode any relationship they attempt to form and confirm their isolation. Out of one evening's encounter Pinter distils the essence of a lifetime's tragic experience of unrequited love. Whatever narrative circumstances the play calls to mind, especially in its conclusion, the audience as a result of Pinter's chosen line of approach are quite free from the pressure to judge: a balance of sympathies is maintained throughout — no easy feat given the subject matter — to offset the varieties of despair in the characters. As the lights intensify then slowly fade on the final tableau of two abjectly prostrate bodies and one unyielding, silent observer of their pain, all the sadness of their tortured union crystallises into one profound image that prints itself indelibly on the imagination. Each of the characters has danced to the measure of some private, instinctive, self-consuming rhythm and the resulting pattern has celebrated not harmony but an impulse to discord, fragmentation and loss.

The richness of texture in *Old Times* and its creative ambiguities in performance could be admired even more in retrospect, when one compared it with several plays later in the decade that attempted a similar kind of structure or a like theme. Caryl Churchill's *Traps* (Theatre Upstairs, 1977),[5] for example, examines the lives of what one might loosely term a commune of four men and two women; Act One is in an urban tenement by night, Act Two in a rural cottage by day; situations, fragmentary episodes in relationships, are played out but the motives of the characters, as the dramatist herself claims, cannot all be reconciled; they are to be supposed rather "as living many of their possibilities at once" [Author's Note]. None of the brief duets, trios or ensemble pieces is to be viewed as a flashback or a fantasy sequence; everything is to be played as real for the duration of the time it takes to play through, however inconsistent it might appear beside what happens immediately before or after it. Acted with the commitment of the young cast at the Theatre Upstairs, *Traps* did evoke through its freewheeling form the excitement and challenge of creating a new style of living and showed how difficult it is wholly to escape more traditional attitudes, expectations, jealousies. Though the groupings continually changed, the tensions that controlled these dispersals and realignments were the ones common to an orthodox marriage. The difference was that here was a limited chance for change and manoeuvre, though that in time, given so frequent (not to say constant) a pattern of change, came to seem more like an escape from relationships rather than a development of new forms of bonding; a kind of emotional restlessness prevailed which was perhaps the ultimate trap: the possibility for change seemed to aggravate the potential for conflict. The need for absolute trust in such a variable emotional climate became increasingly apparent and the characters' discovery at the last of a certain stillness in renewing their sense of a corporate identity by taking a (hilarious) communal bath and sharing an evening meal — simple rituals totally uncomplicated by sexual tensions — was deeply moving. But though the structure of the play initially gripped the imagination for its startling shifts in tone, it never really allowed one to penetrate beneath the surface of situations; *Traps* became as a result an oddly theme-less play and the manifold inconsistencies in the characters' responses to each other came in their own way to be predictable and somewhat wearing: *volte face* after *volte face* seemed engineered for the fun of it and the concluding rituals impressed because they were just different rather than satisfying for being organically necessary. Despite a resemblance to Pinter's structural method in *Old Times*, *Traps* appeared, in contrast with his profundity of insight, a *jeu-d'esprit* of the imagination.

Several of E. A. Whitehead's plays through the decade have examined the subject of marital breakdown through the more traditional mode of realism, where, as the sparring between the partners gets nastier and more vindictive, different areas of experience are searched through to replenish their stocks of ammunition for the fight and the psychology of the combatants is exposed in increasing detail and complexity. In *Old Flames* (Arts, 1976)[6], mother, divorced wives and current girlfriend unite to dissect the luckless Edward and reveal how complete an emotional cripple he is and in the process show their own lacklustre, parched and shrivelled psyches. Though he chooses as his structural method a process of relentless diagnosis, Whitehead's plays, like *Traps*, tend to be all a brilliant surface because the experience is wholly transmuted into talk. The characters articulate what they have tried to be and hear about how they have appeared to others; the accounts are matched and the misunderstandings and deliberate misconceptions are recognised, sometimes admitted; so searing an honesty prevails that one is rather left wondering what could have attracted the partners to each other in the first place. (One is not surprised to find in the grimmest of the plays, *Old Flames*, that images of cannibalism recur.) What is rare in these plays is a moment such as that in *Alpha Beta* (Royal Court, 1972)[7] when the husband retrieves his son's cycle from the garden and, as he dries and cleans it, reminisces about the first old bike his parents bought him; the tensions suddenly relax between him and his wife as the one memory sparks off others and they temporarily forget their resentments in joking about the children. Here a wholly believable past is captured that intimates why, for all the wrangling, she tries every species of blackmail to get him to return to her and he cannot bring himself to take the irretrievable step of turning separation into divorce. They are held together by the vestiges of a rapport that once sustained them; yet their shame at losing this is the source of their spitefulness, each believing the other to be the one responsible for its loss. Elsewhere the characters are required to *explain* the complexity of their dilemmas. Consider Mrs. Elliot's attempt at a fair appraisal of her husband:

You're a real old Catholic missionary at heart. (*Laughs.*) Maybe you should have gone to Outer Polynesia! You're drawn to people . . . like me, once . . . who are lonely, or shy, or . . . in some way, incomplete . . . and you can't rest until you . . . *complete* them. You offer them *your* vitality, *your* resilience, *your* confidence . . . but instead of saving anybody, you're actually enslaving them. (*Pause.*) It's funny to hear you going on about not 'owning' people, because in fact you insist on owning any woman you're in love with . . . that's your price . . . you have to *own* her — heart and mind and body, and past and present and future too! You . . . infiltrate . . . every particle. (*Pause.*) I feel sorry for you because I think you're innocent. (*Pause.*) But that's why you're so dangerous . . . because when you've satisfied your missionary zeal . . . when you've got your new convert, now dedicated, completely committed to you . . . what happens then? (*Pause.*) You drop her! BUMP! Down to earth again. And off you go galloping on your next crusade! [p. 64].

This is a subtle piece of writing and one can see it as a necessary attempt to effect a balance of sympathies between the characters by showing them trying to be fair to each other; but there is no experience in the play against which we can test its truth; it has to be taken by the audience on trust. Interestingly, it could almost be seen as a commentary on Pinter's Deeley, but there lies the difference and the source of Pinter's superior artistry: he allows us to live imaginatively through the consciousness of a man like Deeley and discover in the play of forces that shape his mind such a subtle truth about him and why he is such an individual. *Old Times* departs from realism but in the interests of a greater verisimilitude. Similarly, a little later in the throes of exasperation, Mr. Elliot utters self-pityingly: "Yes, it's true . . . Marriage is one of the few surviving forms of ritual slaughter" [p. 68]. Again what Whitehead expresses as statement, Pinter asks us to encompass imaginatively as a state of mind realised first through Kate's extended metaphor defining how she saw Anna and Deeley "dead" and then, when the others are compelled to admit the truth of her vision, as a veritable ritual played out in mime. All Whitehead's plays are patterned out of a sequence of psychological discoveries; but he never takes advantage of the multiplicity of theatrical styles available to the modern dramatist, as Pinter does, to invest an audience's growth in insight with the quality of revelation, where 'idea' is subsumed in experience and may embrace much more than the characters themselves apprehend of their predicament.

One could be forgiven for supposing from the form, focus and many of the incidental themes of *Old Times* that Pinter was well versed in Proust's fiction, but on his own admission it was not until he received Joseph Losey's commission for a filmscript of *A La Recherche du Temps Perdu* in 1974 that he had read more than *Swann's Way*.[8] *No Man's Land* (Old Vic, 1975)[9] seems imbued more with the quality of Proust's lifestyle than his novel: the closed room where daylight is sealed off to facilitate a greater concentration on one's art — "You're tucked up, the shutters closed, gaining a march on the world"; the dedication to work that hovers on the verge of the obsessive; the immersion in things past that intimates a need for consolation for emotional inadequacies then and an ensuing emptiness now. Pinter seems to be invoking facts from Proust's life concerning his pursuit and jealous possession of calm as the only condition in which to create, in order to examine darker, more ominous states of mind than it would be fair to ascribe to Proust himself. It is as if a certain balance has been lost, as if a possible extension of Proust's world — one meticulously staved off by Proust himself — has come into being. By a characteristic twist of the imagination Pinter has seen how easily a world like Proust's could beget a black travesty of itself, how readily a dependence on servants "to do our living for us"[10] could lay one open to their greed and treachery to the extent that the desired guardians of one's sanctuary would be transformed into the keepers of one's prison, converting dependence into enslavement. Hirst is losing the authority to command and direct the forces that once sustained his world and made for his success as a writer; the servants of his art — both his actual retainers and, more figuratively, his powers of mind — are becoming restive and predatory. If *Old Times* is about the death of the heart, *No Man's Land* is about the death of the imagination.

John Bury's setting for Peter Hall's production was dominated by three features: a wall of bookshelves; a huge bay of curtains parted only once to let daylight blindingly penetrate before they were closed again at Hirst's bidding to end so "distasteful" an intrusion — "Put the lamps on. Ah. What relief. How happy it is" [p. 86]; and a giant table stacked not with writing materials but with glasses and quantities of drink. Were the ironic connotations of apse and altar deliberate? The muse had long since departed this shrine to be replaced by "the great malt which wounds" [p. 32]. Though the first of many toasts to be proposed in the course of the action called on 'art', 'virtue' and 'continued health', what was clearly celebrated by the term 'health' was an irredeemable dejection:

SPOONER: No. You are in no-man's land. Which never moves, which never changes, which never grows older, but which remains forever, icy and silent.
Silence
HIRST: I'll drink to that. [p. 95].

But it was to take the movement of the whole play to bring us to that awareness.

We entered this secluded world as Hirst was welcoming into it a new and chance acquaintance, Spooner, who it is implied has insinuated himself into Hirst's regard when he found him drinking alone in a Hampstead pub. They renew their drinking and Spooner begins more elaborately to introduce himself, not in factual terms concerning achievement but through what he considers his more solid attributes: his intellect and integrity as a poet; his precision of insight; his candour; his self-sufficiency. He is, he claims, a man of discipline and dedication, strong because he is beyond needing the love of others. Assurance of a kind certainly is implicit in the ease with which he manipulates the intricate syntax of his periods, yet the appearance belies the manner: his crumpled clothes and general air of seediness are in marked contrast to Hirst's dapper elegance and curt style of address; and he hovers, unsure of the effect he is having, as if continually expecting to be asked to leave; he relaxes fully into a chair only when Hirst drinks to his "continued health". As Hirst has till now been unyielding, a listening presence, except for the expression of some formal politenesses, Spooner has had to work hard to sustain the conversational flow. For all his easy control of the complex syntax, his sentences have an odd mode of elaborating a phrase or a rhythmic pattern till an idea is lost in absurdity:

May I say how very kind it was of you to ask me in? In fact you are kindness itself, probably always are kindness itself, now and in England and in Hampstead and for all eternity. [p. 17]

The tone of this hovers disturbingly between embarrassment at confronting so unresponsive an individual, and insolence, a wary testing of his ground to see how far perhaps he can go before provoking an outburst and unsettling Hirst's apparent calm. Moreover the convoluted way Spooner has of presenting his notions often leaves his own relation to an idea ambiguous to a degree that seems suddenly and cruelly exposing:

SPOONER: . . . I was about to say, you see, that there are some people who appear to be strong, whose idea of what strength consists of is persuasive, but who inhabit the idea and not the fact. What they possess is not strength but expertise. They have nurtured and maintain what is in fact a calculated posture. Half the time it works. It takes a man of intelligence and perception to stick a needle through that posture and discern the essential flabbiness of the stance. I am such a man.
HIRST: You mean one of the latter?
SPOONER: One of the latter, yes, a man of intelligence and perception. Not one of the former, oh no, not at all. By no means. [pp. 16-17]

Hirst in his longest sentence to date here replies in a manner that echoes Spooner's own; but is he simply seeking clarification of the point at issue or offering a subtle rebuff, suggesting he sees Spooner as a poseur? It certainly causes Spooner to gravel for want of matter; he can do no more than assert his strength, but his repeated denials that he is "one of the former" lack the energy of conviction. It could express hurt surprise at Hirst's failure of perception and judgement. Or is Spooner sounding a note of alarm at having himself revealed perhaps more than he intended? Courtesy prevails but it is not an unsullied tone; malice and insult lurk suspiciously close even if their forms are not clearly defined. The pursuit of a friendship seems to mask a wish to spar and to wound. The intellectual ambience has an ominously predatory quality that makes the drinking obsessive rather than convivial.

Hirst and Spooner were played by Richardson and Gielgud, whose tone and impeccable timing of lines in relation to each other's performances teased every comic nuance out of the dialogue. They had previously in the decade achieved considerable success together in David Storey's *Home* (Royal Court, 1970) as two old men who in distressing circumstances seek cautiously but with great charity to establish a friendship and find in each other some degree of trust through which independently they may reach out to a new kind of life and personality.[11] *No Man's Land* found them together again and in an analogous situation; but, whereas *Home* gave them an opportunity to explore the range of their talents for expressing unsentimentalised pathos, Pinter's play encouraged them to reveal other aspects of their stage personalities to show how, subtly but insidiously, Hirst and Spooner are compelled by inner drives to frustrate all efforts at amity.

Gielgud has of late developed a marvellous line in self-parody. One recalls his headmaster in Alan Bennett's *Forty Years On* (Apollo, 1968) being trapped by his own grandiloquence while celebrating forty years of school and national history into the perception that the values that have sustained his long career are a joke to the young: they are not stirred by his rhetoric, they just enjoy it as a comic turn. Or there was his Sir Geoffrey Kendle in Charles Wood's *Veterans* (Royal Court, 1972) — an affectionate portrait of Gielgud himself filming the role of Lord Raglan in *The Charge of the Light Brigade*, which was scripted by Wood. Here was a man at war with his own diamond-bright integrity as an artist, whose every wish to be generously disposed towards others was continually undermined by his irrepressible honesty, so that he was forever in pain at being betrayed into uttering what sounded at best like tactlessness and at worst like calculated bitchery — "They should be such good friends you know, they're both insufferable". Gielgud has begun since the Seventies to mock the seriousness that was formerly a hallmark of his stage-personality; he has in fact contrived to achieve marvellous comic effects by undercutting the melodiousness of that famous voice in its attempts at pathos, exposing how it is so secure a technique that he could easily rely on it to do its work at the expense of spontaneity or commitment. He has the wit and the humility to question the value of his greatest strength as an actor — his voice; to test his delight in his mastery of it for signs of indulgence and put such a diagnosis of his own expertise to the service of a particular kind of characterisation. In casting him as the decayed, rather reprobate, Hampstead intellectual, Spooner, Peter Hall and Pinter gave Gielgud a vehicle to explore his talent for self-mockery through a character whose derisory wit constantly robs him of his intellectual and emotional goals. Spooner cultivates impersonality as an artist: "My only security, you see, my true comfort and solace, rests in the confirmation that I elicit from people of all kinds a common and constant level of indifference" [p. 17]; his wit appears designed to preserve a necessary distance from others: "What is obligatory to keep in your vision is space. The present is truly unscrupulous. I am a poet. I am interested in where I am eternally present and active" [p. 20]. Yet he manoeuvres continually for a place in that closed world of Hirst's, intruding on his private memories and visions, willing Hirst to need him, trying (at first by devious means, later by abject ingratiation) to bridge the very distances he insists Hirst should keep from people if he is properly to merit the epithet 'manly'.

Since his much praised Peer Gynt (1944) and his Johnson in Priestley's *Johnson Over Jordan* (1939), Ralph Richardson has repeatedly excelled at a particular kind of bluff, apparently down-to-earth figure who, despite a strong vein of commonsense, has a lyrical vein of fantasy in his make-up or a strange perception of the supernatural. Never an actor, or so it is said, to enjoy contact with an audience (he prefers to think of them "as a cage of bloody tigers that will bite you" if you let them get in command), he has become over his career, as Kenneth Tynan has so admirably shown in his study of Richardson's style, "a master of all the stratagems of self-protection". Tynan continues: "He has always been extremely wily if he suspects that an attempt is being made, in Hamlet's phrase, to pluck out the heart of his mystery".[12] If he convinces in communicating moments of metaphysical apprehension on the part of the characters he portrays, it is because he respects their inherent mystery. He possesses an astonishing knack, deployed usually in emotional climaxes, of suddenly beginning to play quite privately to himself; he refuses at such times to wear his heart on his sleeve and he instils awe in an audience by making them feel privileged to be witnessing so supremely intimate an experience, so intense a communion with the self. There was no flamboyance, for example, in his handling of Borkman's compulsion to escape to the mountaintop in Peter Hall's production for the National Theatre of Ibsen's late tragedy (1975); nor was there histrionic display in his playing of either the vision Borkman is vouchsafed of the wealth lying within the rock beneath his feet that surpasses human understanding or of his dream of the power that would fall to him who possessed that unparalleled wealth. All was quiet wonder that the imagination could encompass such a vision and infinite sadness that his failing strength placed such possibilities beyond his grasp, the mind and circumstance cruelly mocking the man. If there was pathos in this recognition of his vulnerability, it was because public appearances had so obsessively dominated the thinking of this Borkman and his wife throughout the earlier scenes of Ibsen's play; the inner life had meant little to either of them, and now he in particular was realising the danger of this. Long before the waking nightmare that afflicts Hirst at the end of the First Act of *No Man's Land*, Richardson had revealed the man to be haunted; nameless terrors hovered on the edges of his sight compelling him to relentless drinking. As Spooner prosed on about their encounter, about his life as a "betwixt twig peeper" [p. 18] on Hampstead Heath, about his self-suffiency and his brilliance, Hirst remained steely, tense. He appeared to be listening to Spooner with only half his mind; Spooner's pauses would compel him back to full attention, when he would let fall a terse but devastatingly apt rejoinder to set his visitor going again, his tone never defining itself precisely as interest or criticism or boredom. Repeatedly in the long opening scene of the play Richardson's eyes strayed to his left to an otherwise empty area of the stage and then hastily withdrew. There was a certain dryness, a world-weariness about his Hirst and always this suggestion that a deeper reach of the mind was luring him away from his immediate preoccupation with Spooner. (Front stage left was the area where later his nightmare of an unidentifiable figure drowning in "blinding shadows, then a fall of water" [p. 47] was to manifest itself provoking a breakdown or fit; and it was an area that Hirst noticeably never entered until at the very end of the play when he decided to break with Spooner forever; when he returned from it to his centrally placed chair, it was to commit himself to a spiritual void as his enduring condition of mind, the "no-man's land" of the final toast.) It is at Hirst's command that the moods in the play change; he who dictates, once Spooner relaxes within his study and settles into a chair, the strange situational games which follow, and invests the other three characters with particular roles, identifying them with persons from his past as he lives through some crisis of conscience in the depths of his psyche. Given Richardson's particular style of acting, his conscious privacy, his command of metaphysical suggestion, he was ideally cast as this voyager through a dark night of the soul.

To confront that journey Hirst needs a guide or a companion. Alert to the implications of Hirst's sudden use of a metaphor — "you find me in the last lap of a race . . . I had long forgotten to run" [p. 32] — Spooner senses the nature of Hirst's appeal and his desperation; he converts the metaphor immediately into an image with more precise connotations of death and gives himself a firm role in the event: "Let me perhaps be your boatman. For if and when we talk of a river we talk of a deep and dank architecture" [p. 33]. He seems to be speaking out of the very heart of Hirst's terror and the very precision appears tactless and cruel, particularly since he goes on to force his interpretation on Hirst with an insistence on his own generosity in offering to help that is positively crude. When, instead of replying, Hirst remains silent, clutching frantically at a chair or table to maintain his balance, Spooner calmly derides his incapacity. Hirst calls out between gasps of breath as if trying to stem great waves of horror — "No-man's land . . . does not move . . . or change . . . or grow old . . . remains . . . forever . . . icy . . . silent" [p. 34] — and collapses; he surfaces, dazed, to fall again and yet again, before crawling away humiliated to bed. Spooner encapsulates the moment in flippant verse: "I have known this before. The exit through the door, by way of belly and floor" [p. 34]. This jeering note has become increasingly Spooner's tone since he settled comfortably into Hirst's room. Immediately after he had ceased to prowl about the set and had esconced himself firmly in the chair next to his host, Hirst had unexpectedly confided a fact about his past — his ownership of a country cottage; Spooner accepted the intimacy as an attempt to establish a point of rapport with himself and sought to encourage its development. Continuing, Hirst told with considerable sensitivity of a particular rural custom that has obviously moved him deeply:

In the village church, the beams are hung with garlands, in honour of young women of the parish, reputed to have died virgin.

Pause

However, the garlands are not bestowed on maidens only, but on all who die unmarried, wearing the white flower of a blameless life. [p. 29]

It is a private symbol, an epiphany; the sharing of it is in consequence an act of trust. Spooner, however, intellectualised both the incident and their shared mood in a fashion that was insulting for being so totally destructive:

I am enraptured. Tell me more. Tell me more about the quaint little perversions of your life and times. Tell me more, with all the authority and brilliance you can muster, about the socio-politico-economic structure of the environment in which you attained to the age of reason. Tell me more. [p. 30]

A spirit of mockery seems to possess him, Hirst's every utterance being seized and fantasized upon as a means of taunting him with accusations of being gutless and unmanly. Moving with care and slow deliberation as if trying to husband his failing powers, Hirst sought comfort in more drink before trying (ineffectually) to silence Spooner's inanities by throwing a glass at him. The metaphor he then voiced of the race he had long forgotten to run seemed a last abject appeal for sympathy, which was why Spooner's stark redefining of the image only to find in it further impetus for his derision sounded both profoundly insensitive and vicious.

The emotional cycle of this long opening scene establishes a structural pattern that repeats itself throughout the play, the form of *No Man's Land* being a kind of fantasia on a theme played with increasingly subtle variations. Always heavy drinking provides a focus for the encounters; this creates a mood in which intimacy is possible by relaxing inhibitions and defences, but it also provokes a state in which individuals are most vulnerable to fears they normally hold repressed. Sensibilities and powers of intuition are sharpened only to make one both acutely conscious of one's inner torment and astutely perceptive of the disabilities in others. Relief from private misery lies in ceasing to hold back for the sake of politeness a malicious urge to tear aside the shreds of dignity with which another individual seeks to hide his abject nakedness and expose to him a truth he knows about himself but cannot openly admit. In encounter after encounter throughout the play, an amiable approach masks in various ways an invitation to a game of oneupmanship, which at a deeper psychological level is a trial of spiritual strengths. When Foster, Hirst's manservant, puts the light out on Spooner, it is both horseplay and a test of how resilient he will prove at the prospect of being benighted. The great malt, as Spooner affirms, truly wounds: camaraderie quickly turns to boasting or outright hostility; an atmosphere of togetherliness can provide excellent cover for being brutally frank: "Do forgive me my candour. It is not method but madness. So you won't, I hope, object if I take out my prayer beads and my prayer mat and salute what I take to be your impotence?" [p. 33]. All four characters in turn emit cries for help only to meet with deflating, cutting or patronising rejoinders. Without his forcing the analogies, the masculine preserves of pub and club are deftly intimated by Pinter; the conversational routines that typically go on there between random drinking companions are explored and shown to mask either egocentric displays of prowess or rituals of unmanning. Foster and Briggs the two servants, being younger with more robust energies, are cruder in their tactics of aggression and more whining in their self pity than the older men but their predicament is essentially the same. What Hirst and Spooner bring to their sparring is longer experience and a cultured upbringing that make their barbs more sharply angled and more lethal. Spooner can effortlessly put down Briggs's affable tediousness in recounting how expertly he once directed Foster to Bolsover Street with a superior aside about Rumanians being the only respectable exponents of the craft of translating verse. Briggs quietly nurses a grudge but mouthing meaningless obscenities is his only resource when later he attempts to retaliate and gain the upper hand. With Hirst Spooner's methods must be much less transparent: in Act Two Hirst appears to mistake Spooner's identity and, thinking him an old Oxford friend, swaps tales of war-experiences and exploits with women, including that friend's own wife: "Admitted you were a damn fine chap, but pointed out I would be taking nothing that belonged to you, simply that portion of herself all women keep in reserve, for a rainy day" [p. 69]; Spooner bides his time till Hirst's smugness is at its ripest, then begins to intimate a sequence of infidelities amongst Hirst's circle which Hirst himself appears not to know about, believing himself to be the only Lothario. When he has quite unsettled Hirst's calm, Spooner unleashes a venomous attack on his "insane and corrosive sexual absolutism" [p. 76]. Real or imaginary, there is enough half-truth in the accusations that fuel Spooner's moral outrage to catch Hirst quite off his guard. As the battle reaches its climax, it is in insults about each other's art as poets that the animosities find expression:

HIRST: This is scandalous! How dare you? I'll have you horsewhipped!
SPOONER: It is you, sir, who have behaved scandalously. To the fairest of sexes, of which my wife was the fairest representative. It is you who have behaved unnaturally and scandalously, to the woman who was joined to me in God.
HIRST: I, sir? Unnaturally? Scandalously?
SPOONER: Scandalously. She told me all.
HIRST: You listen to the drivellings of a farmer's wife?
SPOONER: Since I was the farmer, yes.
HIRST: You were no farmer, sir. A weekend wanker.
SPOONER: I wrote my Homage to Wessex in the summerhouse at West Upfield.
HIRST: I have never had the good fortune to read it.
SPOONER: It is written in terza rima, a form which, if you will forgive my saying so, you have never been able to master. [p. 77]

The envies, hatreds and insecurities the exchange uncovers are legion. The inconsequentialities that govern the direction the repartee takes are funny, but also alarming for the pettiness of spirit they reveal. What a waste of the imagination lies in the meticulously polished syntax of their remarks, keeping up a show of courtesy and decorum while delicately exploring the surface of the opponent's psyche to trace the wounds and open the scars! So much malevolence is insinuated through niceties of grammar and vocal emphasis; so much ill-feeling festers and stifles real creativity.

Hirst, despite his success, is unproductive; he cherishes the marks of his profession like museum-pieces; trying to placate Spooner after the previous outburst, Hirst dangles before him the prospect of being admitted to his study; he gloats almost childishly over the possessions to be seen there: "I am prepared to be patient. I shall be kind to you. I shall show you my library. I might even show you my study. I might even show you my pen, and my blotting pad. I might even show you my footstool" [p. 78]. It is as if admiration is necessary to him to convince him of his continued success. But admiration lies dangerously closer to envy than to affection. Having only a circumscribed life in the present as a result of Foster and Briggs's ministrations, Hirst looks to find his freedom in his past. In the list of treasured possessions he might deign to show to Spooner, it is his photograph album which occupies pride of place — a secret world to which he alone has the key, though Spooner as his contemporary might find his way about there, were he granted admission. Relaxed reminiscence with footstool and album seems all that can now stimulate his imagination. But could his youth have been as idyllic as he claims? He talks of that age as a world of grace, tenderness and ease, yet it seems despite the photographs curiously unredeemable from time except as an array of names and facts. Only if it found some emotional release in him would that world live again; till then, as Hirst says, it remains a world peopled by ghosts who possess all their emotion "trapped" [p. 79]. And it seems he prefers it that way so as not to disturb his own equanimity: an album can be opened and closed at will, its contents subject to deliberate choice. When that world first finds dynamic expression in Hirst's dreams, the figures that reach out to his imagination are "bastards" that terrify him; the elegance suffocates; the beauty is "all poison"; and always there is that insistent image of the drowning one [pp. 46-47]. When again Hirst's past comes alive in the play through shared recollection with, as he supposes, Charles Wetherby (the role in which he suddenly casts Spooner), it is not depicted in terms of its social brilliance but of its covert life, the undercurrent of illicit passions and predilections, never fully understood because of necessity so secret, that as a result still activate guilt, outrage, questioning and pride. Because unresolved, the emotions of that time live on, waiting for the involuntary movement of consciousness that will give them the chance to manifest themselves. Invariably their visitation proves a nightmare.

Hirst's brisk confidence, his courtesy, what remains to him of the gracious etiquette of his youth are a stance, a mannerism, like the room he inhabits — a sanctuary. Welcoming Spooner there neither strengthens his hold on the pose nor helps him exorcise his ghosts, but keeps his consciousness in exquisite tension. Spooner might have proved the Good Samaritan that Hirst needs, had his claim to a complete impersonality been a secure one; but he slips too easily into the various roles Hirst asks him to play for him to maintain a proper detachment; and he invariably seeks through the role he adopts some way of expressing his own sense of injured merit:

My career, I admit it freely, has been chequered. I was one of the golden of my generation. Something happened. I don't know what it was. Nevertheless I am I and I have survived insult and deprivation. I am I. I offer myself not abjectly but with ancient pride. I come to you as a warrior. I shall be happy to serve you as my master. I bend my knee to your excellence. [p. 89]

The will to serve requires selflessness and detachment. Spooner constantly seeks personal references and associations in Hirst's reminiscences and asserts them to Hirst's discomfort. When Hirst's nightmare reaches a pitch of hysteria, Spooner answers him: "It was I drowning in your dream" [p. 47]. He rudely condenses Hirst's frightening vision to a metaphor referring to his own state of desperation that previously goaded him into abusing Hirst's generosity and casting aspersions on his manhood. Far from acting as an apology to calm Hirst, this pushes his hysteria over the edge into complete collapse. Even Spooner's final obsequious imploring for a place as secretary in Hirst's entourage is motivated more by the desire to bask in another's reflected glory and know the success he covets at second hand, than by genuine respect for Hirst's position as an established artist. Jealousy, rancour, self-distaste make his show of humility a pretence: desperate for patronage, Spooner's gestures of help are invariably patronising. His last appeal to be allowed to arrange a public appearance for Hirst (in itself so insensitive a request of a man so determinedly private) is greeted by the silence it deserves and Hirst's insistence that they change the subject. Each needs the other, but the admission of a need is anathema to them both, exciting either derision or distaste.

Spooner is so devious he will survive: lacking any fundamental dignity he will be content to play whatever role his fancy or the mood of other succeeding hosts might dictate; he is utterly shameless. But for Hirst there is no such future; the nightmare experience has shown him that. He has penetrated to the interior of his being, apprehended its nature and learned that nothing can relieve the horror. His final decision is to accept his own judgement of his impotence; he drinks now not to escape dejection but to confirm its truth as abiding. The last section of the play is patterned out of fragments of speech that circle about each other with an incantatory rhythm while the speakers rapidly shed all trace of the personalities they have projected throughout the action and become like the "humming" ghosts Hirst previously dreaded [p. 47]. All this evokes in its extreme stylization the vortex into which his consciousness is entering as he raises his glass aloft in a token salute: the maunderings of drunkenness and dotage through which perception grasps at oblivion. The intimations latent within the setting that this is a place of ritual are finally borne out; but the communion is with death not life. Spooner tonelessly reiterates Hirst's own description of one of his waking visions: "You are in no-man's land. Which never moves, which never changes, which never grows older but which remains forever, icy and silent". And Hirst greets the prospect now with absolute calm: "I'll drink to that" [p. 95].

If *No Man's Land* has a weakness it lies in the younger characters, Foster and Briggs who, though they have a necessary part to play in the sparring matches and by their vigour and brusqueness offset the nostalgia for a vanishing gentility which Spooner and Hirst share, do not have a vital function in the overall narrative. The audience is not allowed to enter into their individual characters at all deeply; the focus is almost entirely on Hirst and Spooner, even when Hirst is not actually on stage. His final capitulation secures their future status as his guardians, but we are given little information about why that security is so essential to their livelihood that they jealously fend Spooner off when he tries to establish himself in their *ménage*. *No Man's Land* does not quite achieve the perfect structure of *Old Times* which defines a situation in a way that permits us both to register it objectively and to experience it from the private perspective of each of the three protagonists. It must, however, be admitted that, in performance, Gielgud and Richardson's characterisations were rich enough to compensate for a certain monotony and predictability in the writing for Foster and Briggs.

Always the master of surprises, Pinter decided late in 1979 to salvage an abandoned work that he had completed in 1958, a companion-piece to *The Caretaker*. *The Hothouse* (Hampstead, 1980)[13] was far from being its match in quality, lacking the density and the drive of Pinter's writing at its best. Where it excited most were those points where it seemed to be anticipating the material and methods of *No Man's Land*: in the jockeying of the bureaucrats Roote, Gibbs and Lush for the office of command. Eileen Diss's setting — all white walls and laminated desks, gleaming filing systems and taut black leather upholstery — was a bureaucrat's dream of impersonal efficiency. (It was a telling detail that the painting that graced the staff-lounge at the mental asylum which is the scene of action was a print of Van Gogh's 'Sunflowers', but with his vibrant colours muted to tones of buff and grey on a white ground.) Here was neatness, system: living up to this ideal of order proved to be the test of the characters' powers of leadership and the stimulus to their intellectual gymnastics, for the play is like a perverse, adult version of the child's game, I'm the King of the Castle. As so often with early Pinter, it was the earnestness of the game that provided much of the humour, together with the characters' deliberate circumscribing of all experience within their obsession about discipline: "A death and a birth. Absolutely bloody scandalous! Is it too much to ask — to keep the place clean?" [p. 129]. Roote, the senior administrator, is ailing, losing control; Gibbs and Lush, his lieutenants, are ambitious; they enact a war of nerves, subtly undermining each other's assertions of authority. All three see this as a questioning of their manhood. Gibbs's courtesy, unfailing deference and pernickety exactitude appear to Roote to be a constant criticism of himself, a projection of the man he ought to be. Lush is more flamboyant, acquiescing sympathetically to Roote's rhetoric about the crippling pressures of leadership, only to turn the rhetoric with apparent innocence into questions about why Roote bothers to maintain so exhausting a role. Lush is disturbing because, being the smart-Alec type, he barely troubles to conceal his awareness that the order they maintain is entirely dependent on their corporately respecting the poses they each choose to assume. Gibbs inhabits his mask so completely he appears inhuman and Lush subjects Gibbs's habit of mind to a joking cynicism. Gibbs is too obsequious to be true; Lush all too true in his impertinence; both are a threat to Roote's sanity and stability. Whether working alone or together, they leave Roote with nothing but vehemence as a way of expressing his authority: "Don't think I can't squash you on a plate as easy as look at you" [p. 84]. Time and again they prove him impotent to fulfil the demands of his office. All along Roote has been shown to be helpless to act without precedents but by the end he cannot perform functions for which there are precedents since Gibbs and Lush have stripped his work of all the mystique through which he convinced himself it was a vocation and have exposed it as simply routine:

GIBBS: I've come to hear the Christmas speech, sir.
ROOTE: Well, why don't you make it? You're dying to make it, aren't you? Why don't you make it?
GIBBS: It's your privilege, sir.
ROOTE: Well, I'm sick to death of it! The patients, the staff, the understaff, the whole damn thing!
GIBBS: I'm sorry to hear that, sir.
ROOTE: It's bleeding me to death.
(LUSH *rises*.)
LUSH: Then why do you continue?
ROOTE: Because I'm a delegate.
LUSH: A delegate of what? [p. 130]

Where *The Hothouse* suffers is in not realising till too late within its action the threat from the offstage world that gives a dangerous edge to the men's exercises in brinkmanship. Things are falling apart, for all Roote's assurances in his Christmas message to the inmates that the institution is a united family held together by faith in the prevailing structures of power; and this is because the officers are obsessed with the fact of power rather than committed to the responsibilities that should accompany it. The patients are escaping their cells and mustering forces to rebel and take a lethal revenge. The imminence of this is not sufficiently clear or sustained in the audience's awareness to give a dimension of manic absurdity to the dialogue or to generate tension and impetus. The repeated pattern of sounds that from time to time arrests the action onstage — a drawn-out sigh, a keen, an echoing laugh — is eerie but too imprecise and too stylised to have the ominous anarchic note that is called for. Setting Spooner and Hirst's gambits on the brink of the grave, making them all-too-conscious of their predicament and giving their desperation — their dread of being impotent, meaningless, unmanned — a metaphysical dimension, secures for the dialogue and action of *No Man's Land* a complexity and energy quite lacking in *The Hothouse*. By abandoning the kinds of narrative considerations he observes in the earlier work (the need for consistency, explanations, a logic to the pace and mode of development) in favour of structural discontinuities accompanied by wholesale changes in pace and tone, Pinter conveys his audience imaginatively inside the experience that is *No Man's Land* so that, by virtue of the form, they share the characters' disquiet and know the urgency of their need to find a meaning. Much of the dialogue of *The Hothouse* plays satirically with easily recognisable conversational formulae apparent in men's rites of combat and self-assertion; the dialogue of *No Man's Land* does this too, but the wit has more brilliance, as the satire is conducted over a greater range of tones and there is a continual pressure at work compelling the characters to test the various formulae to see how readily they can be shaped to articulate apprehensions that lie on the edges of sight and experience just eluding precise definition, intimations of mortality visiting men who have denied in themselves the visionary gleam. Obsessed with their masculinity, Hirst, Spooner, Foster and Briggs have ceased to be either human or humane and so have lost any precise or certain sense of individuality.

Some way into Pinter's *Betrayal* (Lyttleton, 1978)[14] one of the characters comments on the subject of a new novel his wife is reading (we are in the world of publishers and literary agents): ". . . not much more to say on that subject, really, is there? . . . Betrayal" [p. 78]. It is a characteristic Pinter flourish risking either an audience's dismissal of his play as so much old hat or, if the audience is engrossed, as they regularly were with the first production, risking a concentration of their attention on his method, the virtuosity of his style in reinvigorating a jaded topic at the expense of the experience itself. Manner then treads dangerously close to mannerism. There is no denying *Betrayal* is an immediately accessible play. It has a precise narrative line making for completeness and inevitability. A complex of experiences has not been condensed into a symbolic action making for density of texture and a power of allusion as in *Old Times*, beside which *Betrayal* appears a simple tale, simply and wittily told; and there are none of those startling shifts of identity and tone that make for an alert, if troubled, response to *No Man's Land*, where the sheer precariousness of events makes for excitement and a pervasive sense of danger. The darker aspects of consciousness — fantasy, nightmare, hallucination — are kept firmly at bay by Robert, Jerry and Emma: a sudden panic, an impulse to cry, a few vague nostalgic yearnings, a deliberate decision to get drunk — these are the controlled, utterly civilised ways in which needs, regrets, guilts, waves of anger manifest their presence in the lives of this trio. The opening two scenes show us pairs of characters (Jerry with Emma then with Robert) toying with syntax, questioning the formulation of each other's questions. The concern with style here has none of the venom of Spooner and Hirst's sparring matches; the characters know each other too well to have any desire to search out and deflate poses. If one questions another, it is to confirm his suppositions and make the other know the extent of his knowledge. The tone now is not deadly but somehow deadened, the questions not keen but evasive, tired; curiously there is little bite or tension:

the appetite for knowledge satisfied, the recourse is invariably to nonchalance: "It doesn't matter" [p. 29]; "Well, it's not very important, is it?" [p. 35]. Jerry meeting Emma two years after she ended their affair is abstracted more by the hangover he is nursing than by her news that she and her husband, Robert, are separating; he observes the conversational routine they established together over the years: "I ask about your husband. You ask about my wife" [p. 15]. Emma acquiesces and the talk is kept on a level of generalities; she seems constantly on the brink of tears yet her words and her manner are decisive. It is as if she is concerned less about being emotional with Jerry than with questioning the need to be emotional at all: "It's all gone. . . . It's all, all over" [pp. 29-30]. If in a later scene Robert and Jerry, waiting together for Emma, investigate a platitude with inane seriousness about why boy babies cry more than girl babies and decide after intensive cerebration that it must have something to do with the difference between the sexes, there is no subtext of aggression such as we might expect, only a sense again of hollow conversational forms. The men's friendship (it goes back to school and college days and Jerry's being best man at Robert's wedding) has dwindled, like the affair, to routine: it is perhaps safer than facing up to their real situation. Jerry at this moment is basking smugly in his confidence that he and Emma have been "brilliant" at keeping their affair secret from everyone, and most especially from Robert; and Robert will not admit he knows about it lest he chance to end a good business relationship and lose face with one who has been taken in over the years by his stance of controlled detachment. (He reads Yeats and aims at cultivating the gaiety that transfigures dread.) The moment is funny but the hollow tone and the conscious sense of a formula, the somewhat mechanical quality of the dialogue, risk the charge of mannerism, that Pinter is being merely Pinteresque.

The matter-of-fact, limpid tone is refreshing after the claustrophobia of the two earlier plays, *Old Times* and *No Man's Land*, where there was either no chance of changing ground or, if the chance offered, one moved only to what looked eerily like the same place. For Pinter the multiplicity of scene-changes in *Betrayal* seemed almost prodigal — through bar, hotel, restaurant, lounge, study, flat, bedroom, a scene in Venice, constant talk of trips to the States, Robert, Jerry and Emma have a freedom denied most of Pinter's previous creations; but it is a freedom that exposes their essential bloodlessness. They talk of having a home as they move from room to room; but it is a notion, an idea, not a fixation, as it is for Rose, Stanley, Davies or even Spooner and Hirst, a hunger that keeps the will, the nerves, the imagination at full stretch. The trio talk of roots, of enduring values like friendship, but they live on the surface of life and as such are the sport of time. Once again John Bury designed the perfect setting to complement the action: faced with the need to effect rapidly so many scene-changes, he devised a huge carousel divided into three segments by high, wing-like walls. As it moved inexorably onwards between scenes to a remote tinkling music, the image it called to mind was the whirligig of time bringing in its revenges. Whereas Pinter's other plays since *Landscape* and *Silence* have taken place in a timeless present, *Betrayal* observes a meticulous chronology; it is less the mind's processes of recall that are being actualised now than the very process of ageing: *Betrayal* pinpoints an erosion of vitality, passion and spontaneity through the deceptions played by the trio on each other and themselves. The profundity of the waste, the subtle momentousness of the betrayals is the more telling for the mundane obviousness of the circumstances of the adultery.

Our double perspective on to the events is created by a dramatic structure which heightens our appreciation of loss by reversing the chronological order. We begin with Emma's futile efforts to reawaken Jerry's concern for her at the moment her marriage to Robert is crumbling and pass back through her cold-blooded ending of the affair she has come to find tedious — "The fact is that in the old days we used our imagination . . ." [p. 53], through her admission of her adultery to Robert and its repercussions on all three pairings, to the savagely lusty pass Jerry made at Emma while drunk at a party, which is where it all began. The mannerism of the opening scenes is the token of the spiritual wasteland, the grey mediocrity the characters have brought on themselves by affecting not to care.

As the play progresses those early scenes gain a wealth of irony in retrospect. Jerry, for example, during the affair is haunted by the memory of once picking up Emma's daughter, Charlotte, on impulse and throwing her again and again up to the ceiling while his and her families stood by, surprised and laughing; the memory excites them to love-making. It seems bound up with a wish to father a child by Emma (a child being the centre of his notion of a home). In the play's opening scene it is Emma who initiates a recall of the memory of Jerry's playing with Charlotte; Michael Gambon as Jerry responded according to form, but his "Darling" was so chillingly clumsy and flat that it at once exposed to Emma the absurdity of her intention of soliciting a renewal of Jerry's passion. The moment became merely an exercise in nostalgia.

Repeatedly through the scene Emma asks if Jerry remembers the past, if he thinks of her, as if she is seeking reassurance that she ever meant anything to him. Nostalgia is a mood the characters cultivate as if finding in it a security, a certainty, that eludes them in the present. Consider how frequently Robert breaks out of his hauteur to speak rapturously in Emma's presence of the games of squash he and Jerry used to enjoy. His motive seems less the need to insult his wife by talking of an idyllic because simply masculine world from which women and their complicating irresponsibilities are excluded than a wish momentarily to recover the relaxed physicality, the intimacy of his youth with Jerry (an assurance implicit, as Peter Hall directed it, in their easy grasping of hand and shoulder that we see in the final scene immediately before Jerry turns his physical attentions to Emma). Recurring clusters of topics of conversation nicely highlight both the characters' suppressed but unresolved anxieties about knowing and not knowing and the moments of illumination that come too late, sadly, to be of use and so confirm the characters in their apathetic belief that none of it really matters. Consider how Robert seems to harp on about whether or not Emma is looking forward to seeing Torcello again in Scene Five; it is, we discover, a place they first visited together shortly after their wedding; we already know that they visited it on Jerry's recommendation, he and his wife Judith having been there previously. It is one of several "recommendations" by Jerry that Robert stresses in the scene in shaping pressures around Emma till she confesses that she and Jerry are lovers, thus confirming his suppositions. We learn subsequently, however, that in the event Robert went to Torcello early alone and read Yeats in the dawn light. The context now is Robert's first business lunch with Jerry after discovering about the affair. To Jerry's astonishment Robert gets progressively drunker and curses the literature he makes his living by, especially the modern novels that he claims Jerry and Emma find so thrilling. The mood is disquieting because one is not sure how serious Robert is being; the denunciation of modern literature has a comic extravagance about it and is the funnier for Jerry's bemusement at what he patently considers is just a pose on Robert's part. The first actual mention of Torcello in the play comes in the second scene the night after Emma has told Jerry of her imminent divorce and intimated that she has told Robert everything about their former affair. Having sustained a total indifference to the morality of his relationship with Emma while he thought it was a brilliantly kept secret, he is now well-nigh speechless with guilt lest it might jeopardise his friendship with

Robert. Robert calms him down by admitting he has known for years and that it has made no difference to their relationship; he had supposed Jerry knew of Emma's confession. To try and prove to each other that their bond has in no way suffered, the men begin to chat about what they are currently reading. Jerry acknowledges a new admiration for Yeats and recalls Robert's passionate eulogy once of the delight of reading Yeats in the dawn on Torcello. There is a flash of recognition from Robert — "So I did. I told you that, yes" [p. 46] — and a long pause in which the pattern of resonances is followed through before, with a quickly reiterated "yes", he changes the subject. It takes much of the play to fill out that gap of silence, so evidently meaningful, that pains Robert. If he supposed that Jerry *knew* that Emma had informed him about the affair (and she had an excellent opportunity to do so on her return from Venice but perversely kept silent, when Jerry recalled losing one of her letters and living in panic lest Judith find it), then his introduction of Torcello into the conversation in the restaurant and the grotesque clowning which follows can be seen to express Robert's utter astonishment at Jerry's absolute coolness (as he supposes) in the situation, which calls the bluff to his own attempts at detachment. And Jerry's seeming control survives unscathed throughout the lunch, despite Robert's flirting more and more perilously with the prospect of bringing out into the open the subject that is actually taxing his thoughts — the fact of an affair between his wife and his best friend. To Robert Jerry's apparent indifference and nonchalance beggar all description, however progressive morally he prides himself on being. Talking in the very first scene of their reasons for separating, Emma mentions that Robert has betrayed for years with other women. Do the infidelities, perhaps, date from this lunchtime encounter with Jerry? Does Robert's long silence of recognition embrace regret that on that earlier occasion in the restaurant he was perhaps too clever and read too much into Jerry's stance?

In a play that invited us to relish such a texture of retrospective ironies, it seemed wilful of Peter Hall in an otherwise beautifully paced and accented production to break the action with an interval, thereby intensifying the possibility of his audience misconstruing the play's opening. Elsewhere his attention to visual detail ideally complemented Pinter's verbal artistry. Jerry, for example, after Emma has engineered the ending of the affair and the sale of their flat, swaying forward, reached after her yet remained prosaically rooted to the spot, a posture which exactly mirrored his drunken lurching that mesmerised her at the party.

The way their flat passed from a brightly pristine to a shabby condition evoked both their failure to make the place the home they covertly wish for and the tawdry sentimentality of their hope of ever doing so. Buying a new tablecloth to brighten the place is no proof of their success; their very exuberance at such moments was a betrayal to delusion.

It would be wrong to suggest that the power of the play lies all in its retrospective patterning; knowledge of the consequences of particular decisions between the characters brings at once a density and sharpness of emotional definition to the later scenes. Consider the penultimate one where Emma breaks the news to Jerry that she is pregnant. Remembering her control over the ending of the affair, we notice that again she initiates the conversational flow. She sets a loving, domestic mood (Jerry must relax with a drink while she finishes preparing a special casserole), casually mentions his wife, Judith and asks if she is ever unfaithful, questions whether Jerry has ever thought of changing his life. Jerry responds by listing all Judith's capable virtues as reasons for decidedly not breaking with her — "all that means something" — even though, as he finally admits, he "adores" Emma [p. 129]. He chooses a cautious hold on security and Emma confides that she is pregnant by Robert. How much of this is calculated, how much spontaneous? Is she testing Jerry before deciding on the paternity of her child, estimating the depth of feeling that lies behind his adoration? Or is this perhaps a first kindly effort to force their separation? Since a certain deadness sets into Jerry after this, is his final, quiet, uninflected "I'm very happy for you" [p. 130] genuine or a recognition of his failure to meet Emma's expectations? The conversational surface sustains a relaxed intimacy but there is an undertow of yearnings and rejections hardly apparent to the lovers but sensed poignantly by us through the meticulous shaping and placing of the scene. It completes a pattern of encounters between Jerry and Emma in which she senses a need to make a decision (whom she should claim as Ned's father; whether she should inform Jerry she has confessed to Robert; whether they should formally end the affair by selling the flat; whether (an impulse this) there might be a future for her with Jerry when her marriage is terminated); each time clearly she hopes for an outcome that is the opposite of that forced on her by Jerry's lack of daring and commitment. His lassitude, moral and imaginative, continually forces her to a decisiveness that belies her feelings. Jerry plays out his life according to a formula and, if Emma's manner verges on the frantic, even the hysterical, it is because she realises the extent to which that weakness in him has the power to restrict her freedom and her attempts at honesty. Pinter's structure wittily enhances our discriminations.

The form of *Betrayal* imposes formidable demands on the actors and the skill of the initial cast was impeccable, pointing (though never forcibly) the pattern of echoes and resonances within the dialogue and exploring the psychological nuances such patterning suggests. Jerry's complete acceptance of his mediocrity, as Michael Gambon projected it, became an act of monstrous egotism, since it rendered him incapable of engaging imaginatively with anything other than his own easy equanimity. Stalwart because unthinking, all too easygoing, he was insufferable in his very ordinariness; his very presence seemed to provoke in Emma a silent questioning of the worth of her betrayals. Robert's gesture of comforting her after Jerry's departure in Scene IV, that released the tears that she seemed ever to be trying to hold back, established this point finely; but it needed the stage-presence Gambon created to invest the moment with a telling degree of pathos. Gambon excels at portraying men whose big stature is not matched with a corresponding largeness of personality for want of a developed *moral* imagination: Brecht's Galileo (Olivier, 1980), Shakespeare's Antony (Other Place and the Pit, 1982-83) and a host of Ayckbourn roles have shown him at his best.

The *cor anglais*-like timbre of Penelope Wilton's voice found ample scope for its special quality in Emma: a rich lower register that is engaging and seductive can thin out to a reedy sobbing note or a chill, insistent vindictiveness; always, even at its fullest, there is a hint of imminent sadness. Penelope Wilton has succeeded over the Seventies in portraying emotionally generous women who are rendered shrewish by discovering the willingness of others to take advantage of them — Ottoline Morrell in *Bloomsbury* (Phoenix, 1974), for example, and a rewardingly subtle study of Shaw's Julia Craven in *The Philanderer* (Lyttleton, 1978), in whom the New Woman is constantly doing battle with the old Eve to a degree that it would be easy to caricature but which she presented with considerable sympathy. Always Miss Wilton seems to find the core of vulnerability in a character out of which to develop her performance (it is in part the happy product of that tear-stained voice), and in her Emma this lay in an impulsiveness that set at risk all her efforts to sustain a cool, rational front and so jeopardised the choices on which she tried to base an emotional security that she was left ever more rawly exposed. She made the role a haunting study in self-betrayal.

Daniel Massey's Robert, a world-weary failed aesthete, was a virtuoso creation, never funnier nor more pathetic than when cursing the literary world that provides his livelihood since he feels it stimulates a rapport between other people that excludes him. The conception was thought through to the finest particulars: how the elegant arabesques traced in the air by his tapered fingers revealed the thrill Robert gets from his verbal felicities, especially in the scene where he seeks to ascertain how accurate his suspicions are that Emma is having an affair without actually appearing to pry. Massey's fine *heldentenor* rose excitedly to a falsetto cry on her admission that was exquisitely pitched between anguish and triumph at the success of his ploys, while the hands were fists now, clenching when he realised how established the affair was — *"Five years!"* — till the knuckles all but burst the skin [p. 86]. This made perfectly credible his remark that he is not above hitting Emma on occasions, though not from any kind of moral standpoint: "I just felt like giving her a good bashing. The old itch . . . you understand" [p. 41]. Yet what an admission that is — the more unnerving for the casualness of the phrasing — from a man who sets such store by adopting a relaxed, bemused acceptance of the ways of the world! It was a most expert and delicate piece of high comedy acting, showing how the more Robert sought to suppress pain in the interests of being open-minded and liberal the less human he became. How far short of his Yeatsian ideal of a fine nonchalance, *sprezzatura*, he fell! Robert's calculated indifference was a decidedly cheap imitation of the real thing. Together the three actors made *Betrayal* a comedy of modern manners that was very civilised; the strength of the play is that it ultimately disturbs us into questioning whether being "civilised" is not the worst betrayal of all, when as here it means being beyond the reach of passion.

Interestingly David Mercer chose to pose that same question in his last play, *No Limits To Love*, (Warehouse, 1980)[15], and to explore the idea in the context of an adulterous relationship, where openness is the rule (it is a *ménage à trois* for Marna, Edward and her lover Hugh). Mercer works within a more traditional idiom of stage realism than Pinter does, but the greater articulateness of his characters compared with those in *Betrayal* is more than a matter of dramatic method: "talking things through" is their means of sustaining an equilibrium in the relationship, it is their way of keeping their powerful egos in control, of creating a communally agreed integrity. This instantaneous forthrightness can be just routine intellectualising or even a grasping wildly at straws rather than a considered explanation of one's behaviour, and the brittle humour of the play quickly alerts the audience to the precarious nature of the balance the three claim they have achieved. Far from connoting a relaxed affability, the witty banter carries a snide, derogatory thrust:

HUGH: How long have you had this house is it?
EDWARD: Twelve, thirteen years.
HUGH: Yes and you've had Marna around for ten. . . .
EDWARD: Funny way to talk about marriage. Having somebody around.
HUGH: I always get the impression that's the way you look at it yourself.
EDWARD: I was alone when I moved in here. No carpets. No furniture.
    (*Pause.*) Girl I knew — Polly something or other — used to sit there. On that very spot. On the bare floor. Drinking champagne all day and playing "Bridge Over Troubled Waters". (*Pause.*) What a golden summer that was. Wild. Way out. (*Pause*). I believe Marna was assisting in one of those abortive French revolutions at the time.
MARNA: I wouldn't put it quite like that.
EDWARD: Yes you were. I saw you on a barricade. (*Firmly to* HUGH:) In Paris. She was a kind of idealogical groupie in those days. Absolutely in her element digging up cobblestones.
MARNA: I took some medical supplies over, that's all.
EDWARD: Yes. So you did. Considering all the pharmacies were open at the time I thought it very eccentric of you. [p.3]

Egotism has been refined to pettishness but not refined away; it can quickly flare up in horseplay, calculated viciousness or great arias of hatred in which the three re-tell their past lives not so much out of a wish to come at truths about themselves as to find an explanation of why and how each came to be caught in the slough of despond that is their shared present. Their culture (Edward is a professional cellist, Marna is involved in Human Rights, Hugh is a history don) has proved no safeguard against intellectual debility. The metaphor from Bunyan is apt, for Mercer has described his play as a "comedy of absense" [p. viii], a kind of social morality in the tradition of Coward's *Design for Living*. As we watch the process of talking things through at work, we come to realise that it is a formula for exorcising instinctive responses; depriving themselves of the right to be spontaneous has robbed all three of originality and imaginative energy. They are shadows of the individuals they could be and they know it:

EDWARD: I expect we shall go on till one of us dies.
MARNA: I expect so.
EDWARD: But all these years. I've watched myself in horror. In despair.

(*Pause.*) Such a long procession of years. (*Pause.*) With the most unaccountable longings and yearnings. As if there were some other Edward waiting to be born. Waiting for a signal to exist. (*Pause.*) An absolutely bloody magnificent new self. A creature of humility and light. Of love. A person of exemplary tenderness and compassion. [p. 67]

The suppressions Pinter's characters practise in *Betrayal* are secret so that the pain each suffers is aggravated by the (erroneous) belief that the affair is of but casual importance to the others involved; only the audience is aware of the true extent of the emotional devastation. In *No Limits to Love* the suppressions are vocal and public; the trio are conscious of each other's pain, even if they choose to disparage it or treat it with contempt. With them it is a deliberate choice not to be generous, whereas Pinter's characters dread admitting to an emotional need or asking for generosity, as if to talk of feeling openly were to break some decorum essential to social and cultural well-being. For them the possibility of benevolence can never be entertained and so their ending is a despair fostered by uncertainty and self-doubt. Mercer — true to the morality drama — believes in the possibility of change: while pain can be admitted, his characters are not wholly slaves to their ritual for extinguishing feeling and personality. He introduces a fourth character to the group: Otto, a psychoanalyst of German extraction, genuinely courteous, suave because his cultured background has invested his physical presence as well as his intellect with a quiet, unassuming grace. (Edward Petherbridge played the role to perfection as a man for whom style was in the best sense a complete way of life; ever-alert being a trained listener, nothing escaped his attention or was deemed unworthy of his notice; his calm seriousness gave him instantly a stature beside the others.) The psychoanalyst with the dulcet voice, the man who has made a profession of talking things through, elects to administer a psychic shock to break the tensions that bedevil the household: he shoots Hugh when he is at his most callous, not to kill, simply to hurt him enough to unsettle his obnoxious smugness. It is a brilliant *coup de théâtre*, quite unexpected in a play that has seemed till now a particularly witty, if predictable, exercise in sardonic Seventies realism; and it heralds in Act Two a series of psychological reversals that astonish yet are wholly convincing, as one by one the trio find the courage to act as spontaneously through impulse as Otto. Hugh cries like a child in Otto's embrace; Marna, feeling her sensibility and Edward's have been abused enough by Hugh, suddenly "springs at him landing on his back like a cat out of a tree. They go down together, thrashing and flailing. . . . She kneels astride him sobbing and pummelling" [p. 63]. Otto takes Hugh away as patient or lover or perhaps as a generous gesture to Edward, whom he admires, to leave him free to find a future with Marna. And Edward, whose perennial lot it has been to nurse Marna through her post-affair depressions, finds her asking him to play for her (earlier she had admitted to Otto that seeing Edward lost in music, seemingly at one with his cello was to her a thing of exquisite beauty). The play ends with her seated beside him entralled in the gathering darkness as he begins to play. (Howard Davies' choice of one of Bach's sonatas for unaccompanied cello, robust and jubilant, for the R.S.C. production was particularly felicitous.) If the play avoids sentimentality in its conclusion — it too is robustly jubilant — it is because Mercer shows from the start how intensely his characters long for change, to break free of the stranglehold imposed by the *ménage* that they feel they have been so clever in creating together but which has forced each of them to adopt a mean little pose, a travesty of the real self within. Mercer's description, a "comedy of absence", is somewhat misleading: *No Limits to Love* is more a comedy of discovery that there are no limits beyond which love cannot find some means of expression. Mercer's conviction of this is the source of the play's dynamic energy, verbal and structural: "We are cut off, trapped, shaped and self-shaped; and somehow the glorious creature that could be man (I imply nothing Rousseau-esque) is like that wonderful line in the Donne poem: 'A great prince in prison lies' " [p. viii]. Grotesques — Mercer's own word — his characters may be, but, broken and humiliated by their acts of desperation, by the end they find a valid human dignity. Where *Betrayal* charts love's passing and becomes an elegy for the spiritual waste that ensues, *No Limits to Love* explores how passion, once embraced, initiates a progress to spiritual ease.

The remarkable feature of Pinter's most recent work is his power to adapt the recognisably idiosyncratic features of his style to subject matter at a far remove from his earlier thematic preoccupations. The manner in which the opening scenes of *Betrayal* seem a near-parody of his idiom and dramatic method to evoke the world-weary dessication of the three characters' sensibilities heralded a series of similar experiments in *Other Places* (Cottesloe, 1982).[16] As the title implies, all three plays explore exclusively private states of being.

In *Victoria Station* Pinter's device of the interrogation that is sustained to the point of frenzied despair by the questioner is deployed to render a state of complete wonder: "I think I've fallen in love. For the first time in my life" [p. 60]. The young taxi driver does not evade the controller's questions out of malice or fear; his answers are purely mechanical, for his mind is engaged elsewhere cautiously testing a state that has transformed his modes of perception and response, though he remains unsure whether this is for good or ill. Exasperating and intrusive though the controller's voice is, at least it represents the familiar and so offers the driver a degree of security against which to measure the quality of his new experience. It could all be cloyingly sentimental — the young man's words certainly are: "I think I'm going to keep her for the rest of my life. I'm going to stay in this car with her for the rest of my life" [p. 60] — were it not for his anxiety — "Don't have anything to do with 135. . . . Don't leave me. I'm your man. I'm the only one you can trust" [p. 54] — and his bewilderment at the all-consuming nature of his passion, its power to create an intense present obliterating all certainties and responsibilities. The technique of the interrogation here defines a loss of self quite different from Stanley's traumatised state in *The Birthday Party* or Lamb's depersonalising ordeal in *The Hothouse* to test whether or not he has the makings of a bureaucrat. Though it was cleverly staged by Peter Hall and John Bury (the dimly-lit Controller's Office loomed out of the darkness behind and above the driver's Ford Cortina), one wondered whether the full poignancy of the piece might not be better served by radio where one could more readily suppose two voices making fragile contact across an unknown distance of night-time London, since their *voices* are all that the controller and driver 274 know of each other. Radio would increase the eeriness of the driver's inconsequential replies, the fact of his being *lost* in a more than physical sense.

Family Voices was broadcast prior to performance at the National Theatre and radio seemed the preferable medium in a way that would not be true of *Silence* to which it is close in style. In *Silence* the three characters are inescapably and painfully present to each other in memory; *Family Voices* is concerned more with parting, loss and the factors that make for a continuing separation. The mother addresses her absent son — "Darling. Where are you? The flowers are wonderful here. The blooms. You loved them so. Why do you never write?" [p. 69] — cajoling, ingratiating, seeking his wheareabouts, hoping for some recognition of her existence. Her reminiscences of experiences shared with him in his childhood give way as time passes to emotional blackmail — "Darling. I miss you. I gave birth to you. Where are you?" [p. 76] — and subsequently to vehemence, threats, cursing, sarcasm — "Do you think the word love means anything?" [p. 82]. The son tells of his situation in a house shared by members of a family called Withers; but as the circumstantial details mount up, the account seems increasingly a work of fiction revealing nothing of his real self, while apparently confiding all. Are the stories a product of sheer indifference towards his parents or strategies to preserve a privately nourished integrity won with difficulty from the reach of an all-too possessive parent whose lifestyle with its cosy middle-class decorum has proved suffocating? When the son contemplates returning, a third voice speaks of his father's sorrow: "I have so much to say to you. But I am quite dead. What I have to say to you will never be said" [p. 83]. Is the nature of family ties such that these strategies for independence will ultimately bring only guilt? Are they temporary prevarications masking an intention to return some day, that might in time prove too late? Is this ideal of escape ever really possible either in place or time? And is that knowledge not the source of the mother's confident and insidious power and of the father's grief? Whatever the word 'love' may mean, its responsibilities are found to be exacting and ineluctable. Though the title refers to *voices*, the style has a detached formality, lacking in idiomatic energy, what one might term a composed quality, as if the characters were mentally formulating letters that may or may not be written and posted. The effect of writing is often to distance emotion, alienating the reader with whom one seeks to connect; one has to trust to a generous reading and where trust is absent or uncertain then the style may communicate that fact by a certain self-consciousness; and Pinter captures this tone in both mother's and son's voices exactly. It is through tone that Pinter defines how love that is caring can become constricting, even ultimately destructive of the relationships it seeks to cherish. Radio focused one's attention so pointedly on tone that one sensed a cold and hardening formality in the mother and an impersonal geniality in the son exacerbating the emotional distance between them to great tragic effect. In the stage performances the three characters were presented as portrait-silhouettes sharing an ornate frame, till a spotlight illuminated individual speakers in turn. It was a nicely judged visual irony, but the necessary sense of *apartness* — deliberately sought by the son, dreaded yet compelled on him by the mother — was lost and with it much of the tragic intensity. Though beautiful, the stage image John Bury created did not seem as perfectly in sympathy with the play as was his richly allusive, metaphorical setting for *Silence*.

By far the most substantial of the three plays that make up *Other Places* is *A Kind of Alaska*, yet one wonders if its impact would have been so profound in performance, were it not preceded by *Family Voices* and *Victoria Station*: for like the one it enquires into the dangerously self-consuming aspects of care and like the other renders the experience of an awakening into an acutely painful transcendence. Deborah is the subject of a scientific miracle: the victim for nearly thirty years of sleeping sickness, her life simply "stopped" till the discovery of the drug that would effect a cure. She has been tended by a younger sister, Pauline and her doctor-husband, who had faith that she would be restored to them: "I lifted you onto this bed, like a corpse. Some wanted to bury you. I forbade it. I have nourished you, watched over you, for all this time" [p. 34]. They have grown old in pursuing this care; Pauline's existence has on her own admission been little more than widowhood as a consequence of her husband's devotion to Deborah. Now their ambition has been fulfilled, Deborah has regained consciousness and they are caught between elation at their success, an exhausted relief and a certain dread both for their own future, now that a life's purpose has been completed, and for Deborah's. Her access to consciousness proves a mixed blessing: she is, as Hornby says, at once "still young, but older" [p. 7]; she has the mind of a precocious adolescent in the body of a middle-aged woman. She has slept through the years when an adolescent acquires the qualities of maturity like tact or generosity and so has no sense of obligation or gratitude for the care lavished on her so relentlessly; her mind has awesomely skipped a gap in time and is conscious only of immediately perceived fact — that if the woman beside her bed is truly Pauline then she has "changed. A great deal. You've aged . . . substantially. What happened to you?" [p. 29]. Deborah is not wantonly callous, just forthright, like a child stating only what falls readily within the limits of its understanding and quite oblivious of its power to hurt. The pain is the more acute for Pauline's barely controlled excitement as her husband's success: "You're looking at me. Oh Deborah . . . you haven't looked at me . . . for such a long time" [p. 26].

Pinter's technique of rapid inconsequential shifts in the direction of his dialogue gains a new impetus here in depicting a consciousness voraciously exploring its immediate experience, trying to explain its condition to its satisfaction by relating perceptions to known facts, but perpetually falling short of any degree of comprehension because it cannot encompass the fact of twenty-nine years of silence and inanition. This is a frightening innocence. Even when Deborah wonders if something shameful has occurred to explain her presence in this unknown bedroom with a stranger — "You've had your way with me. You made me touch you. You stripped me" [p. 12] — her mind cannot conceive of this as more than a flirtatious lark: "Did I make eyes at you? Did I show desire for you? Did I let you peep up my skirt? Did I flash my teeth? Was I as bold as brass?" [p. 11]. There is no sense of her real age, not even when she discovers that, like Pauline, she has breasts. Her attention is recalled repeatedly by Hornby to the present; quietly he enumerates the details — her mother's death, father's blindness, his being cared for now by the eldest sister, Estelle, who never married — but Deborah's mind skates over them referring to parties, friends, family patterns of behaviour, as if what Pauline and Hornby talk of as the past were but yesterday. At the close of the play Deborah confidently asserts what she *knows*:

You say I have been asleep. You say I am now awake. You say I have not awoken from the dead. You say I was not dreaming then and am not dreaming now. You say I have always been alive and am alive now. You say I am a woman.

She looks at PAULINE, *then back to* HORNBY.

She is a widow. She doesn't go to her ballet classes any more. Mummy and Daddy and Estelle are on a world cruise. They've stopped off in Bangkok. It'll be my birthday soon. I think I have the matter in proportion.

Pause

Thank you.   [p. 40]

Her mind has toyed with the idea of her age — "I must be quite old. I wonder what I look like. But it's of no consequence. I certainly have no intention of looking into a mirror" [p. 39] — but the imagination has not grasped the reality of what it means for *her* to be in her mid-forties; and till the imagination can assimilate that, then Pauline and Hornby's period of caring is far from over. The medical miracle may have happened but a greater awakening remains to be achieved. When Hornby first tells Deborah the truth — "I woke you with an injection" — her imagination actually encompasses the greater truth by a joking reference to fairy tale: "And am I beautiful? . . . And you are my Prince Charming. Aren't you?" [p. 19]. Hornby is too overcome by the tragic irony of it all to reply and Deborah lashes out in fear or desperation: "Oh speak up. (*Pause*) Silly shit. All men are alike. (*Pause*) I think I love you" [p. 20]. She is aware briefly that the whimsical mood is mere wish-fulfilment, that there is nothing happy for ever after about this sleeping beauty's awaking; but the imagination shrinks from the need to explore that moment of pain. Will that pattern of recoil continue to be the mind's practice, seeking security in a never-never-land of perpetual youth, free of adult responsibilities, an object life-long of others' care?

Judi Dench was an admirable choice for Deborah. Her voice has long retained command of its youthful inflexions and her stage persona is noted for a passionate impulsiveness and carefree zest. She has given a spirited account of Shakespeare's heroines in the past: to her Beatrice, for example (Stratford and Aldwych, 1976–77), she brought a full-bloodied gaiety; hers indeed was a "wild heart" but one all too willingly tamed for her Benedict (Donald Sinden), the very force of feeling and complete trust quite subduing her earlier reservations about matrimony. This unqualified trust, a willingness to immerse herself totally in the emotional truth of a moment without irony or scruple is a hallmark of her style;[17] she can convey innocence and purity of intent with a fierce radiance. This was a considerable gift when she was a young actress. What is remarkable is that the gift has stayed with her as she has matured without hardening into caricature or becoming a parody of itself. She uses the technique sparingly now, usually to portray moments of transcendence when a character briefly steps out of time and recovers a state of pure joy not known since youth, when the consciousness rises free of the trammelling responsibilities and emotional compromises of age. A notable example was her Mrs. Boyle in O'Casey's *Juno and the Paycock* (Aldwych, 1980), suddenly blossoming in the days of her husband's apparent prosperity and finding a girlish charm and exuberance at the tea-party of Act II, a vivacity that years of menial struggle had suppressed but never wholly extinguished until tragedy closed in on her and she became again the tight-lipped, managing woman, indomitable but joyless. For a fleeting moment, as she linked arms with her daughter, Mary, and shyly joined her in a duet for the assembled guests, the lines of toil dropped from her features and one might have supposed the two women were sisters, so complete and infectious was their gaiety.

For Deborah Judi Dench deployed this technique to disconcerting effect. The face was clearly that of a woman in her mid-forties; the voice touched an occasional mature rasp but mostly sustained a sunny, untroubled timbre, redolent of late childhood verging on adolescence, throughout the character's fluctuating moods: her exuberance; the sibling rivalry — "Sisters are diabolical. Brothers are worse. One day I prayed I would see no one ever again, none of them ever again. All that eating, all that wit" [p. 18]; her precocious delight in big words; the giggling delivery when touching on *risqué* subjects; the pique and the easily bruised dignity — "Bit of a cheek, I think, Mummy not coming in to say hullo, to say goodnight, to tuck me up, to sing me a song, to warn me about going too far with boys" [p. 20]. When she was annoyed, one caught briefly an authentic middle-class tone of command quite dated in its inflexions. Occasionally the mind sensed some discrepancy but could not account for the strangeness: "I sound childish. Out of . . . tune" [p. 12]. With the repeated attempts to explain the situation — was it a hotel by the sea and were waves those distant, muffled sounds? Was it a tent in the Sahara and she a victim of the White Slave Trade or a prison and she completing a sentence for some unknown crime? — the voice always carried a tone of amused disbelief, as if each were an entertaining but recognisably *tall* story. Even at the last the note was of bright, matter-of-fact confidence ("I think I have the matter in proportion. . . . Thank you"), though her body had shown itself to be grotesquely uncoordinated after years of disuse and subject to a type of fit that contorted the spine and set the limbs trembling. Never a hint of self-pity intruded: the dissociation of mind and body was absolute and the consequent challenge to Pauline and Hornby's care formidable. What price such love as theirs that nursed such a consciousness into being?

Fortunately we have two performances by which to gauge the richness of this play, since, shortly after Judi Dench, Dorothy Tutin essayed the role of Deborah for a television production with Paul Schofield as Hornby and then recreated this in the theatre with Colin Blakely (Duchess, 1985). Where Judi Dench gave us a precocious adolescent caged in a middle-aged woman's body, the inner life frighteningly at odds with physical circumstance, Dorothy Tutin offered a ravaged, cavern-eyed woman whose efforts at self-expression were confined within the idioms and rhythms of a teenager. Only occasionally did the inner compulsion and the verbal phrasing truly match and the heavy lines of her face relax into a radiant smile. As Kate in *Old Times* Tutin had intimated unfathomable deeps to the character's mind whither she privately voyaged to the deliberate exclusion of others from her life; here as Deborah she conveyed an impression of the horrendous nightmare that was her long sleep, the sense of a soul's confinement, which she lacked the vocabulary and the conscious, formulated experience to begin to define for others. The image of "dancing with someone dancing on your foot all the time, I mean

all the time, on the same spot, just slam, slam, a big boot on your
foot, not the most ideal kind of dancing, not by a long chalk" [pp.
25–26] was avidly seized on for its possibilities to help convey her
plight but soon proved, as the mind explored it fully, to be
inadequate to her bitter task. Her eyes were wild with frustration.
Always one was conscious of her eyes — defiant; wary at the
incongruity of herself beside her perceptions of Hornby and
Pauline, at the failure of anything seemingly to make sense;
terrified, like Winnie's eyes in *Happy Days*, at being caught
between two dimensions of reality, between "that time" and this.
Whereas Dench achieved pathos by showing a candid innocent soul
awaking unawares into a world of historical and human change,
decay and intricate complexities of feeling, Tutin achieved it by
presenting a mind, shaped by alien forces, struggling to find its
place in an ordinary world dimly remembered from some past
time, when it had been experienced through the irresponsible,
fictionalising perceptions of childhood. "I sound childish. Out of
. . . tune" here carried a wealth of implication: awareness,
judgement, recoil, disbelief, despair. But at the end she began
cautiously to explore Hornby's view of her situation: "*You say* I
have been asleep. . . . *You say* I am a woman". She appeared to
be keeping a safe distance still between herself and factual reality:
was her mind entering a process of change and renewal or was it
objectifying experience the better to detach itself and retreat from
the pressures of commitment? Tutin held the climax poised between
possibilities, a frightening challenge to Hornby and Pauline's
further care.

   Inevitably these two different readings of Deborah's role affected
the playing of Hornby and Pauline. Peter Hall's production seemed
a study in kinds of tormented innocence. Paul Rogers with Judi
Dench was a kindly, avuncular Hornby, the old-style family
doctor, who had patiently set his sights on a cure and doggedly
worked to effect a miracle, never imagining the possible
consequences, determined till the end that with the best of care all
would be well. Anna Massey as Pauline was a frail, bony lady:
married yet, oddly, the archetypal wasted spinster in appearance,
wholly unfulfilled in herself, a sad token of the cost of her
husband's preoccupation with Deborah's case, and desperate that
the cure should work to prove that her own life of abnegation had
been worthwhile. A fragile and dwindling hope was the one spark
of life in her; the poise, the cultured voice were the attributes of one
whose adulthood had been a continual test of fortitude and
stoicism. Paul Schofield's Hornby was a watchful presence, gentle

but firm of voice, a clinical mind studying every change in his patient so as to forestall any lapse in her condition and *will* her to recovery. His was a solicitous, powerfully contained figure, yet strangely *maternal* in his control of the sick-room and possessive in his care. The detailed account of that caring had a quiet but deliberate tone that would clearly brook no opposition or denial; yet one knew that this patient would not bend easily to his subtle will. All those years ago he had determined on effecting a cure and he would not be baulked of his objective: Deborah was a challenge to his professionalism. Blakely's Hornby had a scientific but unimaginative mind that studied the awakening Deborah with detached curiosity, playing along with her shifting moods as if trying to understand her, she being as remote and *other* to him as he to her. When Pauline intruded, he flared up in anger at the loss of further objective study of his patient and at his inability to advise his wife how to proceed with her sister. As he withdrew from their interview together and slumped in a chair, a dark silhouette against the hospital window, his was the weary, humbled resignation of a man who had excitedly reached for a miracle and found only tragedy, an outcome which he might have surmised professionally but which he had failed to prepare either himself or his wife to expect. Susan Engel played Pauline as a decent, ordinary woman joyfully expecting the return of a loved sister to that normality she had known since childhood — middle-class, urbane, comfortable — but who was hurt to the quick by the Deborah she discovered; she was confused, betrayed in her simple affection by cruel circumstance; and she rapidly sensed and accepted the lifetime of further demands her sister was going to make on her stamina. There was a near-hysterical edge to her voice as she shared Deborah's memories of their childhood, as if she were recalling too the years deprived of innocent pleasures since her sister's life "stopped" altogether. Clearly she had hoped that that time was ended for good but was realising that it might be her continuing burden indefinitely. Tutin's Deborah hovered finally on the threshold of hope; but one was left wondering whether her loved ones' care, which she needed now more than ever before, had not been tested beyond its resources.

The two productions showed the immense potential of Pinter's work for inventive actors: here were two quite different readings of *A Kind of Alaska,* each quite viable and profoundly tragic, both intimating the wealth of insight into human character and the workings of consciousness that had been refined into the imagined situation and dialogue. All three combinations of actors moved beyond the immediate circumstances to depict complex family and professional loyalties being measured against the erosions of time, for Deborah's awakening throws into sharp relief each character's nostalgia for an innocence and joy untroubled by responsibilities. All the actors presented the basic situation of the play as a moment of truth for the characters they portrayed, when their lives were being weighed in the balance of their own clear-eyed scrutiny. For Hornby and Pauline there was the poignant awareness of how inexorably compassion wears away the human spirit. Pinter meticulously shares an audience's imaginative sympathies between his three characters; both productions were impeccably attuned to that equipoise.

Within a short while of its composition, two actors assumed the central role of Nicolas in *One For The Road*:[19] Alan Bates (Lyric Studio, Hammersmith, 1984) and Colin Blakely (Duchess, 1985). A short, angry work influenced by his involvement with Amnesty International, it marks, according to Pinter himself, his farewell to playwriting. Scenes of interrogation have recurred throughout his plays in which a questioner has sought to penetrate a victim's defences, search out his weaknesses the better to demoralise him totally; they have been frightening episodes because they have evolved, often casually, out of domestic environments, growing with a seemingly natural momentum out of familiar conversational routines. Whereas such scenes have disturbed by revealing the potential for sadism hovering within so much human, so-called civilised, behaviour, *One For The Road* is a study of a mind for which sadism is a profession that is politically sanctioned, a *created* part of the *status quo* aiming "to keep the world clean for God" [p. 23]. Never has Pinter imagined a character so mercilessly evil, who does not need to resort to threat or an outburst of anger or abuse to cow a victim into submission. Henchmen elsewhere perform the vile business. Power in Nicolas is absolute; he has no wish to lose his suave composure; with the recalcitrant he can simply wait since time is wholly at his command. He does not need to show his strength because of latent insecurities in himself, which the interrogation is a strategy designed to hide, as in many such scenes in Pinter. What we watch here is a corrupt authority re-shaping dissident minds to a pattern of its liking by searching in them for the roots of fear. These are strategies designed to ensure people conform.

The play is profoundly shocking because the torture is directed relentlessly against the loyalties and affections that make for a secure family. What renders Victor, Gila and their child so vulnerable to Nicolas is the strength of the love that exists between them as husband, wife and son: so much of their self-respect as individuals is bound up in their respect for each other. The child's very openness when under question in the second scene, his lack of suspicion of where the questions may be tending and to what end, defines a complete innocence possible only in a sheltered and loving home. The security of that home is so much a part of the boy's consciousness that he takes it on trust; yet he is casually asked by Nicolas while discussing his liking for aeroplanes to define precisely *why* he likes his mummy and daddy. The terms of endearment make the cruelty even more pointedly callous. Nicolas is planting a seed of doubt in the child's mind about an allegiance, a piety so innate that it informs his whole condition of being: it is an act of real sacrilege. It is a mark of Pinter's skill that he can make tone in so short a scene convey so much about the child's past and likely future. We are given just long enough from the standpoint of our own security to open ourselves imaginatively to the implications of the boy's innocence before he is abused more grossly than if he had been physically hurt.

Nicolas's technique throughout is casually insidious. Victor enters slowly, evidently in pain, bruised, his clothes torn; the least move from Nicolas makes him wince and cower. Nicolas almost at once adopts the cheerful camaraderie of a drinking companion in a pub, sneaking in yet another "one for the road"; he talks confidentially about his way of life, his beliefs, his success with his boss, "the man who runs this country" [p. 12]; he appears frequently to be on the point of changing the subject and getting down to serious business ("Tell me . . .") but never does so, at least not directly. Instead he slips in a remark about Victor's wife or child: "You're probably wondering where your wife is. She's in another room (*He drinks.*) Good-looking woman. (*He drinks.*) God, that was good"; [p. 7] or "Is your son all right?" [p. 10]. Neither remark informs of any precise danger to Victor's family; the manner is relaxed, off-hand, as though the matter were of only incidental interest; but each in the circumstances is calculated to set a tense and suspicious mind racing with nameless fears. The orgasmic luxury of the drinking, while mentioning Gila and her looks, hints at other possible appetites and satisfactions hideous for a husband to contemplate. Nicolas is a master-hand as teasing into play what Henry James called "the imagination for disaster", till Victor capitulates completely: "Kill me" [p. 13]. Death would be too easy a solution for a connoisseur of pain the like of Nicolas: control over Victor physically he already has; now he possesses Victor's will and spirit to direct or extinguish as he chooses: "Look at me. (*Victor does so.*) Your soul shines out of your eyes" [p. 14].

Only with Gila is the tactic openly brutal in an attempt to destroy every vestige of her identity, because she owns a more resilient spirit than her husband. The simple-enough question, "When did you meet your husband?" [p. 17], is followed by the intricate "Why?" that questions the very fabric out of which the self is created, the patterns of chance and choice which shape one's life and its values. Mention of her father occasions an outburst of villification: "Are you prepared to defame, to debase the memory of your father? . . . How do you dare to speak of your father to me?" [p. 19]. Sacrilege is now imputed to her. When Nicolas returns to the matter of where Gila met her husband, she changes the factual detail — it is no longer "in a room" but "in the street". Is this her strategy of prevarication in self-defence or has Nicolas begun to make her fashion her life's story anew into a fiction generated by fear and self-loathing? Nicolas changes the subject to her immediate predicament:

NICOLAS: Where are you now?
Pause.
  Where are you now? Do you think you are in a hospital?
Pause.
  Do you think we have nuns upstairs?
Pause.
  What do we have upstairs?
GILA: No nuns.
NICOLAS: What do we have?
GILA: Men.
NICOLAS: Have they been raping you?
She stares at him.
  How many times?
Pause.
  How many times have you been raped?
Pause.
  How many times?
He stands, goes to her, lifts his finger.
  This is my big finger. And this is my little finger. Look. I wave them in front of your eyes. Like this. How many times have you been raped?
GILA: I don't know.
NICOLAS: And you consider yourself a reliable witness?
He goes to sideboard, pours drink, sits, drinks.
  You're a lovely woman. Well, you were. [pp. 21–22]

The tonal shifts are deft, dazzling and vicious: a taunting glee ("Do you think we have nuns upstairs"); solicitous concern ("Have they been raping you"); prurient curiosity ("How many times?"); bullying; sarcastic triumph when he gains his larger objective and makes Gila question her own veracity; and finally naked insult. By the end of the scene Nicolas has compelled Gila to see herself as utterly worthless by tricking her into an apparent admission of her failure not only as wife, daughter and mother, but also in truth to herself and her own perceptions. He has contrived to make her doubt the essence of her integrity. But even as he dismisses her as too abject a nonentity to merit his further attention, Nicolas ensures he leaves her mind in an ecstasy of apprehension: "You're of no interest to me. I might even let you go out of here, in due course. But I should think you might entertain us all a little more before you go" [p. 22]. This momentarily relaxes the pressure only to renew it the more acutely, when that temptation to hope implicit in "might . . . let you go" is cunningly stifled by a reassertion of power and control with the qualifying "in due course". How terrible the perversions of language and meaning contained in the one word "entertain" and the manifold horrors intimated by "us *all*"! Yet they define the full scope of Nicolas's evil with a rare precision.

Just how precisely is conveyed by the final scene where Nicolas is letting Victor go. Humbled, mutilated, Victor still cannot escape Nicolas's depradations into his psyche. Cheerfully indifferent to Victor's condition, Nicolas insists they drink together as if parting friends: "Go out. Enjoy life. Be good. Love your wife. She'll be joining you in about a week, by the way. If she feels up to it"; and as for the child, "Oh, don't worry about him. He was a little prick" [p. 24]. Having broken Victor completely, Nicolas can afford to assume a total indifference: it expresses his confidence that Victor has no future free from the shadow of his power; he has left his mark on every aspect of his victim's social and private self. Physical rape and maiming are constant threats in the play, but what we witness is a man's pleasure in invading, conquering and subjugating three independent spirits by destroying in them the capacity to love and leaving them naked, raw and ashamed. With unerring skill and tact Pinter has made us *know* human depravity from within.

Alan Bates presented a Nicolas of silken-voiced charm, an aristocratic type whose studied elegance of looks matched a studied elegance of manner that delighted in carefully contriving brief, frightening glimpses of the intellectual thug that lurked within.[20] He relished the cerebral acrobatics by which he mesmerised and trapped his victims. The horror of the performance lay in the extent to which evil was to this Nicolas quite genuinely an *art*, a creative expression of his innermost self and subject in his personal view to impeccable criteria and a rigorous intellectual discipline. He clearly had the power to kill and no compunction about doing so; but that to him would be to admit defeat: his art lay in bringing his victims "by degrees to mortification",[21] then giving them not the hoped-for release of death but the lingering torment of a new lifestyle of his devising. Colin Blakely offered a Nicolas who seemed more of a jovial butcher, his face puffed and blotchy with the relentless drinking, his cheek muscles constantly flexing in the silences. The impression was of a brute force just kept in check by a prodigious effort of will, as though out of a tender concern for his victims: the strong man being deliberately gentle with his physical inferiors and being the more unnerving for the show of care and the restraint. His questioning whether Victor was "beginning to love me" [p. 12] and his addressing the child as "my darling" [p. 17] seemed deeply offensive for their abuse of the relationships in which such overtures of intimacy would be natural. But these moments seemed to hold the key to Blakely's characterization, as did the moral fervour of the outrage he voiced against Gila when she spoke of her father. Forcibly restraining his own will to violence, preferring to re-make these lost souls (as he sees them) in his own image as "soldiers of God" [p. 22] was for Blakely's Nicolas — as for many an inquisitor of old — an act of *love*. In both characterizations the perversion of language and of values was all-consuming; both performances created a man who believed evil to be his good, where the sadism was not a random impulse but an expression of the *total* self. The play amply supported the psychological discriminations that went into the shaping of each interpretation. Since *Landscape* and *Silence* Pinter's technique has continued to open out as he has reached for new, evermore demanding terrain to explore in voyaging deeper and deeper into the nature of consciousness. Whatever the developments of his style, he has remained quintessentially the actor's dramatist.

CHAPTER TWO

NEW FORMS OF COMEDY: AYCKBOURN AND STOPPARD

The posthumously produced *What the Butler Saw* (Queen's, 1969)[1] showed what a genius the theatre lost in the tragic death of Joe Orton. Brilliantly the play broke all the rules to find a unique style that blended the irreverence and daring of farce with the miraculous discoveries of pastoral romance and the verbal ingenuities of the comedy of manners. Every conceivable style of comedy found a place in Orton's depiction of the dangers and the exuberance of a world in which the Id is allowed total freedom of expression.[2] The best comedies to follow in the wake of *What the Butler Saw* have been those that have similarly sought to push against the boundaries of traditional comic form and carry them beyond the predictable and the formulaic.

Alan Bennett's *Habeas Corpus* (Lyric, 1973)[3] was a fair match for Orton's technical virtuosity. With no attempt to pretend that we were anywhere but in a theatre, Bennett presented us with a host of recognisable stereotypes from traditional farce: a middle-aged doctor with a lascivious imagination; his gargantuan wife, outwardly the sternest of prudes but a smouldering sexpot within; his despairingly flat-chested sister and acne-ridden, hypochondriac son; a celibate cleric, aptly surnamed Throbbing; a pillar of society, who is huge in ambition, influence and power but immensely short in stature; a seeming virgin who is far from it and her stentorian Tory mother, who is also a woman with a *past*. The gallery of grotesques is not dissimilar from Orton's but Bennett's motive is decidedly different. Where Orton is liberating (taking his characters through mayhem to purge them of their inhibitions so they no longer need to be furtive but can shamelessly face the light of day, true to what they are),[4] Bennett is nostalgic: his characters are funny because they are trapped between a great inner yearning for a permissive society and an equally intense dread that, if circumstances allowed them to express their secret selves openly, they would totally lose their recognisable identities. When the sheerly vertical form of the spinster, Connie, develops magnificent, Rubens-like contours (by aids far from natural), the Canon, her fiancé, is ecstatic:

Gently we can lead each other on as together we explore all the alleys and pathways of the body. Just think of it. . . . Together we shall be in the forefront of Anglican sexuality. Perhaps I might even write a frank and fearless account of our activities for the *Church Times*. Oh such sin. Only it won't be sin because we shall be married, married and allowed to do what we want. Married and FREE. [p. 53]

Connie's transformation, however, goes no deeper than her falsies and Throbbing increasingly finds freedom a less exciting prospect than sin. Mayhem abounds — the doctor comes close to public disgrace and divorce and, anticipating the latter outcome, his wife goes in pursuit of several potential replacements; Sir Percy Shorter the pillar of society is discovered to be the sometime virgin's long-lost father, but at the last he marries her mother thus righting all past wrongs. The *status quo* is firmly re-established and permissiveness confined for the future to the characters' imaginations. Not surprisingly the closing tone is wistful:

Dying you'll grieve for what you didn't do. . . .
So this is my prescription: grab any chance you get
Because if you take it or you leave it
You end up with regret. [p. 75]

While Bennett can see farce as providing a useful safety-valve for an ordered, institution-prone society, he seemingly cannot determine its function in a permissive world. Clearly he would regret the passing of the old familiar stereotypes (Michael Billington aptly described the play in his *Guardian* review as "an animated McGill postcard").[5] Dr. Wickstead's final advice to the audience is "He whose lust lasts, lasts longest" [p. 75]. Presumably lust, and with it farce, in Bennett's view will last as long as the libido is confined to purely cerebral activity, imagining but never quite realising a world of unlimited freedoms.

Nostalgia has been the hall-mark of Bennett's plays: *Forty Years On* (Apollo, 1968)[6] offers an affectionate parody of cultural and social values between the wars from the stand-point of a public school headmaster whose situation is blissfully unaffected by the pressures of time and change; *Getting On* (Queen's, 1971)[7] takes a compassionate look at the middle-aged in their envy of the young for their freedom from responsibilities and their apparent fearlessness of self-expression; and *The Old Country* (Queen's, 1977)[8] explores a dated, fantasy view of England cultivated by a group of former spies now exiled in Russia in order to offset the bleak realities of the régime with which intellectually, but not emotionally, they have chosen to identify. Wistful regret becomes more strongly marked in each of these works and the last two are firmly set in the realist mode. Not since *Habeas Corpus* has Bennett experimented with the form of comedy where the whole process of caricature and stylisation, the conscious theatricality of it all, had an organic relation to his theme. The play was a personal statement about the nature and limitations of farce as a genre, which Bennett clearly felt was under threat in a permissive age.

Interestingly the best of Peter Nichols' plays seem designed as commentaries on the form and function of certain styles of comedy too. He has a gift for parody which he has several times exploited to depict the moral inadequacy of what passes for popular entertainment when it loses touch with realism. *The National Health* (Old Vic, 1969)[9] juxtaposes the sweat, mess and exhausting routine in a hospital ward of largely terminal cases with a melodramatic soap-opera about love among surgeons and nurses, the squalid, makeshift struggle of the one contrasting with the expensive, mechanical efficiency of the other which allows time for the medical personnel to become absorbed in their romantic attachments. *Privates On Parade* (Aldwych, 1977)[10] offsets the tatty revue numbers of an E.N.S.A. troupe touring the allied camps near the battleline in the Far East with the grim, sporadic violence and the moral anarchy of warfare; this theatre peddles tinselled fantasies to distract men whose minds are otherwise wholly centred on devastation, travesty-images of the culture the war was intended to salvage for posterity. *Poppy* (Barbican, 1982)[11] explores the British involvement in the Opium Wars with China through the medium of Victorian pantomime, where the Dick Whittington story of the local lad who miraculously makes good gradually evolves into a portrayal of how the nineteenth-century ethos of Self-Help could easily degenerate into an excuse for exploitation, greed and lust. The fortune-hunting Principal Boy and husband-hunting Dame become increasingly sinister figures although very little change is made to their traditional patter. Where glamorous spectacle would have provided the climax to pantomime, a nightmare of carnage occurs — the consequence of seeing colonial and economic politics in simplistic terms with Queen Victoria as the Fairy Godmother, force of good and right, and the Emperor of China as a menacing Demon King. In all three plays the aim of the satire is political: to expose the conventions, the theatrical artifice of the form of popular theatre being parodied as so much capitalist propaganda inducing an uncritical acceptance of values that are inhumane.

These are Nichols' most flamboyant experiments with technique. His comedies exclusively in the realist mode tend to be more earnest, less concerned to experiment to extend the province of comedy into new fields of investigation. The commonest subjects of West End comedy and farce are still romantic — courtship, marriage, infidelity. Where Bennett shies away from the freedoms the permissive age allows, Nichols seizes the chance for a greater explicitness paradoxically to bring a degree of moral rigour to the popular format which it does not normally sustain.

Chez Nous (Globe, 1974)[12] explores whether the new sexual freedoms can affect the middle-aged deeply, however staunchly they may uphold the concept of permissiveness. Dick, a paediatrician, has published a book, *The Nubile Baby*, advocating a greater degree of sexual experimentation amongst the young as the major part of their education. True to his precepts his fourteen-year-old daughter has conceived and given birth to a son but the family has shrouded the matter in secrecy for fear of the effect of adverse publicity on Dick's career; Liz, his wife, is bringing up the child as her own. Phil and Diana, long-standing friends, are alone let in on the truth and a pattern of circumstances reveals that Phil is the baby's father, as a consequence of being seduced the previous summer by the 'nubile' Jane. Lengthy recriminations inevitably follow which show how much the apparent harmony of both marriages is the result of extensive compromises by the partners, which at heart they each profoundly resent: generosity can be abused and taken too much for granted or felt to be so; frustration can be misinterpreted as malice. The one passion they all four share is the longing to wipe the slate clean and start a fresh relationship in which sexual fulfilment might be freed of attendant responsibilities. If the others resent Phil, it is because chance has permitted him to live out their most secret and tenacious fantasy. Dick and Diana are spurred on by the situation to admit a long-suppressed affection for each other and plan to elope into serene adultery. Though Phil briefly lived out with Jane the idyll the others long for, it is the joys and cares of fatherhood that now preoccupy him and Liz sees that as a threat to her reawakened maternal instincts. Circumstances show that the two couples are mismatched (Dick and Diana dislike children; Liz and Phil are instinctive parents); the proposed elopment might effect a valuable change for them all; but Diana shies away at the last moment from the challenge preferring to live with the security of the *known* relationship, even though that entails living with the awareness that by contemporary permissive standards hers is a failed sexual experiment.

In *Chez Nous* Nichols takes advantage of the new permissiveness to make actual, viable possibilities for his characters what previously in traditional comedy and farce were only covert yearnings in the protagonists to break out of the barriers of conformity and respectability, to be as young in habit as in heart and to quest for heights of rapture free of all thought of consequences, to find *romance*. What are usually illicit hopes are here realisable goals, but the couples procrastinate, effect more compromises, retreat to the boredom of the *status quo* and deal a cruel blow to their self-respect. *Chez Nous* has a bitter edge to its humour in that it articulates openly motives and meanings which usually in domestic comedy and farce are presented in terms of situation. The *status quo* that comedy conventionally re-establishes in its dénouement, though free of dangers, invariably seems a bleaker reality than when we first encountered it; formerly the possibilities for change were apparent, here they are exhausted. Implicit in *Chez Nous* is a criticism of the form and function of conventional comedy as lacking the courage of its convictions in being content to stop at wish-fulfilment rather than reaching out for wholesale change. The play challenges the audience to question how permissive their own values are by implying the chance of a different, healthier outcome to the situation than that the characters choose to effect. Perhaps it is of the essence of comedy, as it is of Dick's best seller, *The Nubile Baby*, that its freedoms are fantasies of the mind not experiences of the heart.

Passion Play (Aldwych, 1981)[13] covers similar ground in terms of plot but goes more searchingly into the effects of compromise on the mind and personality. Kate, a young woman in her twenties, embodies the pleasure principle but in its darker aspects as it affects the lives of Eleanor and James: amoral, irresponsible, mindless, self-centred. She seduces the innocent James into adultery and enmeshes his life with Eleanor in a tangle of lies and deceptions; Eleanor resorts to a psychiatrist and a suicide-attempt before the marriage can achieve a compromise that both partners can live with. But Nichols contrives to give us a second play that runs concurrently with all this. At the point where James begins to lead a double life and Eleanor discovers it, each is provided with an alter ego (Nell and Jim), the intimate voices within who speak to and for their private selves. For once we hear what inwardly fills the silences when a character tries to regain calm and register the pain that lies behind the stiff-upper-lip and the brave wit when that character seeks to create the impression of being totally self-possessed. The inner selves are cunning, calculating, abrasive, shameless, histrionic, vindictive, naked, hurt. But little of what Jim and Nell utter gets *spoken*: the anger, the humiliation, the passion. Eleanor and James are, as the device of the alter ego implies, too preoccupied with their own thoughts to listen to each other any longer; they cease to know themselves as a couple, lose the intimacy, the openness together of the play's opening scenes, which had its own kind of freedom. *Passion Play* is, like *Chez Nous*, a bitter comedy, much of the laughter being produced by our shocked appreciation of the gap between the spoken and the felt. As the play advances James and Eleanor become increasingly shallower individuals: they let the situation become a stalemate, bleak, habitual, routine, and Jim and Nell's passionate self-assertion gives place to self-pity till at the last they silently play out James and Eleanor's private fantasies — he of undressing and mauling the naked Kate; she of packing and leaving. James and Eleanor have dwindled into the caricatures that are the stock types of conventional domestic comedy — the ageing lecher with the rampant imagination and his up-tight, shrewish wife. *Passion Play* suddenly makes it difficult for us to laugh at such types: caricature is reductive and Nichols makes us conscious of the extent of the loss of humanity involved in the process. While using the conventional material of domestic comedy in these two plays, Nichols contrives to make us think more rigorously than usual about the nature, conventions and assumptions of comedy as a form and so question our own relation with it as *popular* theatre.

If Nichols like Bennett is suspicious of the anarchic potential of comedy and farce, Michael Frayn like Orton delights in it and seems perennially fascinated by why, once individuals congregate in groups, they seem to experience the need to create a corporate mayhem. *Alphabetical Order* (Hampstead and Mayfair, 1975)[14] finds the staff of a national newspaper rebelling against the super-efficient Leslie, the assistant in the cuttings library. Punctilious, orderly, she reorganises the research library and their lives into neat compartments, and is too humourless to note that their constant jokes express their contentment with the muddle of the way things are. Quiet but dogged, she transforms the stage-space into a streamlined image of her own mind; the staff reluctantly acquiesce to it all, until they hear the paper has folded. Jubilant, they scatter the now useless files of cuttings to the winds and gambol about like children in a snowstorn as papers shower down about them everywhere. What Leslie never appreciates is that the staff both sought out the former muddle of the library and cherished their ramshackle lives as acts of resistance against the pressures of being efficient and disciplined in their work. Deprived by her for too long of that escape, they desecrate her world now in a spirit of carnival, regardless of what to her is the gravity of the situation. The outburst is savage but undeniably dynamic and invigorating. So too is the drunken rout in *Donkeys' Years* (Globe, 1976) that transforms the staid figures of the establishment who return for a gaudy night at their former Oxbridge college. When they arrive, they are all struck by how the place seems not to have changed since their student days and by the end of their dinner they are back at their undergraduate japes, debagging, defenestrating, chasing the Master's wife over the chapel roof, as if time has stood still. That they are all portly men in their prime adds to the absurdity, as does their fear that their antics might get leaked to the press; but Frayn's aim is not satirical or condemnatory; the laughter he creates is warm, recognising that figures burdened with authority need to relax occasionally in a period of licence and misrule, to recover some of the freedoms of youth.

For Frayn, farce is an open not a furtive celebration of our primal needs and instincts; even when he takes sexual instinct as his subject he avoids the tone of engrossing naughtiness and the claustrophobia typical of conventional farce. Unlike Bennett he finds it possible to create farce in a permissive world partly because he refuses to use stock figures in familiar locations. In *Clouds* (Hampstead, 1976)[15] three reporters — two English, one American — are being taken on a fact-finding tour of Cuba by an official guide and a chauffeur; four men and one woman spend much of the play in the close confines of a car or in adjacent hotel rooms. Ostensibly they are studying a new world in the making, are "floating free of money and greed" [p. 19]. But Frayn, by the simple device of limiting his setting to a group of five chairs which the cast rearrange against a background of blue sky and mounting cloud, creates the effect that they are travelling in a void, cut adrift from their private ties and sanctions. What the characters increasingly grow conscious of is their physical proximity. The Englishman, the American and the guide begin to compete for Mara's attention, are suspicious if she appears to favour one in any special way; the more confined the space they share, the more they over-react to her presence. The tensions finally explode in a night of macho fisticuffs, which is kept hilariously funny by being presented as a series of *tableaux* seen in flashes of lightning during a tropical storm so that one appears to be watching a sequence of stills from an old silent movie. Fleeing from the mayhem Mara turns to the chauffeur, Hilberto, for protection. Till now he has been a slow, quiet type, who has kept very much to himself, but it is he who finally gets the lady. The last scene returns us to the car: the three suitors, covered in bruises and sticking plaster, share the back seat; Mara sits beside the driver; she chatters on excitedly about the sights they are passing, while the previously silent Hilberto periodically lets rip with an ecstatic "whee-heeee!" [pp. 83-84). Frayn may be writing a permissive farce but he chooses to make his effects by witty implication. *Clouds* has the clarity of line of a fable but its celebration of the waywardness of sexual instinct as a force that can undermine intellectual pretensions and political zeal is free of all sense of the guilt that generally affects the tone of farce: as in *Donkeys' Years*, sheer joy prevails.

That there is a wealth of difference between his own style of comedy and conventional farce, Frayn makes abundantly clear in *Noises Off* (Lyric, Hammersmith, and Savoy, 1982)[16] by contriving to stage two farces simultaneously — one is a parody of the traditional saucy variety called *Nothing On*; the other is a portrayal of the backstage life of the troupe who are performing it on a provincial tour. Farce in performance demands an exceptionally high degree of discipline if the split-second timing on which its rhythm depends is to have effect; the actors involved need physical, even at times athletic, expertise so that the moments of catastrophe will appear funny (because executed with grace and brio) and not painful, as such experiences would be in real life. All the normal demands on an actor — concentration, sensitivity to the ensemble nature of the work, self-awareness — are in farce heightened by the exceptional demands that the form itself makes for pace, speed of attack and absolute accuracy of judgement. Conventional farce tends to exist in a moral and social void; and, true to type, *Nothing On* takes place in a never-never-land of tax exiles, sheikhs, burglars and estate agents; it is a world where extra marital *coitus* is constantly interrupted by such bizarre improbabilities as the re-appearance at every romantic turn of a previously misplaced plate of sardines. The cast whose work we watch inhabit another self-enclosed world. Good ensemble work depends on trust; but what, Frayn asks, if the wayward instincts explored in *Clouds* were to begin to upset the equanimity of that backstage world? The show, of course, must go on at any cost; and the precise cost in this instance is the rigorous attention, the discipline of the performers. Farces the like of *Nothing On* are usually generated by a group of characters obsessed with sex; but what ensues in *Noises Off* is a farce less about sex than about perception.

Act One introduces us to the cast as they rehearse *Nothing On* so we appreciate the given norm (in the form of the play to be staged) and the variables (the precariously balanced temperaments of the actors, which might jeopardise the precision of the farce in performance). Act Two takes us backstage a month later as a matinee is about to begin and a hurried exchange intimates that the volatile *jeune premier* suspects rivals in his relationship with the female lead. The show (belatedly) goes on while the cast at the risk of their concentration set about calming the aggrieved Garry and Dotty; since silence must prevail offstage during a performance, their efforts have to be confined to mime. Garry and Dotty, as farce requires of its leads, begin sailing in and out of the many doors in the set at breakneck speed, constantly re-emerging back-stage at a point where the mimed scenario seems to corroborate their worst suspicions of each other (though we know that everyone is innocent and acting for the best). The cast now have to cope not only with the performance but with Garry's murderous rage and Dotty's malicious reprisals: entrances are mis-timed or made through wrong doors; bizarrely inappropriate props are seized in the rush for the stage; physical agility is impaired as actors discover too late that their costumes have been tampered with; hearing silence on-stage, they assume someone has missed a cue and race to stand in for each other only to discover the required actor has simultaneously entered through a different door in the set; throughout it all the young starlet, who has not yet learned the necessary art of improvising to adjust to the prevailing situation one finds oneself in on-stage, repeats her role like clockwork, regardless of what is happening around her. We are left to imagine from the noises off the manic tempo that the performance of *Nothing On* has acquired; but it cannot compare with the frantic hysteria that prevails in the rigorously respected silence backstage, as the cast race for the haven of the interval-curtain whatever the consequences. Act Three gives us a front-of-house view of *Nothing On* six weeks further on in the tour; by now the script and the stage business have degenerated to surreal nonsense; the tone, pace, mechanics of farce are there but the slender thread of logic by which farce makes possible the improbable has been severed and we are lost in a maze of inconsequentialities. Given the battered, wary-eyed fashion in which the cast go through their routines, it seems the Marquis of Queensbury's rules have long since been abandoned backstage. The feeble struggle to preserve some sense of decorum on-stage only intimates the savagery of conditions prevailing behind the set.

Anarchy breaks out because Garry and Dotty at a crucial moment have only a partial view of events and that dangerously limits their perceptions. By his artfully conceived structure, Frayn makes us conscious of the extent to which farce itself is a carefully engineered partial view that keeps the painful consequences of human fallibility at a distance. In Act Two Garry is *heard* falling headlong down the flight of stairs that dominates the set of *Nothing On*; after a moment's silence, the only other actor on-stage asks in awed tones "Are you all right?" [p. 104]. The audience rock with laughter: we have watched Garry so given up to rage he has not noticed Dotty tie his shoelaces together; we know from Act One that he has a rapid run down the stairs at this point when he returns to the action of *Nothing On*; our expectations are aroused and satisfied by the prolonged noises off. The incident is further enriched by the *sotto voce* question from the fellow-actor: it is woefully inept in the circumstances but the whispered tone implies he feels it is desperately important to keep up a pretence that the spectacular mishap is part of the script. And indeed Garry miraculously recovers and the dialogue continues. Farce performed well excites the imagination to break free of the need to care: the fierce pace never allows us time to register horror or even pause for thought, while the actors' prowess in presenting misadventure with seemingly effortless panache suggests that the characters they impersonate live beyond pain and surprise and have an indefatigable resilience. The credible artifice that is farce is wholly dependent on the virtuosity of the performer; the device of the play-within-a-play in *Noises Off* takes us right inside the process of farce and shows in the gap between accomplishment (the performance of *Noises Off*) and disaster (the performance of *Nothing On*) what these technical skills are and why the discipline they impose on performers is so fundamental to the success of the genre. The sustained and accelerating movement in Act Two between the off-stage play and on-stage mime is designed to achieve a succession of meticulously calculated entrances which required of Frayn's actors a tour-de-force in ensemble playing that was exhilarating to watch. The synchronised brilliance of it left one weak with laughter and wide-eyed in amazement. *Noises Off* is a superb celebration of the art of the actor.

If Nichol's and Frayn's experiments with the form of domestic comedy and farce seem intent on defining the nature and function of these two styles, Alan Ayckbourn's prolific output seems designed to question whether what till now were believed to be *necessary* limitations in these styles of comedy, the "carefully engineered partial" views of events referred to above, are really necessary at all. By imposing a series of quite arbitrary limitations on himself (usually the consequences of writing primarily for the small-scale Library Theatre in Scarborough), Ayckbourn has steadily transformed the subject matter of comedy and farce making them a vehicle for stringent psychological analysis, especially of the waste lands of the middle class sensibility. Ayckbourn has said that he felt his progress as a dramatist demanded that he should "try and get more comedy from character and less from artificially induced situations".[17] Interestingly the more that character has become his focus the more he has begun to blur the dividing lines between different styles of comic writing: satirical comedy can suddenly erupt into farce (*Ten Times Table*); domestic comedy can pass through farce into a dark, mordant mood (*Just Between Ourselves*); while black comedy he has redefined as a dispassionate view of a middle-class household that is "positively knee-deep in home truths" (*Living Together*).[18]

One of Ayckbourn's first West End successes of the Seventies, *How the Other Half Loves* (Lyric, 1970), offered an image which has proved emblematic of the directions in which his more recent plays would move: two rooms intersected on stage so that characters ostensibly in different locations could work beside or around each other while being quite oblivious of the other's presence. This illustrates not only Ayckbourn's immensely inventive way with settings (he has never found it essential to have quantities of doors before he can create farce) but also his preoccupation with the invisible walls that people create around themselves. Obsessional minds have long been the butt of comedy and Ayckbourn is not averse to exploiting this device; what is unusual is his increasing tendency to shift our perspective suddenly so that we perceive the unconscious motive that generates the obsession, which quite changes the quality of our laughter. The obsessions are not sexual but rather the products of minds coping with a totally shallow, benighted existence as in the case of the wives in *Absurd Person Singular* (Criterion, 1973):[19] "When you've lain in bed for any length of time, on your own. . . . with just your thoughts, don't you find your whole world just begins to crowd in on you? . . . . You just lie there thinking, oh God, it could've been so much better if only I'd had the sense to do so and so — you finish up lying there utterly filled with self-loathing" [p. 87]. Or the obsessions may be compensating for an emotional void in the characters' experience as with Sarah and Annie in *The Norman Conquests* (Greenwich and Globe, 1974), who despise the ramshackle Norman but are helpless to stave off his advances once he promises them a little happiness. When Ayckbourn does turn to an apparently conventional setting and idiom in *Bedroom Farce* (Lyttleton, 1977),[20] it is to show that the express desire of the occupiers of all three bedrooms is for a good night's sleep. That they are prevented from this by the squabbles of Susannah and Trevor has got nothing to do with infidelities enjoyed or planned; it is simply that Susannah and Trevor can only find peace when they have totally discomfitted everyone else (when they do finally get together, they quite unconcernedly dispossess Kate and Malcolm of their bed for the night). *Bedroom Farce* is not about adultery or permissiveness but is a wry look at the quixotic ways in which couples contrive to live together amicably; it is less concerned with the capriciousness of wicked instincts than the waywardness of affection in regulating marital harmony.

Much of Ayckbourn's comic invention is directed at marriages in which that pattern of adjustment is not fair to both partners. Desperation provides the momentum for many a conventional farce where "desperate" takes the meaning "reckless"; Ayckbourn pursues this line but will suddenly shift his perspective to explore the darker significances of "desperate" as "extremely serious" and "without hope". Act Two Scene One of *Just Between Ourselves* (Queen's, 1977)[21] shows the genial Dennis esconced in his private den at the back of the garage preparing a birthday treat for his mother, Marjorie: it involves decking the place out with coloured lights and giving a final sanding to a new workbox he has made for her. Throughout his efforts are disrupted by first a neighbouring husband, Neil, and then his wife, Pam, giving their respective accounts of why their marriage has failed. Pam gets very drunk on the birthday wine. Dennis's attempt to extricate her from his car into which she has tumbled is viewed by Marjorie, who now inopportunely arrives, as scandalous; her scathing innuendoes attract the attention of Dennis's wife, Vera, whose inadequacy as a spouse for her son has been relentlessly the subject of Marjorie's conversation. Marjorie sees the scene with Pam as vindication of her opinion and this drives Vera to breaking-point. Fortunately the flex on Dennis's sanding drill is too short for Vera to reach Marjorie's face when she grabs it with lethal intent. Seeking to protect his mother, Dennis abandons Pam who falls prone over the steering wheel, sounding the horn which is Neil's signal to switch on the fairy lights and arrive with a candlelit cake singing "Happy birthday to you!". Here are many of the hallmarks of good farce: the monster mother-in-law about to get her come-uppance; the mouse cornered once too often who becomes a raging fury; the helplessly inert body getting in everyone's way; the misunderstood accident that gives rise in the spectator's mind to a string of lubricious interpretations; the inappropriately timed arrival of an unsuspecting innocent into a seeming madhouse; and the credible domestic detail (the too-short flex) that just stops the situation short of tragedy. It is all too fast-moving for us to stop and think of the degrees of desperation that have brought the situation about. There are times — and this is one of them — when Ayckbourn appears to distrust farce for engineering that partial view which obviates our need for care. Those two characters sharing a stage-space in *How the Other Half Loves* but ignoring each other can be funny or callous depending on one's perspective and how attuned one's sensitivity is. In *Just Between Ourselves* Ayckbourn's interest is in character not situation. The short second scene of the Act shows Vera, now in a catatonic daze, seated in the garden in mid-January rather than share the house with Marjorie while Dennis, ever-genial, vows his wife is getting better by the day. The situation is bizarre but it leaves the audience profoundly uneasy. The opening act had intimated the tensions between Vera and Marjorie — but to his wife's pleas that he help more around the house (Vera is too polite and too timid to speak openly of how Marjorie tyrannises over her) Dennis turns a deaf ear. His den is his sanctum, his means of creating harmony between himself and his world. As the play goes on Dennis's genial joking, the camaraderie of his "Just between ourselves now" is seen to be a strategy for keeping painful experience at bay. His recurrent snorts of laughter in time cut our laughter dead because by the final scene we realise the extent to which in seeing Dennis's world as the stuff of farce we are sharing his deliberately limited perspective. Doubtless we no more see ourselves as cruel than Dennis does; but, by changing perspective, the play shames us into caring. Ayckbourn cleverly manipulates the form and nature of farce to make us aware how holding unquestioningly to certain attitudes and assumptions we unwittingly do violence to others.

Not all Ayckbourn's experiments with the form of farce are as successful as this or the bravura technical achievement of the three interlocking plays that make up *The Norman Conquests*. *Sisterly Feelings* (Olivier, 1980)[22] attempted to explore the play of chance and choice in shaping the individual life by creating a structure in which the two leading actresses could twice during performance opt at the toss of a coin to play one of two alternative scenes. The fact that all the possible combinations led invariably to the same final scene meant that the structure became imprisoning rather than liberating. Two sisters are seen contemplating whether or not to pursue an affair with a handsome stranger; the final scene shows them back with their respective partners. One admired the ingenuity of the transitions between scenes, but the emphatic assertion of the *status quo* at the end made the sisters seem little more than dilettante flirts while the overall theme seemed to be that the comfort of the known will always have a stronger attraction than the risky and the unpredictable, which rather runs counter to Ayckbourn's claim that he believes characters should "retain the dignity of resolving their own destinies".[23] The structure seemed too elaborate for it all to be an anecdote about people lacking the courage to be unconventional and singular; there is scant sense of human dignity involved in that observation on character.

Ayckbourn has also several times tried to make his social criticism covertly political. That there is a power-hungry Hitler inside little Sydney Hopcroft in *Absurd Person Singular* is evident from the way in the first act he scares his wife Jane into being a slave to his passion for order and cleanliness; the final image of him making all their friends dance to his orders and play humiliating party games, however, seems too stark a transition at the close of an act that, though already dark in mood, has looked with compassion at the spiritual desolation of Eva and Marion, the social demise of Geoffrey and the marital *angst* of Ronald. It is not that the insight is misguided — such lost souls could credibly be swept up into the schemes of a rising entrepreneurial demon like Sydney — the problem is that the dramatic method has shifted into the surreal and expressionistic without due preparation. In a play that has moved like *Just Between Ourselves* from comedy of manners through farce to a sombre realism, the transition is one too many and so the whole structure suddenly risks seeming contrived. The Fascist overtones are discomfitting in the wrong way; as they are in the frankly allegorical *Way Upstream* (Lyttleton, 1982):[24] the pirating of a private launch touring the rivers of England (this ship of state) by a petty dictator goes unchallenged till the submissive Alistair rebels when his wife Emma is threatened with walking the plank; the worm turns, gains control of the boat and steers through Armageddon Bridge to sunlight and a naked frolic, as if Eden has been regained. The ultra-realism (a navigable boat on a stage full of water) did not merge well with political allegory, and the farce-convention (little man makes good) by which the play achieved its conclusion reduced the portentous to the bathetic. The boundaries of comic expression resisted stretching in that fashion. *Ten Times Table* (Globe, 1978)[25] succeeds while it remains a satirical comedy about the way factions on committees polarise each other to wider and wider extremes till the real purpose of their coming together (here to organise a civic pageant) is lost sight of as the will to power seizes everyone's imagination uncontrollably. As the day of the pageant approaches the two sides are clearly intent on turning the simulation of a chapter of local history (the army's suppression of a labourers' revolt) into a genuine battle. The Socialists are particularly keen to re-write history and convert what was formerly a martyrdom into a decisive military *coup*. The shift to farce for the final scene during the pageant misfires because Ayckbourn seems uncertain about what is the appropriate tone to sustain here: there are hints of black comedy (an offstage wounding and an offstage rape), but the dominant mood is that of a jolly skit on amateur dramatics with a bizarre hobby-horse and ill-fitting costumes, drunken actors and a deaf pianist who blithely plays on through the riot. Surprisingly for Ayckbourn, the end was misjudged in being *comfortable* (a descent into whimsy) when shock was called for. One is left wondering with these three instances whether Ayckbourn's much-boasted facility for conceiving plays in the few days that precede the date allotted for their rehearsal might not, given the newness for him here of the subject matter and the consequent problems with tone, have merited some pause for study and revision. *Ten Times Table* fails for want of the conviction to follow through the logic that its progress through four excellent scenes has set in motion. Overall Ayckbourn is at his best reinvigorating the forms of domestic comedy, when his technical virtuosity makes us *feel* how life's richest comic ironies are from the standpoint of the victims utterly catastrophic.

Stoppard is another prolific dramatist whose work tends to fall short of the best when it becomes overtly political. His richest and most rewarding comedies are those that experiment with the possibilities of comic form to illuminate the nature of imagination. Like Ayckbourn, Stoppard is preoccupied with the way individuals' desperation and recklessness spring from a deep-rooted despair at the over-tidy efficiency, pragmatism and self-interest of the modern world, where commercial values risk governing every aspect of the human condition. His finest plays — *Rosencrantz and Guildenstern are Dead, Jumpers, Travesties* — are essentially about blindness, usually moral blindness, which is equated with a dangerous failure of imagination in the characters, who cannot engage adequately in consequence with the world in which they are situated. The cleverness of his art is to make us engage with those worlds far more subtly than the characters can do themselves and, since *Rosencrantz and Guildenstern are Dead*, Stoppard has generally achieved this by deploying an art of travesty, where much of the humour depends for its effect on the audience's familiarity with the plot, conventions or style of a well-known play or popular theatrical format. Travesty perhaps needs definition here. It is not with Stoppard simply a matter of destructive burlesque, a debunking (as in several of Peter Nichols' works) of a form of theatre he finds morally questionable; nor is it a self-conscious exploration as with Bennett and Frayn of a particular genre in order to reach some psychological understanding of its nature and its relation to an audience's needs. Stoppard's usage is quite different too from the structure Ayckbourn has devised for his most recent work, *A Chorus of Disapproval* (Olivier, 1985),[26] which looks at an amateur operatic society's rehearsals of *The Beggar's Opera* and draws some ironic parallels between the cupidity and lusts of Gay's characters in Hanoverian England and the actors and actresses who now impersonate them. The difference between Ayckbourn's and Stoppard's use of travesty is that one produces a closed, the other an open form of comedy. Ayckbourn's prevailing irony infers that, though times and fashions change, humankind will still find subtle ways of transgressing the biblical commandment against coveting a neighbour's ox, ass, and wife. While there is great ingenuity in the way the parallels are drawn, the play's development does become increasingly predictable, which is not helped by the device of playing what is chronologically the last scene of the play first in the actual performance so that the outcome is clear from the start. As a consequence the characters have only a limited freedom within which to develop, being confined by the structure Ayckbourn has imposed on the action and the pessimism it infers. Travesty in Stoppard enriches rather than questions one's appreciation of the play that acts as his prototype; travesty becomes itself a creative act of the imagination.

How this operates to create an open-ended rather than a predictable dramatic structure can be seen in the play that established Stoppard's reputation in the Sixties. Stoppard admits to having "enormous difficulty in working out plots", so using another work for a "basic structure takes a lot of the pressure" off him.[27] *Rosencrantz and Guildenstern are Dead* (Old Vic, 1967)[28] borrows Shakespeare's plot from *Hamlet* and weds it to a dramatic structure imitated from Beckett so that the familiar is suddenly made strange. The world of *Hamlet* is viewed through the minds of two minor characters who are frankly just devices necessary to Shakespeare's plotting, thankless parts for the actors concerned as they are given none of those distinguishing features that make minor characters in other Shakespearean plays live in the memory. They are *types* in the pejorative sense but as such for Stoppard emblems of common humanity. Beside Hamlet they lack stage-presence, charisma, personality; and that mediocrity — apparent even to them — is a cause of intense anguish: they want to *mean* something, but for that to be possible they need to find a structure of meaning for the world they inhabit, to determine the scheme within which they appear to have a place. All they have to go on, however, are the observable facts of life at Claudius's court. The world of Shakespeare's *Hamlet* is compounded of blood, love and rhetoric; Elsinore is a place where love is corrupt, adulterous, or self-regarding, where blood is shed so that lust may be satisfied, and where guilt is disguised or dismissed by rhetorical evasion. The only certain reality there is death, as the bad end unhappily and the good unluckily in a "climatic carnage by poison and by steel" [p. 90]. Frightened by the horror, madness and confusion about them, Rosencrantz and Guildenstern try to seek the comfort of rational explanation but, given that so many people at court are actors assuming masks to disguise their real motives, the facts inevitably do not add up to anything very conclusive. Elsinore, as we know from our familiarity with Shakespeare's play, cannot be defined in terms of appearances: explanations lie beyond logic. In their quest for meaning, the pair often play games in which they simulate being Hamlet or Claudius but their efforts always stop short of imaginatively inhabiting the minds of the individuals they impersonate. They stick relentlessly to facts and miss the meaning. Guildenstern "plays" Hamlet and Rosencrantz interrogates him about the causes of his melancholy:

To sum up: your father, whom you love, dies, you are his heir, you come back to find that hardly was the corpse cold before his young brother popped on to his throne and into his sheets thereby offending both legal and natural practice. Now why exactly are you behaving in this extraordinary manner? [p. 36]

Through acting they reach out at a perception of Hamlet's predicament but, just when a little lateral thinking is called for, they shy away from their premises because they are based on intuition.

Acting is used throughout the play as a metaphor for the workings of imagination. Theatre may be such stuff as dreams are made of, but dreams can give us access to reality and the art of the actor, Stoppard implies, is a *surreality*. Guildenstern yearns for a mystical experience, a "timeless moment" which will give him some transcendent insight into the nature of being — a visitation by a unicorn or a "bird out of season dropping bright-feathered on my shoulder"[p. 19]. He is visited instead by a troupe of players: waiting for Godot, he gets what out of a sense of insult he dismisses as "a comic pornographer leading a rabble of prostitutes"[p. 19]. Yet, having played in their persons many parts, the actors have an emotional assurance, a confidence in their readiness to adapt to all occasions that aggravates the mounting panic in Rosencrantz and Guildenstern to the point of hysteria. Given their work in tragedy and melodrama, the actors are quite familiar with the base extremes of human nature: their stock-in-trade is blood, love and rhetoric and so they are perfectly at ease in Elsinore.

It was a masterstroke of Stoppard's to have the players *act* in dumb-show: their mime, balletic, passionate, larger than life in its exaggerated gestures yet mesmerically beautiful in its grace and control, creates a marvellous sense of another dimension of experience, stylised but immediate in its power to captivate the imagination. It is a fine evocation of *surreal* truth, which Rosencrantz and Guildenstern dismiss at their peril. Given our enhanced awareness of its significance, we can apprehend that the players are showing the risks of life at court and the trap that is being sprung around Rosencrantz and Guildenstern by minds politically more astute than theirs. But the luckless pair merely register shock at what to them is "not a good, clean show suitable for all the family" [p. 46]. Stoppard excels at defining through comedy states of dangerous innocence, minds alarmingly closed to new areas of awareness.

This is not to suggest that Rosencrantz and Guildenstern are simply victims of circumstance: the presence of the players' mime in the play holds out for them the possibility of recognition and change; they could come to share our level of understanding. But their apathy is inexorable, because, as the numerous games with words slowly reveal, they share a neurotic and self-pitying obsession with death:

Stuffed in a box like that, I mean you'd be in there for ever. Even taking into account the fact that you're dead, it isn't a pleasant thought.

Especially if you're dead, really. . . . . I wouldn't think about it, if I were
you. You'd only get depressed. Eternity is a terrible thought. I mean,
where's it going to end? [pp. 50-51]

All the games with logic, as with Beckett's Didi and Gogo, are a
desperate fending off of the silence in which nameless fears can
possess our imaginations. Recalling Shakespeare's play we know
that just these same fears of death, of the apparent meaninglessness
of existence, of the duplicity of the court are haunting Hamlet's
imagination and undermining his sanity too. His passionate
dilemma is theirs; their words constantly echo his; his actions and
responses constantly mirror theirs; but they cannot break out of the
mental trap of their obsessions to experience any kind of fellow-
feeling. Repeatedly Hamlet traverses the rear of the stage while
they are immersed in their anguish; we know he is in the throes of
one of his great soliloquies; to them, if they chance to notice him,
he is merely "talking to himself"[p. 85]. This want of imagination
is felt increasingly to be an ethical failing and the comedy darkens
towards its close as we come more readily to understand why for
all their anguish they have excited our laughter. On board ship and
bound for England, they once again enact a little play about their
arrival with Hamlet at the English court; Rosencrantz is carried
away by his performance, being totally identified for once with the
role he is playing (the King of England), and breaks open Claudius's
letter:

ROS: (*efficiently*): I see . . . I see . . . well, this seems to support your story
    such as it is — it is an exact command from the king of Denmark, for
    several different reasons, importing Denmark's health and England's
    too, that on the reading of this letter, without delay, I should have
    Hamlet's head cut off——!
    (GUIL *snatches the letter. ROS, doubletaking, snatches it back. GUIL
    snatches it half back. They read it together, and separate.*)
    (*Pause.*)
    (*They are well downstage looking front.*)
ROS: The sun's going down. It will be dark soon.
GUIL: Do you think so?
ROS: I was just making conversation. (*Pause.*) We're his *friends*.
GUIL: How do you know?
ROS: From our young days brought up with him.
GUIL: You've only got their word for it.
ROS: But that's what we depend on.
GUIL: Well, yes, and then again no. (*Airily.*) Let us keep things in
    proportion. Assume, if you like, that they're going to kill him. Well, he
    is a man, he is mortal, death comes to us all, etcetera, and consequently
    he would have died anyway, sooner or later. Or to look at it from the

social point of view — he's just one man among many, the loss would be well within reason and convenience. And then again, what is so terrible about death? As Socrates so philosophically put it, since we don't know what death is, it is illogical to fear it. It might be . . . very nice. Certainly it is a release from the burden of life, and, for the godly, a haven and a reward. Or to look at it another way — we are little men, we don't know the ins and outs of the matter, there are wheels within wheels, etcetera — it would be presumptuous of us to interfere with the designs of fate or even of kings. All in all, I think we'd be well advised to leave well alone. [pp. 79-80]

This is their existential moment: they have a direct call on their imaginative sympathy, which is a chance to break the causal chain of events leading inevitably, did they but realise it, to their own deaths. Guildenstern dismisses logic, justice and friendship as irrelevant to the issue, having no claim upon them. And he does so all in terms of the *easy* reality of death. Cant and apathy damn them irrevocably. The universe of Shakespeare's *Hamlet* brings nothing but panic to the logically minded. Rosencrantz and Guildenstern are at sea on a tide of incongruities. We are encouraged through travesty to extend our imaginations and make the connections they cannot and find new patterns of insight, even as Hamlet does in confronting the same experiences. Stoppard's comedy is nothing less than a plea for the necessity of art as a teller of surreal truths. As such it invites us to look again at Shakespeare's tragedy (in a sense such a familiar landmark in our culture) and rediscover the sanity of the vision that sustains it. The parody is not destructive but affirmative in its intentions: travesty is elevated to the status of high comedy.

The panic of the logically minded is Stoppard's theme in *Jumpers* (Old Vic, 1972)[29] and once again his chosen dramatic strategy is surrealism, which excites even as it bewilders the imagination with startling images. Consider the opening: a seemingly drunken night-club singer struggles lamely to find her tune and flees the stage in tears to be replaced by a striptease act; a perfunctory display of acrobatics follows, through which an elderly professor wanders complaining about the time and pursuing the singer, who is now on the verge of hysteria and demanding that someone, somewhere surprise her. As if to comply, the acrobats form a shaky pyramid till their efforts are rudely halted by a gunshot and the bloody collapse of one of the team; the lights go haywire then contract to a diminishing spot on the singer clasping the corpse, her dress splattered with gore. It is a mad world we enter, though by the end of Act One *nearly* everything is found to be capable of explanation.

It is as if the performance of a symphony had begun with the scherzo which was then followed by the first movement, so that we only gradually perceive where all the brilliantly fragmented themes had their derivation. This proves to be a recurring device in the play: when Bones, the detective investigating the murder of the acrobat, arrives to inspect the scene of the crime and rings the bell of the house where it took place, the door is opened to him by a man (George Moore, the elderly Professor) who is holding a bow but no arrows and some lecture notes in one hand, a tortoise in the other, has shaving cream all over his face and appears to be clad in little other than a bath towel and a pair of spectacles. Having watched the stages that have led up to George's answering the bell, we see nothing incongruous in his condition till Bones reacts as if he is confronting a lunatic. Again, there are perfectly sound explanations but they require patience and sympathy to determine — qualities which, as the play unfolds, are found to be dangerously lacking in the world it reveals.

It is not a specific play that Stoppard is travestying here but the conventions of the popular detective mystery (play or novel). The whodunnit implies a universe in which justice will operate, in which an acceptable code of rightness will prevail, so that it will be possible to prove who did it and why. The form presupposes such ethical security. Stoppard however poses a different premise: what if such trust were misplaced and itself a mere fiction, if power rather than right prevailed? *Jumpers* explores the horror of a world in which ethics have ceased to be given universal accord; where the appointment to the Archbishopric of Canterbury is a political not a religious matter (the present incumbent we learn is a former Minister of Agriculture promoted because of his familiarity with flocks and shepherds); where values, being deemed an exclusively personal matter, can be dismissed as of only *relative* significance. Consequently we watch a murder committed; observe the body being efficiently disposed of in a large plastic bag; see a figure of the political establishment (the Vice-Chancellor, Archie) casually use his wide-ranging influence to re-define the murder as suicide while of tidy, if unsound mind (McFee, the corpse, having thoughtfully crawled into the bag before pulling the trigger on himself, being Archie's interpretation of the scenario in his role as coroner); and watch him and the singer (George's wife, Dotty) blackmail Bones the detective into acquiescing to this view of the events. In the play, the one serious question — who killed Professor McFee and why — never gets answered; it is evaded or dismissed by the characters as irrelevant. To confront the question openly would, we see, be too disturbing for them, too intrusive on their pursuit of self-interest. The brilliantly streamlined efficiency of farce here evokes an utterly heartless world in which people are valued according to their use. Archie and his like foster mayhem as a cover for their sinister practices.

What is remarkable with *Jumpers* is Stoppard's facility like this in giving a new organic purpose to traditional devices and effects of comedy. Since classical times much humour has been derived from the situation of two characters talking at cross-purposes, where each is so obsessed with his own particular perspective on events that ironic misunderstandings rapidly multiply. Bones is convinced that Dotty is responsible for the murder and that George is seeking to protect her from arrest by admitting guilt himself; George, ignorant of any murder occurring the previous evening, believes that Bones is simply making routine enquiries about the lateness of the party at his house, which he personally tried to stop by making an anonymous phone-call to the police complaining of the noise:

BONES: Well, your wife says you can explain everything, and you say you are wholly responsible, but——
GEORGE: Are you still going on about that?— for goodness sake, I just lost my temper for a moment, that's all, and took matters into my own hands.
BONES: Because of the noise?
GEORGE: Exactly.
BONES: Don't you think it was a bit extreme?
GEORGE: Yes, yes, I suppose it was a bit.
BONES: Won't wash, Wilfred. I believe you are trying to shield her.
GEORGE: Shield who?
BONES: It's quite understandable. Is there a man who could stand aside when this fair creature is in trouble——
GEORGE: Aren't you getting a little carried away? The point is, surely, that I'm the householder and I must be held responsible for what happens in my house.
BONES: I don't think the burden of being a householder extends to responsibility for any crime committed on the premises.
GEORGE: Crime? You call that a crime?
BONES: (*with more heat*): Well, what would you call it?
GEORGE: It was just a bit of *fun!* Where's your sense of humour, man?

[p. 59]

We enjoy the absurdity of this, but the device also highlights Stoppard's ethical theme: here are two characters so utterly self-absorbed that they never stop to listen or imaginatively engage with why they appear to be shocking each other so, why each man's every statement increases the other's apparent outrage. They are talking *at* not *to* each other.

George is a philosophy don who is writing throughout much of the play a lecture on "Man, Good, Bad or Indifferent"; he is trying to prove the existence of God as a counter-theme to his argument that mankind seems to find it a personal imperative to cultivate a moral sense. All societies, he reasons, even savage tribes and cannibals have an instinct for piety, for deeming certain patterns of behaviour right and proper. The need is intuitive, innate; and if pragmatic logicians see that as irrational, then, he counters, all that is best in culture is a monument to irrationality: "if rationality were the criteria for things being allowed to exist, the world would be a gigantic field of soya beans!" [p. 40]. With great relish he demonstrates that much of what passes for logical thinking is utterly ridiculous in terms of experience. But despite his avid concern, this belief in ethics is not an active principle with George: it is a cerebral stance, an intellectual charade, a game. Like the many witty talkers in Shaw's *Heartbreak House*, George plays no formative role in the society he endlessly criticises. The news that blares forth from the television set in his wife's bedroom, which he ignores as so much noise, shows that in the world outside his flat the legends of heroic endeavour and altruism that once sustained his creed throughout the nation are being alarmingly re-written by circumstance: the triumph of a British moon-landing has been marred by the discovery that the space capsule has been damaged by the impact and has power to take only one passenger on the return flight; Scott and Oates, the two astronauts, have been seen "struggling at the foot of the ladder until Oates was knocked to the ground by his commanding officer. . . . Captain Scott has maintained radio silence since pulling up the ladder and closing the hatch with the remark, 'I am going up now. I may be gone for some time' " [p. 23]. George scarcely registers that his opponent in the debate, McFee, is dead or that his own wife is undergoing a traumatic mental breakdown. Dotty hungers for metaphysical belief, for a romantic and spiritual dimension to existence, a place in life for imagination. She has lost her hold on sanity, now that the moon is a compassable entity and no longer a figment of the artist's vision, a symbol of mystery and emblem of his trust in the unknown, Her poetic sensitivity has no means of expression left open to it. Though George ought to be capable of giving her the assurance she needs, he is utterly absorbed in using morals as an excuse for verbal ingenuity. Philosophy to him is no more but words, words, words. Dotty's all-consuming desperation seems to him nothing but sexual frustration; when her anguish does finally impinge on him he resorts to the plaintive: "You mean you're bad again. I'm sorry . . . How was I supposed to know you were . . ." [p. 33]. From a husband, the remark is damning in the extreme. Much of the laughter that their scenes together provide springs either from observations like this which are true to self but unwittingly callous or from remarks which each calculates to be witty at the other's expense, so keeping an emotional distance deliberately between them. It is as if they are afraid of their need for each other. When Dotty rounds on George with "Haven't you invented God, *yet?*" [p.34], her disdain is clear but, in exasperation at being denied the comfort of his physical presence, she is actually disparaging the very quality in him that could afford her psychological relief. Where Nichols' Eleanor and James in *Passion Play* individually watch themselves becoming comic stereotypes, Stoppard's George and Dotty are kept apart by a cruel streak of superiority that goads each to see the other as a caricature: scatter-brained professor, dead to all but his "dreamland debating society" [p. 32] and frigid shrew, "whose relationship with her husband stops short only of the issue of a ration book"[p. 32]. For all its corruscating wit, flights of intellectual fancy and ingenious structure, *Jumpers* is a decidedly *dark* comedy.

The problem for the performers is to hit a proper balance: it is all too easy, as amateur productions have shown, to play George and Dotty as the caricatures they appear to each other to be. If this happens, then Dotty quickly loses all sympathy and George's ideas cease to gain an audience's assent in *principle* but seem to be just another aspect of his antic disposition. In consequence, the challenges which the play should offer in positioning George's lecture alongside a farce depicting the extremes to which overly pragmatic, materialist and permissive ideologies may lead are obscured. Stoppard's irony is that George is having to defend what hitherto has been deemed common-sense against charges that such attitudes are dated and impossibly utopian. Michael Hordern, for whom the role was conceived, contrived to be an endearing eccentric, whose irascible temper and shafts of satire were clearly not very successful lecture-room strategies to keep erring students up to the mark; and they were damagingly inappropriate in handling his difficult wife. His George Moore was a man who did not have the rigorous command over the flow of his ideas that he supposed, and so was likely to tie his intellect in knots when he used ideas as a means of self-display. But he could suddenly be overtaken by the force of his own moral vision and find a verbal fluency and succinctness of definition which left him humbled in awe at his achievement and at the power inherent in the sheer momentum of ideas that enabled him briefly to transcend his pettier, fumbling self. Conceptualising could be a source of demoralising agony or of great inner radiance for Hordern's George: it was the *sporadic* flow of inspiration that made him self-conscious, tetchy and uncaring. Diana Rigg as Dotty used her charismatic beauty to offset the darker sides of her role — a woman whose evident warmth George took cruelly for granted. Moreover she had an acute intelligence that could wield the language of song-lyrics as metaphors for her subtle soul-searching. When she capitulated to Archie's sexual advances, it was out of a need to be valued for some quality in herself and no longer be seen, as by George, as an object for dispassionate intellectual scrutiny. If in her final moments with George her voice took on a hard, bitter edge, it was because she realised that, had he been more caring, she would not have had to sell herself short and trade on her physical charm to win some vestige of identity. In the 1985 revival of *Jumpers* at the Aldwych, Paul Eddington and Felicity Kendal chose to explore beyond the witty banter of George and Dotty the profound emotional need they have for each other. They contrived to articulate a subtext of feeling beneath the level of language, of loneliness both physical and spiritual which neither partner manages to engage with honestly. The failure of imagination, that is so central to Stoppard's work, was in their playing essentially a failure in tenderness. The compact bedroom set for this production with a centrally placed bed encouraged them regularly to sit together (the more expansive design for the National Theatre kept Hordern and Rigg largely apart and him absentmindedly on the move) so that the waves of attraction and recoil in the dialogue were matched by an unconscious sensing of and retreat from each other's physical proximity. When they gave way in time to malice and spite, they both seemed taken aback by the bitterness of their tone. It was reluctantly (rather than as with Rigg a matter of deliberate choice) that Felicity Kendal's Dotty fell more and more under the spell of the ingratiating, predatory Archie; her being content to be merely used sexually intimated the sheer depth of her desperation. As Eddington's George lost touch with Dotty so his consciousness increasingly lost touch with reality; when he accidentally killed his pet hare and tortoise, there was a sudden bleak awakening to the greater loss; his instinctive appeal as he fainted with shock was to Dotty.

The whodunnit moves logically to a firm conclusion, but there is no simple solution to Stoppard's comedy. Having begun with a surreal scherzo, he ends with a surreal coda, reiterating his argument through a sequence of equally disturbing images as we enter the nightmare realisation that activated George's fainting away. It is a world where language has ceased to have any meaning whatever and morals are what those in power deem for their own current convenience to find appropriate behaviour. Total anarchy prevails: Archie reels off utter jabberwocky to rapturous bursts of applause; the jumpers reappear and during their act this time the Archbishop of Canterbury is assassinated and clearly at Archie's command; Dotty swings aimlessly above it all in a star-spangled void; and George's efforts to impose order on the chaos collapse as ideas and words begin to disintegrate on his lips. It is a dazzling, glossy but heartless spectacle, a foreshadowing of the mindlessness that would overtake a world that lacks imagination and belief. We are left to question the outcome of George's moment of recognition, whether he will have the strength to act on the intuitions he is grasping through dream. It is a savage black farce that Stoppard precipitates us into here, but one technically far better integrated into the development of his play than Ayckbourn's conclusions to *Absurd Person Singular* and *Ten Times Table*. It is a conclusion that leaves the burden of responsibility and choice firmly with the audience by recapitulating all the issues of the play with a startling immediacy.

Not surprisingly for one so adept at parody, Stoppard is much preoccupied with the integrity of words and suspicious of styles that camouflage sinister intentions or deck out commonplace thinking with ostentatious effects. What was an incidental theme in *Jumpers* (but one that came sharply into focus in the coda, when Archie spoke gobbledegook but with the oratorical emphases and the kinds of intonations that provoke mass applause) has become an increasingly urgent concern of Stoppard's in several one-act and full-scale comedies over the last decade. Some seem almost like commentaries on the more intricate dramatic structure of the earlier play; others borrow heavily from the comic devices Stoppard first experimented with there, especially the intrusion of seemingly surreal experience into a work that otherwise observes realist conventions, which is provocative, disturbing at first but ultimately prophetic of the way the plot will develop. The right use of language is a matter of imaginative scruple but, whereas in *Jumpers* the theme was explored through a complex dramatic structure that juxtaposed intellectual comedy with black farce to pinpoint the divergence between stated principles and social practice, in the later plays the subject is treated either in a Shavian fashion as an issue for open debate (*Night and Day, The Real Thing*) or is quite simply illustrated (*Dirty Linen, Every Good Boy Deserves Favour, Dogg's Hamlet, Cahoot's Macbeth*). In varying degrees with these plays it is clearly the political implications of the use and abuse of language that have stimulated Stoppard to write and the sense of urgency he feels (already implicit in the format he created for the coda to *Jumpers*) introduces a markedly didactic quality; as his theme narrows in compass, travesty ceases to be Stoppard's organising creative principle and the resulting dramatic structures are consequently less intricate, less rich in allusion. The theme tends to be *presented* rather than explored as a process of mind in one or more of the characters: we are conscious of Stoppard thinking and are less imaginatively engaged with why a particular character thinks in the way he does.

Though a full symphony orchestra provides Stoppard with a fine image of a totalitarian society working in concert to a common rhythm, *Every Good Boy Deserves Favour* (Festival Hall and Mermaid, 1977)[30] risks trivialising its subject through its wish to achieve a solution to a work that is ambitious in intent but of necessity limited in scope. The more powerfully certain scenes are acted — young Alexander's canny teacher manipulating the laws of Euclidian geometry into a lecture for the child on the need for conformist thinking; his father on hunger-strike keeping himself sane by memorising letters to his son in rhyme (he is denied paper) that speak, despite the simplistic expression, of his love for his child and his respect for the child's integrity as his motives in continuing his stance against the evil consequences of conformism — the more the conclusion uniting father and son seems a descent into sentimental fantasy. The play is not helped at this point by a score (by André Previn) that, setting the child's soprano piping "Everything can be all right" to a harp continuo, is overt and limp pastiche of Benjamin Britten. This is a travesty (in the pejorative sense) of the play's high seriousness: pain like that which the play begins by defining in some nicely judged comic scenes cannot be assuaged by a fairytale dénouement: the attempt is embarrassing.

Dogg's Hamlet, Cahoot's Macbeth (Collegiate, 1979)[31] first contrives with astonishing rapidity to teach the audience a code-language (Dogg); gives us the first scene of *Hamlet* in translation into that code showing how much intonation alone can define sense and meaning; then concludes the first act with a translated version of *Hamlet* (in fifteen minutes) with a reprise of the whole play by way of encore (in three minutes) that communicates what a surprising amount of the play's essence can be conveyed if the cutting is judiciously done. Act Two opens with a chamber production of *Macbeth* in the manner of performances by Czech dissident actors, which is interrupted (at the point where we expect the fatal knocking at the castle gate) by the intrusion of a Police Inspector who condemns the performance as treasonous individualism. The situation is saved by the arrival of a stranger speaking Dogg which he rapidly teaches the cast; this allows them to continue to play the tragedy in code to the utter bewilderment of the police, who cannot think of a law they can bend to apply to this situation which would allow them to arrest actors and audience. The point is deftly made that tyranny excites subversion, that the human mind will always ingeniously make a bid for freedom. What seems at first a destructive travesty of Shakespeare turns steadily into a creative rendering of how the mind evolves a strategy to frustrate pressures to conform. The play is a fantasy but one that exhilarates rather than embarrasses, because through travesty the audience is made to participate in the process of intellectual subversion. Stoppard's didactic impulse has, as with *Rosencrantz and Guildenstern are Dead* and *Jumpers*, been subsumed within the creation of his entire dramatic structure. Travesty here illuminates how the exercise of imagination can safeguard the mind's health.

Dirty Linen (Almost Free, 1976)[32] exploits the furtive aspects of sex-farce to show how as a form it encourages double standards rather than liberating an audience from such hypocrisy. A select committee of the House of Commons is investigating newspaper allegations of affairs between at first twenty-one, later one-hundred-and-nineteen, Members of Parliament and a "Mystery Woman". It is a cover-up manoeuvre, since most members of the committee are secretly implicated. Their secretary turns out to be the unknown mystery and she advises that they write a single paragraph by way of report "saying that M.P's have got just as much right to enjoy themselves in their own way as anyone else" [p. 42] and just call Fleet Street's bluff. The parodist in Stoppard has fun with mimicking the various styles in which cant and hypocrisy are couched by the press and by Parliament; but *Dirty Linen* is a slight piece, pushing innuendo to wearying lengths. The satire is aimed at too obvious and hackneyed a target so that, like many of the sex-farces it is ridiculing, it is all surface and no substance.

Night and Day (Phoenix, 1978)[33] is a much more incisive study of the mentalities that create the jargon favoured by the popular press; like *Jumpers* it is another of Stoppard's comedies about the hell of the morally dispossessed and free-ranging. We watch a trio of reporters at work somewhere in Africa as an attempt by one part of a nation to secede and become independent threatens to turn into full-scale civil war. They are hungry for newsworthy action; irritated that the "bloody thing wont catch fire" [p. 23]; desperate, not for accurate facts during the confusing political manoeuvres between Mageeba, the President, and the rebel leader that precede hostilities, but for a story — and preferably one big enough to make their rivals "sick". The aim is only incidentally to enlighten their potential readers; the over-riding ambition is to be first with a breakthrough. For that they will virtually commandeer a private house (the Carsons are too polite not to admit white visitors, however pushing); double-cross each other for the chance to gate-crash a private visit to the house by Mageeba in the expectation of getting an informal interview; toady to the African leader hoping that flattery will win his confidence. They will risk even death for a scoop. "It's all bloody ego", as Ruth Carson says. "And the winner isn't democracy, it's just business" [p. 91]. Mageeba knows that too and cunningly runs circles round Wagner, one of the reporters, by playing the innocent as Wagner extols the virtues of a free press. "Does freedom of the press mean freedom to choose its own standards?" [p. 84], Mageeba questions with a sudden withering sarcasm; this pointedly demonstrates how offensive Wagner's own standards are to an African leader and to a black nation anxious to create a new identity for itself. Who ultimately controls the policy and tone of a newspaper — the politician, the businessman, the individual reporter or the reporters' union — is left an open-ended debate; but what remains alarmingly clear is that truth as meaning genuine facts in news is a decidedly relative and manipulable entity. Milne, the idealistic, younger reporter believes that "junk journalism is the evidence of a society that has got at least one thing right, that there should be nobody with the power to dictate where responsible journalism begins" [p. 61]. But by what standards do you then judge what *responsible* journalism is? He and Wagner both work for what is ostensibly a responsible weekly and their methods and ethics are manifestly different; and it is Milne who is accidentally shot pushing his luck too far in the race for a front-page headline.

Night and Day is a mordant comedy that explores the gap between individuals' stated values and their actual, usually instinctive behaviour. Comedy thrives on incongruity; it leads inevitably to the mayhem we expect as the climax of the farce. With

Night and Day the mayhem is unusually distanced: for Stoppard the plot is surprisingly clear-cut and simple; the surreal opening sequence in which by night a jeep is seen caught in a sweeping arc of searchlights, which then isolate a fleeing figure who is suddenly killed by a burst of gunfire, resolves by the light of day into the nightmare of an exhausted reporter faced with yet another war-assignment. Guthrie's dream becomes a reality for Milne who is shot while trying to drive into the rebel army's camp. The mayhem in this comedy, as the opening implies, largely lies within. Though his subject is the division between his characters' intellectual and instinctive selves, Stoppard does not evolve a complex dramatic structure to define this; instead he employs the device of having one character, the businessman Carson's wife, Ruth, speak her thoughts aloud. It is a clever redeployment of the technique of the ironic aside in effect, but one that carries more weight here than it does conventionally. Ruth embodies Stoppard's theme about the disassociated self by playing in her person two parts, neither of which content her. Intellectually she despises the men about her, especially Wagner; she enjoys demolishing his opinions as vulgar, commonplace; she senses Mageeba's cat-and-mouse game with him and relishes Wagner's humiliation; her view of him is affected by the deep hurt she sustained when her private life was the subject of scandal-mongering by the gutter press during the divorce that preceded her marriage to Carson. Sexually she is aroused by Milne's youth and vigour of mind but her hope of seducing him never reaches beyond the realm of fantasy; Carson is a colourless figure defined entirely by his business interests, who hardly intrudes on Ruth's mind-life. Loneliness and a hunger that (like Dotty's) is as much metaphysical as sensual drives her to offer herself to Wagner with the grim recognition that the two of them are alike in being divided against themselves, though he is too thick-skinned and jaded to be aware of the fact while she is caught in a vortex of self-appraisal and disgust.

What is remarkable is Stoppard's ability to convey this bitterness through comedy. The device of Ruth's inner voice is perfectly judged: its irony deflates masculine pretensions in the various debates with pithy scorn; it sits relentlessly in judgement on Ruth's own public utterance, speaking for a mind that is quick-witted, incisive, penetrating, but dangerously clever, because clearly it is the voice of a boredom that engrosses Ruth's whole consciousness. Stoppard excels, as did Coward in plays like *Design for Living*, in devising styles of wit that speak for minds stretched to breaking point and sensibilities that operate at the very nerve ends. Ruth's wit is funny but brittle given its acute tension. It is also a welcome diversion from the earnest tones of debate that occupy much of the play; the device is particularly well used in the early stages of the interview with Mageeba to intimate that more is perhaps going on than Wagner is aware of, that he has met his match in craftiness and pretence. Even Ruth's final capitulation to the man she despises is framed in a witty conceit. Wagner is working at Carson's telex machine when Ruth enigmatically invites him to her bed ("You can use the phone upstairs if you like"); he is not dull-brained when such an opportunity offers and replies in an equally enigmatic but characteristically laconic style ("I thought you didn't want to be a tart"); Ruth empties a bottle of whiskey and throws integrity to the winds ("How do I know until I've tried it?"). Wagner continues to sit at the telex "tie loose, cigarette in mouth", while she leans against the machine. In her mind's eye she suddenly sees it as the "familiar piano-player-plus-singer" scene; we hear a distant piano and her inner voice murmurs a few bars of 'The Lady is a Tramp' till Wagner breaks off her play of thought by tearing his copy out of the machine. To her terse question "Is that it?", he replies as tersely, "That's it"; and the play ends [p. 94]. Fleeting stage-picture and final exchange humorously capture the casual, bleak quality of the encounter. For all her efforts at integrity, circumstance proves Ruth to be at heart as much a tramp and opportunist as Wagner. The irony is she knows it but that does not stop her. The last laugh is on her.

Night and Day is a good play but far less adventurous in its dramatic technique than any of Stoppard's other full-length comedies. The one device that keeps it from a complete adherence to realist conventions comes to be almost over-worked as the source of laughter in the play, tartly funny though most of the 'inner' Ruth's observations are. It is as if the theme of language as an index to integrity proved too serious an issue when applied to the public realm of news and the media. The one female character in the cast has a rebellious inner self; but why have none of the men? The recent production with Glenda Jackson of O'Neill's *Strange Interlude* (Duke of York's, 1984) showed that the device of the inner voice can encompass a wealth of comic (as well as tragic) effects. For once Stoppard appears to be too preoccupied with arguing out his subject to allow his invention free-rein with his chosen technique. Some of his inspiration for the play obviously derives from Evelyn Waugh's *Scoop*; but the play in no way attempts to travesty material from the novel, presumably because Waugh's critical perspective and sense of outrage are too close to Stoppard's own for him to be capable of outdoing Waugh's satire.

The problem facing Stoppard with his particular mode of travesty must be the need to choose as his base a play or style of drama familiar to his audience (Shakespeare, Wilde, the whodunnit); *Rosencrantz and Guildenstern Are Dead* becomes a more enjoyable experience the more one appreciates the degree to which even in its finest details the play is shaped by the instinct for travesty. Two recent works have shown Stoppard confronting this problem with only varying degrees of success. *Rough Crossing* (Lyttleton, 1984)[34] was a complete failure because Stoppard demonstrated scant respect for his original, Ferenc Molnar's *Play at the Castle*; the Hungarian play is a study of types of intricate emotional blackmail, but Stoppard made Molnar's tightly crafted plot an excuse for satirising techniques of exposition and dénouement in third-rate comedies, the humour of which quickly palled. It was a thin play, less a travsty than a meagre adaptation, devoid of the complex texture of ideas and wit that Stoppard creates with seeming effortlessness at his best. *The Real Thing* (Strand, 1982)[35] was a more interesting case showing an attempt to do something new with travesty: here the technique does not control the whole dramatic structure but is used intermittently to provide a commentary on Stoppard's own dramatic style and highlight his preoccupation with language and sincerity of feeling; the play shifts between realism and more fanciful, not to say fantastic, forms of theatre to develop and substantiate a debate about the nature of truth and artistic honesty.

We begin with a husband accusing his wife of adultery; it is carried off with a certain panache in the high style of Coward and his West-End imitators: upper lips are decidedly stiff and the crisis is seized by the characters, particularly the husband, as a chance to revel in wit as self-display. There is little sense of hurt or outrage:

MAX: Aren't you going to tell me who it is?
CHARLOTTE: Who what is?
MAX: Your lover, lover.
CHARLOTTE: Which lover?
MAX: I assumed there'd only be the one.
CHARLOTTE: Did you?
MAX: Well, do you see them separately or both together?
   Sorry, that's not fair.
   Well, tell you what, nod your head if it's separately.
   (*She looks at him.*)

Heavens
If you have an opening free, I'm not doing much at the moment.
Or is the position taken?
It is only two, is it?
Nod your head.
(*She looks at him.*)
Golly, you are a dark horse. Do they share a flat and pay a third of the rent each or what? How does it work? I'm interested in the logistics, you see. How do they all get away at the same time? Do they work together, like the Marx Brothers?
I'm not upsetting you, I hope?
CHARLOTTE: You underestimate me.
MAX: (*Interested*) Do I? A string quartet, you mean? That sort of thing?
(*He ponders for a moment.*)
What does the fourth one do?
(*She raises her hand.*)
Got it. Plays by himself. [p. 14]

In the second scene we see the same woman but with a different man who equally appears to be her husband. Stoppard plays along with this situation long enough for us to wonder whether this wife does indeed have a 'husband' in every port, before subtly informing us that the first scene we saw was in fact a play written by the real-life husband, Henry, in which his actress-wife, Charlotte, was appearing. This second scene challenges and questions the dramatic idiom of the first and the values that are implicit in that idiom. In the play-scene from "The House of Cards", the wife is merely a 'feed' to the husband's brilliance; in life, Charlotte is firmly in control of the conversation. The tone now is infinitely more complex: as she perceives, "The House of Cards" is a kind of wish-fulfilling fantasy, a compensation for Henry:

CHARLOTTE: What an ego trip! Having all the words to come back with just as you need them. That's the difference between plays and real life — thinking time, time to get your bottle back. "Must say, I take my hat off to you, coming home with Rembrandt place mats for your mother." You don't really think that if Henry caught me out with a lover, he'd sit around being witty about place mats? Like hell he would. He'd come apart like pick-a-sticks. His sentence structure would go to pot, closely followed by his sphincter. You know that, don't you, Henry? Henry? No answer. Are you there, Henry? Say something witty. [p. 22]

Charlotte's marriage is on the brink of dissolution: Henry has fallen passionately in love with Annie, another actress, but the matter is still secret. The tone of the second scene is as brilliant as that in "The House of Cards", but the cleverness is brittle, has a tense, bitter edge to it. One cannot be sure whether the wit is intended to wound or whether it is playful *badinage*, a stiff-upper-lipped control of emotion or sly, calculated bitchery. The third scene exactly mirrors scene one: Annie tells Max, her husband, that she is in love with Henry. Max loses all control, declines into incoherent abuse and barely audible sobbing, then tries physically to assault Annie but the movement turns into a desperate embrace. Throughout Annie is blank, unresponsive. Travesty in these three scenes is working as a form of criticism, establishing a recognisable theatrical norm and testing it for realism. Language and tone are being explored as indices of feeling, and a conventional dramatic idiom is seen to deploy humour in an effort to keep detached from emotion and a proper engagement with character.

The main focus of the play which follows is on Henry's voyage of self-discovery through loving Annie. As a writer he desperately wants to express this new-found exuberance with her in his art but is frustrated repeatedly for want of an appropriate language: "Loving and being loved is so unliterary. It's happiness expressed in banality and lust" [p. 41], he moans. "I don't know how to write love. I try to write it properly, and it just comes out embarrassing. It's either childish or rude. And the rude bits are absolutely juvenile" [p. 40]. Banality and cliché he abhors as abuses of language; worse is the contemporary fashion for reducing philosophy to slogans to be printed on T-shirts — "Sophistry in a phrase so neat you can't see the loose end that would unravel it" [p. 68]. Henry has a moving humility before language as the medium of his art: "I don't think writers are sacred, but words are. They deserve respect. If you get the right ones in the right order, you can nudge the world a little or make a poem which children will speak for you when you're dead" [p. 55]. The fact that Henry is a dramatist and Charlotte and Annie actresses allows Stoppard to accentuate Henry's dilemma by quoting other kinds of love-drama, other modes of emotional expression. Interestingly Stoppard chooses to *quote*, not travesty.

At the time of their elopement, Annie is rehearsing in a production of *Miss Julie* and Henry's dilemma over a language for loving is juxtaposed against her learning her lines for Strindberg's masterpiece. As Annie remarks: Strindberg is not concerned with *stated* emotions (in the manner of "The House of Cards") but with a sub-text; his dialogue is "steaming with lust, but there is nothing rude on the page" [p. 41]. The two of them begin to read together one of the exchanges in which Julie and Jean enter into their mutual seduction. There was a problem here in performance: Stoppard's stage direction suggests the passage be " 'read' without inflection" [p. 40], and Roger Rees and Felicity Kendal carried this rather to extremes, as if they were inwardly embarrassed by the sudden shift of style; the episode came across in consequence as rather perfunctory. Preferably the actors should begin flatly enough but, as the writing gets a grip on their imaginations and fuels their discussion about art and sincerity, they should begin to act in earnest so that the quotation from Strindberg is felt by the audience to have significance. Here is an intricate language of love, charged by anyone who knows *Miss Julie* with a profound wealth of meaning beneath its surface banter: the class difference (mistress and servant) and various attendant social barriers and taboos are tacitly being broken and that excites Julie and Jean erotically; they are entering a forbidden world. Beneath the prosaic dialogue, there are intimated surprises, discoveries, fears; but all the time an irresistible impulse is driving them on inexorably to sexual fulfilment. There are no tensions like these for Henry and Annie; in a permissive world, they know no barriers or taboos; they share a freedom and openness with each other beyond Strindberg's imagining; but it is that very freedom that seems Henry's undoing as a dramatist. To sense the full meaning of the episode does require a familiarity with *Miss Julie* and to the uninitiated the moment can seem over-intellectual. *Miss Julie* is not part of the national consciousness in the way that *Hamlet* and *The Importance of Being Earnest* are; and *The Real Thing* does not allow time for an exposition of Strindberg's scene to give the uninformed spectator an insight into the reasons for Stoppard's reference to it. It makes some impact through its obvious-sounding difference from the dialogue in the rest of the play, but the subtlety of its reference may well escape the audience, especially given too lame a rendering by the actors as happened with the first cast.

Much the same can be said of the other literary reference in the play to Ford's *'Tis Pity She's a Whore*. Annie is this time playing the piece in Glasgow in the role of Annabella who is wooed by her brother Giovanni to commit incest. The scenes for brother and sister are written with a passionate eloquence and the young actor, Billy, who is playing Giovanni, uses the intensity of these scenes with Annie to seduce her into adultery:

BILLY: I marvel why the chaster of your sex
  Should think this pretty toy called maidenhead

So strange a loss, when, being lost, 'tis nothing,
And you are still the same.
ANNIE: 'Tis well for you;
Now you can talk.
BILLY: Music as well consists
In the ear as in the playing.
ANNIE: O, you're wanton!
Tell on't you're best; do.
BILLY: Thou wilt chide me, then.
Kiss me:-
(*He kisses her lightly.*)
ANNIE: (*Quietly*) Billy . . .
(*She returns the kiss in earnest.*) [p. 64]

Again Stoppard is inviting us to draw parallels and contrasts. Is
Annie succumbing like Annabella to the attraction of a relationship
that should be taboo? Is Annie too in her professed amorality also
a whore? Ironically when Henry wished he could write in the
Renaissance manner with "complete artificiality. Blank verse.
Poetic imagery" [p. 40], Annie laughed the idea to scorn; yet
circumstance shows that that idiom in the right emotional context
has the power to bewitch her imagination. Again Stoppard could
be accused of being over-intellectual (a situation not helped by the
actors who for a second time were directed to play without feeling
as if the scene were just a word-rehearsal to memorise lines and
cues). It is essential that the audience take the scene from Ford
seriously, because our awareness of it should underlie all our
responses to Henry in the rest of the play. He wishes to prove his
love a whore, to rage like another Othello, but cannot. Throughout
Act Two of *The Real Thing* Stoppard demonstrates that love is not
a feeling that can be stated in the way Henry yearns for, but a total
condition of being. It is what Henry comes to be and to do that
defines the meaning of love as 'the real thing'. He learns to live
beyond jealousy and accept Annie's amorality and discovers that
love is not just a question of fidelity any more than fidelity is a
matter simply of monogamy. He starts the play, as Charlotte
wistfully acknowledges when she is too late to profit by the insight,
as one of the last Romantics, an utter innocent in a permissive
world for whom one loving relationship can still be all-consuming.
(Roger Rees, as his Nicholas Nickleby (Aldwych, 1980) showed,
excels in playing sterling, honest souls, vulnerable in their very
openness, gentle men whose iron-hard integrity wins respct; he can
play goodness with an unembarrassed fervour that saves it from all
suspicion of sentimentality, and that is no easy feat as the

limitations of the actors who succeeded him in the role of Henry[36] quickly proved.) Annie shatters his ideals and expectations: Henry compromises with his artistic standards and re-writes an inferior play by another hand for her, because she believes in its author and feels his work deserves a hearing; he accepts her relationship with the young actor on her terms and generously leaves her free to pursue it, winning her gratitude because "you allow me to behave well towards him without having to be furtive"[p. 79]; and when Annie says "I love you", he knows she means it, that what she experiences with him is 'the real thing'. When Henry finally comes to state what love *is*, it is paradoxically not in terms of love at all but in terms of morals:

I can't cope with more than one moral system at a time. Mine is that what you think is right is right. What you do is right. What you want is right. There was a tribe, wasn't there, which worshipped Charlie Chaplin. It worked just as well as any other theology, apparently. They loved Charlie Chaplin. I love you. [p. 79]

The comic absurdity of that central image of the tribe's idolatry of Chaplin is nicely calculated to provoke a laugh: the earnest and the ludicrous are held in a careful balance that cleanses the expression of love from sentimentality and pretentiousness. As played by Rees, it was an unselfconscious experience of pure rapture.

Just as *Dogg's Hamlet, Cahoot's Macbeth* teaches us a language, so *The Real Thing* with its echoes of Coward and quotations from Strindberg and Ford educates our sensibilities and fine tunes our ear to show how style shapes language to create tone and how it is tone that intimates complexities of feeling. The scenes between Henry and Charlotte (in marked contrast to those between Henry and Annie even at their most painful) define a marriage which has lost the intimacy which allows for total honesty under any circumstances; later, after the divorce, the mood between them relaxes to an easy friendship undercut by Charlotte's recognition that she previously misjudged Henry and, judging him by her own standards, brought their separation on herself. The scenes between Henry and his adolescent daughter, Debbie, intimate a profound affection and, in him, an unforced expression of care beneath all their mutual teasing: they can argue without tempers getting involved or Henry asserting an adult superiority. Faced with the prospect of "Cuckoldry", Henry muses: "And I'm supposed to score points on dignity. I don't think I can. It'll become my only thought. It'll replace thinking" [p. 74]. Yet his dignity is precisely what he does retain, because he never ceases to respect the integrity of others' feelings. Henry's journey from innocence to experience is not a matter of moral or emotional collapse, rather it entails finding viable personal moral standards that will allow him to maintain his self-respect in an otherwise permissive world. (Felicity Kendal's effervescent stage personality — her very voice seems to gurgle with laughter — was an ideal foil for Rees's Henry, being utterly charismatic even while admitting she is not a type who can "come up with the proper guilt" to order [p. 39]. Annie's amorality does not prevent her recognising pain in others, even when she cannot experience either pain in herself or remorse for causing it in others. (That Felicity Kendal could make a success of both Annie and the love-lorn Dotty recently shows her to be an actress of considerable imaginative range.) *The Real Thing* is a comedy about a man who needs to care and who, caring, can create. Stoppard's dramatic structure teaches us how to listen with as scrupulous an attention as Henry's to the ways language defines the essence of character and the quality of relationships. If we respond to Stoppard's strategies, we become part of the play's creative process.

If one has reservations about *The Real Thing* (that, though fine, it is not Stoppard at his very best), that is because the play lacks the dimension of surrealism and fantasy. The play's method puts us in tune with Henry's creative scruples, but that does not involve Stoppard in fashioning a new dramatic structure for comedy which takes us inside the workings of Henry's consciousness so that we share his very mode of perception, as we do with Rosencrantz and Guildenstern or with George Moore. The form of *The Real Thing* is conventionl apart from its use of pastiche and quotation. Perhaps Henry is too positive a figure: it is the flawed, limited or prejudiced consciousness which seems to excite Stoppard's greatest feats of invention, quintessentially so in his masterpiece, *Travesties* (Aldwych, 1974).[37]

The whole piece is a fantasy spun with great elegance out of two simple historical facts: that James Joyce, Tristan Tzara and Lenin were all living and working in Zurich during the first World War; and that Joyce mounted a production of *The Importance of Being Earnest* there in which a young man, Henry Carr of the British Consulate, achieved success in the part of Algernon but afterwards took Joyce to court in an attempt to recover the money he spent on some trousers for his stage costume. Carr was subsequently satirised by Joyce as a minor character in *Ulysses* and he is precisely the sort of man whose life is relegated to the footnotes of history; but it is he and neither of the artists nor the social reformer that Stoppard chooses to put at the centre of his comedy. What is amazing is that from such simple beginnings such a complex dramatic structure has been created drawing inspiration from Wilde's play and Joyce's novel: the agility with which so many ideas are brought into play, contrasted and interwoven in a sequence of memorable dramatic conceits is a virtuoso display of wit.

At the heart of the play each of the great men is allowed a statement of his aims in life; the conflict of ideals between them creates a debate on the nature of art and its relation to society and politics, a debate into which Carr enters to put the common man's invariably philistine and conservative point of view. Tzara, expounding the theories of Dadaism, demands revolution, the smashing of traditions, so that a clean start can be made. "Artists and intellectuals will be the conscience of the revolution" [p. 83], he asserts, while believing that social change will be accompanied by a change in conciousness; but he finds that "the further left you go politically the more bourgeois they like their art" [p. 45]. Lenin bears that out for, though he speaks of equality and freedom, he wishes ruthlessly to curtail the freedom of artists and intellectuals: they are, he says, "irresponsible people" [p. 88]. He despises bourgeois life and its values but cannot disguise his nostalgia for the bourgeois art of Pushkin and Beethoven: the *Appassionata* moves him to tears but the challenge that poses to his ideals he refuses to take up, preferring to crush the insights music affords. Lenin will have no truck with the inner life and the emotions. Joyce glories in his lack of a social conscience and our shock at his satirising the war-effort goes some way towards substantiating Lenin's criticism of artists:

> Who is the tranquil gentleman who wont salute the State
> Or serve Nebuchadnezzar or proletariat
> But thinks that every son of man has quite enough to do
> To paddle down the stream of life his personal canoe.
>
> [pp. 49-50]

Tzara abhors such art-for-art's-sake attitudes: "For your masterpiece", he tells Joyce, "I have great expectorations". With an eye to *Ulysses* and with an oddly prophetic intuition of Joyce's later novel, he accuses: "You've turned literature into a religion and it's as dead as all the rest, it's an over-ripe corpse and you're cutting fancy figures at its wake" [p. 62]. But though Tzara dismisses Joyce's experiments with fiction as sorting "language into hands for contract bridge" [p. 42], his own experiments with simultaneous verse do not sound so very different in effect. He simply chops up other people's poems with a pair of scissors and re-arranges the words to form a poem of his own. Being disciples of Freud, the Dadaists believed the libido should be given free expression in art; rooted deep in the subconscious, it was, they felt, the source of the spontaneity they most prized in art. (Stoppard cannot resist the chance to out-Tzara Tzara and transforms Shakespeare's "Shall I Compare Thee to a Summer's Day" to a verse with urgent erotic overtones that quite startle its recipient [pp. 54-55].) Little or none of Tzara's revolutionary zeal ever gets into his art and his postures are easily deflated; as Joyce informs him: "You're an over-excited little man, with a need for self-expression far beyond the scope of your natural gifts" [p. 62]. And so the debate continues with each man justifying himself and detecting the weaknesses in his opponents' arguments. But each is seen to have a quality of dedication to his life's work which he will perfect even at the expense of his own life. Each in his own way went on to transform the cultural life of Europe.

Stoppard's chief problems with this play must have been firstly how to offer enough exposition about these three figures so that we can appreciate the point of the debate about art and society; and secondly how to shape that debate into an artistic unity. He solves the first problem by making Tzara, Lenin and Joyce exaggerated caricatures of their real selves to give us a powerful sense of their individual personalities and a grasp of the close connection between their respective personalities and their ideas. The second problem he confronts by making all the caricature acceptable as a travesty of the truth by projecting the whole experience of the play through the memory and consciousness of Henry Carr. In old age Carr is trying to write his autobiography, describing especially his relations with his great contemporaries — a curious pastime since we discover at the end that he never actually met either Lenin or Tzara and his encounter with Joyce was not exactly amicable. Still, as he keeps reassuring himself and us — the four of them were all in Zurich together. When his wife tries to point out his fallacies with fact, he snaps back: "Oh, Cecily. I wish I'd known then that you'd turn out to be a pedant! Wasn't this — Didn't do that — 1916 — 1917 — *What of it*? I was here. They were here. They went on. I went on. We all went on". But Cecily is adamant: "No, we didn't. We stayed" [p. 98]. That Henry Carr *stayed* has, we realise, more than one level of significance.

Just as Joyce needed the *Odyssey* to create a structure within which he could contain the fluctuating consciousness of Leopold Bloom, so for his plot-line Stoppard takes Wilde's *The Importance of Being Earnest* and uses it loosely to give a shape to the roving fantasies of Carr's dream life. The only things of note in Carr's social existence were the "blighty wound" which got him out of the trenches and into the safety of Zurich, his ever-stylish trousers and his success as Algernon in Joyce's production. Like so many other autobiographers Carr in his memoirs is struggling to give importance to a rather grey life, to create something out of nothing. It is a prodigous feat of the imagination aimed not at eliciting the truth about himself but at compensating for the harshness of reality. Stoppard with his gift for parody has a field-day. There is the struggle with style and rhetoric to disguise as melodrama what hindsight has proved to be downright incompetence:

Lenin and I in Zurich. I'd got pretty close to him, had a stroke of luck with a certain little lady and I'd got a pretty good idea of his plans, in fact I might have stopped the whole Bolshevik thing in its tracks, but — here's the point. *I was uncertain* . . . And don't forget, *he wasn't Lenin then!* . . . So there I was, the lives of millions of people hanging on which way I'd move, or whether I'd move at all, another man might have cracked . . . [p. 81]

Then there is the quest for the right tone and the precise and telling epithet to *place* an individual in the pen-portrait:

To be in [Lenin's] presence was to be aware of a complex personality, enigmatic, magnetic, but not, I think, astigmatic, his piercing brown (if memory serves) eyes giving no hint of it. . . . As I shook the hand of this dynamic, gnomic and yet not, I think, anaemic stranger who with his fine head of blond hair falling over his forehead had the clean-shaven look of a Scandinavian sea-faring — hello, hello, got the wrong chap, has he? — take no notice, all come out in the wash, that's the art of it. [p. 23]

Though the attempt here is to be discriminating, the mannerism of the style with its hesitant qualifications reveals not so much the character of Lenin as the inadequacy of Carr's knowledge, Language is a more subtle truth-teller than Carr realises — that indeed *is* the art of it. Carr's whole process of reminiscing can be summed up as an attempt to recover his self-esteem: through injured pride, spleen, wish-fulfilment he tries to sustain in his dream-life an eloquence and decorum denied him in reality. He is trying to live with the easy grace and articulate brilliance of a character in a Wildean comedy and with a debonair vivacity that history and his own prejudiced, fallible nature prevented him from ever achieving. This is, of course, to approach the central debate about the nature of art from a different but related perspective: of what value is it, if it is largely compensation for the writer's own inadequacies?

The action of the play — the movement of Carr's mind — is

erratic; the train of his thoughts is constantly jumping the rails. Continually he sets up new possibilities to contemplate, new fantasy-confrontations with the three giants of our cultural history, and attempts to get top-side of them. But even in his private dreams the figures of authority have a terrible tendency to get the better of him:

I dreamed about [Joyce], dreamed I had him in the witness box, a masterly cross-examination, case practically won, admitted it all, the whole thing, the trousers, everything, and I *flung* at him — "And what did you do in the Great War?" "I wrote *Ulysses*", he said. "What did you do?" Bloody nerve. [p. 65]

Truth will out; but, when this happens, Carr breaks off his fantasy, goes back to the beginning and starts a fresh line of approach. His resilience is indefatigable and, though it provides our laughter, it provokes our sympathy too.

Each of Carr's memory-episodes, his wish-fulfilling fantasies, evolves out of a situation in *The Importance of Being Earnest* and is dramatised for us as an affectionate pastiche of Joyce's experiments with style in *Ulysses*. Joyce at one point, for example, interrogates Tzara about the principles of his art and this is offered to us as a parody both of Lady Bracknell's interview with Worthing about his marriage prospects and of the catechism-sequence when Bloom asks Stephen about his circumstances and prospects as a would-be artist in working-class Dublin as the two men fall drunkenly asleep.[38] Joyce in real life had some notoriety as a writer of limericks, so when he first appears in the play the dialogue erupts into doggerel stanzas which delightfully mimic the obsessional formality of the business of introductions and tea-table conversations in Wilde's comedies:

(GWENDOLEN *and* JAMES JOYCE *enter*. BENNETT *remains by the door.* GWENDOLEN *and* TZARA *are momentarily transfixed by each other. This is hardly noticed as* JOYCE *has made it his own entrance.*)

JOYCE: Top o' the morning! — James Joyce!
         I hope you'll allow me to voice
         my regrets in advance
         for coming on the off-chance —
         b'jasus I hadn't much choice!
CARR: I . . . sorry . . . would you say that again?
JOYCE: Begob — I'd better explain
         I'm told that you are a——
TZARA: Miss Carr!
GWEN: Mr. Tzara!
JOYCE: (*seeing Tzara for the first time*) B'jasus'. Joyce is the name.

GWEN: I'm sorry! — how terribly rude!
Henry — Mr. Joyce!
CARR: How d'you do?
JOYCE: Delighted!
TZARA: Good day!
JOYCE: I just wanted to say
how sorry I am to intrude.
CARR: Tell me . . . are you some kind of a poet?
JOYCE: You know my work?
CARR: No — it's
something about your deliv'ry——
can't quite——
JOYCE: Irish.
CARR: From Lim'rick?
JOYCE: No — Dublin, don't tell me you know it!
GWEN: He's a poor writer——
JOYCE: Aha!
A fine writer who writes caviar
for the general, hence poor——
TZARA: Wants to touch you for sure.
JOYCE: I'm addressing my friend, Mr. . . .
CARR: (gulp)   Carr.
GWEN: Mr. Tzara writes poetry and sculpts,
with quite unexpected results.
I'm told he recites
and on Saturday nights
does all kinds of things for adults.   [pp. 33-34]

(A feat of memory and perfect timing this requires of the actors, since it gets funnier in performance the faster it can be played). Even the eerie opening of the play in Cecily's library (another of Stoppard's surreal inventions) has its parallel in Joyce. Tzara sits creating a nonsense poem by extracting words on scraps of paper out of his hat: "Eel ate enormous appletzara"; nearby Joyce is dictating *Ulysses*: "Deshill holles eamus", which his secretary promptly echoes; in the next bay Lenin and his wife Nadya whisper urgently in Russian, while Cecily keeps trying to instil silence with a prolonged, sibilant "Sssssssh!" [p. 18]. It is a mad farago of language but, as the play unfolds, we learn how to interpret what is going on. The technique has its counterpart in *Ulysses* in the chapter that Joyce sets in the Ormond Street Bar which begins with a phonetic rendering of all the sounds to be heard there by way of a prelude; the strange phrases then find a context of meaning as the chapter develops.[39] Most of the scenes in *Travesties* have this complexity of resonance, literary and theatrical; the exception involves the episodes with Lenin who resists inclusion in the parody (the play's one serious weakness). As one who is revealed as ruling according to inflexible principles and who wishes to impose fixed patterns of behaviour on others, Lenin ought perhaps ideally to have been paired with Lady Bracknell (both in their respective ways believe that financial considerations permeate every aspect of human experience) but Stoppard fights shy of that possible travesty. Lenin affords a necessary critical perspective on the debate about art and interestingly shares many of Carr's prejudices; as a force for social change who also poses a sinister threat to the introspective, self-conscious artists, he has perhaps too complex a role to be integrated at all easily into the play's satirical scheme. Maybe Stoppard's point in handling Lenin as he does is that the artists in Zurich should have attempted to integrate him into their circle and not have kept their distance for the future benefit of Russian intellectual life, but that is to begin entering the realm of wish-fulfilment which in the play is Carr's exclusive territory. Whatever Stoppard's aim, it lacks clarity of definition.

Like *Ulysses*, *Travesties* is a masterpiece of comic irreverence but there is a serious purpose behind the high spirits in the way the play offers us a sensitive analysis of Henry Carr's mind. The form of the play — long monologues alternating with scenes of comic fantasy — actualises the different levels of Carr's consciousness. The monologues explore the region of the mind where consciousness is ordered into articulated thought; the fantasies give us access to the richer creative reaches of Carr's subconscious. What we watch are the workings of the mind of a man caught in 1917 at the point of change in our cultural destiny where Modernism in the writings and art of men like Joyce and Tzara revolutionised our ways of perception. Carr is essentially conservative and his monologues show him trying feebly to describe his great contemporaries in traditional terms since Carr is troubled by Modernist assertions that reality is fluid, evanescent. He prefers the old conception of the stable ego and his autobiography is an attempt to impose fixed, predictable, factual interpretations on his life in Zurich but reality constantly eludes him. If Carr relishes the characters in Wilde's comedies, it is because they have no trouble in asserting form over feeling; they compel life to submit to decorous and acceptable patterns of behaviour. Lenin is conservative too in this and has an absolutist power to impose form over feeling, to insist that only certain patterns of behaviour are socially acceptable. Paradoxically in his fantasy-life Carr, for all his prejudices, comes much closer to defining the quintessential achievements of men like Tzara and Joyce. Travesty brings us to a subtle apprehension of truth: though in his social self Carr is a nonentity, in his mind-life, like Joyce's Leopold Bloom, he has a dynamic, colourful personality which the old traditional modes of perception would never have penetrated. The dazzling technique of the play is at once an exposition and a reaffirmation of the values of Modernism. Stoppard confidently takes us through surrealist fantasy into the world of extended reality which is consciousness and actualises on stage the workings of imagination. Like much surrealist art, *Travesties* invites us to wonder at the miracle of the human mind. The form of the play during its performance invited us to relish the art of the actor too, as John Wood bridged the many time-shifts by effecting lightning transitions between the tetchy octogenarian Carr, frenziedly composing his memoirs, and his dapper, callow, twenty-year-old self, the epitome of mindless upper-class poise. Wood's gift for vocal mimicry was the perfect vehicle for Stoppard's parodies, while the slightly manic intensity Wood tends to instil in the pace of a performance ensured the play sustained the quality of a wild dream as Carr's old and young selves dissolved, the one into the other, and then magically re-formed. The old device of one comic actor impersonating a range of roles in a single play gained a new and startling vitality.[40]

It is Stoppard's facility in taking the familiar and transforming it into the strange which is a continuing joy in his artistry; it is the essence of his technique of travesty. By far the best comic writing since the Seventies has involved the creating of new forms for comedy and farce. Several notable plays especially by Bennett, Nichols and Ayckbourn seem to be testing the limits of comic expression; Nichols and Frayn have become preoccupied with the implications of form in comedy and have explored why comedy and farce have traditionally employed the devices they do. For Stoppard comedy is a liberating exercise of the imagination and his career shows him exploiting the possibilities of form to illuminate the protean workings of consciousness. At his best Stoppard invites an audience to experience comedy in the mind at play.

CHAPTER THREE

MONOLOGUES AND SOLILOQUIES: SAMUEL BECKETT

The monologue and the soliloquy have had a longstanding place in the drama since its very origins. The monologue, growing out of the messenger speech of classical tragedy, tends to involve a large element of narrative and to presuppose an audience. Even where the monologue evolved into the tirade, the narrative content was not lost since the tirade usually involved some statement of how a particular character saw, interpreted and responded to a pattern of events; it is a public assertion by a character of the nature of his private perceptions. That the tirade embraces invective, denunciation, even on occasion abuse, is because it is frequently used as a device to characterize the individuality of mind of one who chooses to deviate from the social norm of the given world of a play and who frequently luxuriates in so doing. Attack is such a character's mode of self-defence. The soliloquy is quintessentially intimate: a conversing with one's self apart, a searching for some understanding of that self in reaches of the mind where one is too utterly vulnerable to contemplate sharing one's knowledge with another. Both devices require of an audience empathy and judgement but to interestingly different degrees: the monologue/tirade by virtue of its somewhat provocative stance makes the stronger appeal to judgement through understanding; the soliloquy in its very nakedness reaches beyond critical responses to an audience's sensibilities, making its appeal to the sense of a common bond in human frailty. 'Judge not lest ye be judged' is the Bible's advice[1] and these two dramatic forms exemplify this to a nicety. The monologue/tirade takes a tone that is assured and judgemental of the world that the character inhabits and so invites judgement. The soliloquy is hesitant, enquiring, nervous; if anything it is critical of the self which this journey into the interior reveals and so tends to suspend judgement. A number of contemporary playwrights — Nichols, Frayn, Osborne, Wesker — in a move away from conventional forms of realism have recently begun exploring the possibilities these devices open up to the drama; two — Beckett and Barry Collins — have created entire works for single performers, which daringly confuse the boundaries between monologue, tirade and soliloquy in the effort of dramatising with exquisitely judged tact material that an audience might normally be expected to shy away from in fear or revulsion.

Peter Nichols in *Forget-Me-Not Lane* (Greenwich and Apollo, 1971)[2] makes his play unfold the narrative of his central character: Frank at forty searches his past to explain why he is the man he is. Certain episodes that blossom in his memory are played out in full (another actor plays Frank when young) but the focus is directed at the older Frank, who provides a commentary in the form of a continuing monologue that connects the incidents and shapes the narrative to define his present self. But the very act of *shaping* events to a pattern is a form of judgement on experience, however tolerantly done; though this is a journey into the self, the chosen mode is monologue not soliloquy and it has a strange air of calculation about it. Our first image is of Frank packing a suitcase apparently intent on leaving his wife and family and the ensuing journey through memory appears to be a vindication of his right to be a free man; however, the closing seconds of the play show that this is all a fantasy, a dream of leaving, indulged to avoid the hassle of packing for a holiday. What seemed a brave self-defence turns out to be the fanciful projection of a role that guilt would never allow Frank play in reality. The clear-sighted, confident monologuist bears no truth to self.

A more recent play by Nichols, *Born in the Gardens* (Globe, 1979)[3] makes an unusual use of soliloquy. The play is largely taken up with defining the eccentric lifestyle of the elderly Maud and her son Mo. Contentedly self-absorbed, both are in their way innocents and rather appealing for that. Maud's two other children are worldly and apparently successful. Called home to their father's funeral, Hedley and Queenie find their mother and brother's unconventionality too disturbing, too compromising to their principles not to interfere. Maud excites Hedley's "over-developed sense of duty"; he feels society would expect him to establish her in his London home. Queenie wants to take Mo away to find himself in the sexual liberation of California. Both aspirations seem ludicrously commonplace and are met by Maud and Mo with serene indifference. That the 'normality' of Hedley's and Queenie's worlds is not the delightful prospect they insist on is made clear through the use of two soliloquy scenes. Each is overheard telephoning that other world. Hedley is found to be caught in a tangle of deceptions: his life in London involves a mad wife and a mad secretary/lover; his mistress, the recipient of his phone call, forces him to ask himself, what is the *point* of adding to the *mènage* a mad mother. That she cries then rings off when he can find no answer to that but a laugh, leaves him utterly nonplussed, which is indicative of her desperation and his utter chauvinism. Queenie's perceptions of the good life are wholly circumscribed by clichés, as is very evident from the article 'Springtime in Merrie Englande' she dictates as magazine copy to her lover Mark back in the States; it is equally evident that the Californian sexual paradise is not without its treacheries and jealousies: Queenie suddenly realises another woman has been listening in to her intimacies on an extension. The soliloquies are the stuff of cheap fiction, a perspective that enables us both to judge Hedley and Queenie's outrage over their mother and brother with some irony, and to delight the more in Maud and Mo's child-like self-sufficiency, which is not without its own shrewd sense of the truth. Maud's final observations on Hedley and Queenie are wickedly apt: of him, "Gone and never called me mother" [p. 73]; of her, "And she's an alley-cat, tell her that" [p. 74].

Michael Frayn's *Benefactors* (Vaudeville, 1984)[4] like *Forget-Me-Not Lane* uses the device of retrospective narrative but shares it systematically between the four characters, who quite overtly tell a tale to the audience; changes of voice are less frequently occasioned by genuine dialogue than by the desire to juxtapose different, private perspectives of opinion on events:

DAVID   Basuto Road. I love the name!
JANE   Basuto Road. How I hate those sour grey words! [p. 1]

The surface interest of the play is provided by a satire on current practices in town-planning and architectural design; but the dramatic method highlights a quite different theme, where Frayn's concern is less social than moral in discriminating how kindness and charity can easily become or be interpreted as patronage, how a vaunted social conscience can often be a means of avoiding issues of conscience in one's personal life, and how pity can be debilitating or, worse, cruelly insulting. Repeatedly the method of juxtaposing four independent monologues throws the attitudes of David and Jane with their organised, no-nonsense approach to life into relief beside the responses of Colin and Sheila, who are the objects of their concern; the effect is to show the extent to which care in David and Jane springs from a smug self-satisfaction that is vicious; they are too busy being successful ever really to *feel* and the consequence of this for both marriages is devastating. The monologue technique ensures the audience remains detached, critical, alert to the implications of tone.

John Osborne has been the master of tirade as a volley of invective since his first play. Most of his early heroes attacked the complacency of the world about them out of a passionate loathing of shoddiness, cant and self-delusion. Theirs were the voices of men baulked in their efforts to realise socially or personally their visions of a finer condition of being. In recent work like *The End of Me Old Cigar* (Greenwich, 1975)[5] Osborne deploys a similar technique but the invective has lost its dynamic energy: vision in Lady Regine Frimley has been reduced to a consuming hatred that renders her somewhat ridiculous long before she is halted in her plot to overthrow the Establishment by exposing every echelon of power as riddled with vice. She plans to inaugurate a Feminist Revolution but she is activated less by an imagined world of realisable possibilities, as Osborne's Luther is, than by a revulsion from men and sexuality. She inveighs against man's abuse of woman for political ends yet can conceive no way of effecting a revolution other than by exploiting her women friends as sexual objects for the purpose of blackmailing men in high office. Act one builds to the expected tirade from Regine; from the beginning she has lashed out in scorn at any other character's use of cliché: it reveals, she argues, a slovenly mind trapped in attitudes promulagated by the *status quo*. But, given the floor, Regine has no *pure* language at her command; Osborne invests her speech with slogans culled from extremist feminism and a vague, cheer-leader style of rhetoric:

Believe me, from what I've seen, the female mind and body is a holy miracle of ingenuity and divine invention. Blake has nothing on HER visions and explorations. That's why we're here. That's the *message*. [p. 37]

And the tirade lacks a sense of direction and climax. Well before her schemes founder, Regine has been marked by Osborne as a failure for want of genuine inspiration and so the outcome of the plot is wholly predictable. Osborne has created a character in whom he has no belief and the resulting play is heartless and cynical. Regine's long monologue is devised as a judgement upon her; paradoxically, in judging her, Osborne exposes his own artistry and its values to question.

Wesker has similarly used monologue, tirade and soliloquy within larger dramatic structures since his trilogy; but *The Old Ones* (Royal Court, 1972)[6] returned to the devices for a highly innovatory purpose. Monologue, tirade, soliloquy all define in his characters their apartness. Old age can be a time of withdrawal into memories, forgetfulness, rancour, frustration — all occasioned by loss of physical vitality. This is Wesker's subject but he is concerned to show that these qualities can be accompanied by defiance: there is no going gently into death for any of the ageing Jewish brothers and sisters who make up his characters. They mostly live alone and talk to themselves through the day (the staging requires several small rooms to be visible); but there is nothing maudlin in this.

Teresa is a translator and her dialogue with herself about her work reveals a mind acutely responsive to nuances of language and tone and an infinite patience in striving for accuracy of interpretation. Her detached critical spirit refuses to let her take refuge in self-pity and her very clear-sightedness can bring her consolation:

You know, darling, when a person *really* feels lonely? Not when they're alone and no one comes to see them — in such a case you can go out to people, even if they don't ask. No, it's when they don't have in their heart one little bit of a wish themselves to see other people. It's *not* having appetites for contact, that! That, my darling, makes for real loneliness. You, you're lucky, you're *not* lonely — you *want* contact. But who? That's your problem. And where? And when? (*Pause*) And why? I always forget why. Such a memory! My memory is so bad that when I went to the psychiatrist to get it seen to I'd forgot why I came. (*Pause*) No! That's not true. It's funny but it's not true. Who can afford a psychiatrist? Jokes! Even jokes I have to tell myself, and *that's* not funny, darling. My poor darling.
[p. 50]

The energy of her mind, its stringency, is its own reward. Millie lives entirely in the past oblivious of immediate circumstance; she inhabits memory with a clarity that suggests for her it is a present reality. She talks unaware whether she is alone or in company but, far from being an object of pathos in this, she excites a kind of wonder, for Millie is totally free of anxiety, of any sense of the pressure of circumstance; even remembered tragedies are devoid now of pain. Age has brought her release from any sense of self in a total acceptance of all she has experienced without question, grudge or remorse. Each of the soliloquy-scenes invites us to view old age imaginatively from within and find that it is not a state to be pitied — or rather *states*, for what impresses Wesker is the rich diversity of ways that human consciousness faces the challenge of age. There is Manny's ceaseless reading in quest of passages from literature and philosophy that reflect his own belief that life is a matter to rejoice over, balanced by his brother Boomy's equally endless quest for passages that support his creed that all life is vanity. Victims they may be of their quixotic attitudes, but the prodigious range of their reading is astonishing and their thirst for confirmation of their ideas a joy to behold. Both men are indomitable; and so too is their sister Sarah who noticeably and aptly has no soliloquy, for her will to live finds its resource in action, in making, organising, welcoming the need to do things for others.

To isolate the soliloquies is perhaps to put a false emphasis on a play that has a subtly varying technique. That pity however well meant can be an inadequate response is dramatised as an explicit issue in three scenes involving Sarah's daughter Rosa, who is a careers adviser in schools. We see her, in what is staged as a series of monologues, approach three different sets of teenagers; her first two attempts are appalling failures because her anxiety to help is too apparent; she speaks out of her own ideals not out of any engagement with the school-leavers' specific condition:

After all, I think insufficient attention is paid to what is likely to make us feel fulfilled. Society isn't very good at that yet, is it? It's a bit of a monster actually. Eats up everything, indiscriminately. [p. 19]

Not surprisingly the boys' response is a mixture of jeers and slow hand-clapping. In a moving scene where she is at loggerheads with her mother, Sarah, she suddenly realises how like each other they are — "I'm not really criticising you. How could I? Everything *you* are, I am" [p. 56]. Rosa sees that love is essentially a recognition of a common bond between one's self and another. She should speak to the teenagers direct from her feelings — Sarah has no time for tact — and not hide behind soft platitudes that at once intimate that the children are about to encounter hardship (the social process is cruelly indiscriminate) yet try to palliate the blow (it is no more evil than a fairytale monster). When we next see her confront a class, she no longer compromises her honesty:

You won't even find the job you want, most of you. So get that straight, firm in your heads. It's a big world in which control rests with other people, not *you. Not* you. (*Pause*). Good. You're listening. It makes a change. I don't say any of these things happily. I don't approve of this system I speak about and, in my own way, I fight it. I only tell you of it in the hope of stirring you to the challenge. [p. 61]

She recognises the hatred in their eyes that her honesty excites, warns them that hate is a sterile emotion but frankly admits it is "the diet most of you will live with from now on". Rosa has given her social conscience a genuine voice and she can communicate with her audience because it is a voice unsullied by pity. This is a voice that speaks directly out of care, not a voice conscious of its tones as the mark of a caring person; pity can dangerously imply judgement and, by implying it, invite it.

Wesker takes care not to idealise his old people: they can be stubborn and cantankerous. His dramatic technique is flexible enough to yield some choice moments of comedy. When the elderly go visiting each other, private soliloquy does not always give way to dialogue, rather soliloquy interweaves with soliloquy, so utterly absorbing is the dialogue with the self. When Jack calls on Millie and tries to convince himself that she is not mad but that she'll give him tea, company and "homemade bread pudding", Millie gazes out of the window lost to all sense of time and occasion, living through a memory of her daughters. If the moment is comic not pathetic, it is because the rhythm of the scene is utterly relaxed: neither character is aware of intruding on the other or of giving offence. The effect of this scene is in marked contrast with one in which young Rudi visits his aunt Sarah to tell her of the latest in a line of vocations he is pursuing and transforms their conversation into a tirade; he is anxious for her approval but the unrelenting urgency of his speech intimates an inner dread of her criticism; his would-be enthusiasm sits in judgement on itself. It is the resistance of the old ones against the urge to judge that is the key to their inner strength; they are beyond praise or blame.

It might appear from this that Wesker's aged folk are locked in solipsistic worlds, but this is not so: they have a tremendous sense of a family identity. Throughout the play Sarah is preparing to bring the group together to celebrate the festival of Succoth, appropriately in the season of autumn harvests. Not being orthodox Jews, they have to read instructions about conducting the rituals: their efforts are gauche, shy, and they struggle to keep an appropriate dignity; but the spirit of the ritual takes over gradually and they all relax publicly into the selves they have been till now in private. The stage is alive with sound and movement, and Manny suddenly finds the courage in *himself*, not in his reading, to apostrophize joy as the instinct to be unashamedly one's self. This final tirade is an exuberant personal vision, but the artistry of the entire play through its subtle counterpointing of soliloquy and monologue affirms its truth. *The Old Ones* enacts its meaning.

Barry Collins's *Judgement* (Cottesloe, 1974)[7] as its title suggests confronts head-on one issue we have found to be central to the use of the monologue. A full-length play for single performer (at

Bristol, Peter O'Toole; in London, Colin Blakely), it explores an incident in the Second World War recounted briefly by George Steiner in *The Death of Tragedy*. When the Germans in retreat left a number of captured Russian officers locked in the cellar of an abandoned monastery, "two of them managed to stay alive by killing and devouring their companions" [p. 9] before they were released eight weeks later. The play is the story, "my history", of one of the survivors. Clearly such a subject could become an exercise in sensationalism. How to allay an audience's nausea must have been for Collins a major preoccupation. Nausea implies loathing, aversion, a turning away in disgust — judgement. Officer Vukhov realises this from the moment of his wished-for freedom:

In the close confines of our four walls I had begun to consider the freedom of release as absolute, my future vast and uncontained. . . . Now on the faces of my bearers, I recognised my error: I saw repulsion, I saw disgust. . . . Who, or rather, what was I to walk, composed, from such a torment? [pp. 87–88]

In that shift of pronoun, Vukhov recognises the ease with which men resort to judgement rather than seek to imagine and understand. Vukhov can only be accommodated within the scheme of things if he is categorised as other than human. Yet what does it *mean* to label him 'cannibal'? Judgement implies guilt and guilt presupposes responsibility but as Vukho repeatedly asks: of what is he actually guilty? It was an episode of warfare; both sides had committed atrocities; so is he personally guilty in being a victim of circumstance? Throughout the tone is unemotional but deliberately challenging: an assertion of the self as human being not as monster. The very technique of the monologue-form invites judgement yet, in asserting the truth of his identity, Vukhov is not insisting on a unique difference in himself but appealing to a common humanity. Against the urge to judge he mounts a plea based on the idea of necessity. Collins brilliantly exploits the nature of the dramatic form he has chosen to make the dilemma of judgement a direct experience for the audience too: Vukhov's appeal is to our empathy but in a situation that more readily activates our critical detachment.

Collins's one touch of sensationalism happens within seconds of the play's opening, when Vukhov places before him a "silent witness": it is he tells us "the thighbone of Officer Lubianko — to be precise, the left thighbone — sharpened, you will note, to a point — on the stone floor of our cell — for the purpose of killing Officer Rubin — my brother, Rubin — I confess it — for killing comrade Officer Rubin, at one eventual moment of trial — had it come to that — between him and me — Rubin and Vukhov — the two last of our seven. . . ." [pp. 11–12] The fact of the cannibalism is as yet unrevealed and what shock we experience is offset by our growing attention to language and tone: Vukhov's manner is matter-of-fact, indeed his concentration is absolutely on *facts* — the weapon, its source, making, intended purpose; no specious rhetorical flourish appears to link the definition of his objective, a "killing", with the description of his victim as "my brother"; "trial" seems to carry a specific, not emotive or symbolic meaning (the indirect reference to the five lost colleagues suggests a meaning more precisely relating to combat and, by implication, the survival of the fittest than to any concept of justice); and the carefully placed interjection — "had it come to that" — introduces the idea of necessity as the pressure shaping the event. The careful organising of the speech suggests a mind prepared to accept the inevitable.

As Vukhov's history unfolds, these qualities persist and their significance becomes clearer — the attention to detail; the care with language; the scrupulous concern that a listener's response should be a properly reasoned one (repeatedly he forestalls possible emotional reactions); the composure, the unerring rationality of it all. Though his story is about death and dismemberment, it is not about anarchy and violence. Once the men accepted that, for any of them to survive, they must accept submission to necessity, then events — he tells us — followed a pattern that gradually imposed on the group a strange decorum, making the killing and eating of human flesh a kind of ceremony which ensured no loss of respect for the several victims. What might in a different context appear gruesome facts — the preserving of the heads in a special part of the cell, for example, the faces turned to the wall "their eyelids closed . . . as solemn, as private, to us, as undisturbed, as in a tomb" [p. 25] — intimate from Vukhov's perspective a profound reverence. Necessity compels the men to pass beyond the fundamental taboos of Western culture and they find that the savage consciousness creates its own code of values; it is the instinct to create a moral system in the face of even vicious circumstance that emerges as the fundamental trait that defines *human* kind. This is why Vukhov resists all judgements that rob him of human stature. He asks us to share his perception as it became conditioned by circumstance and appreciate that a man can calmly accept the need for his own death, as several of his colleagues did, and submit to it as a willed sacrifice; that, as the numbers dwindled to three by an implacable momentum that exacerbated the tension between them, the murder of one rendered insane by terror became an act of mercy. When the cell was finally broken into, Vukhov was found cradling his 'brother' Rubin in his arms and attempting to feed him, yet beside him — already sharpened — was the "silent witness" prepared lest one final "trial" prove necessary. Vukhov describes how the Russian officer who first saw them there reeled away to retch; yet by degrees he has led us carefully to see that his situation has been brought about by a logic, a human and humane logic, that renders impossible any judgement of the spectacle by us as nauseating or obscene.

As the play unfolds we begin to appreciate why Vukhov is so intent on recording facts, why his account of events is devoid of any emotionally charged epithets, why his intellegence is quick to detect and forestall the possibility of a judgemental response to any of his words. At the moment of his release, his energetic mind could immediately think through the line of attack by which the Russians had recovered the monastery — "You must have struck north through the birch forest" [p. 24], are his first words to his liberator and on the instant of uttering them, as he now admits, he realised they were a mistake. Had he gone mad or feigned madness, he would have excited pity; but what response, he asks, is possible to a man in his circumstances whose intelligence is unimpaired. Blakeley's stage personality, as has been suggested elsewhere,[8] is very much that of a bluff, good-natured, decent but fundamentally *ordinary* man. This was ideal casting, for Vukhov is at pains to stress that he is an ordinary man in the grip of circumstances that were extraordinary by peace-time standards but not by those obtaining in war. Necessity has compelled him to accept that values are relative; if he has preserved his sanity throughout his ordeal, it is by resisting any judgement on himself and he has achieved this state of mind by accepting the conditions imposed on him by his circumstances absolutely. He vaunts no pride in this, nor attempts to wheedle or cajole his listener through self-pity: the tone is direct, because Vukhov is totally without shame. Confronted by chaos, his mind evolved a new kind of order; to sit in judgement on him is to condemn as evil the mind's instinct for survival. Collins set himself a formidable task in terms of stylistic discipline and the finished play makes equally formidable demands on the actor to resist giving the least hint of histrionic self-display. For Collins and for Blakeley *Judgement* proved a *tour de force*.

Given Beckett's preoccupation with the metaphysical loneliness of the individual, it is not surprising that his plays show him exploring the possibilities of monologue and soliloquy. Pozzo and Hamm both have their monologues that are ostentatious assertions of their power and status — stances which Beckett rapidly undermines through the mannerism of their speech to show it all as so much self-delusion. With Winnie in *Happy Days* the technique changes: it is difficult to draw a dividing line between monologue which is a forthright utterance to captivate her audience, Willie; monologue which is a projection of a cheerful persona aimed at entertaining herself and distracting her consciousness from more troubling realities; and soliloquy when, increasingly in Act Two, that anguished consciousness insists on being heard despite Winnie's frantic efforts to keep it suppressed. (Interestingly when Beckett directed Billie Whitelaw in the role at the Royal Court in 1979 he appeared to have encouraged her to find three quite distinct qualities of voice for these three levels of the mind. The effect was of a tawdry, ageing puppet struggling to play yet again a determined role but being possessed by voices insisting on a new routine — an effect both funny and macabre.)

As Beckett has pursued to ever profounder depths the theme that the quality of consciousness, the play of the mind, is the essence of character, so his exploration of the relationship between monologue and soliloquy has grown more subtle and intricate. Krapp musing to himself when preparing to make a recorded monologue about his past year's experience decides to prepare his mind for the event by listening to a taped monologue celebrating an earlier birthday but becomes increasingly angry with its self-conscious manner, its attempts to impose significance on experiences which clearly have not proved of lasting value to him. The one memory that stills his rage is of making love in a boat, where the style does not struggle to define but effortlessly evokes a mood of peaceful release: "We drifted in among the flags and stuck. The way they went down, sighing, before the stem! . . . We lay there without moving. But under us all moved, and moved us, gently, up and down, and from side to side" [p. 61].[9] Monologue gives place to a tone of intimate rapture; the style does not insist how the listener should respond in a fashion that inhibits all but a critical response but allows the experience to *live* in the imagination. Memory recovers the past with a degree of recall so total that it transcends time and recovers a fresh immediacy. When Krapp comes to record this year's "epitaph", he quickly rehearses the significant events, treating them with an amused scorn (a judgemental tone), then passes into reverie: "Lie propped up in the dark — and wander. Be again in the dingle on a Christmas Eve, gathering holly, the red-berried. (*Pause*) Be again on Croghan on a Sunday morning, in the haze, with the bitch, stay and listen to the bells. (*Pause*)" [p. 63]. It is the introspective tones of soliloquy that touch the heart's truth in Krapp not the rhetoric of monologue.

That *Krapp's Last Tape* has affinities with Beckett's plays written since 1970 and anticipates the direction they would follow was made evident when a revival with Albert Finney was chosen to accompany the first English production of *Not I* (Royal Court, 1973). Again the texture of a given consciousness was Beckett's subject and this time, like Collins with Vukhov, he had turned to the mind of an individual who might be deemed a social outcast, one who would most likely be an object of revulsion or fear if encountered in reality. And, like Collins with Vukhov, Beckett chooses to confront that antipathy head on, to shock an audience into paying attention to what it would seek to evade. As we settle chatting into our seats for the performance, our voices are joined by one, a woman's, that is oddly insistent; its rhythms are disjointed, the short broken phrases being like stabs of pain; the breathless speed of the delivery, interrupted only by quick gasps for air suggests mounting hysteria. Within seconds the audience is silent, tense, the easy discourse frozen, the atmosphere hovering between fear and hostility. Before we can relax into the awareness that the voice is just a part of the play, Beckett confronts us with an even more disturbing experience as the curtain rises on a nightmarish vision: through a claustrophobic darkness a dimly-lit figure of vast height, swathed in black, is seen watching with rapt attention an immense mouth, its lips cracked and livid white, as it pours forth a torrent of anguished sound. (In the Royal Court production supervised by Beckett himself the lower portion of Billie Whitelaw's face was visible; cheeks, chin and lips were painted a uniform white and were lit by a controlled, narrow spotlight from below. As she spoke, the play of shadow and light around her face and within the cavity of her actual mouth gave an illusion of immense lips jabbering in a void. This created a gripping visual metaphor for the play that was lacking in the initial American production with Jessica Tandy, where a pencil-thin spotlight played on the actress's own lips. Unfortunately her mouth was invisible for most of the audience and so the play was robbed of its focus.)

The lips are mesmeric: like the silent watcher, we too are caught up in the torment of this soul. As our concentration quickens, we recognise a pattern behind the seeming incoherence of the gabble of words. Again and again the voice describes a particular experience, the onset of senility or perhaps death itself. While walking in the fields one spring, the woman suffered a kind of seizure and was totally paralysed; her body no longer responded to the commands of her brain; she was quite inert, insensible of bodily pain, incapable of screaming for help, and conscious only of a buzzing in the brain, a "dull roar like falls . . . in the skull . . . " [p. 222] and of a faint light coming and going "such as the moon might cast . . . drifting . . . in and out of cloud . . ." [p. 217], which at a later stage she considers may be the last flickerings of her eye-lashes registering in her brain her dwindling sense of sight. Physically she was at peace: "all dead still . . . sweet silent as the grave . . ." [p. 218]. All silent that is but for the inner voices that make up her consciousness; they, alarmingly, have survived her collapse, have gained an energy beyond her control.

Relentlessly the mind garners facts about her present state, tries to compare them with similar experiences in the past, sifts through memories in the hope of finding some explanation of its present state that would bring insight if not release. Listening, we build up a picture of the woman's former life: seventy years of a grey, loveless monotony changed only by the fact of her seizure. Prematurely born, the child of a casual sexual encounter, she was brought up as a waif in an institution. Never encouraged by anyone's care to make any effort for herself, she has spent her adulthood wandering aimlessly around, practically illiterate and mentally sub-normal, the processes of consciousness lying fallow. She has retreated from the callous indifference of the world about her into the stark, self-absorption of the simpleton:

practically speechless . . . all her days . . . how she survived! . . . even shopping . . . out shopping . . . busy shopping centre . . . supermart . . . just hand in the list . . . with the bag . . . old black shopping bag . . . then stand there waiting . . . any length of time . . . middle of the throng . . . motionless . . . staring into space . . . mouth half open as usual . . . till it was back in her hand . . . the bag back in her hand . . . then pay and go . . . not as much as good-bye . . . how she survived! . . . [p. 219]

The response evoked in her by this image of her former self is one of shocked amazement that she could survive in this near-vegetable state, amazement mixed with reproach and disgust. The detail, "mouth half-open as usual" seems particularly caustic but it is characteristic of the blunt, coarse language with which throughout she refers to her past life. She pities herself as a frail, helpless soul in a godforsaken world but despises and repudiates this view of herself even as she creates it. For the first time in her existence the woman's mind has embarked on a voyage of self-awareness but finds increasingly it cannot acknowledge the identity it discovers. The few memories she retrieves bring with them no wish as with Krapp to "be again"; their recall occasions nothing but shame; her helplessness in the supermarket, bewilderment in a law-court, astonishment at finding her hand wet once with involuntary tears. To the mind's frequent troubled question whether this is all that her life amounts to, some impulse from the depths of the psyche offers an absolute denial: "What? . . . Who? . . . No! . . . She! . . ." The explanation for the form of this denial is hinted at by the last of the memories recalled. Significantly the woman has always described herself as *"practically* speechless"; when after her seizure she began to realise that the mechanics of speech were operating involuntarily and that the stream of sound she could hear was issuing from her mouth, it was not simply because she could sense the movement of her facial muscles but because she recognised the distortions of language as unmistakably like her own past efforts to communicate:

. . . then finally had to admit . . . could be none other . . . than her own . . . certain vowel sounds . . . she had never heard . . . elsewhere . . . so that people would stare . . . the rare occasions . . . once or twice a year . . . always winter some strange reason . . . stare at her uncomprehending . . . and now this stream . . . [p. 219]

When first she hinted at this experience, she did not develop it but retreated into the more comforting memory of herself in the supermarket, secure in her dumb silence. Now the memory is confronted and the recall is total. In the long hours of winter darkness, "always winter some strange reason", a sudden, desperate urge would possess her to speak and to speak *to* someone, to "tell":

then rush out stop the first she saw . . . nearest lavatory . . . start pouring it out . . . steady stream . . . mad stuff . . . half the vowels wrong . . . no one could follow . . . till she saw the stare she was getting . . . then die of shame . . . crawl back in . . . [p. 222]

No one understood her plight, or imagined the cause of her anguish; always her need met with a stare of indifference, distaste, fear or hostility; and that repulsion of her clumsy efforts to make some kind of social contact confirms her sense of herself as an outcast. She reads the meaning in the look that these people give her, senses their dread of her 'otherness'. The viciousness of "crawl back in" with its animal connotations expresses all her humiliation and defeat. With every repetition of the experience, her need has become stronger and her reproach of herself for that need more aggressive. The expectation of defeat is indeed inveterate for she is oblivious of the attempts of the silent, watching presence on stage to register compassion at her rage. The self-sufficiency she cultivates gives her a degree of independence of the world that rejects her, but in her new-found awareness she clearly despises herself for making a virtue of necessity.

It is here that Beckett's complex use of dramatic form becomes apparent. The strident tone, the rush of words are characteristic of the tirade and excite initially a detached response in us; yet when we concentrate on the phrases uttered and their syntax, we find that the content, as distinct from the manner of delivery, has the intimate self-probing of the soliloquy. When the woman tries to speak to another, the intention is to arouse empathy but her manner provokes distrust and criticism. Revolving it all in her mind now, she attempts to ease her confusion by pretending it is all a created fantasy, the monologue of an imagined other (". . . Not I! . . . She! . . .") on whom she sits in judgement. The voice of consciousness speaks in all of us for our quintessential selves but the woman has no quintessential self to affirm and her voice speaks only of chaos, incoherence, meaninglessness. The horror is her only self. With the repeated and yet more vehement denials that this is her experience, the mind has less and less to probe and its activity becomes a mechanical routine remorselessly searching through familiar material, fully aware of the futility of what it is doing but desperate to find something *human* to value. The cycles of exploration get briefer as the futility becomes more and more apparent; mind and voice are caught in a vortex and soon the pace will have become so fevered that meaning will be lost and sound reduced to a scream of rage and despair. Consciousness will have become concentred in the image it most feared but which that fear has willed into being for all eternity. By blurring the boundaries between monologue, tirade and soliloquy in *Not I*, Beckett carries us beyond a nervous detachment (would we not back away from such a confrontation in the public street?) to a willingness to respond to the voice's repeated injunctions to "imagine"; but, even as our pity is touched, the perspective changes again to show us that the woman is beyond the reach of anyone's compassion. For character and audience alike, judgement and empathy are found to have terrifying limitations.

To effect these transitions in his audience's sensibility, Beckett needed to preserve a tight control of their attention, despite the necessarily sustained tone of hysteria. This is achieved largely by subtle techniques of repetition and amplification so that, while the audience are assaulted by a ceaseless volley of words by the Mouth in which the individual word or phrase may be lost, they never fail to comprehend the pattern of significance behind the language. The pacing of the play is meticulously conceived. Details which Beckett feels to be crucial are directly repeated and their importance further emphasized either by the horrified injunction, "imagine!" or by a despairing, cynical laugh, "ha!". Passages where the woman's awareness is undergoing a significant transition communicate this change by a device of steady amplification:

. . . no idea what she's saying . . . imagine! . . . no idea what she's saying . . . and can't stop . . . no stopping it . . . she who but a moment before . . . but a moment! . . . could not make a sound . . . no sound of any kind . . . now can't stop . . . imagine! . . . can't stop the stream . . . and the whole brain begging . . . something begging in the brain . . . begging the mouth to stop . . . pause a moment . . . if only for a moment . . . and no response . . . as if it hadn't heard . . . or couldn't . . . couldn't pause a second . . . like maddened . . . [p. 220]

Though the phrases here get briefer than usual and so the speed of delivery increases, the repetitions and rhythmic emphasis in the passage ensure that the audience do not fail to mark the important transition: the woman suddenly comes to realise that the voice is relentless and this in turn makes her long for peace through sheer desperation. The repetitions capture exactly the woman's frantic search for words adequate to convey her misery; and the way that one phrase intimates the next creates a wave of emotion that breaks only with the shock of her realising that the one word truly adequate to describe her state is 'madness'.

Amplification of a different kind is used to allow the audience slightly to relax their concentration between these waves of emotion. This usually occurs in passages of physical description, where the Voice questions itself until the full circumstantial details are enumerated as if anxious to register any change in her condition however slight:

. . . she did not know . . . what position she was in . . . imagine! . . . what position she was in! . . . whether standing . . . or sitting . . . but the brain — . . . what? . . . kneeling? . . . yes . . . whether standing . . . or sitting . . . or kneeling . . . but the brain — . . . what? . . . lying? . . . yes . . . whether standing . . . or sitting . . . or kneeling . . . or lying . . . [p. 217]

The change to a staccato rhythm here and the short pauses which must inevitably follow the questions allow for a lowering of tension without any loss in verisimilitude. A similar effect is achieved by the refrain concerning the buzzing and the play of light of which the woman is constantly aware. The phrases are not repeated exactly each time; variations are played on their arrangement. While we must be reminded of the continuance of these torments, the variations on the familiar do give our attention some respite between the narrative episodes and the emotional climaxes. Beckett takes great care not to overtax an audience's power of receptivity or emotional stamina.

Not I was not written expressly for Billie Whitelaw though she proved an admirable choice of cast for Mouth. Her stage personality has an earthy warmth, her voice a richly ample tone suggestive at once of profound emotional experience and of great reserves of generosity of feeling — indeed some of her finest creations have been in roles where emotional abundance has rendered her cruelly vulnerable such as Franceschina in *The Dutch Courtesan* (Chichester, 1964); the wife, Eleanor, in Peter Nichols's *Passion Play* (Aldwych, 1981). The delicate burr of an accent gives her voice a pleasing matter-of-factness without loss of any of its distinctive music; even in anger and rage Whitelaw's is a melodious voice achieving its effect by stress and deployment of its considerable range rather than by harshness of attack. The rapid delivery and accelerated breathing that Beckett calls for with Mouth, suggestive of one trying to ride out intense pain, inevitably robbed Whitelaw's voice of all but the least hint of its customary amplitude; it was, as it were, the ghost of her voice, thin, etiolated, strained. Yet that barest hint of its full resources made Mouth's dilemma increasingly poignant, intimating the potential in the woman that lay wasted. Mouth's pain is that she has never given love because she has never known love; just as speech and intelligence in her are not void but undeveloped faculties, so too is her capacity for feeling. The restraints the technique of the play imposed on Billie Whitelaw's wealth of vocal tone and all that that tone normally evokes rendered vividly actual the extent of the deprivations Mouth has suffered.

Beckett has been acutely responsive to the tonal possibilities for his art of certain favourite actors' voices — Jack MacGowran, Max Wall, David Warrilow and Patrick Magee. It was for Magee that he composed *That Time* (Royal Court, 1976), another play for consciousness. A strong Irish lilt was rarely absent from Magee's voice and a beautiful sense of the rhythm not only of a speech overall but of individual words that he could make dance in the listener's imagination (his joy in language as Krapp — 'viduity'; 'spool' — readily communicated the older man's respect for the autonomy and mystery of words which his younger self ignores to his cost; and by exaggerating his own technique into mannerism, he made the grandiloquence of Hamm's monologue with its striving for optimum verbal effect a great source of comedy).[10] Where Whitelaw's voice has an earthiness that saves its emotional power from sentimentality, Magee's, when occasion demanded, had a rough edge which could descend to a bass rasp to express cynicism or contempt; but the tonal scale could rise to a high baritone of a haunting intensity, suggestive of a rapt visionary dimension. A further remarkable quality was his projection — ideal for Beckett's work — of a plangent monotone, purged of emotional colouring, that caressed the ear and never palled because it was accompanied by his customary sensitivity to the rhythmic pulse of language; the seemingly austere tone was found, as we engaged with it, to be alive with energy. Magee's portrayal of Marlowe's Mephistopheles (Lyric Studio, Hammersmith, 1980) a short while before his death showed his range to the full: the biting disdain for Faustus's petty imaginings, the perpetual grief of a mind that has known Heaven, has lost it through foolhardiness and has passed beyond bitterness and remorse to embrace desolation as the unchanging condition of being. The sepulchral monotone, frightening in its implications, made Faustus's unthinking zeal for damnation genuinely shocking. *That Time* equally exploited the voice's evocative potency.

High above the stage through the darkness a face is perceived, seemingly illumined from within in Beckett's production at the Royal Court, the features grey, immobile, set as in a death mask; the white hair spread wide catching the light becomes a luminous halo. From left, right and above voices speak to the face which appears to be dreaming their flow of narrative; if they for a moment cease, the eyes immediately open in a haunted stare, till they renew the flow and the face recovers its impassivity. The visual concentration that the stage-picture exacts helps concentrate the mind and the ear intently on the disembodied voices. (Beckett's theatre has a marvellous way of fine-tuning the senses and through them the sensibility.)

Beckett insists in a prefatory note to the play that the recording should be such that, though the voices are projected from three different sources, they should clearly be one and the same voice. The effect is to be rather like that of Shakespeare's Richard II in his prison-cell playing in his person many parts. The voices are to be distinguished more by the content of their respective speeches (here Magee's responsiveness to rhythm was beneficial) than by tone or pitch. The first, 'A', tells of an attempt in his maturity to return to a childhood haunt that was frustrated: "no no trams then all gone long ago that time you went back to look" [p. 228]; the rhythms suggest a practical, energetic individual. 'B' tells of a romantic attachment and its passing and the rhythms are appropriately more langorous suggesting a deep calm. 'C' does not so much tell a tale as criticise various frustrated attempts to find meaning in life, to give significance to experience: "crawling about year after year sunk in your lifelong mess muttering to yourself who else you'll never be the same after this you were never the same after that" [p. 230]. Magee sustained the monotone throughout his rendering of the three voices but allowed a little of his idiosyncratic visionary quality to permeate the voice of 'B' and intimations of his gruff cynicism to give a slight edge to his rendering of 'C'.

The effect of the three voices constantly interweaving is not of three separate streams of consciousness but rather of three different dimensions of consciousness. The subject matter of the three utterances constitutes three of the primary impulses to compose an autobiography — recall of the freedom and simplicities of childhood; emotional experience; the growth of spiritual awareness and the perception of pattern behind the seemingly random flow of a life's incidents. The voices interweave but never integrate; no unity of being is achieved, only a play of diverse selves. Oddly there is no stress involved in this for the figure; the voices preserve an even monotone and only total silence provokes a response from the face. The mood is one of profound reverie, of letting the forces of the mind roam at will unchecked. Yet as we listen one notices that certain features recur with each of the voices. 'A' recalls that a constant pursuit of childhood was finding a place apart, "Foley's Folly bit of a tower still standing all the rest rubble and nettles . . . where you hid as a child slip off when no one was looking and hide there all day long on a stone among the nettles with your picture book" [p. 229]. 'B' evokes an idyllic setting for love's fulfilment: "vowing every now and then you loved each other just a murmur not touching or anything of that nature you one end of the stone she the other long low stone like millstone no looks just there on the stone in the sun with the little wood behind gazing at the wheat or eyes closed all still no sign of life" [p. 228]. 'C' seems to speak for an older self, a vagrant in search of a comfortable sitting place on which to while away the time: "that time in the Portrait Gallery in off the street out of the cold and rain slipped in when no one was looking and through the rooms shivering and dripping till you found a seat marble slab and sat down to rest and dry off and on to hell out of there" [p. 228]. From childhood the mind seems only to have known contentment when it could find the security of a place apart where it could be free to relax into reverie and the prerequisite for this, a kind of necessary talisman, is the stone seat. The recreation of a childhood habit is essential to the free-wheeling of the mind in adulthood, when, given the exact conditions, experience can be transmuted into reverie. Since reverie is without the pressure of anxiety or tension (the voices sustain that steady monotone without sense of pain or effort),[11] the mind can recover the state of innocence he knew as a boy. The stone seat is a necessary part of the mind's strategy enabling it to "be again". Being a man apart is an essential strategy too, as is evident from 'C's' ensuring if he is in a public place that his presence excites loathing so that people keep their distance.

As the play develops we begin to explore the state of reverie and discover that its freedom from the pressures of immediate circumstance means that its content frequently blurs the boundary between reality and fiction. The love-idyll initially convinces as authentic until the setting begins to grow curiously evanescent: "gazing up at the blue or eyes closed blue dark blue dark stock still side by side scene float up and there you were wherever it was" [p. 232]. The mind seems curiously unable to place the idyll in time: "or that time alone on your back in the sand and no vows to break the peace when was that an earlier time a later time before she came after she went or both before she came after she was gone and you back in the old scene wherever it might be might have been the same old scene before as then then as after" [p. 233]. In time the mind admits it was all imaginary, vividly conceived perhaps, but a fiction nonetheless: "every now and then in the great peace like a whisper so faint she loved you hard to believe you even you made up that bit" [p. 234]. As 'A' almost immediately affirms, life has been a long process of "making up" selves, "making yourself all up again for the millionth time" [p. 234]. The mind has found an ingenious way of preserving its innocence; and it all springs from a childhood game to engross his imagination in order to console his loneliness:

. . . or talking to yourself who else out loud imaginary conversations there was childhood for you ten or eleven on a stone among the giant nettles making it up now one voice now another till you were hoarse and they all sounded the same well on into the night some woods in the black night or moonlight and they all out on the roads looking for you [p. 230]

Like Millie in Wesker's *The Old Ones* this consciousness inhabits the past, but it is a past that is both fluid and often uncertain because experience is a product of fancy not of fact:

. . . the old scenes the old names not a thought in your head only get back on board and away to hell out of it and never come back or was that another time all that another time was there ever any other time but that time away to hell out of it all and never come back [p. 235]

What would be a nightmare condition for most minds is a source of utter serenity: there is no urgency here to sort out the temporal confusion. Make-believe is this mind's necessary condition of being. This child is quintessentially the father to the man but the innocence so cherished and safeguarded at the expense of the perplexities of experience is dangerously close to the childish rather than the childlike. The speech is wholly unstructured; thoughts flow inconclusively into thoughts; questions, exclamations are devoid of rhetorical or emotional stress. The fact that there are three selves is an admission that the body waxes old in time but the mind's condition by contrast is constant. 'C' recalls seeing a reflection of himself in the glass shielding a portrait in a gallery and at first did not even recognise the image as his; when eventually he does, the incident affords no real crisis or awakening: it is dismissed with his conventional platitude — "never the same after that never quite the same but that was nothing new" [p. 230]. Why this is the mind's habitual routine only becomes clear at the very end of the play when 'C' again recalls a fleeting experience which this time did partake of an epiphany:

. . . not a sound only the old breath and the leaves turning and then suddenly this dust whole place suddenly full of dust when you opened your eyes from floor to ceiling nothing only dust and not a sound only what was it it said come and gone was that it something like that come and gone come and gone no one come and gone in no time gone in no time [p. 235]

The memory is the only one in the play to provide a response from the face — a smile, "toothless for preference" [p. 235]. Does the moment of vision please because the platitude into which it resolves celebrates the brevity of life — "dust to dust and ashes to ashes"? Or is it perhaps a gesture of triumph because the platitude reveals the truth about his identity: that he has "come and gone" through time a "no one" because he has preserved his consciousness in a state that recognises "no time"? The serenity comes not from a transcendence of life's complexities but from a studied withdrawal from them. Magee's final smile had a roguish cunning.

Like *Not I, That Time* disturbs an audience by the complex relation Beckett works between the forms of monologue and soliloquy. Each of the voice's utterances is within the mode of soliloquy, a private searching of the mind's experience seemingly to find *that time* which best crystallises a sense of identity. Yet the fact that the speech is unpunctuated robs it of that urgency and incisiveness one expects of soliloquy; one does not feel in the presence of a soul laid bare to its own rigorous scrutiny. The very lyricism, especially in Magee's playing, seemed to displace pain, which is the usual spur to self-analysis. Instead a confident ease prevails quite at variance with the *implied* syntax of the speeches. (In performance it is not possible to present the speeches as a totally unstructured flow of language; the actor for one thing must take breath; but the hint of structuring this entails powerfully intimates the extent to which the feeling is being repressed that normally propels speech into syntax.) The voices are not exploring the self but numbing the self's need to care, telling it stories to ease it of the burden of existing. Even as monologues they make no effort to assert an identity but conjure with language to rob it of all specific relation to experience till words evolve only a consoling world of timeless non-being:

. . . you might as well not have been there at all the eyes passing over you and through you like so much thin air was that the time or was that another time another place another time [p. 234]

Here is the recognisable tone of monologue, even and controlled, but it is not directed out to an audience, only inward to the dreaming self, an eerie, private performance. 'C' once quietly admits that there has only ever been one real turning point in this apology for a life:

. . . never but the one the first and last that time curled up worm in slime when they lugged you out and wiped you off and straightened you up never another after that never looked back after that was that the time or was that another time [p. 230]

Since birth and the coming of self-awareness, reverie in repose on a stone has been this life's epitome. Krapp speaks of his tapes as "epitaphs" for his past life. This consciousness perpetually lives its own death; the imagination inhabits its future tomb fearlessly while the body seeks the repose of the funeral monument. The strategies of this mind in its pursuit of non-being are remarkable: continually the phrasing of all three voices verges on the poetic, but the voices flow on as if oblivious of their own creative potential. This wanton denial of richness in perception and the imagination encapsulates the tragedy of *That Time*.

If the male consciousness explored in *That Time* eludes the pressures of care, that of the woman in *Footfalls* seems preoccupied with whether care is in fact the total condition of existence. *Footfalls* (Royal Court, 1976) is a duet for two women, one seen, one merely heard.[12] It has a kind of musical

structure: the theme is established by an initial scene of dialogue
between the two voices; the two scenes which follow are like sets
of variations on that given theme, the first spoken by the unseen
woman who contemplates the silent figure of the other, the second
by that other who contemplates herself now alone; finally comes
a brief coda. The play establishes first a visual image: a woman
pacing with measured step to and fro, the rhythm and distance
controlled as in a ritual; it is night but the light focussed on the path
she treads rather than on her face and tattered clothing gives a
ghostly luminosity to her presence; the faint shuffle we hear
focusses our attention further on her movement which seems
habitual, compulsive yet more than merely routine. The dialogue
establishes the relationship of the two women as mother and
daughter, the one sick, the other in caring attendance; each is
anxious not to be a burden to the other:

V(oice):   Will you not try to snatch a little sleep?
[*M halts facing front at R*(ight). *Pause.*]
M(ay):   Would you like me to inject you again?
V: Yes, but it is too soon.
[*Pause*]
M: Would you like me to change your position again?
V: Yes, but it is too soon. [pp. 239–240]

The mood is one of tender solicitude, where care signifies total and
selfless devotion. May was born late in her mother's life and her
mother's plea, "Forgive me again. [*Pause. No louder.*] Forgive me
again" [p. 240], suggests that May had hardly grown out of being
the object of her mother's care before her mother had grown in
need of her attention. Now the daughter watches over the mother
as over a child. In answer to her mother's plea, May begins to pace
again; speech is unnecessary, the sound of her movement is
sufficient reassurance of her concern and the rhythm is curiously
consoling like the regular pulse of cradle or lullaby that instils
sleep. The mention of age causes May to interrupt her movement
and ask how old she is. Her mother's reply "In your forties" evinces
the surprising response "So little?" [p. 240], as if the burden of
responsibility had weighed far longer on her shoulders. The mother
is instantly sensitive to the drift of May's unspoken thought and
offers deep-felt compassion — "I'm afraid so" — as her daughter
again begins to pace to and fro. Far from being lulled, the mother
is anxious now whether the pacing intimates some darker
significance, some private anguish or remorse. But she is unwilling
to intrude and compel May's confidence. Respecting her daughter's
integrity, she frames her concern again as compassion: "Will you

never have done?" But, lest that seem like a sharp rebuke, she amplifies after a pause: "Will you never have done . . . revolving it all?" [p. 240]. The slight hesitation before 'revolving' indicates the scruple to find a word that expresses empathy not judgement. The question however halts May who tries to clarify her mother's intended meaning: "It?". Her mother suspects the physical movement is occasioned by some impulse deep in the psyche — "In your poor mind" — but she withholds a precise question, fearing perhaps that she is wrong and that to intrude would be to instil a vein of painful introspection in a mind that may be free of such a tendency. It is a delicate passage of dialogue intimating how love must often face uncertainty out of respect for the mystery of another's being and how the motives for a selfless devotion must not be questioned. The scene is a deeply moving exploration of the boundaries that must not be traversed between people, however close their emotional ties.

The first scene for solo voice carries further these intimations that love involves acknowledging there are necessary limits to one's knowledge of another's consciousness. The mother watches the daughter apart now; the suggestion is that she is dead and a ghostly presence studying May's behaviour, remembering the onset of the pacing in childhood when other girls of her age would be out playing lacrosse. Patiently she records May's movements, knowing every one; she previously intimated that they were so much a part of her consciousness that she could sense the slightest disturbance of the pattern even in her deepest sleep. May's movements in the darkness of the stage before us confirm her expectations. The mood is solicitous, brooding, but broken suddenly (after she has watched the pacing for some time with us in silence) by a tone of joy and wonder at the grace of the movement: "watch how feat she wheels". For all her anxiety she can yet find grounds for a hint of motherly pride. She then recalls how the child carefully established the whole ritual, how the movement alone was not enough but the carpet must be removed: "I must hear the feet, however faint they fall" [p. 241]. Strangely this episode is told as a narrative, the voice carefully assigning snatches of dialogue to two speakers — "the mother" and "May — the child's given name — May". The effect is of a memory recalled which is felt to be significant but whose relevance eludes precise definition, as if the woman were asking how indulging a child's caprice could ever have led to this lifelong habit. Is the mother in any way personally to blame, given the child's unshakeable certainty of purpose? And so she goes on recording May's movements, as doubtless she did consciously and unconsciously throughout life, sure that she is right to apprehend some deep-rooted anguish in her daughter but reluctant to act on the intuition lest it break in some way the bond between them. The hushed, ruminative tone is the voice of soliloquy yet the object of that private enquiry here is less the self than another being; moreover the material is presented objectively as in a narrative monologue, though this is not for the benefit of an external audience but for the woman's own enquiring mind. What Beckett seems to have rendered here is the detachment necessary in love, the ability to hold the mind suspended between possibilities. To a remarkable degree by confusing the boundaries between soliloquy and monologue he has found a voice that characterises empathy: knowing, respectful, unjudging.

With the beginning of the third sequence we appreciate that the light has with each scene grown fainter on the pacing feet and the movement slower. The woman observed in the previous scene now speaks, what she calls a "sequel". The scene seems to be the consequence in time of the mother's dying: deprived of an object for her care, the daughter feels as if her own being has been called into question, her motive in living having gone. Noticeably she revises her initial remark: "A little later when she was quite forgotten, she began to — [*Pause.*] A little later, when as though she had never been, it never been . . ." [p. 242]. The change beautifully defines the scruple we have sensed earlier: 'she' with its possible reference to mother or daughter intimates the degree to which the relationship was a bond of union, the loss of one profoundly disturbing the other; and the change from "quite forgotten" to "as though she had never been" subtly evokes the sense of loss in bereavement as a loss of personal identity in the one left mourning but also carefully removes the querulous tone, the note of self-pity and of blame implicit in the first statement. The extent of the personal anguish suffered is revealed but the selfless devotion of the daughter surfaces to suppress any hint of condemnation of her mother for leaving her thus alone and benighted, the "semblance", as she later calls it, of a living woman. The piety of the relationship is always honoured.

Piety becomes increasingly the subject of the woman's words. She has turned now to the church, pacing not within her mother's room but along a transept "up and down, up and down, his poor arm" [p. 242]. It is as if she has been drawn in sympathy to One who also suffered for the sins of the world and whose life's meaning was defined by that, His emblem through time being the cross He bore. Out of simple beginnings a deeply metaphysical experience begins to be rendered on stage before us. In the previous sequence the daughter had stood for a brief period silent but with her body and senses strained to attention while the mother watched and commented on her, remembering her behaviour as a child. Now the daughter observes that the pacing can be suddenly halted and she be "as one frozen by some shudder of the mind". In the scene that ensues she halts first to envisage the pacing self as a "semblance", a ghostly presence, "a tangle of tatters" through which the church candelabrum shines "like moon through passing rack" [p. 242]. Then she tells a story about an elderly woman, Mrs. Winter, who attempts to share and so affirm with her daughter a moment of strange awareness, an apprehension she experienced at Evensong. In this May announces each speaker's name ("Mrs. Winter" and " 'Amy' — the daughter's given name, as the reader will remember") exactly as did the mother recalling the converstaion with May as a child in the previous scene. Finally May recalls the exchange with her mother with which *Footfalls* began but no longer assigns the words to their respective speakers as for a created fiction; she plays in herself both parts now, while noticeably calling the daughter "Amy" and assuming ever more confidently the mother's role: "Amy [*Pause. No louder.*] Amy. [*Pause.*] Yes, Mother. [*Pause.*] Will you never have done? [*Pause*] Will you never have done . . . revolving it all? [*Pause*] It? [*Pause*] It all. [*Pause*] In your poor mind. [*Pause*] It all. [*Pause*] It all." [p. 243]. The mother in the earlier scene informed us that May still speaks "when she fancies none can hear"; she "tells how it was", the mother confides, but then again revises her remark to "tries to tell how it was" [p. 241]. Clearly the daughter is trying to find words to express some dark metaphysical apprehension that hovers on the boundary of awareness, some ghostly intuition: she talks of herself or another as a phantom-like being; imagines through a narrative how such a being might disturb a sensibility suitably attuned; then lives again in memory her care for her mother, yet as she does so this time enters imaginatively into her mother's mind and, through empathy, realises all the older woman's solicitous concern for her daughter and the extent to which each met and so comforted the other's need. Within memory that cherished past lives on. In the second scene we experienced the dead woman's watch over the living; now the daughter's mind has reached out and embraced the fact of that ghostly presence; the emotional bond between them is not dissolved by death. Again as in the second episode the mode of speech is depersonalised either as at first by a syntactical blurring of the identity of "she" or as later by an objectifying of experience into narrative and dialogue; and yet the voice is seeking to express some of the deepest movements of the psyche, an apprehension of identity in union with another which is quite purged of self-regard. That is the meaning of piety and devotion; and Beckett has exercised a remarkable decorum in creating for such an impulse of the mind an apt style of expression.

But the play does not end there. The faint chimes that herald the start of each scene recur and the light, fainter still, illuminates the path where the figure has walked. The stage direction in the text here reads *"No trace of* MAY"; the implication being that she too is now dead, her relentless pacing stilled at last. And yet in performance this final sequence was not so categorical and finite in its effect. *Footfalls* was staged as the third play in a programme that also comprised *That Time* and *Play*; for an evening we had peered through a near-impenetrable darkness throughout the Royal Court at a series of dimly lit faces whose luminosity seemed eerily to come from within not from any obvious external source. Such rapt concentration, aural and visual, on a darkness that grew strangely visible began to affect the retina and the ear-drum. As the ethereal radiance spread across the stage where May had walked, one could no longer be absolutely sure whether there was a figure moving there or not — "up and down, up and down, before vanishing the way she came" — even as she had previously described herself [p. 242]. She had lived so graphically in our imaginations that the "eye of the mind"[13] reached after assurance of her presence still. The metaphysical apprehension she experienced in the third scene of her mother's "presence" was now felt by us: empathy rather than pity had sustained for her a continuing life in our consciousness. Beckett encourages us to cease to judge May's pacing as obsessional, neurotic, and to honour it as emblematic of a mind whose total absorption in the impulse to *care* is its saving grace. Her life's experience is concentred in her pacing to and fro but that ceaseless movement is seen with time to be an act of love, a giving of the self that "costs not less than everything".[14] The stage image is austere and disciplined[15] but our growing experience of that image is complex and enriching: as through watching May's pacing form we concentrate on darkness, so darkness becomes charged with a rare luminous vitality and we share a moment of vision.

Footfalls, written for Billie Whitelaw, seemed designed to explore the warmth and purity of tone her voice can command; *Rockaby* (Cottesloe, 1982, though written for her in 1981) explores rather its exceptional lyricism and delicacy of touch. A prematurely aged woman with tousled hair, cadaverous face, huge "famished eyes" [p. 279], rocks herself gently to and fro while her voice in rhythm

with her rocking-chair tells the story of her days as the light about
her dwindles. Incongruously she is dressed in black evening wear
and hat of a fashion long dated. As we contemplate the stage image
we detect a more subtle incongruity: the general appearance is
decidedly dowdy and yet, because dress and hat are covered with
jet sequins and the rocking-chair is highly polished, the figure
seems to shimmer; the darkness radiates its own peculiar shine.
The narrating voice is a recorded one that is detached from the
brooding figure, though the latter is roused to echo the voice
whenever it pauses over one particular phrase: "time she stopped".
The story the voice tells is of loneliness and desperation, a
searching for companionship, for a kindred sensibility in "another
creature like herself" but for all its urgency the quest never finds its
goal. The scope of the woman's ambition diminishes as she ages,
but she never relinquishes her basic hope even though in time she
ceases to comb the streets on foot and contents herself with gazing
from her window:

> quiet at her window
> all eyes
> all sides
> high and low
> for a blind up
> one blind up
> no more
> never mind a face
> behind the pane
> famished eyes
> like hers
> to see
> be seen   [pp. 278–279]

But that world without is blank, indifferent, perhaps self-sufficient
and uncaring. A further incongruity manifests itself here. The
words define a restless anxiety; the repetitions and the cyclic
patterning of phrases suggest a relentlessly obsessional mind; and
yet the tone, far from being the breathless hysteria of the Mouth
in *Not I*, is increasingly bemused even serene; the words keep time
with the rhythm of the rocking and the Voice caresses them like a
lullaby. Whatever motivated the sense of crisis is now stilled.

Voice's narrative begins to approach the woman's present
circumstances, telling how she left the window, went "down the
steep stair" and found the rocker where years back her mother in
old age had sat rocking herself to sleep, "all in black/best black",
till eventually she died there:

                    dead one night
                    in the rocker
                    in her best black
                    head fallen
                    and the rocker rocking
                    rocking away   [p. 280]

The image is of blissful composure utterly disarming any fear we
might have of death and yet the chance discovery of the dead
mother could have been profoundly disturbing. The woman's
condition now exactly mirrors her mother's at her death and
presumably her state of mind is identical with her mother's too.
What Beckett has subtly rendered here is the irrationality of our
horror of death, imagined as it so often is from our subjective
experience of the loss of a loved one. The death this woman dreads
motivates her search for a consoling presence to fill her mother's
place and yet a deeper impulse of the psyche knows that that death
is inevitable, that it is "time she stopped" procrastinating, living in
blind fear, and accept the common pattern of existence. In going
deep into the house to don her mother's clothes and take her
mother's place in the chair, she finds her "own other/own other
living soul" [p. 281]; it is a keeping faith with her mother, a re-
union through which the will relaxes and she can accept her coming
death. The grey, harassed existence finds peace and with that a new
sensual delight in the rocking motion of the chair and the embrace
of its arms about her withered form. *Rockaby* marvellously renders
what it means to be absolute for death: the processes the mind goes
through that ease away the pressures that formerly shaped
consciousness and defined character. The woman has "done with
that"; indeed she can talk of "that" as of another life, as her mind
finds itself in the reality of death. From her new perspective, the
horror of the past is transmuted into a haunting poetry. The light
fades as her life ebbs away but a faint shimmer continues to reside
in the darkness. Once again the narrative mode of monologue and
the ruminative mode of soliloquy have been subtly fused by
Beckett to give a dramatic form to a process of the mind so private
that it would normally be deemed one to defy theatrical expression:
the willing depersonalisation of consciousness, the giving up of all
the tensions that define self-hood, in the moment of dying. As a
consequence, during a performance of *Rockaby*, serenity is a state
we do not observe but wholly inhabit in our imaginations.

     The depersonalising of the self that is necessary in experiencing
true empathy seems to be the subject of Beckett's most recent
monologue, *Ohio Impromptu* (1981, performed in London at the

Donmar in 1984). Two figures with flowing white hair, swathed in black, their postures identical, sit at right angles to each other: they are like mirror images. The only distinction is that one reads from a book; the other avidly listens, from time to time signifying his need to have a portion of the tale repeated by rapping on the table-top. His rapt intentness and the evident care with which the reader tells the tale focus our attention as we begin to perceive how closely the tale resembles and explains the situation that we contemplate. The story is of a man suffering an experience of loss, most likely a bereavement, of his refusal to remain in the "shared" place where the "shade"of the departed might comfort him; instead he seeks relief in unfamiliar surroundings, spending his days pacing the banks of an island or watching the point where the two arms of a river "in joyous eddies . . . conflowed and flowed united on" [p. 286]. His nights were a torment of fears and despair till one evening he was visited by a stranger who came at the behest of the "dear" one to comfort him by reading a story "the long night through" [p. 287]. Repeatedly and "unheralded" the stranger appeared, read and departed till one night he announced that the "dear"one had requested him not to return again and, so the story concludes, having told his sad tale this last time the stranger sat on, silently perusing the face of his listener, "buried in who knows what profounds of mind" [p. 288]. Just as in the story, the reader before us now closes his book since "nothing is left to tell" and he and his listener "raise their heads and look at each other. Unblinking. Expressionless" [p. 288]. The stage picture and the image evoked by the story to the eye of the mind are again mirror images of each other.

The narrative tells of a mind fraught with loneliness that was brought comfort by the recounting of a story through which teller and listener "grew to be as one" [p. 287]. And that same process is played out before us: the reader engages imaginatively with his text so that he makes the story live just as vividly in the imagination of his own listener; both men lose themselves to contingent reality in order to inhabit the world of the story. The style of the narrative is measured, devoid of emotional emphasis or rhetoric; the syntax is pared to a minimum — "After so long a lapse that as if never been" [p. 286]; the focus is entirely on the *situation* once the loneliness of the central character is established: no attempt is made to reach after explanations, which is why the tale can engross the imagination in the telling. Perhaps *possess* the imagination would be a more accurate description of the experience. The passages that the on-stage listener most frequently wishes to hear repeated refer to the "dear name" who was the occasion of the tragic sense of loss and whose communications, her "unspoken words", are sensed in the form of intuitions. The central character of the tale rebels against the intuition that he should remain where he and the dear one were "Alone together so much shared" [p. 286], as if his mind recognises that to stay in familiar, shared surroundings would be to risk becoming a prey to sentimentality and self-pity. He chooses the more rigorous path of loneliness in an unknown place that holds no significant memories of a shared past, but his steps take him unconsciously to a spot where his mind can contemplate in the river's progress an image of union and felicity. When the stranger appears with his book he announces "I have been sent by — and here he named the dear name" [p. 287]. The narrative tells essentially how a mind slowly accommodates itself to grief by objectifying the experience till it is free of self-regarding impulses. The strategy of the mind by which consciousness finds an apt decorum to define its sense of pain and loss is, Beckett implies, like the play of the critical faculties and the imagination that accompany artistic creativity, where ideally the artist seeks to depersonalise himself so that the experience which his art seeks to define may be left free to speak for itself. That too necessitates finding an apt decorum, for which a total empathy with one's subject is essential. Be it the writer with the experience that inspires him, the actor/narrator with the text he is to interpret and communicate, or the reader/audience responding to the work of art, the mind must be free of the demands of the contingent self if the imagination is to be *possessed*. Only then will one enter the state of empathy, which is to grow "to be as one" with the subject of a work of art. Memory is a state in which the mind tells the story of one's past over again. Escape from the pain of recollection is possible only when the reminiscing self can rise free of the urge to shape and so distort the remembered past out of self-pity or a wish for consolation; only then can the mind lose its present identity and find empathy with the past self. The play is a brilliant conceit, drawing analogies between two seemingly disparate activities of the imagination to show how every consciousness demonstrates a creative potential which for the health of that mind must be handled with a rigour as consummate as the artist's. When the reader on-stage closes his book and he and the listener sit together, gazing into each other's eyes and "buried in who knows what profounds of mind", we too share the rapt, *informed* silence.

Ohio Impromptu seems at first a monologue, a tale narrated to an objective listener, and yet, the more deeply we enter the experience of the story and appreciate its uncanny relationship with the stage picture we are contemplating, so we perceive it as more akin to the soliloquy, the communion of a mind with itself but one from which all egocentric reference has been scrupulously pared away. The voice that speaks is that of the depersonalised self. David Warrilow, for whom Beckett wrote the play, sustained throughout a full and musical bass, the voice of a sophisticated but dispassionate *reader* not actor; it was a delivery that did not seek to control his listeners' responses but left each of us free to relate to Beckett's precise but evocative style as we would, which was for him and us to engage with that style on a level beyond the merely emotional. Listening became a creative and a cathartic act of the imagination. Repeatedly in his most recent work Beckett has pushed the devices of monologue and soliloquy to their limits in his endeavour to give dramatic expression to the subtlest strategies in which the human mind engages. However deeply internalised his subject matter becomes, it remains crucially dramatic, for Beckett shows how at the heart of the self everyone is of necessity both actor and audience. The apter image to define Beckett's perception of the fundamental nature of the psyche as it is shaped by memory and by imagination would seem to be not the 'stream' but the 'theatre of consciousness'.

CHAPTER FOUR

POETIC NATURALISM: DAVID STOREY

David Storey is uncannily one of his own best critics. In interview with Peter Ansorge for *Plays and Players* (1973) he was particularly dismissive of a "conceptualising streak" in his personality and sought to draw a distinction between himself and younger Royal Court dramatists with a more strongly defined political commitment such as Hare and Brenton by arguing that "plays which are mere illustrations of an idea never become real".[1] *Life Class* (Royal Court, 1974)[2] produced a few months later seemed designed to explore this proposition and almost inevitably fell victim to this very criticism: in comparison with plays like *Home* and *The Changing Room* it seemed contrived, effort-ful. In part the action of the play could be seen as an allegory of the dilemma of an artist like Storey himself seeking to shape life-experience into art without destroying its essential randomness and autonomy by moulding it to fit some imposed personal theory or interpretation. As Allott the art teacher remarks: "The essence of any event . . . is that it should be . . . indefinable. Such is the nature . . . the ambivalence . . . of all human responses . . . love, hate . . . anguish . . . hope" [p. 227]. Storey's best plays — and the finest moments in his less successful ones — have just this quality of the indefinable. It is not a sloppy imprecision; rather the presentation of experience allows several possible interpretations to come into play in his audiences' minds (as likely as not of a conflicting nature), yet each is true to the event and each is felt to be right. The ambivalences, the tensions cannot be resolved; and the vitality of the play, its *naturalism*, lies in that sustained note of irresolution which admits to the richness of human motive. As has been implied, Storey's vigorous output is uneven in quality; what makes a play like *The Contractor* superior to *Life Class* is Storey's ability to capture moments when all the tensions relax and the characters briefly, hesitantly reach for shared moments of *pure* feeling when the tone becomes one of complete harmony.

It is just such a significant moment that Allott contrives to effect in his classroom. Using the raw materials at his disposal — the students whom he holds in extreme contempt as but "pubescent excrescences on the cheeks of time" [p. 162] — he tries to create a "happening" that might teach the class some truths about themselves. Their lewd chatter while drawing from the nude prompts Allott to stimulate the cocky exhibitionist tendencies of one of the young men — Mathews — till in the mood of relaxed licence he attempts to rape the model. The attention of the class and of the audience is certainly captured but the mood is hardly one of concord: shock, disbelief, embarrassment, pruriency animate the spectators on and off stage, while Allott stands bemused, superior, apart. The outcome is destructive because Allott's artistic intention was negative and demeaning to the students — a patronising gesture revealing not an artist's concern but total disdain; not surprisingly the event recoils on him and he is dismissed; the students have learned nothing. The problem with the play is that too much stage-time is devoted to Allott's personal theorising about the state of contemporary art to explain for the audience why he is stage-managing the central event. Most of his words are lost on the students; this is indeed a symptom of his withdrawal from genuine involvement with his teaching. As the audience do understand him, that is to make them enter uneasily into complicity with his schemes to use people. In Storey's terms, Allott is a failed artist and dangerous at that, but the dramatic structure presents him with no viable opponent to challenge or contest his views in a way that would define how sympathetic or critical a stance the audience should take to him. The result is an external, over-explicit play that asks for a limited creative response from its audience. There was however one moment of rapt communication between stage and audience and significantly it involved no talk and did not involve Allott: it was a period of intensifying silence as the students began their day's class, contemplated the model, set to work and, as their drawings took shape, watched her with ever more intent gaze. No two students worked by the same technique; each established his own particular rhythm defining his particular personality and style; but they shared one focus of attention [pp. 166-7]. Here was both diversity and yet union, broken only by Allott's moving amongst the easels subjecting the students' private visions to his critical scrutiny and making them one by one suddenly self-aware. Till his intrusion, this was a spontaneous "happening", quiet, profound, of which the participants, even Allott, were not conscious. The play never achieved such intensity again.

Life Class contains Storey's strengths and his limitations. Unconsciously perhaps, but with some accuracy Storey pinpointed one possible explanation for the dramatic weakness of some of his work when, in the interview with Peter Ansorge, he argued that his plays fall into "three broad categories":

One is what you might call poetic naturalism along the lines of *The Contractor* and *The Changing Room*. Then there's a kind of very traditional literary play like *In Celebration* and *The Farm*. Thirdly, there's the more overtly stylistic play like *Home* and *Cromwell*.[3]

It has been with the first and last categories that Storey has been most innovative and has reached his largest audiences. "Very traditional" and "literary" suggest writing to a proven formula and that in its particular way is also to risk writing a play that illustrates an idea. Storey's two earliest plays for the Royal Court, *The Restoration of Arnold Middleton* (1967) and *In Celebration* (1969) show him caught in the trap of the 'literary' play but also momentarily making a bid for creative freedom by breaking away from its accepted conventions.

There is an eerie sense of *déjà vu* about *The Restoration of Arnold Middleton*.[4] Wrestling with the boredom of marriage and rebelling against his wife's passion for tidiness by installing more and more bizarre historical curiosities in their home, Arnold seems a rather milk-and-water version of Jimmy Porter. A whimsical jokiness has replaced Jimmy's corrosive wit, while the urge to seek a mode for self-expression finds an outlet merely in childish pranks for much of the play. Storey's dialogue has little of the dynamism and the dangerous edge to it that Osborne's has, intimating a pent-up fury in the protagonist — dangerous in the sense that Jimmy's anger spills out of the play-world of *Look Back in Anger* to confront the audience's apathy too. Storey achieves only one episode as psychologically disturbing as Osborne's play and that is when he abandons Osborne's method completely and aims not for realism but a grotesque style of farce. At the close of the first act Arnold returns home from a spree at the cinema and the local pub with his wife, Joan, and her mother, Edie Ellis. Tipsy and gigglesome, the three begin dancing together till Edie breaks away holding her skirt high to waltz alone "with a slow nostalgia" to Arnold's admiration. His response provokes in Joan a malicious, competitive urge. Within seconds she has her mother and herself parading before Arnold, skirts raised, and insisting that he choose: "Who's got the best legs!" [p. 19]. Arnold is detached, apathetic, lost in stupor. What seems an uproarious drunken parody of the Judgement of Paris turns ominous as Joan, verging on hysteria now, becomes increasingly sadistic. She tears at her husband's hair like some frenzied Bacchante and goads her mother into joining her in cutting it off by the fist-full. With splendid theatrical invention and considerable economy, Storey has illuminated for the audience the psychological tensions which underlie the nervy jokiness that Arnold adopts as a characteristic pose and define further the obsessional quality of Joan's fastidiousness about her home. This bizarre yet nightmarish episode exposes the sexual drives and antagonisms, of which that daytime pettiness is the token. The mythical and biblical parallels that are called to mind provoke laughter initially for being such travesties of their prototypes, but they skilfully prepare the way for the primitive ferocity the women have released in themselves by the time the scene ends.

Nothing in the rest of the play can dispel one's memory of that drunken rout because of the creative energy the writing and conception of that episode generate; indeed the restoration of sanity to the Middleton household and the sense of affirmation that Storey works for at the close seem too neat and cosy by comparison. It is difficult to see how the play could have continued that darkly farcical mode (indeed one admires Storey's dexterity in exploiting the idea of drunkenness to allow him to introduce a mode and tone at variance with the rest of the play while retaining a vestige of a hold on realism) but once he sounds that complex note it shows up the rest of his invention as thin and derivative.

In Celebration[5] is set in the same territory — social, geographical and psychological — as Lawrence's *Sons and Lovers.* A bogusly genteel woman is purging her self-disgust at having *had* to marry a man who is her social inferior by compelling him to a life of drudgery at the coal face so their sons can have all the opportunities she feels deprived of: "hygiene — never forgiven him she hasn't. . . . Dig coal he will till kingdom come. Never dig enough. . . . Retribution" [p. 49]. The play's structure — the gathering of the family for the parents' ruby wedding anniversary where, as the effects of the celebration wear off, the sentimental gestures cease and the truths about the past emerge, the easy domesticity being set at hazard by the return to the fold of a hardened, cynical prodigal — was instantly recognisable in a theatre that a decade earlier had launched Wesker's career. The roots of course go back further still past Priestley to the North Country realist tradition of the 20s and 30s, which is a peculiarly English development of a technique evolved essentially by Ibsen.

This is not to say that the play lacks originality. There is a fine vitality to the dialogue especially in the earlier act where the family relax back into the old teasing comic routines they evolved over years of living together to ease away in jokes the tensions generated by inhabiting the confined space of a two-bedroomed house. And old father Shaw (no down-trodden Walter Morel this) offered Bill Owen some rich material out of which to build a study in a particular kind of innocence. Shaw's salvation has been his pride in his work: he rejoices in the peril, the hardship, the challenge of it; work so engrosses his imagination that the spare, factual accounts he gives of digging a seam touch the poetic. Stubborn he may be in wishing to see out fifty years underground (he refuses his sons' offer to help him out financially so that he can retire early), but that sense of work as a continuous test of self frees him from knowledge of his wife's objectives and of her attitude to him and frees him too from any envy of his sons' social advancement. It is a telling irony that the sons to a man believe, given Shaw's self-sufficiency, that he despises the lives he has raised them to; but that is rather a projection of their envy than a true insight into him. When Shaw weeps silently as Andrew, the returned prodigal, denounces his mother asleep upstairs as the destructive fate in all their lives, it marks not the disintegration of the old man's illusions so much as painful astonishment that his son could be capable of such rancour. He sees only the fact of Andrew's vindictiveness, not its possible cause; it is his view of Andrew's existence that is shaken, not his view of himself and his marriage. As Bill Owen played the scene, his tears seemed more a compound of pity and dismay than of self-pity and humiliation: his dignity remained unimpaired.

An equally arresting stage-image occurs in the closing moments of the play when Colin and Steven, who were incapable of countering Andrew's indictment of their mother with any force the previous evening, nonetheless move instinctively with their father to protect her when it appears Andrew intends to accuse her openly at breakfast and stage a show-down. Silently the three men will him to lie about the cause of their row together in the night and he backs down, muttering "Politics" as his excuse. The moment is exciting because so enigmatic. Shaw's motivation is the most clear-cut: a wish not to dispel his wife's contentment over the celebration and to save her from the pain he has recently experienced in being disillusioned about Andrew's 'success'. The brothers' action, though it immediately rings true, is less easily defined: do they believe her to be unconscious of the motives Andrew ascribes to her and so are protecting her innocence? Or, if they consider her more self-aware, are they shielding her from knowledge that her best of motives has had the worst of effects? Or do they perhaps need to defend her illusion that her sons are successful to salvage some hope for themselves in the future, her belief in them being their last possible source of confidence in themselves?

The richness in conception of incidents like these highlights the fundamental weakness of the play: Storey's over-reliance on Andrew, as on Allott in *Life Class*, to articulate and explain the theme.[6] In the early scenes his sharp-eyed watchfulness over the family circle offset by bursts of strident joviality generates both character-interest and tension; we soon see that his concern for others masks a predatory interest in their shortcomings. A solicitor by training, he is deviously gleaning evidence that will substantiate his thesis about the family's and his own emotional impotence. Where the play starts to go thin is in offering no real challenge to that thesis once he begins to expand it (even the dramatic climaxes just described confirm rather than deny its validity). The problem is that Mrs. Shaw herself is so sketchily characterised. Constance Chapman's plump, comfortable personality was a nicely calculated ironic contrast with Andrew's talk of a lethal goddess, but it was not a strong enough dramatic contrast to give the play a structural balance. Mrs. Shaw's carefully delayed entrance in her new celebration outfit and hat to catch the men's attention and approval conveys no insidious implications, nor does her quiet singing of a hymn to express her satisfaction after the family outing in which one by one the men join her; and those are really the only 'big' stage moments the play affords her. Hers is largely an impassive role given no sustained dialogue with any other character. In a play written to a different convention that could in itself be a revealing detail, but in a play where Storey elects to make his points chiefly by statement it creates an emotional vacuum where an emotional vortex is required. If Andrew is right about the household and not just goaded on by petty malice then we need some demonstration of Mrs. Shaw's power to control these men through guilt. *In Celebration* is damagingly 'literary' in that we are required to bring a host of associations from novels and plays about working-class matriarchs to piece out the imperfections of Storey's characterisation of Mrs. Shaw: as presented, she is not a dominant enough stage-presence to carry the weight of significance that is expected of her. While Andrew's characterisation is too much on the surface, Mrs. Shaw is hardly characterised at all.

Henry James once observed that a prime hazard facing the novelist was to crate a structure where "the psychological explanation of things . . . too visibly contracts the problem in order to meet it".[7] It is a hazard with the well-made play in the realist mould and one that Storey falls prey to here. Andrew's lengthy theorising about the ramifications of guilt in his and his brothers' minds carries far less resonance than one of Colin's memories:

> Do you remember when old Snuffler came to see my Dad about my going to university? . . . After he came here Snuffler never spoke to us again. Whenever we met in the school corridor he used to gaze at some point exactly six inches above your head. Talk about the pain of poverty. I still dream about that look. I do. . . . I often wake up trying to convince him that we're not as poor as that any longer. [pp. 42-43]

That encapsulates the play's themes in a way that is both succinct and allusive. The shifting, unspecific pronouns "us" and "your" ring true to Colin's accommodating nature: he lapses rapidly back to working class colloquialisms as he settles in at home; and with his command of two "languages" we see precisely why he is a successful works manager sent out to bargain with the men over labour troubles. But Storey does not sustain the dialogue on that level of imaginative engagement for long, writing from *inside* experience.

It was with *The Contractor* (Royal Court, 1969)[8] that Storey found his idiosyncratic style of 'poetic naturalism', working entirely through inferences and nuances of meaning rather than with articulate statement — a technique that requires the audience to respond creatively to ambiguity and allusion. *The Contractor* has no plot in the traditional sense, more a situation: five workmen erect a large tent which is to be the setting for the reception at the wedding of their boss's daughter. Three generations of Ewbanks are gathering together for what is a momentous occasion in the family's history. In Act One the canvas outer tent is erected; in Act Two it is lined with coloured silk, floored, laid out with tables and chairs and decorated with flowers; in Act Three the tent is struck and taken away. Throughout the workmen's routines are interrupted by visits of inspection from various members of the family: in the first two acts the tone is one of excited anticipation; finally that mood changes to one of satisfaction but also of regret that the momentous has but touched their lives and passed on leaving them all to confront the routine patterns of living once again. As the men work and the family observe, criticise, or give a helping hand, cross-currents of conversation cumulatively give us insight into personalities and relationships; yet it is the rhythm of the particular job of work in hand that affords our primary focus of attention and which always clearly dictates the rhythm of the dialogue.

Two Irishmen, Fitzpatrick and Marshall, are the most voluble of the workers with a characteristic Irish flair for malice. They delight out of sheer devilry, having nothing to lose themselves, in seeing just how far they can go in upsetting their more taciturn English colleagues or the boss. Having the suspicion from an earlier exchange that the wife of one of the workmen, Bennett, has left him for another man, they give their curiosity full play:

FITZPATRICK: That's an interesting proposition.
MARSHALL: It is.
FITZPATRICK: Why certain people . . .
MARSHALL: Who shall be nameless . . .
FITZPATRICK. Come seeking employment . . .
MARSHALL: Of all places . . .
FITZPATRICK: At Mr. Ewbank's place itself.
MARSHALL: Aye.
FITZPATRICK: Tenting contractor . . .
MARSHALL: For all outside . . .
FITZPATRICK: And inside occasions.
(*They laugh.*)
(*Direct to* MARSHALL) Some of course . . .
MARSHALL: Have no alternative . . . No. No. They haven't. That's right.
FITZPATRICK: In a manner of speaking, they have no choice.
MARSHALL: No, no. That's right. They can't be blamed.
FITZPATRICK: While on the other hand . . .
MARSHALL: You're right. You're right.
FITZPATRICK: Some of them . . .
MARSHALL: You're right.
FITZPATRICK: Come here because they're bone idle.
MARSHALL: Like myself you mean.
FITZPATRICK: Like yourself. On the other hand . . .
MARSHALL: Aye . . .
FITZPATRICK: There are those . . .
MARSHALL: Aye . . .
FITZPATRICK: Who have it in them to rise to higher things.
MARSHALL: Higher things. They have.
FITZPATRICK: Who have, within them, Marshy, the capacity to get on.
MARSHALL: They have. They have. You're right.
FITZPATRICK: But who, suddenly — through some calamity on the
    domestic front . . .
MARSHALL: The domestic front . . .
FITZPATRICK: In a manner of speaking . . .
MARSHALL: In a manner of speaking. That's right.
FITZPATRICK: Lose . . .
MARSHALL: Lose.
FITZPATRICK: All interest in carrying on.
MARSHALL: They do. They do. You're right.
FITZPATRICK: Some terrible calamity overwhems them . . .
MARSHALL: . . . on the domestic front . . .

FITZPATRICK: And up, into the wide blue yonder . . . all pride and initiative: gone.

MARSHALL: Aye . . . Vanished.

BENNETT: I'm not above using this, Fitzpatrick!

(BENNETT *has come in and has wrapped one of the muslin ropes: now he threatens* FITZPATRICK *with the shackle end.*)

FITZPATRICK: No, no. Each man to his tools I've always said.

MARSHALL: (*to* FITZPATRICK) A tradesman from his tools should never be divided.

BENNETT: I'll kill you. I bloody will!

KAY: That's enough, Fitzpatrick.

FITZPATRICK: I was merely ascertainin' the truth of the matter, Kay.

MARSHALL: (*to* FITZPATRICK) What's a man's life worth if it's comprised of nothing but untruths and lies?

FITZPATRICK: What is it now, indeed?

KAY: And what's so remarkable about your life, Fitzpatrick?

FITZPATRICK: Remarkable?

KAY: That it gives you the right to go poking so often into other people's.

(GLENDENNING *has come in slowly.*)

A loud-mouth. A wet rag. That doesn't do a crumb of work unless he's driven to it.

(KAY *has crossed slowly over to* FITZPATRICK.)

FITZPATRICK: Loud-mouth, now, I might be. And bone-idle.

(MARSHALL *snorts.*)

But I'm the only one round here who hasn't anything to hide.

KAY: Are you, now. Then you're very lucky. You're a very lucky man, Fitzpatrick. If you don't mind my saying so. [pp. 200-202]

There is great energy of movement here even though the dialogue is highly patterned at first, its rhythm closely related by the director (Lindsay Anderson) to the choreographed rhythm of work (the men are taking up sections of flooring and stacking them). It was almost, as performed, as if the men needed the rhythm of the dialogue to give them the right rhythm for the job as others might whistle or sing to establish the pattern for the alternations of effort and rest. It owes something to the cheekily delayed climaxes of the music hall 'patter' act. Many analogous music hall turns are rituals debunking social superiors. Ewbank prides himself on finding work for men no-one else will employ (one, Glenny, is a genial simpleton with a passion for food, while the foreman, Kay, who clearly from his manner and quiet authority once knew better circumstances, has been imprisoned for embezzlement); but Fitzpatrick and Marshall act with the suspicion of outsiders amongst a group who, whatever their private misfortunes, share a common Northern dourness. A pattern of allegiances is constantly forming and breaking down amongst the men under the influence of

Fitzpatrick's mercurial tongue, for none of them can be sure, not even Ewbank, whether his gestures of friendship are genuine or designed quietly to take a rise out of them. When the sharp edge of his wit touches a raw nerve, the men quickly move to the support of his current victim. Behind the exchange here too is a degree of irritability at the early Monday morning start on a chill autumnal day: summer has passed and theirs is in large measure seasonal employment. The music hall-like nature of the Irishman's 'act' also helps to distinguish their characters with some nicety. Fitzpatrick is brash, irrepressible, subtly menacing in the exuberance of his insults (which leave his victims feeling exposed yet incapable of retaliation other than on a level of brute threat), whereas Marshall has a terrier-like mentality, content to bark in safety from behind a bigger dog (noticeably he never initiates the verbal arabesques but is always gleefully in the supporting role). And what is brilliant cunning in Fitzpatrick, the insatiable *provocateur*, is often malice in Marshall (for like Bennett, he has one, if not possibly two failed marriages on his conscience, as we have learned from a similar exchange).

The play abounds in details which unobtrusively *tell*. On his entrance, the boss Ewbank is described as "wearing a suit which is plain, workmanlike and chunky; someone probably who doesn't take easily to wearing clothes, reflecting, perhaps, the feeling of a man who has never really found his proper station in life. The jacket of his coat is open as if it's been put on in a rush" [pp. 113-4]. No audience, of course, will immediately reach this assessment of Ewbank at his first appearance; but the direction indicates to the actor the kind of impact he should make which further details in the dialogue will cumulatively substantiate and explain. Ewbank's anxiety that this particular job should be first-rate and pass without a hitch since the celebration is a family affair brings sharply into focus insecurities of a more profound kind, as the following intimate chat with the foreman illustrates:

EWBANK: That's a nice bit of canvas, Kay.
KAY: It is. (*Nods, looking up at it*)
EWBANK: They don't make them like that no more. (*Gestures at tent*) 'Least, not if I can help it. (*Laughs at his own humour*) It'd be too damn expensive.
KAY: Aye. It would.
EWBANK (*pleased, contemplating*): Would you believe it?
KAY: Aye?
EWBANK: It's the first time I've hired a bit of my own tenting. It'll go down in the books you know. Pay meself with one hand what I tek out with the other.

KAY: Aye! (*Laughs dutifully*)

EWBANK: I'll never do it again. Never. Never have to.

KAY: No. Well. It's worth making a splash.

EWBANK: Splash? By God, this is a bloody thunderclap! It's not just the tent I'm paying for. God, Christ. I wish it was. No. No. (*To men*) Hang it! Hang it! Hang it! *Hook it up!* That's what they're there for. (*To* KAY) Three or four hundred people here. Bloody string orchestra. Waiters. Chef. I could buy four marquees with what I've laid out here. . . . Ah, well. That's another matter. (*Looks round, examining canvas*) Let's hope it keeps fine. Have you got the lining?

KAY: It's on the truck . . .

EWBANK: No marks on it, Kay. And no marks on this either. (*Indicates canvas*) Four lasses, eh?

KAY: Aye . . .

EWBARK: They'll cost you a packet. If I had four I'd set 'em to work and retire. (*Laughs. Wanders round, examining*) Four. And I can't even manage one. And none of 'em married?

KAY: No, no. They're still at school.

EWBANK: By God. If you had the benefit of my experience you'd never set a lass at school. God Christ, they're only good for one damn thing. And for that you don't have to read a book.

KAY: (*laughing*) Aye.

EWBANK: You've kept your eye on them relieving themselves have you?

KAY: Aye. They've been all right.

EWBANK: I don't give a damn myself. I've told you that already. But I can't have the old lady looking out of the window and not knowing where to put herself. (*To* MARSHALL) Leave that side alone. You want it open to bring the floor in. (*To* KAY) I noticed on the truck, Kay. That floor costs a bloody fortune. When you put it on you want to load it near the front. If a bit drops off it's done. That's a lovely bit of sewing. (*Looking up*) Look at that seam. (*Reads*) 'Made by F. Ewbank to commemorate the wedding of his daughter Claire'. [pp. 138-140]

Despite the confidences imparted to Kay, Ewbank never takes his eye off the men to ensure they take special care and respect of what is to him valuable property. The tent, which all the men have admired for its fine workmanship, is for Ewbank a token of love for his daughter and an expression of pride in his own wealth and achievement. Comically offsetting the pride there is a somewhat puritanical awe amounting even to horror at the expense of it all. (His line the morning after the wedding — "If you can't for one day in your life enjoy it" [p. 207] — is finely balanced between satisfaction and a rueful tone of self-justification.) He cannot take his wealth for granted as his children readily do: consciousness of his working-class background and that he is a self-made man colours his response to it. Though in one sense his place today is in the house, he cannot refrain from regular *sorties* to inspect the work and join in, amiably submitting at times even to Fitzpatrick's joshing as if to prove to himself that his true place is with his men, that money has not set him apart from them or his roots. That he turns to the tight-lipped Kay for moral support is particularly ironic. The foreman is quiet, visibly keeping himself under firm emotional control; his replies are terse, non-committal, the laughter has a dutiful ring in it. Later in the play we will learn that he has known a better lifestyle but was tempted into petty embezzlement to support his growing family: Ewbank knows this (indeed it is he who admits the details to Fitzpatrick) so that his talk here of the financial constraints of fatherhood is a gross breach of sensitivity, though quite unthinkingly done. Ewbank is a caring man for all his temper, but he is a man whose tactlessness can get damagingly in the way of his good nature. Only in retrospect is Kay's pained response fully explained. But that Ewbank turns to Kay as a father also has its significance, for Ewbank is frustrated and perplexed by his children's lack of respect for his way of life. His money, painstakingly acquired, has set them as far apart from their background and from him as it has set Ewbank himself from his origins. Covertly pleased that his son Paul gets involved in the work ("Bloody astonishing. I'd forgotten you'd got hands on inside them pockets") and that he tries to silence Fitzpatrick's tongue when it wags dangerously close to insulting his father, Ewbank is moved tentatively to ask a question that clearly weighs on his mind: "Do you ever fancy this job? This" and he gestures at the expanse of tenting. Paul gazes round then after a moment shakes his head. Ewbank accepts the inevitable: "Aye. Well I'm not surprised". Then with a briskness that shows how casual and wounding he has found Paul's dismissal to be, he changes the subject and the tone to a sour note of self-pity: "Not much thanks you get for it" [p. 182]. Paul clearly registers the pain he has caused: on several occasions subsequently, when left alone together, the two men hang back unwilling to follow family or workmen, trying to find the words, the gesture of affection that would heal the silence between them. Only in retrospect, as the play progresses, does the full weight of feeling in that early exchange between Ewbank and Kay clarify itself, the private anguish that lies in the darker reaches of both men's minds. Within the current of the dialogue the experience of two lifetimes is subtly caught; the passage gathers resonances into itself so that phrase after phrase is loaded with implication. The dialogue is apparently confined to immediate circumstances but it gives us access to a deeper continuum of feeling where a private conscience operates and the two men sit in judgement on their lives.

Many naturalistic plays since Chekhov have achieved a complex tone by illuminating in this way the suffering of individuals within the onward sweep of existence sustained by a particular social group. *The Contractor* does this admirably but does something more besides. As the work on the tent progresses and we come to know the men and the Ewbank family, not only does the patterning of the dialogue with its repetitions and echoes reveal the private fixations troubling each individual consciousness, but another pattern reveals itself — visually — within the routines of actually building the tent. Expertise also fascinates, commands attention and respect. Knowing that actors have had to learn a particular kind of work in order to enact it authentically enhances that fascination further. Skill and labour are transfigured by Storey into art. The tent taking form before us is a thing of beauty and the rhythm of work going into its creation as it gathers momentum seems to take possession of the characters, dissipating the tensions between them and for a time relieving individual minds of their awareness of pain and failure. Here — the sum of their efforts — was real achievement.

Memorably at the end of Act 2 as the tent stands finished, ready, the men having departed, the family enter to see it and do so with a pleasure amounting to awe. The light is radiant. "Is it what you were hoping for?" Mrs. Ewbank asks her husband, the questioning intonation beautifully capturing her awareness of his high expectations and her wish that he be wholly satisfied [p. 185]. Movement has gone into the making of the tent and now the family find they can only express what they feel about it all in the same mode — movement. Spontaneously bride and groom, son and mother, then husband and wife begin to dance but silently, to a rhythm heard only in the mind. It is a moment of pure joy, a discovery of unity in a shared pleasure, a celebration of human endeavour, more enriching perhaps to the family as a group than the public festivities to come.

But the play does not end there. Act 3 sees the tent in the early morning light the day after the wedding. It is in a terrible disarray, part of the muslin torn, chairs and tables overturned, bottles, napkins, paper littering the floor. Having seen it last in a mood of wonder and with some pleasure at their effort, the men are shocked at the mess. As they begin dismantling the structure, the family groups are seen breaking up to return to their various homes. Ewbank and his wife, relieved that the strain is over, accept the general dispersal. Where in the earlier scenes the rhythm of the dialogue pulsed with vitality, it begins now increasingly to dissipate:

EWBANK: (*Looks down at the view, standing beside* MRS. EWBANK) You'd think you'd have something to show for it, wouldn't you. After all this time.

MRS. EWBANK: Well, now . . . (*Abstracted.*)

EWBANK: I don't know. . . . (*Looks round. Then down at the lawn*) Made a few marks in that.

MRS. EWBANK: One or two . . .

EWBANK: (*shivers. Looks up*) Autumn . . .

MRS. EWBANK: (*abstracted*) Still. . . . It's been a good summer.

EWBANK: Aye. Comes and goes.

MRS. EWBANK. What . . .?

(*Pause.*)

EWBANK: Do you know that Kay was had up once for embezzlement?

MRS. EWBANK: They've been had up for a lot of things. The men that work for you.

EWBANK: Aye. . . . Nobody else'll have 'em. . . . I must be bloody daft. Well. I suppose we better see the old uns off.

MRS. EWBANK: Yes . . .

EWBANK: I don't know. . . . What's to become of us, you reckon? (MRS. EWBANK *looks at him, smiles, then shakes her head.*) Never do this again, you know.

MRS. EWBANK: No. . . . (*She smiles*)

EWBANK: Me heart wouldn't stand it.

MRS. EWBANK: No. . . . (*She laughs*)

OLD MRS. E: (*off*) Frank. . . .!

EWBANK: Aye, well. (*Half-laughs*) That's summat. (*They turn slowly, arm in arm.*)

OLD MRS. E: (*off*) Frank. . . .!

EWBANK: S'all right. We're coming. (*To* MRS. EWBANK) Well, then. We better go.

(*They go.*)

The stage stands empty: bare poles, the ropes fastened off. The lights fade slowly. [pp. 222-223]

The mood is elegaic, sad perhaps but relaxed. Behind the parents' sense that a responsibility for their children has now ended was, as it was played by Constance Chapman and Bill Owen, an openness to new possibilities of experience, a shy recognition that they must now be sufficient to themselves in facing old age together and in that perhaps recover a lost intimacy. Spontaneously, as with the dancing earlier, they were drawn to hold each other. Within the rhythms of dispersal, a new movement was beginning. That empty vista of stage space at the close presented as a consequence no threat; we registered a loss — beauty had gone: the tent, the actors, the play itself — but regret was tempered by a sense of freedom, the challenge to work to create meaning within that void afresh, dispersal inviting renewal, which is the rhythm of life itself.

Though his best plays of the Seventies show Storey exploring the possibilities of the style he perfected in *The Contractor* and moving it increasingly towards stylisation in *Home* and *Cromwell* (to the point where in *Cromwell* the dialogue actually hovers between prose and blank verse), he had not yet wholly lost interest in the 'traditional literary' mode. *Mother's Day* (Royal Court, 1976)[9] finds him attempting Orton's vein of black farce but with little success. The *Financial Times* reviewing the play observed that the "farcical invention is tireless, and has the advantage of unlimited permissiveness",[10] but one is left wondering whether this is an advantage. Farce needs a firm sense of norms of behaviour against which to measure the characters' desperate urges to create an alternative permissive lifestyle. There is no logic behind the antics of the Johnson household in *Mother's Day* and so no sense of a gathering momentum and inexorable climax which are essential to farce. Compared with the comic brio of Fitzpatrick and Marshall, more energetic verbally than physically, the dialogue in the farce is surprisingly flaccid and, compared with Orton's, quite devoid of wit. Lines echo an Orton formula — "Mr. Johnson was an inexperienced and vulgar man when he deflowered me and vulgarity has been a plant that has flourished, vigorously, in the manure of his existence" [p. 198]; but the laughter was of brief duration. This is Orton's manner but without his substance; Orton's way like Wilde's is to make florid rhetoric expose the character of the speaker to the core; Mrs. Johnson's observation *says* nothing. *What the Butler Saw* takes a collection of perfectly sane, if oversexed, people who indulge in behaviour which though deviant (like adultery) is deemed acceptable providing it is kept secret and exposes them to a psychiatrist who interprets their frantic efforts to keep the truth about themselves hidden as proof positive of every conceivable kind of Freudian aberration. Though they live theoretically in a permissive society, Orton's characters are vulnerable because they still know shame. The play deliberately confronts the double standards of their world and asks pertinently what is *normal* behaviour and what exactly constitutes madness. But there is no theme of this seriousness generating the mechanics of Storey's farce; invention is pursued for its own sake regardless of meaning. The derivation of *Sisters* (Royal Exchange, Manchester, 1978) is more damagingly obvious: *A Streetcar Named*

Desire has been plundered at every turn for a plotline and, though
the setting is shifted from down-town New Orleans to the post-war
housing estate of some North-country city, there is no disguising
the crib or the lifelessness of the result.[11]

The best of these literary plays is *The Farm* (Royal Court, 1973).[12]
Liveliness this certainly has, because it respects the long-standing
tradition it imitates of northern comedies like *Hobson's Choice* that
get their impetus by exploiting the figure of the overbearing
patriarch. *The Farm* calls the tradition to mind but does not treat it
parasitically as *Sisters* treats Tennessee Williams's masterpiece.
Rather it chooses to add new insights to the theme by looking firmly
at the Oedipal significance that makes the figure perennially so
awesome yet compelling. And Storey makes his point by breaking
with tradition and not giving the audience and characters the
satisfaction of seeing the monster overthrown. The hostility between
Slattery and his son Arthur has been fuelled over the years by Mrs.
Slattery's continuing belief in Arthur's literary talent. The old man's
aggression reflects his disappointment that Arthur should have failed
to live up to the family's expectations as much as rivalry for his wife's
affection. Arthur returns confident that he has something at last to
share with his parents and sisters and perhaps achieve some dignity
in the home: he is to marry. But as his sister Jenny quickly discovers,
the situation is not as simple as that sounds: the twenty-one-year-old
Arthur is to marry a divorcee, twice his age, with two children.
Storey beautifully paces the play towards the inevitable
confrontation of father and son, as each of the sisters and his mother
receive Arthur's news with pleasure changing to apprehension and
an enforcedly cheerful surmise that all might perhaps turn out well.
As the news continually gets a mixed reception, Arthur's self-
possession gutters. The sisters intuitively know their father will have
a field-day and deliberately postpone going to work to watch for the
explosion; they sympathise with Arthur — 'He'd be very foolish to
bring someone — or something — he values into this" [p. 83] — but
their father's vituperative energy enthrals them even as it shocks.
Storey meticulously judges the balance between comedy and cruelty
in the expected climax:

Over forty. . .? What's that mean then? Fifty? . . . *Sixty*? She's not a bloody
octogenarian, is she? . . . By go . . . Be wheeling her in a bloody bath-chair
next . . . [p. 63]

Malicious delight quite revitalises the drunken old reprobate; years
of disappointed hopes for Arthur find their release in a jubilant
denunciation of his shortcomings. Arthur is totally unmanned. He

had intended bringing his fiancée to the farm that evening, but in the event he asks her to return to London and there he makes his mistake. His father goes out of his way to give the woman a proper welcome to the family home and is profoundly wounded by her non-appearance: "Thy did quite right. If thy'd brought her back I'd have probably been reconciled. You realise that? When it comes face to face — with her, or you, or you . . . with whoever they bring in here — I soon step back . . . I don't have a bite. You realise that? All bark . . ." [p. 84]. The carefully preserved comic note throughout the show-down substantiates that last point. Father and son have each misjudged the other's point of vulnerability and the separation that ensues seems final. The play ends on an equivocal note: at breakfast the next morning Arthur is conspicuously absent and Slattery is a model of boisterous fun; leaving us questioning the value of his moment of self-recognition and remorse. If *The Farm* has a weakness it lies in the presentation of the sisters as too-knowing commentators on the action, who do not leave the audience much room to move imaginatively within the situation. If one resents their presence at times, it is only because they suggest that Storey underestimates the power of his art to define by implication and lacks trust in the audience's perceptions.

No such loss of faith was evident in the plays that built on the achievements of *The Contractor*. *The Changing Room* (Royal Court, 1971)[13] proved to be another play of celebration, not of work this time so much as physical prowess. Fifteen men gather together to prepare for a rugger match; they change, are given instructions by their trainer, are massaged, encouraged by the team's chairman, warned by the referee, as he inspects their boots, to play fair. The surface detail is an authentic recreation. What the play really explores — again through carefully orchestrated patterns of dialogue — is how the men are in effect undergoing a ritual to prepare for an ordeal. The match is a weekly testing, a rite of passage. What we watch are fifteen men undergoing a process of complete depersonalisation as the kick-off time approaches and the tension mounts. As they severally arrive in the changing room, Storey characterises each by his way of entering (whether the individual takes note of the group or of a particular colleague or goes single-mindedly straight to the business of undressing), by his attitude to his kit (checking it through only half-consciously as a routine procedure or obsessively to ensure it is to hand in the appropriate order). Some comment at large on the weather or the team's chances, others greeting a team-mate make more random, intimate chat; none of it, however, sustains its impetus for long even when Walsh, the joker of the pack, arrives from a wedding and expansively takes them all into his confidence about his betting and womanising, teasing the more recalcitrant men till they at least acknowledge his presence. He is a big man in every way, totally at ease in himself and therefore good for morale, however daft his antics. As time passes the dialogue fragments, breaks down, gives way to silence as the men begin to think of themselves as a corporate unit, willing a team-mind into being. They are dressed alike now, distinguished only by numbers indicating their positions on the field. Communication is by gutterals and brief interjections, while outside the crowd, moved by a keen anticipation, begins to roar in great waves of sound. The careful preparation of the men, the hushed calming tones of the trainer, the oiling and flexing of muscles and limbs, the final, almost whispered invocation of luck to each of the players like a kind of benediction, work naturalistically yet evoke the stages of a ritual which have opened up the players' minds steadily to a force of primitive emotion, a kind of battle-fury that they can hardly keep in check. The men have gained access to an abnormal quick of attention in body awareness and in animal-like sensitivity to each other's movements.

Act Two contrasts this briefly with the physical and mental lassitude of the Chairman, the Club Secretary and Harry, the cleaner, for whom the match is just another game they are too idle, cold or bored to watch. Then with the prolonged whistle the men return; and trainer, masseur and Chairman set out to sustain the tension and nurture it through the interval. A short way into the second half of the match (heard in play by the audience over the tannoy system that Harry turns on in the changing room), Kendal, one of the men, returns injured, his face a mass of pulp and blood, his nose broken, his mind closed to everything but the numbing experience of pain. He is bathed, dressed, taken away to hospital, pathetically uncoordinated, devoid of every vestige of human dignity. It is a terrible image of the fear the men pit themselves against each week: the fear of pain, of the injury that can jeopardise their super-normal fitness and hypersensitivity in an instant. Yet without that fear, there would be no challenge to them to rise out of the everyday self, and be transfigured.

In the final act the game has been won; the team are taking a noisy corporate bath, horse-play is rife with duckings and chasings and much larking about with a hose of cold water. The tension over, that hypersensitivity relaxed, there is a great release of exuberance as the men gambol about naked with a completely unselfconscious innocence. And the audience is suddenly privileged to watch *play*, game in its purest sense. There have been few occasions when nudity on stage has conveyed such a fruitful dramatic purpose as here, wholly related as it is to the great cycle of feeling the play was seeking to define. This was a moment of Dionysiac exhilaration, an almost childlike joy in the reality of the body and a freedom of the spirit found through pushing the self to a limit of physical endurance. In time, the men begin to dry, don their clothes and with these their individualities before dispersing to their homes and family responsibilities. Each player accepts again the various daily pressures that define his social self from which briefly he had found means of escape; and the older ones are left wondering for how many more seasons they'll have the stamina to face the test.

If *The Changing Room* was not perhaps as completely satisfying an experience as *The Contractor*, it was because of the way that outer world beyond the changing room could be only sketchily realised within the play. The earlier work gave equal attention to most of the characters who, with the possible exception of Maurice the bridegroom, were realised through a richness of detail. Storey set himself an almost impossible task in attempting to give individualising touches to all fifteen players and an overall cast of twenty-two (as opposed to twelve in *The Contractor*) yet, relying as he had to do on modes of dressing and so on for this purpose, the men's everyday selves appeared somewhat caricatured. One could argue that it is Storey's point that the men's recovery through the match of a primitive energy and awareness is a confronting of their truest selves. If that is the point, then it should be made more clearly: it certainly was not the lasting impression from Lindsay Anderson's production. Somehow the play ought to intimate, but does not, why the men are lured week by week despite the evident dangers to submit to this ordeal. What are the consequences of this access to self-transcendence and the ensuing release into a primal innocence? Surely that period of *change* has some lasting effect psychologically?

Perhaps Storey's most daring play to date has been *Cromwell* (Royal Court, 1973)[14] in which he attempted to wed his style of poetic naturalism with a subject of epic, Shakespearian breadth — the fate of a group of Catholic sympathisers in Cromwellian occupied Ireland. It was not perhaps a total success, but it was a far finer play than was claimed by many reviewers who seemed tetchily preoccupied with the fact that Cromwell himself does not appear in the action (though he is in the first two acts everywhere felt, even if nowhere seen; he is the Big One, feared for his seemingly magical powers of endurance and cunning, who seems to hold Fortune and everyone's fate in his grasp). And that was to miss Storey's point which, as befits the demands of naturalism, was to show the impact of an endless civil war on the condition of everyday lives. This was to give the study of private suffering in the onward sweep of a group experience — his achievement in *The Contractor* — an utterly new dimension, especially since that sweep of events that here constitutes the pattern of history is seen to be senseless and futile. Factions form — initially from idealistic religious motives — but then splinter into rival groups; allegiances waver and break down; then factions realign and the battle wearily goes on with the objectives increasingly lost sight of; new ideals stir up a flicker of courage: "the King", "the Church", "the People", "the Country", "God" become the battle-cry in turn and the relentless machine of war goes on destroying life, property, and, above all, man's spirit. What begins in historical fact with Cromwell's invasion of Ireland is gradually transformed by a process of increasing stylisation into an allegory of the fate of the common man's honest soul trapped where "ignorant armies clash by night".[15] (The language and vision constantly call Bunyan to mind.) Storey's setting greatly aided this subtle change of focus: a largely bare stage space where locations were suggested by fitfully glimmering lights evocative of haze, the dim recesses of woods, the smoke of the battlefield. If, briefly, the lights shone vividly on a scene of pastoral calm, soldiers soon appeared and engulfed the place in darkness once again. Through the half-light we saw images sickeningly recur of homesteads sacked and fired, of chains of prisoners roped together and forced groping onward to some unknown destination, of the nightmare silhouettes of helmeted soldiers. At the last the characters choose the absolute darkness of death in the hope of relief.

But it would be wrong to suggest the play is wholly nihilistic. It is more a study of the resilience of the human mind in the face of adversity. Circumstance throws together five characters: the three men are survivors of a party on its way to enlist for the Catholic cause; a woman and her half-witted servant are all that remain of a family group wandering in quest of a decent burial for a deceased grandparent. All have suffered from the English soldiers. Proctor and the woman, Joan, decide to try and create a family and a home to realise the values that the warring factions claim they are fighting to protect. To join a faction, they have found, is to court death in battle or execution as a traitor. But to withdraw to a private world, they discover, is to invite reprisals from either faction. They are always at the mercy of military power. What we watch are humble people trying to live a life they feel to be honest amidst the slogans and the war-mongerers' jargon:

PROCTOR. Have the barn . . . What's broken down by you I can build again.
CLEET. Aye . . . 'tis destruction you see in me . . . and not the promotion of a higher cause.
PROCTOR. One thing I've found of causes . . .
CLEET. Aye?
PROCTOR. No cause is greater than its means.
CLEET. Oppressors are met by oppressor's schemes.
PROCTOR. Then oppression makes reflection of itself — and calls it revolution . . . change . . . the end to discontent . . . And change it is . . . the beggar usurps the horseman and takes the whip himself.
(CLEET *turns aside*.)
CLEET. All I have need of now is rest . . .
PROCTOR. Well, rest I'll not deny . . . nor food . . . [pp. 66-67]

The quiet assurance of Proctor here is the token of a slowly maturing strength that comes from struggling with Joan to find ever new inner resources to rely on. He too had earlier been a "monomaniac fool"[p. 47] fighting out of the belief that "without ideals no man can live" [p. 50] and needing "badges, stripes, emblems that tell one who and what and where I am"[p. 59]. But life with Joan changes that; when Cleet taunts him for being a coward, a no-man wanting a little security, Proctor's answer is firm: "A brave man makes his life"[p. 65] and argues for creative toil rather than death-dealing, however sound the cause might be. Out of humanity he shelters the injured Cleet but the English come searching for him and Proctor's home is fired, his child within it, and he and Joan have to learn to live beyond heartbreak.

Joining them in their fortunes are two labourers, O'Halloran and Logan, who are brothers across the centuries with Fitzpatrick and Marshall, wary loafers whose loquacity is constantly their saving grace, born survivors whose only allegiance is to their own skins:

BROOME: And you?
O'HALLORAN: Oh . . . oh . . . If you're looking for recruits, your honour . . .
LOGAN: I've always got the colours muddled up . . .
O'HALLORAN: It's the uniforms you see . . .
LOGAN: Which side is which . . .
O'HALLORAN: Left or right . . .
LOGAN: Facing front or facing back.

O'HALLORAN: I could never decide, you see, myself . . .
LOGAN: Always needed someone like your honour, your gracious
    worshipful honour, to do it for me. [p. 42]

Scurrilous they may be, but in adapting themselves to all occasions
they show an energy of mind lacking in the dogged soldiery that
frequently threatens them. Their senses are finely tuned to danger
yet they show no fear, for they have the confidence that they can
turn any man to their will by activating in him a contempt for them
as worthless. But in playing out this chosen role as the scum of the
earth, they are free of the constraints of political necessity that bind
others. They know a joy in living and find zest and excitement in
accommodating themselves to the pattern of events which none of
the other characters share. At the last they and Proctor part. The
violence about them reaches apocalyptic proportions as they come
to a river: behind is the clash of arms in the night, before them only
a deeper darkness. O'Halloran and Logan cower back but Proctor
and Joan, trusting in their faith in each other and an inner vision
of finding a haven of peace, enter a boat and journey onward. They
ask the ferryman about the farther shores but his awareness is
confined to his task:

BOATMAN: The stream is all I know . . . its shoals, its rocks, its crevices
    . . . its gleams . . . the pattern of its light at dawn and dusk . . . the
    rushing of its waves . . . its stillness when it floods or lies, dwindling,
    in a summer heat . . . I know the river, and the manner of the boat; that's
    all. [p. 78]

(The boatman is made very real despite his clearly symbolic
function.) Joan and Proctor disembark and the boat instantly
recedes:

JOAN: See . . . the boat has drifted in the stream . . .
PROCTOR: He plies the oar . . .
JOAN: For the first time in our lives we have no turning back.
PROCTOR: Fool: to the front . . .
JOAN: He plunges in the dark.
PROCTOR: The darkness thickens . . .
JOAN: Do you hear those cries and shouts?
PROCTOR: Are others moving in those fields that we knew before?
JOAN: And beyond the darkness . . .
PROCTOR: Do you see the light?
(*Fade.*) [p. 79]

This is a compelling stage image — the journeying onward, the
monumental resilience, the courage to be open to new possibilities
despite horrendous past defeats. Yet boatmen, river and night are
traditional emblems of death.

Is the intimation of Proctor's last desperate question that retreat into the self for whatever ends ultimately exacts a death of the spirit? Or is the tone positive and has the pursuit of vision brought its reward? The ambivalence of this ending makes the sordid reality of the war-torn world the characters have felt compelled to leave behind them even more terrible to contemplate. Is it possible ever to find honourable shelter from the inexorable machine of war? It is Storey's achievement that he can invite his audience to frame such questions without resorting in the play to overt rhetoric. Statement in this play is never assured fact, however dogmatically it may be uttered by men like Cleet, but always hypothesis circumscribed by the facts of war. Hardship, loss and pain shape the characters' ideas, which in Proctor's case change under the pressure of events: grief makes him a thinking man. Storey records that process but the ambivalence of the conclusion shows he hesitates to endorse Proctor's view; he can but respect the effort of the man not to be consumed by despair nor brutalised by circumstance. Always there are the wayward tides of the battle evoked by the ever bare and darkening stage, a place of uncertainty and fear, only dimly apprehended and the more ominous for that, a constant threat to human dignity and achievement. Stage-space and lighting became powerful metaphors as Storey turned to great creative advantage the limitations of the Royal Court for coping with elaborate scene design. The conception of *Cromwell*, despite a misguidedly slow-paced production by Anthony Page, was a radical development of the history play and made for superb poetic theatre.

In *The Contractor* and *The Changing Rom* the group event set up a counter-rhythm to the routine of individual lives, one that allowed the characters to escape temporarily from the pressures shaping their private selves; in *Cromwell* Storey experimented with a situation where that counter-rhythm was a frightening and destructive force compelling the characters to seek security within the private consciousness. *Home* (Royal Court, 1970),[16] arguably Storey's most perfect exploration of his idiosyncratic style, studies the dilemma of individuals who are freed of all social pressures, all need for effort: living in a mental asylum, they have all lost a public identity and inhabit a strange vacuum governed only by the passage of time and the routines of meals and sleep. Within the play virtually nothing happens in terms of external action and little is said that could be described as meaningful. Rather it is a play where action and meaning are entirely bound up with questions of tone and nuance.

Two men, Harry and Jack, chance to meet in a garden; they seem acquaintances but not of long standing (it is not established until the second scene that they are inmates of an institution) for there is a certain reserve, a wariness in their talk; but confidences about their families and about past experiences begin to slip into the conversation displacing the generalities, the jokes, and commonplace remarks about the weather, clothes, the newspapers. Even then they seem sedulously to avoid any directly personal observations. Carefully they reach for the tone of intimacy without committing themselves to its substance. There is an air of faded gentility about the men with their neat but rather worn clothes; their somewhat formal manner suggests a meeting in a club or some holiday spa — the shyness of men who have an interest in each other but who have been educated to restrain their emotions and not push any relationship beyond the bounds of courtesy:

JACK: I remember I once owned a little boat.
HARRY: Really.
JACK: For fishing. Nothing very grand.
HARRY: A fishing man.
JACK: Not really. More an occasional pursuit.
HARRY: I've always been curious about that.
JACK: Yes?
HARRY: "A solitary figure crouched upon a bank."
JACK: Never stirring.
HARRY: No. No.
JACK: Can be very tedious, I know.
HARRY: Still. A boat is more interesting.
JACK: Oh, yes. A sort of tradition, really.
HARRY: In the family.
JACK: No. No. More in the . . . island, you know.
HARRY: Ah, yes.
JACK: Drake.
HARRY: Yes!
JACK: Nelson.
HARRY: Beatty.
JACK: Sir Walter Raleigh.
HARRY: There was a very fine man . . . poet.
JACK: Lost his head, you know.
HARRY: It's surprising the amount of dust that collects in so short a space of time. (*runs hand lightly over table*)
JACK: It is. (*looks round*) Spot like this, perhaps, attracts it.
HARRY: Yes . . . (*pause*) You never became a priest, then?
JACK: No . . . No.
HARRY: Splendid to have a vocation.
JACK: Tis . . . Something you believe in.

HARRY: Oh, yes.
JACK: I could never . . . resolve certain difficulties, myself.
HARRY: Yes?
JACK: The hows and the wherefores I could understand. How we came
   to be, and His presence, lurking everywhere, you know. But as to the
   'why' . . . I could never understand. Seemed a terrible waste of time to me.
HARRY: Oh, yes.
JACK: Thought it better to leave it to those who didn't mind.
HARRY: Ah, yes.
JACK: I suppose the same was true about dancing.
HARRY: Oh, yes. I remember turning up for instance, to my first class,
   only to discover that all the rest of them were girls.
JACK: Really?
HARRY: Well . . . there are men dancers, I know. Still . . . Took up
   football after that.
JACK: To professional standard, I imagine.
HARRY: Oh, no. Just the odd kick around. Joined a team that played in
   the park on Sunday mornings.
JACK: The athletic life has many attractions.
HARRY: It has. It has.
JACK: (*pause*) How long have you been here, then?
HARRY: Oh, a couple of er.
JACK: Strange — meeting the other day.
HARRY: Yes.
JACK: On the way back, thought to myself, "What a chance encounter."
HARRY: Yes.
JACK: So rare, these days, to meet someone to whom one can actually
   talk.
HARRY: I know what you mean.
JACK: One works. One looks around. One meets people. But very little
   communication actually takes place.
HARRY: Very.
JACK: None at all in most cases! (*Laughs*)
HARRY: Oh, absolutely.
JACK: The agonies and frustrations. I can assure you. In the end one gives
   up in absolute despair. [pp. 22-24]

What we are watching here are two men creating a friendship but
even the finally admitted confidence that their previous meeting
was a pleasure for them both has to be couched as a generalisation:
"One works, one looks around. One meets people. But very little
communication takes place". In retrospect we appreciate that each
knows the other is an inmate like himself and, given that
knowledge, each recognises that there must in the other's
consciousness be areas of pain and trouble. Their reserve is in fact
an act of extreme care, meticulously avoiding giving hurt or
embarrassment. Jack usually initiates a flow of talk invariably by

reminiscing about a relative ("I had an aunt once who, for a short while, lived near Gloucester" [p. 27]); he has a fascination for other people's lives and for the anecdotal details by which they live in the memory as uniquely individual. Subsequently we wonder whether the memories are all a play of fancy — that "once" in the reminiscence about the aunt near Gloucester gives a slightly odd turn to an otherwise factual statement — but even then they express a great wish to belong, to have a family, be on good terms with a community, have the friends, relatives, acquaintances who confirm one's identity. Harry is altogether more reluctant to communicate, preserving a shy edginess in his replies — "Oh, yes" is his recurrent response, as if surprised by his growing interest. He seems at times incapable of saying anything that is clearly affirmative yet he seems anxious, even at times desperate, that the talk should continue and will suddenly relax into the confidential himself. On the surface the long exchange skates lightly from subject to subject, never pausing long enough for serious insights to develop; the two minds seem to take comfort in cliché and in commonplaces; and yet, as played by Richardson and Gielgud, something quite profound was happening behind the language which the development of the play was to confirm. The two men were hesitantly building structures of feeling, both discovering areas of experience in each other's lives which, since they were evidently a source of pain, were deemed *taboo* for future comment (they both retreat uneasily from mention of their wives) and noting others — their war records, their past hobbies — which were obviously *safe* subjects for discussion. With great delicacy they seemed intent on discovering how not to wound each other. When, later in the play, mistakes are made and pain is unwittingly given, grief will be expressed by the one hurt in silent tears, while the other will wait patiently (usually commenting on the weather) to rekindle an involvement and restore equanimity. Cliché is their protection from realities too cruel to contemplate. The long first scene is a moving display of tact, courtesy, intuition that leaves the men with a carefree air and a sudden access of vigour as they decide to take a walk together:

JACK: All correct.
HARRY: Cane.
JACK: Cane.
HARRY: Well, then. Off we go.
JACK: Off we go.
[HARRY *breathes in deeply: breathes out.*]
HARRY: Beautiful corner.

JACK: Tis.
[*Pause: last look round.*]
HARRY: Work up an appetite.
JACK: Right, then. Best foot forward.
HARRY: Best foot forward.
JACK: Best foot forward, and off we go.
[*They stroll off, taking the air, stage left.*] [p. 39]

They give place to two women, Marjorie and Kathleen, who provide a sharp contrast: they are earthy, forthright, gossipy and lewd. Their talk is relentlessly, even obsessionally physical: Kathleen has painfully swollen feet; Marjorie anxiously ensures their skirts are well down below their knees; theirs is a relationship founded on shared recall of the miseries of their lives *outside*. Though they criticise the running of the institution, they enjoy it (both admit to being "regulars"), because it affords them escape from meagre, loveless lives trapped in squalid marriages and meaningless jobs. Here they can live a leisured existence like *ladies*, even if they lack the necessary style and manner that make for a true gentility. They share a repugnance for sex, agreeing that it is all men ever think about and yet it totally consumes their imaginations inspiring them to read innuendo into the most harmless remarks. As Marjorie observes with grim satisfaction: "Seen it all I have. Rape, intercourse. Physical pleasure" [p. 75].

The men return, invigorated by their walk and ripening friendship, and genially endeavour to include the women in their mood of well-being. Marjorie and Kathleen hanker after a different quality of life and one offers itself now; they quickly respond to the invitation but are so much the victims of their past that they cannot sustain the ensuing mood of concord for long. They misjudge the men's motives, misprize their good nature and shatter the fragile bonds of sympathy Harry and Jack have established with each other. It would be callous if it were not done quite unknowingly, but the women are totally without self-awareness and are hardly conscious of their loss; they are quite without shame. The men's courtesy and all the generous impulses it stands for wither before the women's forthright questioning, for they have no respect for privacy. Observing a foible or mannerism in Jack or Harry, both Marjorie and Kathleen will comment on it, even satirise it, mercilessly:

KATHLEEN: Here. . . .
[HARRY *looks across*]
He really what he says he is?
HARRY: How do you mean?

KATHLEEN: Told us he was a doctor. Another time he said he'd been a sanitary inspector.
HARRY: Really? Hadn't heard of that.
KATHLEEN: Go on. Know what inspecting he'll do. You the same.
HARRY: Oh, now. Certain discriminations can be . . .
KATHLEEN: I've heard about you.
HARRY: Oh, well, you er.
KATHLEEN: Making up things.
HARRY: Oh, well. One . . . embodies . . . of course.
KATHLEEN: What's that, then?
HARRY: *Fancies* . . . What's life for if you can't. . . . [*Flutters his fingers.*]
KATHLEEN: We've heard about that an' all. [*Imitates his action.*]
HARRY: Well. I'm sure you and I have, in reality, a great deal in common. After all, one looks around: what does one see?
KATHLEEN: Gawd . . . [*Groans, feeling her feet.*]
HARRY: A little this. A little that.
KATHLEEN: Here. Everything you know is little.
HARRY: Well . . . I er . . . Yes . . . No great role for this actor, I'm afraid. A little stage, a tiny part.
KATHLEEN: You an actor, then?
HARRY: Well, I did, as a matter of fact, at one time . . . actually a little . . .
KATHLEEN: Here, little again. You notice? [pp. 59-60]

How misplaced are Harry's hopes! And Jack fares no better:

JACK: I had a cousin once . . .
MARJORIE: Here, you got a big family, haven't you?
JACK: Seven brothers and sisters. Spreads around, you know.
MARJORIE: Here, you was an only child last week.
JACK: A niece of mine — I say niece . . . she was only . . .
MARJORIE: What you do it for?
JACK: Oh, now . . . [pp. 75-76]

But worse is to follow, the women have no scruples or tact: when they sense a private pain, nothing can hold back their curiosity:

KATHLEEN: Your friend come in for following little girls?
HARRY: What . . .
KATHLEEN: Go on. You can tell me. Cross my heart and hope to die.
HARRY: Well . . . that's . . .
KATHLEEN: Well, then.
HARRY: I believe there were . . . er . . . certain proclivities, shall we say?
KATHLEEN: Proclivities? What's them?
HARRY: Nothing criminal, of course.
KATHLEEN: Oh, no . . .
HARRY: No prosecution . . .
KATHLEEN: Oh, no . . .
HARRY: Certain pressures, in the er . . . Revealed themselves.
KATHLEEN: In public?

HARRY: No. No . . . I . . . Not what I meant.
KATHLEEN: I don't know what you're saying half the time. You realise
   that?
HARRY: Communication is a difficult factor.
KATHLEEN: Say that again.
HARRY: I believe he was encouraged to come here for a little er.
KATHLEEN: Here. Little.
HARRY: Oh, yes . . . As it is, very few places left now where one can be
   at ease. [p. 62]

Shameless herself, Kathleen never for a moment suspects Harry
suffers shame or feels shame for his friend in this crude unmasking.
Attempts by Harry or Jack to redeem the situation, to put
themselves and their motives in a true perspective are rapidly
frustrated; the women are relentless:

JACK: Respect for the gentler sex, I must say, is a fast diminishing concept
   in the modern world.
HARRY: Oh, yes.
JACK: I recollect the time when one stood for a lady as a matter of course.
HARRY: Oh, yes.
MARJORIE: Know the kind of standing he's on about.
KATHLEEN: Oooooh!
JACK: Each becomes hardened to his ways.
KATHLEEN: Oooooh!
JACK: No regard for anyone else's. [p. 54]

Storey beautifully sustains a balance between comedy and pathos.
Harry's belief that "The essence of true friendship . . . is to make
allowances for one another's little lapses" [p. 53] is heartfelt for it
expresses a personal need to care; but, while Jack can recognise the
need for compassion, the women cannot begin to comprehend his
meaning: nothing in their past experience can enlighten them to the
value of his concern. Both men are reduced to tears at their failure;
though the women treat self-pity as the one luxury in their lives,
they cannot recognise the need for pity here; Marjorie finds wildly
funny the incongruity between the men's constant concern lest it
rain with their own repeated "splashing", as she calls their weeping.
Ultimately Jack and Harry's only resource is silence: they refuse to
recognise the women's presence any longer and so compel them to
leave.
   Alone again, they exchange a few pleasantries before reaching
for some explanation of it all. Jack hazards the remark: "If a person
can't be what they are, what's the purpose of being anything at
all?" [p. 83]. It is a painfully ambiguous observation. "What they
are" (inmates of the asylum) is an awareness they would seek to

escape from, as is the reality of their equally vulnerable selves which have brought them here. We have had doubts all along about the men's identity, since we are unsure how much of what we have heard can be believed; but they chose to believe in each other, in the *persona* each sought to project to stifle the inner sense of disgrace. Each recognised in the other the wish to create an acceptable self that another person could trust in and, in trusting, authenticate; hopefully in this way each could escape the shame of being in a home for unacceptables. Each cherished in the other the need for a little human dignity. Words may have failed them, words may only have articulated *fancies*, but behind the words a wealth of meaning has been conveyed by tone. In the breakdown between language and factual truth, Storey has found a means of defining the nature of love, its terrors and its strengths, in a fashion that is quite unforced (no "conceptualised" theatre, this) and quite without sentimentality. By their corporate effort, their care, Harry and Jack have briefly created a relationship which is finer than the sum of their individual selves and we are left wondering whether it has the power to withstand the derision of Kathleen and Marjorie. We see them finally in a bare void, weeping. Perhaps the ambiguity of Jack's statement about the need to be accepted for what one is, coming so soon after Kathleen and Marjorie have unashamedly expressed some truths about the men's condition, implies they have been robbed of the courage to persevere. Now that the areas of pain only sensed before are known as harsh facts, their play with illusion for the sake of appearances may lack the motive and the impetus to continue. When finally they take refuge in the conversational formulae that have graced their past exchanges together, the words fail to take wing, to provoke an answering response, except when Jack voices his sense of loss:

HARRY: Amazing thing, of course, is the er.
JACK: Oh, yes.
HARRY: Still prevails.
JACK: Oh, my goodness.
HARRY: Hendricks I find is a . . .
JACK: Oh, yes.
HARRY: Moustache . . . Eye-brows.
JACK: Divorced.
HARRY: Oh, yes.
JACK: Moral fibre. Set to a task, never complete it. Find some way to back out.
HARRY: Oh, yes.
JACK: The sea is an extraordinary . . .

HARRY: Oh, yes.
JACK: Cousin of mine . . .
HARRY: See the church.
[*They gaze off.*]
JACK: Shouldn't wonder He's disappointed. [*Looks up.*]
HARRY: Oh, yes.
JACK: Heart-break.
HARRY: Oh, yes.
JACK: Same mistake . . . Won't make it twice.
HARRY: Oh, no.
JACK: Once over. Never again. [pp. 87-88]

And yet their weeping is a *shared* condition, an admission of a common vulnerability. The light fades from the stage evoking a long dusk descending on their individual lives and on their particular style of living. Gracious gentility, courteous charm seemingly have no place in an aggressively matter-of-fact world: the full pathos of their predicament is that the men are outsiders at every level of their existence. Incontestably in friendship they found a time of joyous transcendence and a certain truth to feeling.

Storey has claimed that for him the ideal play is one that leaves the audience much of the work of creating a sense of inward detail.[17] But such a play does require expert direction and a cast sensitive to the possibilities of inward detail, who will stimulate an audience's sensibilities to flow in appropriate directions. The casting for *Home* was ideal. Richardson and Gielgud were perfect embodiments of a vanishing age. Both have a gift for unforced pathos: one recalls Richardson's debonair grace, the voice ripe with experience, soon lifting Gielgud's Harry out of his quiet melancholia; and Gielgud's suppressed tone and rather chilly politeness warming to Jack's conversational ploys as his voice steadily took on its familiar musical colouring. Disillusioned by Marjorie, Richardson's Jack slumped throughout his entire frame as if the life had gone out of him, the eyes dilating with a secret terror before they glazed over in an effort to distance himself from her power to hurt. Gielgud became monumentally still at the point of Harry's defeat, frailly tall, the eyes narrowing to extinction until the facial muscles tightened and mouth and brows looked like seams of craggy rock. At the close Richardson resorted to an almost child-like helplessness and Gielgud produced an ethereal timbre, as if Harry could barely speak for inwardly suppressed sobs. The women were finely distinguished too: Dandy Nichols' Marjorie was sharply raucous and uncompromisingly vulgar, while Mona Washbourne's Kathleen with her print frock, silk scarf and decent coat clearly thought of herself as 'above' Marjorie and, though she enjoyed and fostered her friend's bawdy, squealed in merriment behind her hand like a naughty schoolgirl rather than guffawed hugely as Marjorie did, her whole torso shaking in time with her cackling hoots. Lindsay Anderson's pacing of the production was judged to a nicety, allowing time for characters and audience to register unspoken responses while not letting the overall tempo to go slack; in a play about the crucially hesitant development of a relationship that was no mean feat. His success lay in sustaining a disciplined ensemble, permitting neither the playing of the women to become crude caricature (one never lost touch with the pain in their lives — Kathleen's suicidal urges, Marjorie's various compulsions) nor their coarse humour to control to any significant degree the audience's view of Harry and Jack. It is rare that audiences and actors share such intensities of silence as one experienced with *Home*.

Early Days (Cottesloe, 1980)[18] seemed in performance almost designed as a study of the stage personality of Sir Ralph Richardson; the part of Sir Richard Kitchen suited him admirably: the boisterous fun that can mask a slily-timed thrust at an intellectual inferior; the volatile mind and the stylishly poised body; a zest for life acting as foil to a sensibility boldly reaching after intimations of another world, another time; a consciousness that can inhabit past, present and future with fearless vigour. *Early Days* observes an old man dying. There is none of the shame or the evasions that colour Jack's existence in *Home*; Kitchen as he claims himself is "a sport. I don't like keeping quiet about anything" [p. 32]. Sir Ralph always relished the part of likeable old reprobate. In the final scene Kitchen is sleeping in his daughter's garden, where he is found by his granddaughter and her fiancé; Gloria in hushed terms gives an account to Steven of Kitchen's public life, the facts such as doubtless will appear on his decease in a *Times* obituary:

Grandpa went out to work at twelve. He ran errands: he bought a shop. He went into politics when he was twenty-five. He joined the wrong party. At that time it believed in breeding. If he'd had a little he might have got on farther. He was the longest serving Minister of Health. Then he made a speech which was critical of his colleagues. He became a dark horse: people mentioned him when they thought of an alternative leader: he was on the ballot paper for the party-leadership two years after the war and came out third; when the time came to make his challenge he'd lost support. [p. 50]

Storey places this moment perfectly: it is exposition which is non-exposition, for there is nothing here of the man whose volatile temperament has fascinated us through the three previous scenes. Storey has no illusions about his character: Kitchen's behaviour can clearly be maddening to the rest of his family. His daughter and her husband barely tolerate his endless criticism of their marriage, his reiterated suppositions about his son-in-law's philandering and his pressing Mathilda to take a lover:

KITCHEN: Why do you let him abuse you?

MATHILDA: He doesn't abuse me.

KITCHEN: You're a woman of sensibility. Of taste. I have never seen a more sensitive child.

MATHILDA: You have a false image of him, Father. My life isn't bound up with Arthur's the way my mother's was with you.

KITCHEN: Promiscuity with him is like a disease: it hangs around him like the air he breathes. Scent, perfume, lotion. Cream. The man is like a fetish. What does he do with all these women?

MATHILDA: He came home especially to see you today.

KITCHEN: You believe he loves me like I love you.

MATHILDA: He does.

KITCHEN: You believe none of these things I say about him.

MATHILDA: It's not your concern.

KITCHEN: You've given him everything, Matt! How can you attract another man? Get rid of him. Men like that are ten a penny. They destroy everything around them, Matt! Believe me. I've seen it!

MATHILDA: I married him twenty-five years ago. I'm too old to start my life again. [p. 28]

Her refusal to answer his accusations ("You believe none of the things I say about him" — "It's not your concern") at first suggests deliberate evasion; but then Gloria, who shares her grandfather's willingness to speak out, challenges him with facts about his own past that cause us to revise this view. Kitchen's treatment of his own wife was, in Gloria's eyes, shoddy and his veneration now of her memory is so much sentimentality:

GLORIA: Your achievements, Grandpa, are a pile of dust. The one person who loved you you callously destroyed, by doing those very things you accuse my father of, with your obscene calls and grotesque abuse and your promenading of your genitals in the village street. You used her, Grandpa, but you won't use us.

KITCHEN: You'd better call that doctor back! I won't stand for abuse like that in my house.

GLORIA: It's not your house. It's my house. It's my mother's house. It's my father's house: it's where you live on sufferance! [p. 38]

No-one but Gloria can be bothered to dispute his comments on their lives; they have grown weary of him, and of his priapic exploits and lubricious imaginings. "Obstreperous" is Mathilda's word for him as of an unruly child, whom she must resign herself to tolerate. What a terrible end for a once-respected public figure: to be patronised by people waiting for him to die, who feel obliged to show signs of care out of duty and respect! Yet as Storey presents them, their tolerance reflects adversely on themselves, not on Kitchen. Wanting sympathy, they cannot see as Gloria can that the public figure has found an unexpected freedom in the privacy of age and retirement. When her father callously remarks that they ought to "shove" Kitchen in a straight-jacket, she is outraged: "He's lived in one all his life: he's only now got out of it" [p. 43]. Their lives seem meagre, peevish beside his; and how he despises their tones of respect! Gloria and the village doctor delight him because they are not afraid to speak their minds to him; they treat his dogmatism, his teasing, even his exhibitionism in a forthright manner and he relishes the challenge; his intelligence longs for stimulus, the thrill of debate, of witty repartee. Only Gloria, whom he entertained as a child with poems and fantasies, can understand Kitchen's exuberant imagination in its need for *play*:

KITCHEN: I devoted more time to you than I did to my daughter. And now, after all these years, she doesn't like me.
GLORIA: I like you a lot.
KITCHEN: How much?
GLORIA: A lot.
KITCHEN: You'd shoot me tomorrow if you got the chance.
GLORIA: I wouldn't.
KITCHEN: The day after.
GLORIA: Never.
KITCHEN: In my father's time they believed in God.
GLORIA: So what!
KITCHEN: Now all you believe in are ideals. As if anything has ever been changed by grasping at one faith instead of another.
GLORIA: "Don't like my music —
             Don't like my song:
             Don't run away —
             You may have it wrong!"
I remember you when I was young — all your little songs and ditties. Remember your last Party Conference, do you? (*Sings: 'Men of Harlech'.*)
             "Here am I!
             Alone and thwarted . . .
             Full of hope,
             And not down-hearted!"
(*They laugh.*)
You had a moustache. Quite fancied yourself. Telling Grandma how the world was made by special people. [pp. 34-35].

Spontaneity is what they enjoy in each others' company, witty shifts of subject, the unpredictable response, the lapse into memory and shared intimacies. Quality of mind is the true index of vitality in this play and for Kitchen the mind is a place of adventure, an enriching of experience by an imaginative living through possibilities, which Mathilda or Kitchen's companion, Bristol, can counter only with deadly platitudes.

KITCHEN: I walk around the house and I think, "The people here are mad. They go on as if they know what they're doing." They don't. No one does. Yet they go from A to B as if that were precisely what they intended.

BRISTOL: We all have a destiny to fulfil.

KITCHEN: I wonder. (*Pause.*) Can you smell the blossom? I've been somewhere else I can never recall — odd sounds, smells, odd incidents and encounters, occasionally bring back a fragment, like a headland glimpsed, or a peak of a mountain: is it a continent, I think, or only an island?

BRISTOL: I travelled far when I was younger. [pp. 12-13]

Irritated by the constant surveillance of his movements, Kitchen keeps his annoyance in perspective by turning the whole situation into an elaborate joke about Russian spies and the attraction of becoming notorious by defecting in old age to a *dacha* ("already furnished") within sound of peasants singing or the howls of wolves. To people with no sense of humour this is just further proof of Kitchen being wantonly tiresome, spinning a tissue of hurtful lies. Because Mathilda, Benson and Bristol cannot appreciate the lighter side of Kitchen's temperament, they cannot sense its darker reaches: the unsolved, riddling memories from his childhood that persistently take root in the psyche and intrude on his awareness when the conscious mind is relaxed; the deep-rooted guilts about his wife, Ellen, how he used her and was unfaithful, guilts which were too painful to discuss with her when she lived and which cannot now be placated. As death closes in on him, the mind becomes a prey to the uneasy heart.

KITCHEN: (*Light fades, strengthening around his figure*) I can't see you if you stand behind. I was telling Matt . . . So tall, I thought the bridge would fall. So high, the people on it looked like flies. (*Pause: looking up.*) All those strange faces gazing down . . . Ellen . . . (*Turns.*) Ellen! (*The light, which has accumulated around his figure, is suddenly extinguished.*) [p. 53]

It was a fitting end for that great spirit to suddenly close in on itself and cease; and the stage-image exactly mirrored one's sense of the illuminating intelligence in the man being extinguished on the instant. *Early Days* is a swan-song; Kitchen called on the full range of Richardson's genius and proved the richest of his final appearances at the National Theatre, because Storey gave him every opportunity to infuse the role with his own tremendous appetite for life.

David Storey has not been alone among Royal Court dramatists in exploring the possibilities of a poetic mode of naturalism. Peter Gill established himself primarily as a director at the theatre with a range of productions of Lawrence's plays which were remarkable for their attention to details of voice and movement in charting the ebb and flow of affection and antipathy through which Lawrence defines the quality of working class life amongst the Nottinghamshire mining community. A sensitivity to the way environment affects the play of emotions within a relationship is similarly a strength of Gill's work, though one that took time to come to fruition. The two plays Gill wrote in the 'Sixties, *The Sleepers Den* (Theatre Upstairs, 1969) and *Over Gardens Out* (Theatre Upstairs, 1968),[19] seem thin in retrospect beside the richness of texture in *Small Change* (Royal Court, 1976), yet its conception would scarcely have been possible without these earlier experiments in a more traditional style. Both plays explore the emotional poverty of lives lived in confined spaces where identity is worn relentlessly away by the drudgery of struggling to 'make do' financially and spiritually. The sheer effort to keep a home together for her mother, brother and daughter in *The Sleepers Den* debilitates Mrs. Shannon's will to survive, while the adolescents of *Over Gardens Out* endeavour to create a degree of imaginative excitement for themselves by indulging in childishly dare-devil antics and petty thieving yet cannot see any *point* in what they do: it is as much a routine as the round of jobs, household chores and churchgoing that make up their parents' existence. Gill excels at stirring an audience to care for bleak lives centred on a deep-rooted anguish which is the more searing for being beyond the reach of definition. The characters experience a profound sense of loss without ever to their satisfaction knowing why. Theirs are lives that at best can see but *small change* in their circumstances; yet they possess one's imagination in the theatre because of Gill's ability never to disparage the emotional intricacies that the characters are prey to. *Over Gardens Out* begins to anticipate the structural design of *Small Change* with its fragmented scenes that tell no precise story in the way of realism but capture isolated aspects of the youths' lives at home and at play. It is a kind of theatrical impressionism, juxtaposing seemingly random moments to stimulate in an audience an awareness of the theme. *Small Change* and this play are alike in the demands they make on the actors to be conscious of a theme that should be everywhere felt yet is nowhere precisely stated. *Over Gardens Out* is at its best in evoking the peculiarly tense affection that exists between a working-class mother and her son: she would like to indulge a tenderness he yearns for, yet both hold emotion back out of some vague sense of propriety and a fear they share of trespassing on his growing awareness of his masculinity; a continuing embarrassment is the one token of an emotional bond between them.

Small Change[20] is an altogether more complex play than its predecessors. The fragmentation is more marked and the inner intimated meanings of the play correspondingly richer. The characters are few: two mothers, two sons; the setting in performance was austere: four chairs upon a steeply raked stage that "appeared to be floating" for the play never defines precisely the dimension of time in which it exists.[21] By changing timbres of voice, by speed and flexibility of movement, the sons were now children, now adolescents, now grown men; the mothers youngish, middle-aged, one at times elderly. The play could be imagined as taking place in one son, Gerard's mind as he is returning by train to his Cardiff background when a confused tangle of memories surfaces in his consciousness, the speed of the train lulling him out of time present to a past where the mind glides effortlessly to and fro over the years as the pattern of associations calls forth now this incident, now that:

GERARD: On we zip, the ghost train through other stations and halts. Then the red starts. Dark, dark red. The berries are huge, there was no frost in the spring. Birds are the only wildlife in this countryside. One magpie. Two for joy. So much red it seems like an obsession, so, observe. It's not an obsession. Obsessive about what is there. So many berries and bushes, the greens and reds mixing, each losing its intensity, defocused, mixed so to speak, defocused, confused by their intensity and this speed. Thick with berries like ampoules of oil. The reddening reminds me of harsh winter afternoons with willows reddening in the spring. Red September. Hydrangeas soaked in red. Some trees starting to gleam, glowing, passing, fail and then glow. Single trees like these are creating aureoles in woods. Llanwern turning red with dust. Miles of blue laminated boxes under red dust. The green between the two towns has hedges, they're red. Red pullovers on lovers with a dog, one red arm round another red shoulder. The reens are covered still in their slime, like knitted green silk. Pulling in, past the old town, the Dowlais, the old works is chalked in red madder on a blue ground. Hiding in smoke but not lost to view. [pp. 40-41]

Rarely does memory touch on a momentous event, except for the suicide of Gerard's neighbour, Mrs. Driscoll, and that because it seems to call into being all the emotional confusion and guilt of this particular childhood. What *Small Change* examines is how the compromises the women make with their circumstances affect, often quite unintentionally, the experience of their sons. Always there is warmth but also a fear of emotion, as if it is a luxury out of place in such a grey world. The women hate their life, and the constant struggle it imposes simply to be decent; "It's all a mess, wherever you look. You finish something. You turn around and nothing's been done. And you notice everything. I get up. I think another day" [p. 8]. This lowering of their morale activates an antipathy to the husbands that keep them so subject to toil, and yet as wives they are not unloving: "I don't care about the kids, that's the God's truth and I can't help it, I can't. I've only got any feeling for him, isn't it awful, only him" [p. 9]. Such awkward impoverished confessions together bring some comfort in sympathy for the women; but such intimacies, overheard yet not adequately understood, disturb the sons, fuel in them a drive to get away, to be different, which is not possible for them without severing bonds with their parents that will ever after leave them with a crippling sense of guilt. The boys' childish bids for freedom and later the young men's growing independence call up a black despair in the two women who have endlessly wrestled with that same longing to get away but have willed it to rest silent in them:

MRS. HARTE: You're drifting away from me. I feel a dead failure . . . I
    wish I could come up when you're ill like that. Are you feeling better?
GERARD: Much.
MRS. HARTE: If anything happened to you, I'd lose my mind. When you
    ran away I was so frightened.
GERARD: What do you mean, ran away? I never ran away.
MRS. HARTE: You just slammed out of the house. Now I think you've
    run away for good, haven't you?
GERARD: I'm here, aren't I?
MRS. HARTE: But you're drifting away from me.
GERARD: I can't stay here. I hate it.
MRS. HARTE: Not as much as me. I can tell you.
GERARD: Come back with me.
MRS. HARTE: I wouldn't fit in up there.
GERARD: Come back with me. I'll find a place.
MRS. HARTE: I'd love it, but it's not to be.
GERARD: Why?
MRS. HARTE: Don't ask me, son. That's how it is. I wish I could cry like
    that.

GERARD: Silly, isn't it.
MRS. HARTE: Yes.
GERARD: Come with me please. Oh please. Let's run away together. You
    and me. For Christ's sake don't cry, Mam, it will kill me.
MRS. HARTE: I don't cry.
GERARD: Oh Jesus, you're crying.
MRS. HARTE: I'm not crying.
GERARD: I am.
MRS. HARTE: I'm not.
GERARD: Nor am I, now.
MRS. HARTE: I never cry.
GERARD: I don't much. Never.
MRS. HARTE: You always used to cry.
GERARD: You don't cry.
MRS. HARTE: No. Leave that to everyone else. I'm sorry I couldn't come
    up to see you. But you must know me by now. Too much of a coward.
GERARD: I didn't expect it.
MRS. HARTE: What do you mean?
GERARD: That I didn't expect you to come up.
MRS. HARTE: What's that supposed to mean?
GERARD: What I said.
MRS. HARTE: You can be cruel sometimes.
GERARD: Can I?
MRS. HARTE: When you going back?
GERARD: I don't know.
MRS. HARTE: I expect I'll see you sooner than I think I will. [pp. 28-29]

For Mrs. Driscoll the struggle ends in suicide:

MRS. HARTE: She wasn't a great deal younger than me . . . silly girl. Oh
    she was a nice girl. A really nice girl. She didn't look any different,
    except for the burns on the side of her mouth. [p. 33]

Only the scenes of the boys' companionship evoke a *pure*
emotional tone, a freedom from stress, as they go swimming by the
docks or scramble the cliffs for birds' eggs; even playing truant or
staying out past bedtime has no sense of threat:

VINCENT: Swimming in the dock, light seeps through the heavy
    suspension of oil in the water. Head breaks through the water. Never
    thought one would get there. Out on to a raft. Cormorants. Or climb
    the cranes. Pick up little baby pigeons. [p. 55]

In such matters their parents may scold for form's sake but are at
heart generously disposed. Both men grow up to be emotionally
reticent and the contrasting memory of the ease and intimacy of
their boyhood despite the prevailing social conditions leaves them
perplexed in retrospect as to the significance of their one-time

freedom with each other. Meeting in middle age both Gerard and Vincent feel betrayed. Jokes, a drink together, sharing memories cannot keep long suppressed a vein of resentment:

VINCENT: Oh come for a drink, Ger?
GERARD: No.
VINCENT: Come on.
GERARD: I said no.
VINCENT: You did for me, you know.
MRS. DRISCOLL: Vincent.
GERARD: What?
VINCENT: You did, you know.
GERARD: I did for you?
MRS. DRISCOLL: Vincent.
GERARD: *I. I* did for you? *I* did?
MRS. HARTE: Gerard.
GERARD: *I* did for you?
MRS. HARTE: Gerard.
GERARD: *I* did?
MRS. HARTE: Gerard.
VINCENT: You did, you. know. [p. 45]

The whole play is a rendering of Gerard's growing insight that the worst of pains is living in the past when you cannot "feel safe in its hurt" [p. 50]. Vincent tries to scoff at this: "You've got a war-memorial mentality" [p. 52]; but his every action shows its truth. Both men experience an urge to avenge but can neither specify the crime against them nor name the offender. Neither man can engage actively with the present. The rapid time shifts and the juxtaposing of childhood and adult experiences neatly depict how with both Gerard and Vincent the child is father to the man: the life of the emotions is increasingly for them a confusion, which Vincent refuses to acknowledge and which the shrewder Gerard acknowledges but cannot analyse. Repeatedly the rhythm and speech patterns of youth are echoed in the conversational exchanges of adulthood: the episode where Gerard and Mrs. Harte toy with the sentimental idyll of escaping to a new life together while admitting it is too late to attempt to change anything has its counterpart in a sequence when the boys tired and sulky at the end of a day's play, argue in endless circles since neither wants to be the first to break their mood of shared pleasure and go home:

GERARD: Where you going?
VINCENT: I got to go in.
GERARD: Oh.
VINCENT: Where YOU going?

GERARD: I got to go in.

VINCENT: Well, what's the matter with you then? Eh? Mmmm?

GERARD: I'm going in then. OK. OK?

VINCENT: Alright then, go in.

GERARD: You going in?

VINCENT: Yeah.

GERARD: I got to have my tea.

VINCENT: Alright then.

GERARD: Call for us later then.

VINCENT: OK.

GERARD: Don't forget. Vincent. Vincent!

VINCENT: I won't forget. Go on. I'll see you later.

GERARD: Where you going? I thought you was going in?

VINCENT: I got to do my paper round first.

GERARD: You've done your paper round.

VINCENT: I haven't. I didn't do it.

GERARD: Do you want me to come with you then?

VINCENT: No. I'm not doing it.

GERARD: Why not?

VINCENT: I don't feel like it. All right? Anyway, I'm packing it in.

GERARD: Where you going then?

VINCENT: I don't know. I thought you had to go in. Go on. I'll see you later.

GERARD: No you won't.

VINCENT: Alright then. What's the matter with you? Eh? Mmm? All right then.

GERARD: Nothing's the matter with me.

VINCENT: Well then, go in then.

GERARD: I am going in.

VINCENT: I'm going in an' all.

GERARD: Don't go in.

VINCENT: I got to.

GERARD: And me.

VINCENT: I'll see you later.

GERARD: Aye. Don't forget. [pp. 11-12]

Banal though the speeches may be, the structure of the play creates for them a context through which they develop both pathos and irony: the men will hark back to such moments with a sentimentality that will incapitate them from coping with adult responsibilities. The very stage image of grown men playing children's parts — even though quite unselfconsciously done by James Hazeldine and Philip Joseph and devoid of caricature — was a disturbing one; however fresh and innocent their voices, that image intimated the psychological damage in store.

Perhaps it is here that one can draw a distinction between Gill's work and Storey's. Gill's is a bleaker vision: his characters never break free into moments of wonder, of unsullied joy in just being alive as Storey's can; never for Gerard or Vincent, as for Harry and Jack in *Home*, is there even the frail chance of creating a more satisfying environment. Time circumscribes all experience in Gill's vision with the sense of loss and brings no sustaining compensations: memory is hurtful in both senses and the future wholly grim — "I'll just go on living till I wear away". The two mothers are once seen recalling their youth, whistling and dancing together: "Come on" — "What?" — "Up you get" — "I can't lead" — "Nor can I. Hang on. Here we are . . . my Christ when did you last have a dance?" — "Don't ask me" [pp. 39-40]; but the scene is shot through with poignancy for the audience who have witnessed Mrs. Driscoll's suicide staged earlier and know that such a moment of carefree abandon cannot halt the despair that is sapping her will to live. Throughout *Small Change* in this way the structure sustains the elegaic mood; one is conscious always of the deliberate shaping and ordering of events. While there is a degree of idiomatic freedom within any individual scenic fragment, there is none of the seeming spontaneity in the dialogue that Storey can achieve by relating speech rhythms to the processes of work as in *The Contractor*.[22] The poetic dimension in *Small Change* is consciously worked for; it is there in the very conception and structuring of the play, whereas in Storey's best plays it is a dimension achieved only in performance. Within the terms of their chosen style both dramatists work their method through to the finest details. It is characteristic of how attuned his style is to his vision that even in Storey's darkest plays, *Cromwell* and *Early Days*, the final words are in the one a question ("And beyond the darkness" — "Do you see the light?") and in the other a challenging call from a dying man reaching after a metaphysical apprehension ("Ellen!"). Each instance offers us a resilient mind ever open to new possibilities of experience. Equally apt for Gill's manner and vision is the way in which the syntax of Gerard's last speech precisely renders the entangling labyrinths of his psyche:

GERARD: Try but can't. Won't but can. Will but can't. Shall but don't. [p. 56]

CHAPTER FIVE

POLITICAL DRAMA AND DAVID HARE

Political drama over the last two decades, as John Bull has admirably demonstrated,[1] has become a major constituent of the repertoires of our subsidised theatres, has even at times (*Teeth n' Smiles, Comedians, Accidental Death of an Anarchist*) sustained good runs in the West End. There are many reasons for this. Politically: the complex range of responses by the intelligentsia to the events of 1968, to the American demise in Vietnam and to Watergate; numerous public scandals exposing the potential for corruption in local and national government; the soul-baring at all levels of society that has accompanied the failure of socialism to be the governing party since 1979 or to achieve a united philosophy and intent amongst its ranks. Theatrically: the increasing influence of the oft-misunderstood but always potent Brecht on the quality of much dramatic writing and on production-methods and style; the movement into the theatre at large of a considerable number of actors, designers, directors, writers trained initially at the Royal Court under the aegis of George Devine; the impact of American and Continental concepts of 'fringe' theatre. But that is still not to account for the sheer wealth of political theatre available, the energy, the excitement to experiment which Catherine Itzin has recorded in meticulous detail,[2] where just to be different, to break away from the established norms of theatrical expression, was a political gesture. There has been a massive reassertion of the Aristophanic spirit, a healthy scepticism, after the departure of the Lord Chamberlain as censor, that refuses to see the figures of public life as beyond criticism. The theatre as cartoon rather than as art has learned to match mordant analysis with inventive exuberance, believing passionately in the effectiveness of a "short, sharp shock"[3] to the mind, the emotions, the imagination. Howard Barker's *No End of Blame,*[4] which looks at the events which shape the mind of a cartoonist, expresses this passion for a moment's experience of a searing truth explicitly: "I don't want to be a painter. I hate oils, studios, manipulating colours inches thick. Give me ink, which dries quick, speaks quick, hurts" [p. 11]. But Barker's cartoonist,

Bela, is a brilliant artist and draughtsman trained in the discipline, who chooses to direct that discipline to ends different from traditional modes of expression. Enthusiasm, commitment, imaginative daring are not enough without discipline, as a deal of fringe theatrical activity has shown. The better groups over the period (Pip Simmons, Joint Stock) have enlightened and inspired because of the rigour of their performance-technique and the kinds of rehearsal methods that have gone to the shaping of their productions. The short, sharp shock is most effectively delivered by the skilled practitioner.

The attack on 'art' by much political drama in the period is worth considering further. Bela in Barker's play justifies his choice as follows: "The cartoon is a weapon in the struggle of peoples. It is a liberating instrument. It is brief like life. It is not about me. It is about us. Important art is about us. Great art is about me. . . . The cartoon has only one meaning. When the cartoon lies it shows at once. When the painting lies it can deceive for centuries. The cartoon is celebrated in a million homes. The painting is worshipped in a gallery" [p. 32]. The concept of culture was undergoing severe attack during the Sixties by influential thinkers like George Steiner, who brought to the study of aesthetics a formidable knowledge of philosophy and psychology to question what value culture had if it could not halt a Belsen or a Hiroshima; in China there was the more startling example of the Red Guards' revolution. Anti-art and anti-theatre had a passing vogue; more challengingly, the Royal Shakespeare Company began to examine Renaissance dramatists and the traditional repertoire by the light of twentieth-century theories of theatrical practice — Artaud, Brecht, Kott — to test whether Shakespeare was indeed our contemporary. The need for immediacy and relevance ensured that much new writing in the Seventies deliberately avoided traditional dramatic structures, except perhaps as a vehicle for satire or deconstruction. In practice this generally made for plays shaped out of a heterogeneous mixture of styles: the shock-element often lying in the sudden disjunctions; anything was possible, though too rag-bag a mix could carry an audience beyond surprise till they relaxed into appreciating the medium for itself rather than being informed by the message. Medium risked becoming massage, which was the Fringe's prime criticism of Broadway and the West End. There was a limit to the number of ways you could offend an audience *creatively*. And there came a time when to describe a character as listening to Mahler or reading Henry James became too slack a way of implying that he was a villain. To see culture as necessarily synonymous with Establishment values was a simplistic stance. From a creative angle, the healthy side of this whole argument lay in the distrust of traditional forms and the ensuing urge find new ones.

As political drama has moved steadily from the Fringe into the subsidised theatres, it has been interesting to watch how this debate about style and its relation to a writer's political belief and motives has affected the quality of the plays conceived for these larger venues. Hare and Griffiths have made a wealth of styles and the strategy of disjunction serve an organising creative principle and so have found a necessary discipline; others, especially Brenton and Barker, have tended to make unhappy compromises so that the sum is often less satisfying than the parts. The problem is fundamentally a matter of balance as opposed to emphasis, finding a right relation between character and political context. Cartoon-style theatre has of necessity to simplify, to stylise its characterisations in order to depict lucidly the complexities of situation. Social realism as exemplified by an earlier generation of Royal Court dramatists focusses on the way political change affects individual psychologies. Brecht had found a way of balance in his epic theatre. Were there ways of following his example other than by direct imitation? Hare and Griffiths have consistently found ways of effecting the balance through a controlled flexibility of styles. Many of their contemporaries by contrast lack a certain rigour which might discipline what seems at times an almost prodigal inventiveness.

Howard Barker, for example, has a bravura way with words and a baroque extravagance with plot that generate an undeniable energy and excitement in performance, but one is often left wondering where all the 'go' is going to. Language and situation seem to develop a life of their own that is governed by a pattern of associations and a demand for theatrical spectacle as much as by intellectual design; characterisation as a consequence is fitful and arbitrary. With plays like *Crimes in Hot Countries* (Pit, 1985)[5] and *The Castle* (Pit, 1985),[6] we seem in the presence of an intricate parable with few keys to its application. *No End Of Blame* (Oxford Playhouse and The Royal Court, 1981) is an exception because it works within the form of the biographical play and because it addresses itself to the very problem under discussion: the relation between an artist and the political changes he moves through, the degree to which he can safely distance himself from his times to criticise them the better. The whole play is about the dilemma of balance between subjectivity and objectivity in the satirical artist searching for the humility out of which one has the right to apportion blame.

Stephen Poliakoff also has a rare verbal gift for capturing the wasteland of the imagination of so much popular culture: the frenetic verbosity of the disc-jockey (*City Sugar*),[7] violence in films (*Strawberry Fields*),[8] the fashionable cults they foster and the cheap myths. He is sensitive too to how being confined within such mediocrity can generate a black, self-destructive hate in individuals. *Shout Across The River* (Warehouse, 1978)[9] presents such a girl first at her school's evaluation of her and then as she is in herself. By her teachers she is crudely labelled potential material for a remand home; but Christine in herself, and as her mother comes to know her, is consumed with a genuine disgust at the squalor that is being offered her in return for the privilege of living. This is akin to Hare's subject in *Teeth n' Smiles* and *Plenty*, but Hare actualises on stage far more than Poliakoff succeeds in doing the social contexts that have nurtured the hate. The all-important factor in Christine's experience, her school, is represented by two brief encounters with one of her teachers, Mr. Lawson; and we are virtually asked to take on trust Christine's view of it and its obsession with discipline at the expense of real education. Poliakoff's focus is almost exclusively on how Christine lives with her hate, rather than with how a hate came into being which wholly distinguishes her from her peers. Why has Christine chosen to live her life and destroy it as a criticism of the times? It is because Poliakoff goes only some way towards answering the question that, beside Hare's works, his play seems thin. Much the same criticism can be levelled at *Strawberry Fields* (Cottesloe, 1977). Through its opposition of the bleak horror of a motorway landscape and an idyllic rural haven in the Border Country, Poliakoff actualises the nostalgia and fears of some seemingly ordinary middle-class souls; but he gives us no social dimension which might explain why these emotions push the characters towards joining the National Front and the condoning and practice of violence. The effect in performance was less that of a serious, political debate than a bizarre nightmare. Poliakoff seems to have ambitions for making epic statements about the condition of contemporary England, but he seeks to do this within plays whose structures are on too limited a scale, being over-concerned with character at the expense of political context. Again as with Barker the balance is not finely tuned.

David Edgar's work poses a related but more intricate problem. Immensely prolific, from the first Edgar showed himself capable of summarizing studiously researched political situations in trenchant dramatic statements. Something of a change came over his work after the success of *Mary Barnes* (Royal Court, 1978)[10] which investigates alternative modes of psychiatry in respect of their treatment of schizophrenia as less a form of mental than of social disturbance. Since then his ambition has been to write large-scale social histories that resist the temptation to reduce characters to convenient caricatures. (It is significant in this respect that Trevor Nunn invited Edgar to dramatise Dickens's *Nicholas Nickleby* for the Royal Shakespeare Company.) *Destiny* (Other Place and Aldwych, 1976/7)[11] explores the rise in popularity of the National Front as a consequence of the disintegration of the British Empire; *Maydays* (Barbican, 1983)[12] looks at the history of socialism in England since the War and a recurring pattern of commitment, disillusion and reaction amongst the intelligentsia. Broad canvases, both; but Edgar scrupulously shows the connections between public issues and changing private allegiances. Political movements are defined in terms of individual awareness and consequent choices of action. The panoramic scale is impressive but the concern with individuals is confined very much to social facts and intellectual positions; the overall impression is of a style of documentary. There is not the sense as with Hare's *Plenty* or Griffiths' *Comedians* and *The Party* that political positions are a product of the whole self, affecting every level of one's being and informing every sphere of one's actions. *Plenty* searches deeply into one woman's mind through a span of thirty years in Britain's political decline; *The Party* looks at how the Paris Occupations of 1968 cause a group of British socialists to assess their lives, weighing that present against their past and their likely futures. Edgar by comparison seems almost too ambitious: in each of his plays he takes several characters to give complexity to his analysis — Turner, Rolfe, Clifton in *Destiny*; Crowther, Glass, Grain, Amanda in *Maydays* — whose lives are only briefly and randomly connected. There is a degree of psychological verisimilitude but it is inevitably limited. Edgar's characters are acceptable as types, carefully imagined projections of certain political stances; their attitudes are what fascinate Edgar, rather than the minds that shape those attitudes. Fundamentally Edgar is a historian of political ideas.

Of his generation Howard Brenton is the one who has remained truest to the tenets of the Fringe with its suspicion of the unified work of art and its preference for a technique of dislocations and a will to shock and provoke. His earliest works have a tough, cynical style coupled with a powerful visual imagination that delights in exploiting unusual playing spaces — a chapel, an ice-rink. His aim seems always to make an audience re-think its settled judgements, to go on asking questions instead of being content with answers. *Christie in Love*, (Ovalhouse and Theatre Upstairs, 1969–70),[13] for example, asks us to contemplate murder from a range of perspectives: as an obscenity, an incarnation of evil or as a rite of exorcism, a ritual of revenge by a man terrified of the power of women. The play offers possibilities, not a solution; challenges not confirms. There is, though, an unevenness about the early work: the tight, angry dialogue — best exemplified by *Magnificence* (Royal Court, 1973)[14] — often works at variance with Brenton's other strength, his invention of explosive, almost baroque visual effects. He spoke at this time of his excitement at working with the whole "arsenal of styles";[15] but behind the obvious relish one detects a concern to find a distinctively personal voice and dramatic idiom.

The turning point came with his collaboration on *Brassneck* (Nottingham Playhouse, 1973)[16] with David Hare: one episode seemed to point a way forward for Brenton. The play is about local government from the post-war years to the Seventies, showing how the Bagley family through three generations move from the doss-house to wealth by the clever manipulation of the law and by fostering rivalries, which their position as outsiders allows them to do, in the Tory old-boy network that formerly controlled the centres of power. By such an opportunist trick Bagley Senior is elected Grand Master of the local Masonic Lodge; instantly *"the stage bursts into colour. The Vatican. A huge altar and golden angels"*; a cardinal intones exultantly in Latin: "Habemus pontificem! A great new Holy Father!" A second cardinal appears demanding to know who has been elected; the first replies "Alonso de Borja". At once: *"huge whispers all over the theatre, 'BORJA, BORJA, BORJA', which rise and then explode into music. A huge organ burst. Narrow light on Alfred Bagley dressed as Callistus III, sitting on an enormous throne in a cloud of incense, his hand resting on a small white HERMAPHRODITE"* [p. 34]. A graphic political point is made through a powerful theatrical image as the style shifts briefly from realism to expressionistic effect; the visual metaphor calls historical resonances into play that amplify one's sense of the meaning of the title, *Brassneck* — a Midlands idiomatic term meaning cool, calculating, criminal. The past illuminates the present, while the present offers a perspective through which to re-evaluate history; either way works as denigration, a cutting down of pretentiousness to size. Here Brenton found a method for achieving an epic style that would not rob his anger of its energy. The best of his subsequent works — *The Churchill Play, Weapons of Happiness, The Romans in Britain* — play startling games with time, juxtaposing images of past, present and future to eerie effect so that the juxtapositions in large measure carry the meaning of the play.

Consider *The Churchill Play* (Nottingham Playhouse, 1974).[17] It opens apparently with Churchill's lying-in-state. It is night and a group of servicemen guard the catafalque; they relax, smoke, but are suddenly terrified by a knocking from within the coffin; the lid slides away and the Churchill of the War years climbs out giving his characteristic Victory salute. A voice from the darkness calls for lights which reveal what we have been watching to be a play-within-the-play. A new situation is established: we are in a future age that has realised Orwell's vision in *Nineteen Eighty-Four*; the place is a concentration camp where political dissidents are interned; the prisoners are rehearsing to entertain a party of visitors. Brenton sets the bleak world of a possible tomorrow against a cartoon-style life of Churchill in the agit-prop manner, the larger context questioning the Churchillian rhetoric about fighting for a brave new world. The promise is juxtaposed against a possible fulfilment, the hope against a reality that exposes the common man as the dupe of political propaganda, the constant loser-out, used and betrayed by figures of authority. The juxtapositions define the prisoners' despair and mounting anger that compels them to make a (disastrous) bid for freedom. Meaning in *The Churchill Play* is conveyed largely through dramatic structure rather than through dialogue or discussion: the technique of dislocations working through an audience's senses directly on to their imaginations. The method is powerful as theatre art but has its limitations: the want of debate makes it easy for an unsympathetic viewer to reject Brenton's basic premise.

What Brenton has done is create here a new style of Dream Play but one more specifically rooted in political feeling than Strindberg's prototype. Crucially it is political *feeling* rather than political thought. *Weapons of Happiness* (Lyttleton, 1976)[18] by developing the form makes this distinction clear. The basic situation is contemporary, a strike in a crisp factory which has been taken over by the work force. One of their number, Josef Frank, is a Czech dissident, publicly humiliated by the Russians and, since the Fifties, an *emigré*; he seeks anonymity through fear of reprisal were his whereabouts to become known. He is a man who by choice has no identity, no place, no class — a total outsider who possesses nothing but his memories of past hopes to create a Communist paradise in his native land and of his betrayal by the Russians, who made him a pawn in their power games. Flashback scenes show the constant friction between his intellectual communism and the actuality of communist politics: his very idealism made him useful to Stalin for a time while it served Russia's purpose but soon it made him a threat to be eradicated when his hopes caused him to be critical of Russian failure and injustice. The real Josef Frank was hanged in 1952, but in this Dream Play his presence allows Brenton to juxtapose the nightmare realities of Russian socialism against the kids' play that is so much socialist activity in Britain. Frank's mind-life into which we are continually projected out of the present is a condemnation of the intellectual triviality of the factory progressives, who have no knowledge, no insight, only attitudes and poses:

First book I read 'bout Communism was called *The Evil That Was Lenin*. Think it was meant to put me off. 'Stead it put me on. . . . And I read and read. Shiny books you get from Moscow. And plastic covers, red, from Peking you know? All printed faint. Couldn't understand a word. But I believed in it. . . . I knew it was right! . . . Then I got in with this crowd. Big flashy flats. Lots a cushions and booze. That's how I met Trotsky. . . . I was their pet, in a way. Real, wan't I. The real stuff. Proletarian. Na, they were all right I s'pose. Kept on wanting a poke me rigid though, some of 'em. So I gave that lot up. And I gave school up. Wanted me to do 'A' levels. (*She laughs.*) One teacher, woman, Mrs. Banks . . . You know thirty and raddled with groovy afro hair . . . Said I'd got a go a University. Said if I didn't I'd ruin myself. (*She laughs.*) I mean, I may as well a been a hundred. And I left. [pp. 34-5].

To counter this gaucheness in Janice which Frank considers irredeemably juvenile, he tells her a story, simple in expression but full of the complexities of experience:

There was a violinist. A Jew. At the time of Hitler he hid his race. One day he had to play, it was Beethoven's Violin Concerto, at a concert with Hitler present. At the entrance of the violin, after the orchestral introduction, the violinist found he could not play. In the awful silence he left the platform. After the war, after surviving the camps and many sufferings, he lived obscurely in retirement. It was the violinist's birthday when a friend gave him a gramophone and a record. It was Beethoven's Violin Concerto. The violinist put it on the gramophone. The orchestra played the introduction. The moment for the violin to play came . . . And went. No violin. It was a practice record. The music continued, a mockery. The violinist looked at his hands and killed himself. [p. 36].

There is powerful characterization through contrasting idioms here; but it is the overall stagecraft, the pattern of structural dislocations, that gives the exchange its metaphorical and political weight. Again it is the dramatic structure that actualises for us the suffering of Frank as he lives with futility after having nurtured such profound ideals. *Weapons of Happiness* affords intense, moving analysis through its pattern of contrasts, but it rests very much at the level of feeling; Brenton lacks the sharp, intellectual scruple of Hare or Griffiths and cannot extend the awareness he induces in his audience into debate. A consequence of this is an inability to end the play satisfactorily; the contrasts are, as presented, not resolvable. Frank dies; Janice and her friends establish a new life in the country and she finds she is carrying Frank's child. After the hard, satirical mood of the rest of the play, this Arcadian idyll seems hopelessly sentimental, the more so in that Frank's dying memory is of Stalin laughing hugely and dismissing him with the derisive thrust — "Incurable romantic" [p. 75].

The same difficulty over a conclusion affects *The Romans in Britain* (Olivier, 1980).[19] It is a play about invasion, conquest, Empire, that examines the British military presence in Northern Ireland from a panoramic perspective of the country's history from the time of Caesar's defeat of the Celts onwards. Again there are some startling dislocations: at the conclusion of Act One the Romans, having departed, suddenly return to the harassed Celts dressed now in modern Army uniforms to the sound of machine-gun fire and hovering helicopters. The second act actualises on stage the reverie of a British Intelligence agent as he waits to meet and assassinate an I.R.A. leader; his mind moves in and out of history from the Irish field in the present to the fields of his family farm near Colchester fought over and possessed by Roman, Saxon, Dane. What seems a quiet harvested landscape is discovered to be an object of ravening greed. The dream activates a crisis of conscience in the agent who, waking to find his 'enemies' watching him, tries to share his recent vision. The Irish jeer at this "honourable man having a hard time of it. The assassin humanised by his trade" [p. 98]. Asking "what nation ever learnt from the sufferings it inflicted on others?" [p. 98], they shoot him. The play savagely denies a humanistic reading of history yet its structure of bold juxtapositions offers no more discriminating a judgement. The patterning of the scenes is analogous with the flow of images and ideas through the agent's mind. Given the violence of the ending, the play could as a consequence be seen as a statement of profound nihilism. The limitation of the play's form is that it stimulates premises that have the potential for debate but resists the intellectual challenge. Brenton's plays are consistently ambitious but never daring enough, wanting the rigour to explore the consequences of his finely imagined conceits.[20] Brenton's most completely satisfying plays to date remain his collaborations with David Hare, *Brassneck* and *Pravda* (Olivier, 1985),[21] where his anger and moral outrage sustain a powerful satirical vision and a structure that aims frankly at demonstration rather than debate. There are some characteristic startling juxtapositions of scenes in *Pravda*: the action moves in the opening sequences from the offices of a seedy provincial newspaper to a sports stadium full of athletes in training then back to a London Club; but it is, we discover, of the essence of the tycoon, Lambert Le Roux's mind that he creates power by forging relevances between what seem incompatibles. If he sees a need to make connections then he will make them: what he *wills*, is. That he abuses language and morality in the process never impinges on his conscience:

Childhood, boyhood, manhood. These are special things in South Africa. The hardening of muscle, the sprouting of hair. The coming realisation you are born into a divided culture. Ski-ing, riding, scuba-diving, flying your private plane, you feel all around you — and below you — the tragedy of the condition from which you cannot escape.

No one has tried harder than I through my organisations to untie the knots of the cultural contradictions — black, white — rich, poor — us, them — but people who come from Europe bearing simplistic solutions ignore the grandeur, the scale of what we have inherited from Mother Nature herself.

What I do is a natural thing. There is nothing unnatural about making money. When you are born where I was born, you do have a feeling for nature. [pp. 29-30]

There is real evil here, but the man's undeviating sense of purpose has its fascination. Brenton and Hare do not undervalue their modern, financier-Satan; and his enemies are powerless against him, for, as he knows, they do not possess his energy because they do not know what they want in life. All that motivates them is envy and spleen. One of the most bizarre scenes shows Le Roux at home with his wife practising a Japanese discipline of self-defence: he is lean, svelte, potent, a coiled spring at a pitch of tension to be released in whatever direction his will chooses — a comic image at first in his efforts to assume a Japanese manner and mincing gait, but the physical prowess is soon seen to be lethal, superlatively controlled and directed. The triumphant dynamism of the man in Anthony Hopkins's performance repels even as it enthralls. Structure and meaning are beautifully judged and integrated here. The authors insist with *Pravda* as with *Brassneck* that every detail was a collaborative effort. Comparing these with the plays Brenton has written on his own, one cannot but wonder whether the greater clarity of line here is not the work or at least the influence of David Hare. It argues a creative discipline more typical of his plays than of Brenton's.

*   *   *

David Hare's early plays like *Slag* (Hampstead Theatre Club, 1970) and *The Great Exhibition* (Hampstead, 1972) are almost too brilliant, too exuberantly disposed to wit and satirical plotting. There is considerable theatrical brio in the way he exposes how much that passes for socialist fervour amongst moneyed intellectuals is really radical chic, progressive only as far as current fashions allow. The characters of both plays are looking for alternative lifestyles, more 'real' than the ones they have inherited by their upbringing; but none of them has the courage or the imagination necessary to be genuinely original; articulate they may be on the subject of their difference but they are the dupes of their own rhetoric, ridiculously blind to the degree to which their efforts at revolutionary behaviour are only parodies of the way of life that has conditioned them. Their political stances are poses they justify with intensity, but which they readily change when circumstances dictate. Both plays in performance at the Hampstead Theatre Club had an impromptu, free-wheeling quality like charades; but here lay the snag. Hare's technique is to resort to increasingly bizarre situations to portray how zany his characters are in believing that their solipsism is a fulfilling engagement with reality and this risks diffusing the satirical passion that motivates the plays. It becomes too easy as the plays retreat into fantasy for an audience to dismiss the whole experience as elegant whimsy. The comic method (admittedly very funny) stifles the poignant urgency of the writer's vision.

If *Knuckle* (Oxford Playhouse and the Comedy Theatre, 1974)[22] is a better play, it is because Hare keeps in it a much tighter grasp on his dramatic method. He chooses a dry, taut style of dialogue rather than baroque histrionics to convey the spiritual shoddiness of his characters; though his theme is similar to ones pursued in earlier plays — a would-be rebel's discovery of the moral worth of his background for which he feels an instinctive repulsion but which insidiously compels him to conform to its standards — it is presented now as a mental process which shapes the action of the play; the state of mind is not here an achieved one merely requiring illustration but an enquiring and dynamic one; as a result the hero, Curly's final decision to acquiesce and conform, despite his knowledge of the moral failure and spiritual complacency that that decision will entail, brings the play to a dramatic climax that endorses rather than impairs Hare's satirical vision. Whatever critical attitude we were being invited to take to the characters of *Slag* and *The Great Exhibition*, the sheer energy of the dialogue invested them with a certain glamour, but there is nothing romantic about Curly, however earnestly he champions the cause of truth. He sets himself up as a detective investigating his father's world of City brokers and merchant bankers and learns of the pettiness, corruption and naked greed that lurk beneath the urbanity of such men; but an element of parody that Hare sustains throughout the play puts the audience on their guard against Curly himself, who is cast not in the mould of one of the healthy, assured truth-tellers of Ibsen and Shaw, but in the guise of the aggressive sleuths that people Spillane-style thrillers. Curly may have intelligence but he has little imagination or sensitivity, as is evident from his brutal, staccato methods of questioning others. His motives, he claims, are altruistic; yet one senses that there is a more primal, Oedipal need to humiliate his father, Patrick, judging by the viciousness with which he talks of his father in his absence. When they are alone together Curly instantly loses his sharp cunning and his hold on his cool persona, Patrick's suaveness making Curly's every remark sound utterly crude. When Curly has all the evidence to prove his father's malpractice, Patrick remains wholly unperturbed:

> You wanted me to say I was degraded. Well—
> > (*Pause*)
> I am.
> > (*Pause*)
> O.K.? So now can I please go back to work? [p. 100]

Patrick stays calm because he has long since ceased to be troubled by conscience; his confidence comes from the knowledge that it would be pointless ever to force him to resign on *moral* grounds since his place would be filled by his like immediately. If his demise will have a cautionary value, it will be simply in warning his colleagues of the need to be more careful in future. In an age of cynicism, Patrick argues, the predator is triumphant; Curly may make a spectacle of him but he doubts whether that will effect any change socially, whatever the private satisfactions to Curly himself; and if that is to be the only outcome, can Curly be said to be waging a *moral* crusade? Patrick completely undermines Curly's stance by showing how ill he fits his chosen role, how much at odds it is with his real motive — power. Patrick is master of the situation because he recognises all along one salient fact: father and son both assume roles. But whereas Patrick knows himself thoroughly, studies relentlessly to justify calling himself civilised, so that his mask sits tight, Curly's slips continually, because he is not sure of his motives for adopting one and not sure either if having a mask does not compromise his claims to integrity. That Curly is the one to capitulate in the final confrontation with Patrick is shocking but psychologically inevitable; he has recognised the limits of his power, that ambition is compromised by conscience, but he cannot imagine a way of life different from his father's that he could judge worthwhile. Curly's idealism proves as shoddy as Patrick's so-called culture, no more than the veneer that is a flamboyant personality.

It is in the vigour with which Hare examines the distinctions between character and personality that *Knuckle* finds its moral strength and dramatic excitement. Technique is now perfectly matched with theme. Where the play fails is in trying to give a particular family conflict representative status as symptomatic of a sickness generally prevalent in English society. One admires Hare's ambition here but his effort is too self-conscious and it excites disbelief. Left alone, the young characters — Curly and his acquaintance Jenny — reach out not for intimacy with each other and the audience but for rhetorical complaint: "Money," says Curly, "can be harvested like rotten fruit" [p. 55], while Jenny assures us that "Young women in Guildford must expect to be threatened. . . . I expect to be bumped, bruised, followed, assaulted, stared at and propositioned for the rest of my life, while at the same time offering sanctuary, purity, reassurance, prestige — the only point of loveliness in men's ever-darkening lives" [p. 69]. If we view these moments as expressing the characters' awareness of their vulnerability as cynicism begins to engulf them, then they are credible enough; but the action of the play in both instances has already intimated far more subtly the occasion for this despair so that the bald statement of the fact strikes one as redundant; and there is no excuse for the banality of the writing. If on the other hand the reference here is more than merely personal (the characters are clearly to be viewed as speaking in choric fashion as commentators on the significance of the play), then these statements have to be criticised as travesties of the actual psychological conflicts in *Knuckle*; and that renders their validity

as large-scale social insights open to question. Far better to do as
Arthur Miller in *The Price* or as Trevor Griffiths in *Comedians*
(and Hare himself in his more recent plays) and so shape the action
and dialogue of the play that they reflect the tone and social
attitudes of the time and involve the audience imaginatively in
making the connections, drawing the parallels, perceiving the
larger relevances. These moments in *Knuckle* cause a break in
stylistic unity and psychological verisimilitude (Curly, as we have
seen, is just not knowing enough to bring authority to this kind of
insight); they mark a lapse in the wit and intelligence that elsewhere
make the play so stimulating, if bitter, a moral challenge.

Hare's plays have required increasingly lavish forms of staging
but his next venture, a collaboration with the Joint Stock Company
on dramatising William Hinton's *Fanshen* (I.C.A., 1975)[23] was
remarkable for its pared-down technique. It took the documentary
style which is a hallmark of Joint Stock's work and completely
transformed it by making the very conditions of theatre — stripped
here to their essentials — a metaphor for the political experience the
play was defining. Rather than theatre being merely the vehicle for
conveying documentary fact as can happen with this style of
presentation, the idea of performance became the organising
principle behind the play bringing to the pattern of historical events
a richness of implication.

Fanshen examines the effects of the first six years of the People's
Revolution in China, from the time of the departure of the Japanese
occupying forces till 1949, on a small village community, Long
Bow, situated four hundred miles south-west of Peking. With a
handful of actors — seven men and two women — playing some
forty parts between them with the aid of a few props and lights (no
scenery beyond a number of giant red banners that unfurl to mark
the stages in the peasants' progress towards enlightened self-
government), Hare contrived to bring before us a whole alien
community and its way of life. *Fanshen* proved a superb
demonstration of how, given virtuoso acting and direction, it is
possible to piece out the imperfections of a stage, reduced to its
most rudimentary necessities, with an audience's imaginative
participation, as Shakespeare would have us do to realise fully the
world of his history plays. Having the imagination to create out of
a state of virtual nothingness (psychological and economic) was the
achievement of the Long Bow peasants, after they had broken the
tyranny of the landlords and discovered their rights as individuals
within a community and discovered too the responsibilities that
accompany such rights. For centuries their kind had accepted a

slave's mentality, kept always by debt in a state of submissive dependence on the landlords:

> When I was born my family wanted to celebrate.
> But they had to borrow money for dumplings.
> And so before I could speak I was in debt to a landlord.
> A man stands up to his neck in water so that even a
> ripple is enough to drown him. [p. 29]

Asked questions by visiting Secretary Liu about how they are planning to take advantage of the turmoil created by the Japanese withdrawal and change their status, they ask quite simply to be told the answers; no one has asked anything of them before. But he refuses to give way: "No *you* must think. . . . You must know why you do things" [pp. 21-22]. Arduously the peasants attempt a new division of the land between them, classifying each other's status and apportioning the landlords' goods according to individuals' needs; when this fails to produce a fair division of the soil so that all families have an equal standard of subsistence, then they have to learn to accept failure and begin again.

Time and again solutions like this over land-tenure or how to cope with criminals or punish malpractice are reached and characters and audience sit back pleased with their intellectual efforts; but the next scene introduces a character new to the community who views the solution objectively, having shared in none of the enthusiasm that went into the reaching of such conclusions; he demonstrates a weakness in the previous argument and the process begins all over again. In its capacity to be intellectually unsettling like this, the play meticulously pinpoints many of the moral dangers inherent in enthusiasm and complacency. As Liu advises one of the Work Team sent to assess how comprehensively the peasants of Long Bow have been freed from serfdom: "There are no breakthroughs in our work. There is no 'just do this one thing and we will be there'. There is only the patient, daily work of re-making people" [p. 79]. Re-making and re-making. In *Fanshen* dialectic is truly dynamic. Here it is in marked contrast with many plays of the decade that attempt a dialectical structure — Nigel Williams's plays are perhaps the most subtly argued examples, especially *Line 'em* (Cottesloe, 1980), with its clash between a picket line and a band of soldiers sent to break the strike — but which go no further than carefully articulating two opposed attitudes which are left at a point of stalemate. It is because in *Fanshen* dialectic is a continuing process that a performance became intellectually so exhilarating. Moreover the dialectic involves not struggles between warring factions but choices that will be in the best interests of the community at large and not favour random groups or individuals and where the result will be judged a failure if anyone is left in a state of hopelessness feeling victimised. Experience is constantly the test of the strength of an argument; starting with nothing but their recognition of a corporate need, the villagers can afford to experiment in ways of living and they work together in a state of attentive patience.

Given the current state of political disillusionment in the West which Hare admits is a prime cause of alarm to him — that "cowed" mentality that considers "that most of the experiments you could make with the human spirit are likely to be doomed or at any rate highly embarrassing"[24] — it could have been easy for him to present an idealised, didactic picture of the society of Long Bow; but this he resolutely avoids. There is no disguising the fact that many of the initial decisions reached by the village are rooted in petty jealousies or wish-fulfilment. An old woman at the classification cannot restrain herself: "If we say he's a poor peasant, he'll get something in the distribution and . . . I don't want him to get anything" [p. 50]. When the landlords' possessions are divided amongst the peasants, many cannot resist buying a useless quilt gown or an over-large cooking pot simply to own such treasures, which they crow over with childish glee even though they really need more useful farming implements. The new society produces its bullies — Yu Lai and Wen Te; in time the people have enough confidence to put them on trial and, proud of their courage, are appalled when Liu insists they separate their attitude to the deeds from their view of the men and hate only what Yu Lai has done, not want him dead. Always the appeal is for a rational balance as the essence of judgement. During the Work Team's public examination of the village leaders, the first question the villagers wish them to be asked is how much they personally have made out of the revolution. One of the leaders is criticised simply on the grounds of her attitude and tone of voice:

It's not what she did, it's that — look on her face. . . . Look at you. All the time. I have suffered more than you. I know more than you. I'm a better person than you. . . . Why does everyone bristle the moment she comes in? [pp. 60-61]

There is malice in the outburst certainly and the Work Team are criticised subsequently for allowing it to happen; as one of the Team admits, "I'm a servant of the people but sometimes . . . I find the people very hard to like' [p. 66]. Yet that moment also shows how perceptive the villagers are becoming, how quick to detect both lapses in sincerity amongst their number and subtle touches in behaviour that indicate the tentative growth of self-interest that, if allowed to flourish, might jeopardise their corporate ideal. Brutal and humiliating though the attack is, it marks a new growth in awareness; it is voiced by a man who was himself the object of a rigorous examination earlier; from being compelled then to be wary of his own limitations, he has become a shrewd appraiser of how easily in other people manners can harden into mannerisms. Next the villagers have to learn how to make criticism creative by freeing it of any suggestion of vindictiveness so there is never any loss of trust between them.

What an audience watch in *Fanshen* is the creation by a community of a civilization, a culture, for itself as it faces up to the problems of ascertaining the nature and meaning of justice and equality, and discovers that politics is not a matter of power games but a concern with basic human rights and principles. Within the larger process, each man discovers himself; and it is here too that the actual method of staging and production conceived by Hare proved so felicitous. As the group of nine actors assume a variety of parts by the simple means of a shift in tone of voice, change of expression or by seizing simple props, we are given a wonderful sense of the community trying out roles for itself and gradually, painstakingly achieving an acceptable identity. Every aspect of the theatricality of *Fanshen* conveys psychological insights into this process. A device frequently used requires one character to step out of a mimed *tableau* and comment in a flat, expository manner on his reactions to the event being presented in this way, like Cheng Ch'uer telling of the arrival of the Work Team in the village:

The first day we watched each other, the four of us, unknown to each other, scrutinising every action. [p. 43]

The self-consciousness this technique suggests exactly captures the quality of tension between the four members of the team who are anxious to do well and to find a basis for trust in each other without which they know they cannot win the trust of the village. Then there are the numerous examinations of an individual by the rest of the cast questioning the motives for his conduct in a previous scene, like an actor's performance being analysed down to the minutest detail to test its conviction, authenticity and verisimilitude. Taking up in a different format a theme from Hare's earlier plays, this was the pursuit of character freed from the limiting pressures of personality. The objective narrative manner of the first device and the rigorous self-appraisals were disconcerting for an audience initially but they quickly made one appreciate both how utterly bewildering it was for these people to pass from being nameless, destitute serfs to assuming an individuality and how great a challenge it was too to respond positively to this process of awakening, this discovery of what it is to be a human being with all a human being's attendant obligations. Though the writing in *Fanshen* remains scrupulously dispassionate throughout (such emotions as find expression are intimated through terse, oriental-sounding aphorisms), in performance the play generated a profound sense of wonder. At the beginning seven men and two women, clad alike in grey, walked on to a bare stage; two hours later they had peopled a whole village and a cycle of history in our imaginations. Out of a barren void was called forth a tremendous vitality, chastening and revitalising the mind and the perceptions.

With his next two plays *Teeth 'n' Smiles* and *Plenty*, Hare attempted a more probing examination of the disgust that was voiced by Jenny in *Knuckle* at the way that the life she is expected to lead compromises and betrays the moral and emotional worth she recognises in herself. In performance one felt that her disgust retained a dynamic creative potential denied to despair or a cynicism like Curly's and this gave Jenny a moral stature lacking in the other characters, although with the exception of the one rather poorly written soliloquy the disgust found expression largely through a hard, ironic edge that Kate Nelligan introduced into her voice in the final scenes and an impression she created that her quiet dignity was a tremendous effort of self-discipline. With Maggie in *Teeth 'n' Smiles* (Royal Court, 1975)[25] disgust is vibrantly and aggressively articulated.

The situation of the play is a performance (their last in fact, though none of them yet know this) by an ailing pop group and their lead singer, Maggie, at a Cambridge May Ball. Between their three sets we observe the life-styles of the band, their agent, composer and press representative. It is a horrifying world for its utter mindlessness — the prodigious waste of talent, expertise and intelligence that goes to the making of an art-form that the agent, Saraffian, glories in as inspired "tat". For him, it means money for nothing; and he laughs that an audience can be so eager to be gulled. The band under the pressures of endless travelling and the influence of drugs are just zombies who have quite lost touch with their perceptions:

Barnsley. Halifax. I don't know. They carry me about in a sealed container. And sometimes the seasons change. Or we run over a dog. Or they change the design on my cigarette pack. [p. 24]

Crashing music (the epithet is Hare's) is their only means of self-expression; their sexual relations are casual, crude and perfunctory and, bored with the permanence of each other's company, what little converse they have together is on the level of childish games. If their personalities are in any way distinguishable from each other, it is because their various drugs render them in different degrees either rampantly flamboyant or all but catatonic. It is a moot point whether their music can be designated art when its performance demands such an extinction of the faculties that constitute humanity; under the influence of men like Saraffian it has become just another mechanical industrial process.

This is the twilight limbo that Maggie and her one-time lover, Arthur, the group's composer, entered in the naive hope that they could use performance before such mass audiences to promote a new political awareness in their listeners. The irony is that they needed Saraffian's backing to start their careers when his professed aim is to exploit popular culture for its "damnfool, screaming stupidity" [p. 47]; to him it is just "the obvious repeated many times" [p. 52]. Standards, artistic intentions have no place here; all that is wanted is effect, spectacle to enthrall (however demeaning to the performers) and entice the crowds: "Getting your hands on it. I mean, actually getting your hands on the cash. That is the only skill. Really. The only skill in music" [p. 74]. He treats the band with amused contempt and admits with jovial indifference that in his job he expects to spend a percentage of his time sitting by a hospital bed. It was a brilliant stroke to cast a comedian, Dave King, in this role: his genial, buoyant stage personality matched well with the clipped cynicism of Hare's writing for Saraffian's speeches to make it perfectly clear how effortlessly the agent had stifled Maggie and Arthur's aesthetic and political pretensions. King's Saraffian revelled in cultivating a mean personality so that he could despise people more for letting their need of him overcome their scruples. What makes the irony bitter for Arthur and Maggie is that Saraffian claims as his motive a philosophy which is a perverse travesty of their principles. His game is not exploitation but a war of attrition; comforting rhetoric about being a champion in a class war excuses any and every dishonesty. Create mayhem and thrive is his cause in life, but it is the cheery frankness with which he espouses it that makes him lethal. With the self-congratulatory glee of a magician at a children's party, King on his every appearance produced from his resplendent clothes yet another piece of college plate, 'nicked' to supplement the band's fees. That, in sum, is Saraffian's idea of a significant political gesture: and it was with rapt intensity that King told the bizarre tale of the dons who drank up a whole cellar of priceless wines in wartime to prevent it getting into Hitler's hands in the event of an invasion. Imagination can only be roused in Saraffian by images of prodigal waste.

Arthur's one resource against Saraffian is to cling with a desperate nostalgia to his romance with Maggie. She understands his need but sees its futility and her sarcastic debunking of him in the role of lover is cruel but a token of her lasting concern for him. Saraffian has not bought Maggie's soul; however much she has been used, however vigorously she has played the scene, she has always retained control of her consciousness; addiction to drugs or nostalgia like Arthur's she could temporarily indulge but easily get the better of; some vital spark encapsulating her individuality has continued to burn fiercely and she has cherished it as a kind of controlling intelligence. What is exciting in the play is the means whereby Hare allows this "overself" (as Maggie chooses to call it) to find expression. A searing disgust is all that is left Maggie to fight Saraffian's insidious corruptions but it is a kind of integrity. If Saraffian's world has humiliated her then she blatantly exalts in that humiliation as an exposure of his moral worth (she sees herself as his deed's creature and jokes about being a second Trilby). She works now with a kind of zeal to shock and disgust others out of the apathy that Saraffian takes advantage of. With a cold fury she breaks off her singing and begins to taunt and insult her audience, to make them question why they are there and whether the pop scene really is the expression of revolutionary intent that it is cracked up to be. She exposes the tat, the misery, the obscenity of it all; the paucity of imagination; and she speaks with authority since she herself epitomises the degradation. Indeed she accepts that state as a privilege. In a confidential moment with Saraffian, Maggie tells him without a vestige of self-pity how as a child, playing, she was watched by the local priest:

The sun was shining and he took my head in his hands. He said, inside this skull the most beautiful piece of machinery that god ever made. He said, a fair-haired English child, you will think and feel the finest things in the world. The sun blazed and his hands enclosed my whole skull. [p. 72]

Having achieved this moment of awe, Maggie drenches herself in whisky and taking Saraffian's head in her hands expresses her gratitude for their "Great relationship. Great creative control". As Helen Mirren played the sequence, it was a fearsome parody, a ritual of desecration enshrining Saraffian and his kind as the elect of this world and celebrating the evil that is their power to destroy, prodigally to lay waste beauty and innocence. The ceremony expresses derision and moral outrage, yet it also expresses Maggie's awareness that, but for Saraffian, she would have no such knowledge. It is he who has endowed her with this vision of evil. As the disembodied voice of Arthur is heard to declaim eerily out of the darkness at the start of this scene:

> What matter? Out of cavern comes a voice
> And all it knows is that one word: rejoice.[26]

Till now Saraffian has found it easy to dismiss Maggie's virulent criticism, as the band do, and as the audience are half tempted to do, as just an act: the desperate bid of a second-rate artiste to be noticed at any price. Now there can be no more excuses of that kind. He counters her story of her childhood with what he describes as the formative influence on his life: the witnessing during the war of a bomb attack on the Café Royal, when he regained consciousness to see thieves crawling amongst the debris and the dying seizing jewelry and cash and viewed them as a symbol of true existence. As he ends Maggie is not stilled with awe but rocks with hollow laughter at his lack of insight, that he can admit no change after a further thirty years' experience. This proof of his spiritual death renews her spiritual strength. Anger and invective have not been in short supply on our stage in the Seventies but they have rarely conveyed such pure moral energy. Pure, because there is for Maggie no moment of triumph, nor hope of one: arrested on a drugs charge (she is innocent — the band have used her luggage to hide their supplies), she welcomes prison with a fierce determination as a new beginning and a form of suffering less futile, less insulting to her dignity as a human being than her present freedom. With the role of Maggie, David Hare has created one of the few characters on the English stage that bears comparison with Genet's figures who similarly choose to be ritual scapegoats for modern society as a vocation, willing themselves to accept their degradation as a way of revealing the moral bankruptcy of the forces that have reduced them to such a state and thereby discovering in themselves a new vigour and dignity.

Hare's skill in stimulating and extending an audience's moral sensitivity in *Teeth 'n' Smiles* was rendered more impressive by comparison with Barry Keefe's somewhat derivative play, *Bastard*

Angel,[27] staged by the Royal Shakespeare Company (Warehouse, 1980), which tries to make up with an involved plot for what is lacking in analytical depth. As in Hare's play the action is divided by the various sets that make up a pop singer's performance but, whereas in *Teeth 'n' Smiles* the two are continuous in time, in *Bastard Angel* the musical numbers are to be understood as taking place in the immediate present and the scenes as part of a recent past so that one can appreciate in the singer, Shelly, a professionalism that demands she rise above the tragic pressures on her life because of her commitment to an audience. That she recognises a responsibility to her public as a performer while losing every vestige of moral responsibility as an individual is an irony that is not creatively explored and it smacks rather of the old stage cliché that the show must go on at any cost. The fundamental moral vision that shapes Keefe's play is similarly stereotyped and uninspired: however responsive the play is on a level of surface detail to contemporary pop culture, there is no imaginative grappling with that way of life to extend one's understanding of it as a social fact. Shelly's success brings her a wealth that allows her to realise her ambition to own a mansion and its estate where she once sang early in her career; her art recognises no traditional values and not surprisingly she lacks the sense of cultural obligation necessary to maintain the house in the style which first aroused her interest in it; progressively she and her colleagues vandalise the house and outrage the retainers she employs. There is potentially a source of thematic interest in the way the energies that allowed Shelly to achieve her ambition are just the ones to render that triumph futile; but again this is given as a fact, not adequately realised as a mental process; its presentation is confined to a sensational scene where Shelly encourages her band to destroy a beautifully prepared dinner party and abjectly humiliate one of her elderly servants. Indeed throughout the play Keefe resorts to sensational incident to invigorate the stock adage he relies on as his principal theme, namely that wealth corrupts. (There are further strands of plot about an incestuous affair between Shelly and a son she abandoned at birth and about a penurious ex-lover who commits suicide when she refuses financial help.) The passionate commitment of Charlotte Cornwell as Shelly did much to redeem the play from absurdity and melodramatic excess in performance but, for all the energy and intensity *Bastard Angel* demanded of its cast, it disappointed for want of an organic intellectual life; the thinking that had gone into its composition was sluggish and predictable, never probing beyond the surface of the subject. The corruption of Shelly is known only by its effects; it is not imaginatively encompassed by an audience as is Saraffian's. Keefe's final appeal is to our sense of pathos as Shelly returns valiantly to the way of life that has made and broken her; there is none of Maggie's relentless battling to salvage some self-respect and find a way onwards from the inertia Saraffian fosters about him. Hare's play is the more satisfying, because it is the more truly radical and liberating.

At the climax of Hare's *Plenty* (Lyttleton, 1978)[28], his heroine, Susan, meets a wartime colleague, another secret agent, in a seedy hotel; as he caresses her, she falls back in a drug-induced sleep; he quickly removes all traces of his presence — "A fine undercover agent will move so that nobody can ever tell he was there" [p. 84] — and leaves; but as he opens the door there is outside not the mouldering dark passage one expects but a shaft of green iridescent light. Instantly the hotel set disintegrates and another, "a French hillside in high summer", falls rapidly into place: in Hare's own production it was a flood of lush greens and golds in a candescent light. It is 1944, and Susan is magically there in a print frock bubbling over with joy at the liberation of France and the success of her mission: "We have grown up. We will improve our world. . . . There will be days and days and days like this" [pp. 86-87]. It was like the transformation scene in pantomime, an analogy we seemed invited to make by the way in which the scene arrived in a rush of painted tabs and flats. It caught exactly the naive quality of Susan's exuberance, the patent theatricality stressing the insubstantial grounds of her hope as rooted in a wave of emotion not in knowledge and understanding. These colours, more vibrant than lifelike, suggested that memory had enhanced the experience in the process of recall; indeed its recovery now was possible only with the aid of drugs. The mode of staging this sequence felicitously enacted a movement of consciousness. In retrospect it caused one to reappraise the action of the play and realise the point of a disturbing factor throughout. *Plenty* passes with great assurance over two decades of English history from the War years, the Festival of Britain, Suez and its aftermath to the early Sixties and these are the years of Susan's prime from her late teens onwards; Hare realises the passage of time with great attention to detail, recording changes of fashion in idiom as well as clothes and taste and the shift in people's lifestyles from austerity to plenty. Each scene has an accurate verisimilitude; but the fact that the play opens in 1962 with Susan deciding to leave her husband and stripping her grand Kensington lounge bare to the plaster and boards — "Everything to go" [p. 13] — alerts one's attention to setting and staging more than is perhaps customary with a work of social realism, where one looks primarily for a convincing background. Faced with the need to effect a rapid transition of scenes, Hare could not respect the conventions of fourth-wall realism except at great cost financially and in time; instead he took advantage of the technical facilities at the Lyttleton to pre-set his scenes on truck stages and roll them into position down tracks set in the main stage floor. As a result the speed of the scene changes, their looming into place out of the darkness and the surreal effect of their scattering as the lights faded, together with the visual effect that the actors were working true to the conventions of realism but on what were clearly stages within a stage, introduced a deliberate note of theatricality into the proceedings, an eerie effect of distancing. The use of a more extreme theatricality at the climax to evoke the movement of Susan's consciousness suddenly revealed the point of the mode of staging throughout: that at one level of interpretation the play could be seen as taking place in a subjective dimension. Each scene has an objective social reality, but the pattern governing the selection and ordering of the scenes is subjective, one mind's process of recall: we watch Susan's increasingly critical awareness of her performance, as it were, on the stage of history. These scenes rolling inexorably out of the darkness were like images rising out of the store of the unconscious, coalescing, sharpening into focus, setting up resonances and a play of associations that dictate the pace of the mind's movement through contemplation to the need for further recall. The play was simultaneously a journey through time and into the interior, both explaining and compelling in Susan the need to let "everything go" in the way of social obligations and retreat through drugs into the dangerously fragile comfort of nostalgia.

The two perspectives we are invited to take on the action impose a dilemma over judgement. In the scene before the climactic re-encounter that Susan has with the wartime agent Lazar, we watch a lengthy quarrel between her and her husband, Brock, which centres on an outburst of such venom that it precipitates her decision to leave him. The structure of *Plenty* enacts, as it were, a loop in time and we are back where the play began but with greater insight into the steady control Susan demonstrated then. Appalled at seeing his own life destroyed by her with what appears to him to be complete indifference, Brock launches into a vindication of his concern for her:

Your life is selfish, self-interested gain. That's the most charitable interpretation to hand. You claim to be protecting some personal ideal, always at a cost of almost infinite pain to everyone around you. You are selfish, brutish, unkind. Jealous of other people's happiness as well, determined to destroy other ways of happiness they find. I've spent fifteen years of my life trying to help you, simply trying to be kind, and my great comfort has been that I am waiting for some indication from you . . . some sign that you have valued this kindness of mine. Some love perhaps. Insane. (*He smiles.*)
And yet . . . I really shan't ever give up, I won't surrender till you're well again. And that to me would mean your admitting one thing: that in the life you have led you have utterly failed, failed in the very, very heart of your life. Admit it. Then perhaps you might really move on. [pp. 78-79]

Every adjective here carries the ring of truth and Brock's accusation that Susan has become mentally unbalanced and is failing to find fulfilment in "the very, very heart of her life" is an accurate perception. Susan in some of her moods would even agree with this assessment of her nature; she is shortly to confess to Lazar: "Listen, I have to tell you I've not always been well. I have a weakness. I like to lose control. I've been letting it happen, well, a number of times . . ." [p. 82]. Yet from another perspective Brock's view seems painfully unjust and unimaginative. Almost immediately afterwards his stance as moral accuser is comically deflated (he plans to phone their doctor to have Susan certified, intending now to play "as dirtily and ruthlessly as you" [p. 79], but — as she knows — it is Easter weekend and the doctor is away); all along there has been a touch of the amiable buffoon about Brock, at least as Stephen Moore played him. Even as he speaks here we carry in our minds the impressive image that reveals the conclusion of this battle royal, the *tableau* with which the play began, of him naked, drunk and sprawling insensible watched over with cold-eyed distaste by Susan. And what is one to make on reflection of the verbs in her confession to Lazar, "like" and "letting", implying that the activity is not so much spontaneous, provided by external circumstances, as calculated and willed from within?

That Susan is something of an actress who enjoys staging a 'scene' seems on the surface again a true judgement. She con-stantly embarrasses others in these 'scenes' but patently their embarrassment springs from more than distaste at Susan's want of 'good form'; at her most flamboyantly aggressive she speaks openly about problems of moral choice that they are using all the resources of their tact and politeness to cover up. Brock is a diplomat (which allows Hare to make national issues, especially the Suez crisis, the subject of his dialogue), and one of his superiors, Charleson, informs Susan, when she tries secretly and unsuccessfully to improve Brock's standing at the Foreign Office, that "Behaviour is all" [p. 72]; tact is the essence of diplomacy. What occasions Susan's outbreaks — and Charleson triggers one off here — is a sense of outrage when she detects that diplomacy and decency are just rituals and mannerisms, empty forms of behaviour that suggest one has taste and good breeding while inwardly one knows one's self to be ruthless and cynical. Charleson admits as much: "The irony is this: we had an empire to administer, there were six hundred of us in this place [the Foreign Office]. Now it's to be dismantled and there are six thousand. As our power declines, the fight among us for access to that power becomes a little more urgent, a little uglier perhaps" [p. 72]. His careful phrasing ensures that words like "urgent", "ugly" convey no emotional or moral stress whatever. Brock appreciates that "Hypocrisy does keep things pleasant for at least part of the time" [p. 75]; it suits, he says, his style. But to Susan this is patronising, an insult to her intelligence; and the demand that she should conform to such an idea of decorum simply because she is his wife is an abuse of her imagination. It is asking her to play a role and *believe* it to be the truth, unlike her role-playing as a secret agent in the war which was a *conscious* deception. Is perhaps Brock's "kindness" to Susan just an attempt to "keep things pleasant for at least part of the time"? If Susan is a failure, it is because she sees no chance of success on the terms that are offered her; when she offends the dignity of others, it is to protect a dignity and moral vision that lie within. What appears a strident exhibitionism is a powerful conscience refusing to let her submit to the self-deceptions practised by others, a conscience activated in her by the process of history. Her awareness of its growth is a sign of her intelligence.

If the play has a weakness it is that in terms of the stage action the origins of this conscience are not as adequately realised as its development. Susan informs others about how powerfully her training as a secret agent has moulded the cast of her mind and the explanation is convincing enough; but one would have liked more than the single scene devoted to the wartime tensions that have made Susan what she is, because that would have introduced more fully the range of themes that *Plenty* will explore. Susan has had to pretend to be a native Frenchwoman and live that lie convincingly for several years with the knowledge that letting the mask slip even slightly could mean death. She "told such glittering lies" [p. 44] in the interests of a national and international need and her one comfort in the struggle to free France was the sense of being part of a collective endeavour, having her respected if largely secret place in an organisation whose members shared a common aim and lived at a pitch of tension induced by fear of failure. It is this experience that makes Susan so acute in penetrating facades of behaviour in others, especially the gentility, the diplomacy that mask the instincts of the shark. The life she pursued in the interests of national freedom is now the common pattern of behaviour of those in quest of plenty in a world where for Susan "everything is up for grabs" [p. 58]. The charade that is Suez epitomises the moral decline. As Susan through marriage to Brock moves into Foreign Office circles, the need to stifle that voice of conscience for the sake of his career makes the agony of disgust, the sense of contamination, more desperate to find a means of expression. The building up of theatrical tension in each scene is a correlative for the psychological pressures mounting in Susan to the point where everything has to go and she has (literally) to speak her mind. Her 'scenes' are in fact her moments of transcendent lucidity; her audiences (onstage and off) are the *actors* inhabiting a world of illusions that her vehemence discredits as shabby and mercenary.[29] The indictment is fuelled not only with the sense of lost moral possibilities, which she fervently believed Europe had the chance to realise in the aftermath of war, but anger that the intelligence and imagination that enabled her to survive that war are faculties that seem to disqualify her from 'normal' living in peacetime. What is finest in her is what isolates her; Susan's nostalgia is for a world she knew of richer spiritual opportunity and, if she grows "selfish, brutish, unkind", it is to protect the truth of that private vision.

One aspect of the play reviewers tended to question was Susan's friendship with Alice, because Alice herself lacks sharp definition. This is true in one sense but that lack of definition is actually the key to her character and the source of Susan's attraction to her as a complete antithesis to herself. There is a curious innocence about Alice, a child-like freedom from conscience; she has a voracious appetite for surreal experience and lives enthusiastically through every prevailing fashion in dress and *mores* (as such she is, of course, a useful device for Hare to establish the social tone of a particular year). Alice floats through life, directing all her energies to living in and for the moment and, while her spontaneity may be judged as amoral, that for Susan is preferable to the super-subtle evasions of Brock's colleagues, and the bluff, unthinking affability of Brock himself. It is a kind of honesty. Being so much a product of the time, Alice has little sense of social change, of herself as part of the continuum of history, and so, fascinating and relaxing as she is for Susan, she can offer her no lasting help. Every facet of the dramatic method of the play and the wit is directed to illuminate the central dilemma of judgement: how what Charleson and his like view quite credibly as emotional instability in Susan is from another perspective a hunger for moral permanence.

With the roles of Maggie and Susan, battling and vulnerable, by turns frightening and pathetic, Hare is entering territory that has over the two previous decades been the province of John Osborne; and, interestingly, Osborne's most substantial play of the Seventies, *West of Suez* (Royal Court, 1971),[30] is as the title indicates a response to the same political events that shape much of the action of *Plenty*. In some unnamed Caribbean island, a former British colony, Osborne sets an English family on holiday: as he presents it, the world they inhabit mentally and culturally is quite at variance with the political reality they find themselves in and consider themselves above. They have 'gone West' spiritually, since Britain's loss of colonial power, clinging nostalgically to the form of a lifestyle while no longer inhabiting the fact. Asked by a reporter if he adopts a pose, Wyatt, the father, a successful author, answers categorically "Yes . . . because it makes life more tolerable" [p. 72]. How well or ill they each live out a pose modelled on the values of a past they still hanker for is the almost exclusive subject of their discourse. The fragments they shore against their ruin are wholly aesthetic, a precision and elegance of statement as the perfect expression of the self. Words are all that are left any of them as a sign of authority. Wyatt dominates the group in the characteristic style of so many of Osborne's heroes, turning every situation to his verbal advantage. The climax of the play is the interview, when Wyatt, with genial unconcern for anything except his effect on the audience that his attendant family constitute, patronises, insults and humiliates the reporter. (His confidence in his right to do this proves a fatal blindspot: the play ends with his sudden and brutal assassination by a group of islanders.) His daughter, Frederica, is shocked by his performance: "You get away with it all. Bad manners. Laziness. Cowardice. . . . Hurtful indiscretion. And we're all supposed to be stunned by the humour and eccentricity of it" [p. 79]. It is a fair comment on the tone and effect of Wyatt's tirades. If his death shortly afterwards by way of reprisal disturbs us for its arbitrariness, it is because Osborne has turned the tables on us making us see how easily we have let Wyatt's wit and entertainment-value disarm out moral judgement. (Wyatt was played by Sir Ralph Richardson at his most genial.)

Here too is a world where "behaviour is all" with dangerous consequences.

Where Osborne differs from Hare is in leaving his sense of the dangerous complexity of the tenor of the times at the level of feeling: even his urging on his audience an awareness of the need for moral reappraisals is conducted at that emotional level in the final *coup-de-theatre* when Wyatt is shot and meets the "ludicrous death" that has been his one dread. There is little attempt to define why nostalgia is the dominant mood or why in Wyatt it takes the complex form that it does, compelling him to adopt that particular pose. Nostalgia implies profound social change but, beyond the fact of the island's independence and an account of a BBC programme on Europe since 1945 (which one of the characters reads aloud from a newspaper thereby exciting Wyatt's scorn for its sociological jargon), history is not shown to be a dynamic pressure on the characters' lives as it is in *Plenty*. There is curiously little tension in *West of Suez*, even in the private sparring between members of the family; the nostalgia is not rooted in any definable fears or insecurities and it is not made apparent that the characters' constant verbalising is compulsive, rising from a need to convince themselves and others that their stated convictions are soundly based and not comforting deceptions. The leisureliness makes for imprecision: Osborne risks letting his audience consider him over-enamoured with all the intellectualising and, as a result, judge the final violence as gratuitous. The ambiguity over judgement here is not fruitful; there is nothing like the dynamic transformations of one's response to events on stage that Hare effects with his shifting perspectives. *Plenty* has got the ambitious scope that *West of Suez* appears to aim at but not realise. As a result Hare invests our experience of nostalgia with wholly new shades of meaning that free it of its exclusively pejorative connotations. Katharine Worth has remarked of Osborne's plays generally (but in the context of *West of Suez*) that "the lessons of history are always subordinate . . . to the lessons of feeling".[31] David Hare in *Teeth 'n' Smiles* and *Plenty* would appear to be trying to balance that equation, to argue that for a full understanding of feeling one needs as detailed a sense of history. Working to achieve that balance in *Plenty* Hare has extended the range of dramatic structures available to the dramatist of social realism and charged overt theatricality, as he did in *Fanshen*, with a powerful sense of purpose. What impresses about Hare's work through the Seventies is the seemingly inexhuastible array of styles over which as the need arises he has proved himself master.

If *Plenty* with its chosen production-method frequently called analogies with Pirandello to mind in the way it defined the prevailing social *malaise* through images of acting and a self-conscious theatricality, *A Map of the World* (Lyttleton, 1983)[32] made that connection even more forcefully. At the conclusion of the opening scene, played in the realist manner, the actors began alarmingly to overact, the lighting grew intense but concentrated its focus on the speakers, music began to underscore the dialogue giving it an emotional expressiveness it had lacked previously, a subtly witty discussion in the Shavian manner about the relation of politics and art suddenly gave place to a more commonplace, not to say crude, analysis of feeling — "There's something inside every human being, something suppressed. It's got to come out. I tell you, Simon, cut through to it" [p. 26]. Instantaneously the setting began to disintegrate and a film crew slid into view: director, cameraman, make-up and script assistants, clapperboy and propmen; when the scene finished the actors launched into petty private wrangling with the director.[33] Throughout the play the action will shift between a film studio in the present and a hotel in Bombay in 1976, setting of a United Nations conference on World Poverty. It is Hare's most brilliant dramatic structure to date, fusing a *Fanshen*-like discussion of wealth and poverty with a demonstration of the power of art-forms, especially in a popular medium like the cinema, to destroy experience by making it conform to particular conventions.

The dramatic structure allows us at once to live with the experience and with the process of its distortion into 'art'. There are links at two levels between the worlds of politics and cinema: on the level of character and plot a novelist, Mehta, and the journalist, Simon Andrews, meet in Bombay; at a deeper level Hare examines the way both worlds manipulate experience for good or ill through language. From the moment that our preoccupation with the realist convention in theatre is disturbed by the intrusion of the film studio personnel, who put a frame of new conventions around the play that distances us from it immediately, we become alert to the question of language and context. We observe especially how each character has a private register of language and how in consequence the tone of a particular conversation or discussion is determined by whether the characters choose to set about establishing a common register or whether one character seeks to impose his or her register to the exclusion of all others.

Consider the final encounter between the U.N. secretary and M'Bengue, the representative of Senegal, who has been seeking aid:

M'BENGUE: Mr. Martinson, overnight I have been reading the conditions, the terms, of the aid you are proposing to give. They are stiff.
MARTINSON: They are exacting, yes. No aid is pure. There is always an element of trade in all such arrangements, and trade, after all, benefits both sides.
M'BENGUE: Surplus corn, surplus grain from America, at a commercial price . . .
MARTINSON: Less than the market price.
M'BENGUE: A considerable price.
(*MARTINSON smiles.*)
MARTINSON: Perhaps.
M'BENGUE: The other part of the package, the facility of a loan from the World Bank.
MARTINSON: That's right.
M'BENGUE: At 13 per cent. And not even that is the limit of it. With a demand for changes in the internal policies of our country . . .
MARTINSON: Adjustments, yes. [p. 81]

There is no doubting the source of power here. The exchange encapsulates all that we have learned from the play about the humiliations of being a dependent nation: "We take aid from the West because we are poor, and in everything we are made to feel our inferiority" [p. 40]. Martinson suavely rephrases M'Bengue's criticism to take off its bitter edge, implying that he finds M'Bengue's tone melodramatic, uncivilised, lacking in perspective, in need of "adjustments". There is no attempt to understand M'Bengue's point of view: when the Senegalese in despair is quietly specific — "You throw us a lifeline. The lifeline is in the shape of a noose" [p. 82], for Martinson's strictures will destroy the policies which brought M'Bengue's government into being — Martinson merely shrugs; there is no place for naked emotion in his concept of diplomacy. Decorum should always prevail, however desperate one's need. Yet the play has taught us to treat that decorum as callous, smug.

There is a parallel exchange at the start of the play. The atmosphere is rife with tensions: the delegates at the conference, we are led later to understand, are "longing for a dogfight"; Stephen and another journalist, Elaine, a black American working for CBS, are irritable on account of the heat and the monotony of the debates which are constantly being delayed by members questioning trivial points of procedure. They are joined by Mehta, an Indian now living in England, who is a model of old-style English behaviour — neat, coolly elegant, relaxed and witty; he is a fashionable social novelist who has been invited to the conference as a guest speaker. He realises at once that he has fallen into the company of journalists, is wary but wishes to pursue the acquaintance; being a dedicated philanderer, he has instantly grown interested in Elaine. Stephen at once is on the attack, supposing Mehta dislikes journalists given the title of his recent novel about the profession — *The Vermin Class.* Mehta eyes him shrewdly and launches into a bravura style of interview, urbane but exceptionally patronising and not unlike Wyatt's performance in similar circumstances in *West of Suez.* Here is the professional writer going through his public routine. While Elaine, the more experienced journalist, is merely bemused, Stephen is appalled at the way as serious an issue as the state of culture in developing countries, especially those with communist sympathies, can be made the excuse for a flow of derogatory jests. He challenges the assumptions implicit in Mehta's tone and manner that the West can do little to help the need of developing countries beyond setting them the *example* of its own civilised condition: "You mean you are saying . . . even as someone reaches up to you to be fed . . . 'Oh, no I can't fill your bowl . . . but I would — please — do — like you to admire my civilization, the cut of my suit!' " [p. 19]. Challenged, Mehta immediately assumes command of the situation — "I have known many men like you" [p. 20] — and with some relish demolishes not the terms of Stephen's argument, but, more subtly, the grounds on which he appears to set himself up as an opponent to one who is a recognised authority. As Stephen quietly replies: "Actually you haven't argued at all" [p. 20]. Mehta has merely imputed to Stephen Marxist tendencies and a university-trained idealism of the kind that finds enjoyment in making people feel uncomfortable by discussing world poverty in embarrassing situations. He has fabricated a character for Stephen with no basis in ascertained fact, seeking merely to discredit him; he never calls Stephen a fool outright, but it is the drift of Mehta's every remark — that he is young, an idealist and so one who hardly merits the charity of a serious argument. But the journalist like the novelist is an artist with words and Stephen is alert to all of Mehta's rhetorical ploys, above all the attempt to demoralise by speciously ascribing opinions to him which are then held up to ridicule:

MEHTA: Well, ask yourself if your heroes are very pro-women, your
    Lenin, your Castro . . .
STEPHEN: He is not *my* Castro.
MEHTA: This ludicrous, long-winded bore who speaks for eight hours on
    end, who won his battles by speaking whole villages to death — they
    reeled over, bored in the face of his speeches — this man (we do not say
    this, it is long forgotten) who was once an extra in an Esther Williams

movie. Splash! It is the right noise for him. Splash and yawn!
STEPHEN: There, you're doing it again. I haven't mentioned Castro. [p. 21]

The biblical maxim — judge not that ye be not judged[34] — is apt here, for Mehta's rhetorical technique lays him open to criticism as the victim of a sickening world-weariness; it is fitting that his cultivated *ennui* should have global dimensions; the apathy, the indifference implicit in his laid-back 'style' are all-consuming. This has in fact been implicit in his stance from the first, though it might have been interpreted initially as a disarming humility. Asked on his arrival if he is "speaking tomorrow", he replies: "Yes. A chore. To be frank. The neccessary prostitution of the intellect. So much is demanded now of the writer which is not writing, which is not the work. The work alone ought to be sufficient. But my publishers plead with me to make myself seen" [pp. 16-17]. "The work alone ought to be sufficient." Why? Because there the tone of authority can go unchallenged? Solipsism is a dangerous stance for the *social* novelist. One has a further reservation: how much is Mehta's only-cock-in-the-yard manner with Stephen simply a mating display for Elaine's benefit? Unlike his opponent, Stephen does not force these questions into the open; his tactic is to shape the discussion to leave them framed as possibilities, implying he supposes Mehta has enough intelligence to perceive his drift.

Increasingly as the play develops Hare makes the audience suspicious of Mehta's wit and indeed embarrassed at their own tendency as Westerners to laugh at it. In the context of the conference it seems undeniably cheap. As M'Bengue, who wishes to prevent Mehta addressing the delegates, argues: "Jokes . . . are a product of security. If one is secure, one may laugh at others. . . . Humour, like everything, is something you buy. . . . The luxury of the rich who are sure of what they have" [p. 41]. Wit like Mehta's can easily misrepresent, be a wanton or a calculated distortion, either way showing a lack of real engagement, of real charity with its subject. As M'Bengue admits: "indeed the surface of things *is* funny, if you do not understand how that surface comes to be, if you do not look underneath" [p. 41]. M'Bengue chooses to use the conference to make a moral and political stand against Mehta as representing Western values at their most unacceptable. His charge is simple: "You lack respect" [p. 39]; and M'Bengue's dignity is unassailable, because he can touch a point of conscience in Mehta that questions his identity at its most fundamental: "a black man himself, though of course, because he is Indian, it is not how he sees himself: he thinks himself superior to the black man from the bush" [p. 41]. Is Mehta with his cult of a Western sensibility any less absurd than the young English and Americans he denounces who explore Oriental mysticism and "cast doubt on the value of their own material prosperity" [p. 66]? If they are guilty of the ultimate in hypocrisy, is he not guilty too? Stephen sympathising with M'Bengue suggests a compromise: that Mehta be allowed to address the conference if he will first read a statement admitting that fiction by its very nature is an unreliable witness to social and historical truth. Hare has meticulously made the issue a matter of cultural as well as personal integrity. Mehta is trapped into agreeing to a second debate with Stephen. On the personal level the issue is further complicated by Peggy Whitton, an actress-model, who — though formerly attracted to Stephen — has become Mehta's latest conquest: as a gesture of American liberalism, she brashly offers herself to the intellectual champion.

Peggy's naivety is extreme: there can be no victor in what is essentially an exploration of the nature of integrity, as both men fully realise. Integrity is not a static, finished entity but is constantly in the making and never, as Stephen argues, beyond recovery. Mehta defends his satirical art as the way of balance in a world that has lost a proper sense of proportion. He claims it is his duty to define the absurdity of the world, "this universe of idiocy" [p. 68] as he sees it, where the young rush "to discredit the very civilization their grandfathers worked so hard to create" [p. 66], and where diplomacy and culture are enshrined in "the palace of lies" [p. 68] that is the United Nations, a monument to bureaucracy at its most inept. Writing is for him a constant wrestling with conscience and integrity: "I am told to point it out is bloody-minded and — what — 'unhelpful'? And yet to me, I am telling you, not to point it out is worse" [p. 68]. Stephen disputes none of this; for him the crucial issue is motive. He contends — but not with any wish to disparage Mehta's genius — that "everything you say, everything you propose, is from a position of superiority and hopelessness" [p. 69]. If this wounds, then so much the better: it may force Mehta to bridge the distance that his too fastidious artistry has set up between himself and the historical and political process as a lived reality: "the more you write, the more isolated you become. The more frozen" [p. 70]. The only contacts Mehta now makes are with girls like Peggy who easily succumb to the aura of his reputation. (Elaine was too knowing.) "What is left in you that is not disdainful, that is not dead? Only jealousy and lust" [p. 71]. Mehta has argued that mankind has only one enemy and that is self-deception; Stephen retaliates that Mehta's whole mode of arguing is in its way self-deceiving: his way is not wisdom but a cynicism bred of a despair that things might ever change. Mehta trounces ideals in others especially the young because he has lost his belief that "we may change things"; his basic concept of culture is essentially fatalistic, that it is a *received* condition of being. Stephen refuses to see the debate as a contest; the outcome is immaterial to him for its real value has been in forcing him to take stock of his own opinions and see that he has devoted too much of his life to apologising for his beliefs as idealistic through accepting over-readily "the picture the world has of an idealist as a man who is necessarily a clown" [p. 73]. Dialogue and action beautifully complement the progress of the debate: there is no anger now in Stephen as in the first exchanges with Mehta, only a genuine concern for Mehta as a man and as an artist and a growing assurance that in arguing he is finding a better self, a moral stature which for too long he has suppressed out of defence for the views of seniors he knows at heart are wrong. The debate is a process of illumination and he hopes it is as profoundly so for Mehta and Peggy as it is for him.

The dramatic structure shows how that hope was realised. Mehta has made of the experience a novel, "a moral story", as an act of contrition for his own past and as a memorial to Stephen, who shortly after the conference died in a train accident in India. For him too the experience involved an unexpected moral choice: "the novelist is accused of dalliance and asked to put a value on what he has seen as a passing affair" [p. 75]. But beyond that his philosophy of culture has been held up to question as little more than dilettante dalliance also and the writing of a new style of autobiographical fiction has clearly been for him a process of discovering more permanent values for art. Peggy too has grown beyond an "easy promiscuity" and her unthinking pursuit of fun; she is now Mehta's wife. For all three the debate occasioned the shaping of a new identity.

But Hare is anxious that the growth in discrimination should embrace more than the characters central to the debate: his audience is not to rest in a static relation to the play; and it is here that the Pirandello-like complexities of the dramatic structure find their justification. Mehta's novel is being adapted for a film and the "moral story" is being traduced into a "romance". What Mehta chose to imply about the intimate lives of his characters is being made explicit, while the momentous debates are to the director of the film simply "boring". (M'Bengue at one point tersely points out that "boring" is "the white man's word for everything to which he does not wish to come to terms" [p. 40]; repeatedly throughout the play a character using the epithet stands condemned.) The film, seeking stereotypes, dismisses the heart of the novel as "too literary, too talky" [p. 75]; its preferred focus is on sex and death. The train accident is an excuse for lavish spectacle whereas the tragedy confirmed in Mehta and Peggy their new-found resolution; Stephen's death invited not sentimentality but a sharpening of their moral scruple out of the sense of necessary obligation: "for all the bitterness, for all the stupidity . . . we admired this man" [p. 76]. All the delicate psychological nuances of the novel are being travestied. The distress for the audience is as acute as when in *Six Characters in Search of an Author* the Father's encounter with the Step-daughter in Madame Pace's shop is unintentionally but cruelly guyed by the actors who, trapped within the routine of their technique, are blind to the horror they are perpetrating. Hare contrives to give us scenes which enact the substance of Mehta's novel and the distorted version of this which is finding its way on to film; some of the arguments in the book are being filmed, but the cast expect them to be cut. Peggy on visiting the set is appalled; but Mehta, who could legally end the charade if he chose, is moved by the extreme youthfulness of the actors playing Peggy and Stephen, by their eerie resemblance to their prototypes in life, their humility before the fact of his art — they carry his book in their minds at least, they assure him, and promise that "all the warmth, all the kindness we can bring, we will bring" [p. 80]. The Peggy-actress has in fact collapsed in tears while rehearsing one of her scenes, suddenly conscious of the reality of what she has been playing; the actors are not without imagination but are constrained by unyielding conventions that are dictated as much by their audiences' expectations as by the limitations of the director's creative talent.

The surprising element in the final encounter between the novelist and the film world is Mehta's increasingly relaxed and understanding tone, particularly as we have grown so critical of Angelis, the director, and the crudeness of his art. M'Bengue and Stephen had found Mehta wanting in sympathy because he lived without hope. How corrosive the former Mehta's wit would have been at the expense of Angelis and his actors! Interestingly now he does not force the tone of the conversation or seek to dominate it; he listens, observes his differences of opinion over the objectives of book and film; the fiery will to sit in judgement on others flares up briefly but is quickly doused by his growing interest in the two actors, his delight in their youth, their wish to share their enthusiasms with him, their concern to try and preserve some vestige of the integrity of his art. There is a graciousness and distinction quite new to Mehta that expresses itself as the play closes in sharing with the actors an unaffected joy, even laughing with them at the travesty that the film will doubtless be: "For the rest, of course, let it be toplessness . . . And bad dialogue. What else?" — "No sauna scene so far, but we're expecting one" [p. 80]. At the last he is a man with the quiet conviction of one who has found himself, who can rise above a situation which he might previously have deemed insulting to his genius and reputation. By creating in his audiences a sense of outrage at the way the film is desecrating the novel, Hare gives them a measure against which to gauge Mehta's freedom for the remarkable moral and imaginative awakening it has entailed: writing the novel has been for him an intimate experience of catharsis. It is difficult through the medium of drama to convey the frustrations and joy of being a creative writer but Hare has devised a dramatic structure that does precisely that, allowing his audiences to sense the degree of scruple necessary if one is to be true to one's vision and not be seduced into conforming to jaded conventions.

If the structure of *Plenty* because of its constant shifts in time makes heavy demands on the actors by requiring them to build credible and consistent characterizations in their roles, *A Map of the World* asks even more of its performers by asking them to play in several different dimensions. Peggy, Stephen, Mehta, Elaine, Martinson, M'Bengue appear as the characters in the novel and as the actors playing these roles in the film, while Peggy and Mehta also recur as the reflecting, older, 'real life' selves of the characters whose past experience shaped the novel. But in coping with the challenge this poses, the actors are greatly assisted by Hare's virtuoso command of styles of dialogue and by his rigorous control of the dramatic structure. There is nothing arbitrary about the development of *A Map of the World* for all its many surprises and transformations. The disjunctions continually illuminate and extend the action of the play as a subtle process of debate. In retrospect one begins to appreciate how crucial Hare's involvement in *Fanshen* has proved in helping him to find an individual style and technique. There we watched a handful of actors playing with an array of identities; what began as a necessarily austere production-method developed in significance during the performance adding profound resonances to the theme of the play. *Fanshen* not only evoked a process of history, a turning-over and rebuilding of a community, it also showed how for each individual in that community a growth in consciousness, the creation of a self, had to accompany the larger social movement. Playing with an array of identities in order to shape acceptable private and social dimensions for the self has become the dominant preoccupation of Hare's more recent plays. It excites in him a zest for experiment with dramatic forms where a flamboyant theatricality will initiate a rigorous investigation of contemporary social and cultural issues. With Hare's most recent work a richly illuminating social drama derives from a searching adventure into the state of modern consciousness.

CHAPTER SIX

TREVOR GRIFFITHS

Asked at the time of his first London success what he saw as the function of political theatre, whether it should be propagandist or analytical, Trevor Griffiths replied:

I think it should be analytical *and* descriptive. I think there is a terribly important job to go on doing in journalism, in books, in academy, in theatre, which is to go on offering descriptions, painstakingly to say "No! we have not completely looked at the society we live in, we've not completely examined it". *Analytically* is to take it a stage further, is to say "What do we make of this? How do we evaluate this? How do we judge it? What does it make us when we say this is the way we should live or shouldn't live?" . . . I'm not really interested in propaganda theatre. Though it has a function, I'm not really sure it has a function in the society *we* live in.[1]

Griffiths' sense of the term 'political' is quite distinctive: it is not for him synonymous with the didactic, the polemical; 'analytical' carries suggestions of enquiry, curiosity and scepticism, as he develops it here; and above all the stress is on character — *what does it make us,* if our views are such, or such. Even though two of his stage-plays realise tense historical, political situations, his approach constantly invites us to watch what the conflicts reveal of the personality and sensibility of the individuals involved in them. His plays explore the ways political attitudes affect the sublest movements of the human psyche and in this his artistry has a weight and scrupulous attention to detail lacking in the work of Brenton or Barker. For Griffiths the nature of an individual's political consciousness is reflected in many of his most intimate responses to experience; a character's opinions are invariably explored within a theatrical focus that draws our attention to the speaker's unconscious patterns of behaviour, and the dramatic action is organised so that we are aware always of the private emotions that colour and shape public speeches by controlling the quality of the rhetoric. Though his four full-length plays expound carefully structured arguments, those arguments are always left open-ended: aesthetically the plays are resolved, but the debate that each contains goes on.

Griffiths is an immensely gifted writer with a fine ear for, and marvellous facility with dialogue, but he is also — and this is the mark of the scruple so evident in the fabric and structure of his plays — a shrewd critic of his own achievements, and one all too conscious of the dangers of facility in that a flair for dialogue and parody can be over-indulged. In speaking or writing about his art, Griffiths invariably stresses a compulsion to discipline his fluency and spontaneity, to submit his work to the control of increasingly tighter dramatic forms that will allow "deeper, more intricate meanings" to come into play, "ambivalences, ironies" that prevent any reaching after easy solutions.[2] It is this refusal to accept the slapdash or to rely on popular and proven formulae that gives Griffiths his pre-eminence with Edward Bond among contemporary political dramatists. His is a restless, searching intellect; he neither patronises nor insults his audience but inspires them through the sheer rigour of his imagination. Griffiths' considerable talent for parody gives him an advantage here in that it allows him to flatter an audience into a recognition of conventional responses and opinions only to ease them through laughter into an awareness of the precise degree to which the conventional is divided from the authentic.

Sam Sam[3] (Griffiths' first theatre play written in the late Sixties, though not performed till 1972 at the Open Space) finds in parody both its form and meaning. The two acts contrast the life-styles of two brothers, each called Sam: one is an ironic, working-class stoic; the other a guilt-ridden idealist whose better education has got him established in a profession and a middle-class marriage. The very idea of the contrast intimates perhaps a hackneyed theme, but that is to take no account of the tone of the piece and the boisterous comedy with which Griffiths attacks the familiar. All the bleakness of Sam I's working-class upbringing is presented to us — the drudgery, the relentless routine at home and at work, the lack of privacy and the none-to-easily controlled tensions this provokes in a small, cluttered house — but the last thing Sam suffers is that anger and *angst* that, since Osborne, playwrights have identified with such a condition. For all the physical constrictions, Sam has an amazing mental freedom that is realised through the way this act is structured like a music-hall comedian's turn.

On an empty, darkened stage, Sam jokes away, confiding, teasing, chaffing, always like the stand-up comic working the audience into greater degrees of intimacy yet through his deft flashes of irony ever eluding total empathy. Sam reveals his life with knowing insight but his laughter transmutes what is familiar in his condition into something rich and strange. Instead of protracted stories about his relations with mother, father and wife (the usual substance of a comedian's patter) Sam calls forth out of the darkness brief scenes of family life into which he steps but which he effortlessly breaks free of and dispels when his joke has made its point. It is the freedom of movement which is important and the power to dispel the scenes (the mode of staging realises the point beautifully), for with them Sam dispels the audience's illusions about his state of mind. Each of the scenes is a deadly accurate parody of a particular literary or theatrical approach to working-class life: there is the confrontation of father and son in the manner of D. H. Lawrence, facing each other like snorting stags across the kitchen table ("Hae much more o' thy chelp, my young jockey and I'll rattle my fist about thee"[p. 69]), while mother looks on with "a huge, almost comic black eye"; later comes one of those interminable heart-to-heart talks between mates over a pint, so dear to some Royal Court and television dramatists, where four-letter words and terrible silences make up in the way of realism for what is lacking in the way of artistry. Each scene is played straight and sustained just long enough to engage our imaginative sympathies, then Sam comes leaping out of it to tackle our satisfaction:

How's that then? That a bit better? That a bit closer to your authentic working-class drudgery, is it? 'Course it is. Come on, own up, that's the real thing, innit? Eh? Who was it said Lawrence was more authentic than life itself? [p. 69]

Constantly Sam anticipates and ridicules our stereotyped expectations and directs his mimicry at the condescension latent in our pity and concern:

I bet you're beginning to think what an 'orrible life he leads, aren't you? I bet you're saying, "Christ, the poor benaighted blaiter, livin' in all that lot. What chance has he ever had." Well, actually, it's got nowt to do wi' chance. Nothing whatsoever. You see . . . there's two sorts of person. There's them as have it up here . . . And there's them as have it down here . . . You lot, yours'll be up there, if you've gorrit anywhere . . . Mine's down there. 'Swhat makes me so cocky. Irresistibly cocky, you might say. [p. 68]

"Cocky" is precisely the quality of the humour that abounds in Sam's act. If Griffiths exposes our liberal attitudes to the test of ridicule, it is because he wants us to engage with a quality often denied to the working-class sensibility, but one celebrated richly in the art of the music hall: the imagination and intelligence which is vested in a humour that can accommodate itself to the very worst of situations yet even in doing so can discover a source of never-failing resilience. Sam I turns every aspect of his life into a subject for laughter and, though its range may encompass anger and irony, the dominant tone is confident, easy-going and, most important, it is utterly devoid of cynicism. The comedy delights in the working man's life-enhancing capacity for low-cunning, for refusing to go under; the distance that Sam carefully preserves between himself and the audience, that uncertainty he provokes in them about when and why to take him seriously defines his cockiness with exactitude and shows its value: it is essential to his resilience that Sam resist every attempt by the audience to patronise him. Method and meaning are perfectly fused. How can Sam be labelled a prisoner of circumstances while, on his own terms, he is still so firmly in control? He will admit to no class hatred, no envy of his brother's 'established' position:

He's welcome — I mean that. Welcome. I'm happy with my own, here, where I belong. I wanna know where I am. I wanna know the rules. This is my world. [p. 68]

Ingeniously working the rules is his freedom. Played as Sam I originally was by Nikolas Simmonds with what Irving Wardle described as "a prodigious emotional intensity",[4] the remarkable effect of this act was the warmth of affection that shone through, despite all the tensions and ready verbal abuse by Sam's family of each other. There was a tight emotional security in this Sam's life that found its token in the confidence and affability of his relationship with the audience.

Sam II has no such intimacy with the audience and no such freedom to shape his and their perception of his mode of life. Act II is set consciously within a proscenium and the conventions of naturalism that compel surface calm and inner turmoil. It is seen as the mark of this Sam's failure in integrity that he is determined by the theatrical conventions in which he has chosen to play. In the closing moments of the play he is treated in emblematic fashion: abandoned by his wife who finds his unrelieved anguish tedious and sexually unliberated, he seeks consolation in nostalgia by replacing Jimmy Hendrix and Bartok on the record player with Brighouse and Raistrick Brass Band and in cherishing the status symbols, the objects of glass, brass and pottery, with which the set is tastefully decorated. Like many of Osborne's heroes, he despises his wife and her bank-manager father; but, given his passion for 'things' which advertise his culture and standing, his anger lacks real venom and energy and emerges as just petulance. His wife and in-laws easily dismiss him as "childish" and "puerile" because he lacks the insight and the moral fervour of the Osborne prototype that can puncture a victim's pretensions with devastating accuracy of aim. While Sam I expresses himself through his creative cunning, Sam II can only draw attention to himself by an effete jokiness (talking in a bogus, broad accent or spitting whisky over his father-in-law) that arouses only embarrassed distaste. He condemns others as types in terms of fashionable left-wing jargon but is content in himself to be a caricature: he is a victim of the Angry-Young-Man myth.

It was a part of that myth that the middle-class wife should be fragile in her femininity, passive and largely silent, suffering and forgiving, sexual only in exquisitely kittenish ways. Not so Sam's wife, Patricia: she is thrusting, sexually provocative, insistent on establishing her rights in their relationship. When he refuses to recognise how he humiliates her in insulting her parents, she assaults him:

PATRICIA: I really think I hate you. (*She gets up, crosses the room and stands over him*) You. . . . (*She crouches down and hits him across the face, left hand, right hand, a dozen or more times. The blows are hard: blood lurches from his upper lip and nose. He takes it all unflinchingly*) I said I hate you. You . . . guttersnipe. . . . You should have stayed with your own kind, Mr. Shatlock. Down *there*. Where you belong. (*She rides him like a dead crocodile. He is completely flat and inert. . . . They begin a frenzied session. Their lovemaking is hyenal. Patricia retains the upper perch throughout*) What's your name?
SAM: Shatlock.
PATRICIA: Shatlock what?
SAM: Shatlock, madam.
PATRICIA: That's better. Mustn't forget our station must we, Shat-lock?
SAM: No. Madam.
PATRICIA: No. And where do you come from Shatlock?
SAM: Water Lane, madam. Number Three. Water Lane, East Stock-port.
PATRICIA: What kind of district is that, Shatlock?
SAM: Poor, Ma'am. Very poor.
PATRICIA: And dirty.
SAM: And dirty, ma'am.
PATRICIA: Is that why you smell, Shatlock?
SAM: Yes, ma'am.
PATRICIA: You should take a bath, Shatlock. You positively stink.
SAM: Yes, ma'am.
PATRICIA: Give yourself a good scrubbing. (*No response*) Understood?
SAM: Yes'm.

PATRICIA: And come and show me when you've finished.
SAM: Yes'm.
PATRICIA: I want to see you . . . gleam.
SAM: Yes'm.
PATRICIA: Understood?
SAM: Yes'm.
PATRICIA: We'll clean you up yet, won't we Shatlock?
SAM: Yes'm.
PATRICIA: Make you . . . presentable.
SAM: (*close*) Mmm. Mmm.
PATRICIA: Make you *fit*.
SAM: Mmm. Mmm. [p. 77]

In Patricia's eyes Sam II is no more than a working class comic mouthing platitudes about bourgeois decadence and social progress. He is all words and no 'go'; and she recognises the reason for this more shrewdly than he does, which gives her the upper hand. Humiliating him verbally and sexually till she makes him admit to his origins is the only way left to her to break through his smugness to reach to where he can still *feel*. It is Sam II who experiences envy, craving Sam I's apparent satisfaction in life.

Griffiths' structure in *Sam Sam* with its shift of styles and the prescription that both brothers are to be played by the same actor certainly achieves the "ambivalances" and "ironies" he seeks in writing a play. But compared with his later work, it remains a rather precocious and contrived piece. There are incidental weaknesses, partly the outcome of the parodic modes chosen for the two acts. Sam I, for example, can question whether the audience have any real conception of the drudgery that has been his mother's lot in life and he can pinpoint their sentimental illusions about her, but the music hall format does not allow Griffiths to render the nature of that drudgery precisely either; the mother remains throughout merely a 'feed' as does the supporting comic in a music hall routine, an occasion for continuing the dialogue between Sam and the audience. In the second act Patricia's parents are characterised more in the stage-directions than in the given dialogue, where the emotional range is limited to expressions of boredom with each other and disdain for Sam II. The structural contrasts raise some thematic questions which are not resolved. The two halves of the play are linked by a scene in which Sam II is seen preparing a speech on education in the future which he is to deliver at the next Labour Party Conference. In part this highlights the conflicting values and responses in himself as the product of an educational system that has cut him free of the culture into which he was born but which has provided him with nothing as emotionally satisfying in return. But it encourages one to question Sam I's cunning and relative contentment: if education is a privilege, then is the attitude of mind he fosters the reason why he remains socially depressed? Is that brand of humour for all its satirical bite in fact conducive to preserving the *status quo*? Would hatred be a more profitable stand? And, if so, would it be as creative a response as his laughter? How easily can hate be deflected into envy and covetousness which seem to be Sam II's only remaining passions? One senses that Griffiths wishes the ironies to probe more searchingly and be darker in tone than they are, but the structure and the mode of parody prevent that. Interestingly two of his later plays seem to grow out of the experience of the separate acts of *Sam Sam*: *Comedians* from the first; *The Party* from the second. But for all its shortcomings *Sam Sam* remains a vigorous, provocative play in performance, remarkable for what it reveals of Griffiths' rapidity in discovering his particular strengths. Here are all the hallmarks of his later work: a bold, clear narrative line and structure; a marvellous ear for parodying styles of speech and styles of theatrical diction; an ability to use an audience and its responses, both stereotyped and original, in developing his theme; a deft precision in exposing how a character's political attitudes can be at the mercy of his more intimate self-deceptions; and a versatility in conceiving ideas in terms of potent theatrical metaphors.

When the Royal Shakespeare Company mounted *Occupations* (The Place, 1971),[5] they cast in it some of their finest talents in character-acting: Patrick Stewart, Ben Kingsley, Estelle Kohler, Sebastian Shaw. It was a token of the value the director, Buzz Goodbody, saw in the play, for Griffiths was then virtually unknown, and a token of her sensitivity to where the heart of the play lies. Griffiths himself has written of his delight at the "emotional bite" the actors achieved in performance, the "terrible, straining, vaunting excitements".[6] This might seem a curious view to take of a play which explores moral and political failure, were it not for what *Sam Sam* reveals of Griffiths' ability to make the theatricality of a play convey his essential meaning. To criticize the play, as Irving Wardle did of the London production,[7] because its political and moral centres do not coincide is to wish the play to be a far more didactic and doctrinaire work than it is. Wardle justified his view by claiming that Gramsci, the communist intellectual, one of the play's two main actors, is finally dismissed as a simpleton. That opinion of Gramsci is indeed expressed by his political opponent and his apparent political friend surprisingly concurs; but it is not a view that Griffiths' artistry endorses, especially since so much of the play's action concentrates on examining the moral worth of that 'friend' — Kabak. The moral and political centres of the play are more intricate than Wardle would suggest.

The occasion for the play but not predominantly its subject is the occupation by the workers of the Fiat factories in Turin in 1920 and the procrastinations of the Italian Communist Party which prevented the event from turning into a national revolution on the Russian pattern. Gramsci inspires the Turin workers but, in the idealistic belief that the choice of action must be their decision, refuses to lead them. Passionately he exhorts them to "beware rhetoric. Even mine" [p. 45]. That he will not lead the men and encourage armed action infuriates the opportunist in Kabak, a Russian agent, who would be prepared to foment a local revolution in Turin whether or not there were national agreement to support such a development. Against Kabak's image of the work force as any army for the using, Gramsci argues that they are better seen as individuals whose energies and lives could, if misdirected, be pointlessly wasted. Such "love" excites Kabak's exasperation and contempt; but Gramsci defends himself on the grounds of the long-term issues involved in revolution, a perspective for which Kabak has noticeably scant imagination:

Treat masses as expendable, as fodder, *during* the revolution, you will always treat them thus. I'll tell you this, Comrade Kabak, if you see masses that way, there can be no revolution worth the blood it spills. [p. 50]

In Ben Kingsley's performance this was the moment that profoundly illuminated the character he was projecting — a man who, even when burning with political fervour, while addressing the workers was invariably self-effacing. Though crippled and dwarfish, his every movement had, as Griffiths' directions insist, a rare delicacy intimating a beauty of temperament, a care for others that never relaxed, however exhausted or antagonised he might be. Humiliated by the chicanery of the party executive which results in nothing being achieved by the occupations and prophetically conscious of the horrors of a right-wing backlash, Kingsley's Gramsci was profoundly tragic when confronting the workers with the news that they must return to work; tenderly concerned to salvage their dignity and keep their commitment alive, he had to resort to the very rhetoric he had long warned them against:

Today, we have the referendum. It must not be made the occasion for despair and dissolution. Rather we must see it as an urgent lesson from history; as a call for tighter, even more disciplined action. The liberation of our class is not a part-time hobby, and it isn't the work of small minds and feeble imaginations. When disillusion prospers like malaria in a Southern swamp, when a cause has been recklessly squandered by those to whom it should never have been entrusted, only he who can keep his heart strong and his will bright as steel can be regarded as a fighter for the working class; can be called a revolutionary. [p. 66]

A quite different kind of self-effacement obtains with Kabak, the Russian agent, who is present in the West in quest of financial aid for Russian industry and to establish trade concessions but keeps the precise nature of his mission a closely guarded secret: it is, he informs Gramsci, "delicate" and offers that as his justification for taking no public stance over the occupations. Just how delicate his manoeuvres are is not fully revealed even to the audience till the closing section of the play. This technique of intimating through tensions in the playing matters for which an explanation is not given till the denouement makes enormous demands on an actor's creativity, if he is to render that explanation when it comes convincing psychologically, to make it a moment of insight that is genuinely illuminating and not a bathetic underlining of what has long been obvious to a sensitive audience. Too easily it could seem a clever device to provoke suspense. Griffiths lets Kabak command interest by virtue of his constantly eluding definition. Kabak is to be played as a man of rigorous self-discipline; his face, Griffiths insists, must rarely register clues to his state of mind. Yet it is the nature of the inner man in Kabak that puzzles us, seeing that he finds it necessary to exercise this degree of discipline over himself in the privacy of his hotel room. (The audience never sees him elsewhere.) His movements must have the speed and prevision of "one who knows he is being secretly watched" [p. 13]. As one of the state's "professional guardian[s] of the status quo" [p. 58], he is constantly playing under the scrutiny of his communist conscience and is both anxious that he take the best advantage of the situation he finds himself in to further Russia's objectives and conscious that he will have to account for himself to the powers he represents. Kabak has no life outside what the State dictates; it is essential to his political function that he practise self-effacement and be all things to all men; personality has to be wholly suppressed.

Griffiths makes this difficult study in non-being exciting by exploring the degree to which necessity makes Kabak an actor required to play for an unseen audience of powerful critics (his communist superiors) who are willing him to complete his scenario to their satisfaction and achieve the ending that flatters their interests most. Griffiths neither forces the analogy (the agent as actor) through rhetoric nor explores it through soliloquy; he allows it to impinge on the audience's imagination through details of performance. There is Kabak's habit of dressing to suit the part, changing his clothes for the various interviews with the Italians who visit his room to discuss the occupations: impeccable business-suit for travel and in the company of the hotelier; Bulgarian national costume for greeting Gramsci; a suave dressing-gown for bribing the spy, D'Avanzo. For each scene Kabak meticulously arranges the quality and angle of the lighting in his room, deftly creating the appropriate mood (Griffiths' command of stage-space and stage-effects is impressive for its purposefulness); and similarly he adjusts and controls the tone of the exchanges that ensue or at least attempts to do so; but what is noticeable as the play develops is the disparity that often exists between the words Kabak utters and the quality of the silence that establishes itself between Kabak and each of his visitors. Gramsci speaking in public is an extension of the man we see in private; his integrity is complete. But with Kabak what obtains is an exemplary technique; beyond that, however, is an intense self-consciousness calculating the success of every effect. The gap between a surface ease of manner and an underlying tension and watchfulness immediately engages an audience's attention, alerting them to the silences behind words, where Griffiths begins to examine in moral and psychological terms what it takes to be a 'good' Communist and, more importantly, what it *costs*.

Patrick Stewart, who played Kabak, is an actor who has the gift of being able to 'work' silence, communicating the drift of unspoken thought, anguish, even moments of vision through his brooding presence (his Shakespeare in the R.S.C.'s revival of *Bingo* at the Warehouse in 1977 was the most notable attempt at the role to date); and as such he was the perfect foil to Ben Kingsley as Gramsci, an actor who is at his best when a part allows him to act with great intensity directly out of the emotional core of the character. (Hamlet and Baal have proved ideal vehicles for him; and he excels in manic roles like Mosca and Ford where the character's emotionalism is externalised; Shakespeare's Brutus, however, where there is a wide disparity between surface manner and inner emotional turbulence eluded him completely.[8] One cannot envisage Kingsley making Enobarbus the complex tragic figure Stewart presented in Peter Brook's 1978 production of *Antony and Cleopatra*, a man broken by the discovery of his own capacity to *feel*.) Stewart's performance as Kabak was remarkable for the complex nuances of insight he evoked in our imaginations through silence and the degrees of nervous tension he generated in the exchanges that make up the play. Gramsci's dismissal of Kabak's view of the workers as "fodder" proves in time to be an exact criticism of the man himself: "I came to the masses with the same mechanical view of them, and my own relation to them as you have just propounded. Use them. Tool them up. Keep them greased. Discard when they wear out" [p. 50]. The play shows Kabak's constant measuring of his own efficiency, provoked by his fear that he also might outwear use; and, given that fear, it shows too in time the profound psychological anarchy that underlies his will to conform to a prescribed pattern of behaviour. Gramsci's very being presents a constant challenge to Kabak for he embodies a different kind of conscience which Kabak has found it necessary to suppress: moral idealism may have fostered the revolutionary impulse in Kabak but it has given place now to a wily opportunism. For all his attempts at amity with Gramsci, a reserve continually obtrudes. Gramsci comes to understand the nature of this unease at the moment of his personal humiliation and, understanding, characteristically pities Kabak. The silence between the two men never conveys the peace and equanimity of genuine friendship.

How accurate Gramsci's silent condemnation of Kabak is may be inferred through the intimate scenes Kabak shares with his mistress, Angelica, a former Russian aristocrat. She embarrasses him because she compromises his status as a communist agent and he has come to loathe her for, dying as she is painfully of cancer, her condition urges on him responsibilities that his duties as an agent make it impossible for him to undertake. That her claim on him has its roots solely in his emotional needs makes him further despise her: she is his Achilles heel, the touch of vulnerability that makes him human but jeopardises his skill as actor and politician. He speaks soothingly to calm her but prefers to drug her to complete insensibility rather than listen to her fears; he betrays her sexually with her own maid; and, when the reproach (which she never once actually voices but which is instinctively felt by him in her very presence there in his room) overwhelms him finally, he tells her with brutal frankness that she is soon to die. The revulsion for her that motivates his outburst confirms the awareness that they both appreciate but never speak of, that his need of her physically has largely been to boost his peasant pride in having a lady for a lover. The increasing hardness of his tone in referring to Angelica with Polya, her maid, and with Gramsci is a token of both the intensity of Kabak's emotional turmoil and the force of will needed to control it. Kabak's last words to Gramsci, to be spoken with an unexpected softness according to Griffiths' direction, are: "You still love them [the people] too much, comrade" [p. 77]. It seems a last effort at establishing friendship between them and is an expression of Kabak's gratitude that Gramsci has come to offer his help in nursing Angelica after Kabak himself has left Turin. Then: *"Gramsci turns, looks at Kabak for a long time, leaves without answer"*. The silence is profoundly disturbing: it intimates first Gramsci's astonishment at the revelation of a crack in Kabak's carapace implicit in his tone which seems to express *care*; secondly pity that the carapace exists forbidding more sustained expressions of feeling; lastly shock or even disgust, at the hypocrisy of Kabak's words as an attempt to ingratiate himself back into Gramsci's good opinion despite his conniving at Gramsci's betrayal. Gramsci's silent withdrawal is a sign of his moral rectitude and his recognition of the complete moral bankruptcy of Kabak with his commitment to political efficiency.

The nature of that bankruptcy has been established for the audience through Kabak's exchanges with the last of the visitors to his room. This is the one moment in the play when Kabak completely relaxes into a tone of camaraderie and rapport with another individual; and it is with Valletta, the capitalist from the Fiat organisation. They light cigars, settle down with their brandy, and laugh together at what they believe is Gramsci's absurdity in underestimating the power and intelligence of his political adversaries. Valletta outlines to Kabak's admiration his new welfare schemes for the factory workers and his ambition that they too in time "will live Fiat the way I live it now" [p. 73]. It is a chilling moment of relevation, that sudden letting-go of all the tension and Kabak's ensuing calm. It is too a brilliant theatrical and moral climax as Kabak announces his true reason for being in Turin: the establishing of trade links with Fiat at any cost. Valletta's toast — "Business as usual" [p. 72] — which provokes a bray of laughter from Kabak, marks an economically necessary but secret *détente* with the West that quite compromises Russia's stated idealogy as expressed in Lenin's letters to Gramsci and the work force occupying the factories. Gramsci's advice to the workers — "Beware rhetoric" — has a bitter aptness, though it is only in his final silence with Kabak that he recognises the full extent of its relevance. For Kabak the secret agent, socialism is an occupation (in the other sense of the term), where survival requires one to accept and accomodate hazards to such a degree that commitment to any ideology rapidly wears thin. Commitment is possible only to the State, whose objectives are everything and beside which the conscience of the individual is not deemed worthy of consideration. What *Occupations* examines are the monumental suppressions that must accompany such willed self-effacement. Angelica's is the last view of Kabak to find expression in the play: in her "apocalyptic" delirium she confuses him and his like with the cancerous disease erupting under her skin and consuming her very being; and indeed, except for Valletta, Kabak has preyed inexorably on everyone, even — and most subtly — on himself. Both Gramsci and Kabak are betrayed as a direct result of their different kinds of commitment and both are invested with tragic status. It is the purposeful theatricality of Griffiths' conception that releases an audience's imagination into this inner thematic debate. *Occupations* may appear on the page a very cerebral play; but if a production faithfully observes Griffiths' theatrical details concerning lighting, dress, nuances in mood, rhythms of dialogue and the shaping of silences, then it becomes a play richly textured in its emotional and psychological implications, one that does indeed achieve "terrible, straining, vaunting excitements".

The opening sequences of Griffiths' next venture, *The Party* (Old Vic, 1973),[9] underwent considerable revision when the National Theatre arranged for a small-scale version of its production to go on tour. Formerly the play began with a naked couple in bed failing with frantic desperation to achieve sexual fulfilment together, while quotations from Marx, Lenin, Trotsky were projected out of the darkness of their bedroom. There was a somewhat risible quality (obviously unintended) about the incongruities of this which, in his revision, Griffiths turned to his advantage by making even more marked the surreal disparity between various images confronting his audience. The visual element now focussed on towering projections of the Communist authors but these were offered as illustrations to a lecture by Groucho Marx on the economic philosophy of his namesake, Karl — "They do hug the stage these boys" [p. 10]. Not surprisingly, the lecture is an utter travesty of the original thinking, particularly given Groucho's infectious glee at the mere mention of money: "My, how straight you're sitting now. Me too, folks" [pp. 10-11]. Each of the ponderously-phrased idealogical statements has to struggle for credence against the comedian's appeal to his audience's urge to covet. At the mention of Marx's belief that "money is the pander . . . between human life and the means of existence", Olivier (or an actor mimicking him) suddenly appears in a spotlight as Timon of Athens uttering his passionate denunciation of the evils of gold and his belief that its "right nature" is to corrupt all human potential. Delivered with Olivier's customary panache we feel its import on the pulses through the immediacy of the simple phrasing and the gathering energy of the examples illustrating humanity's willingness to be bought. Language is relished for its power to realise ideas in the imagination as potent images of experience. Beside this intensity the ideological abstractions of the communist writers seem flatly unimpressive, although they are repeating Shakespeare's fundamental argument. Their moral indictment lacks his fervour in making an appeal to the intellect rather than the imagination. As the image of Olivier fades away, Groucho remarks: "There's nobody speaking like that anymore, believe me" [p. 11]. Almost immediately he loses the thread of his argument and wanders away muttering to himself about his inability to keep his mouth shut and keep a tight hold on his money. The play which follows is about why there is nobody speaking like Timon any more; the rapid juxtaposition in this fantasy of styles and contrasting tones of speech, ranging through fierce cynicism (Shakespeare), moral earnestness (Marx) and lighthearted, because unthinking, apathy (Groucho), has tuned our ears finely to discriminate how rhetoric reveals the psychology of the mind that shapes it. Style is the expression of the man; it is a way of detecting the private self that controls the public stance.

The Party has virtually no plot; as in the prologue, a range of personalities are explored to illuminate a theme - the current moral failure of the Socialist cause and the psychological malaise that this has instilled in English partisans of the Left. The occasion is a meeting of a group of communist intellectuals at the time of the student uprising in Paris in 1968. Periodically through the play film of these events is projected on to the walls of the elegant trendily furnished house in SW7, where the meeting is taking place over drinks and food, to keep us informed of actual historical facts while we concentrate on the attempts of the group to come to terms with the uprising. The impact of the surreal dislocations of the prologue continues to work on in one's imagination, for there is a deeply ironic contrast between the gathering tension, activity and violence of events on film and the sedate, controlled discussion of the Party as it subsides under the weight of its own inertia. A disturbing sense of unreality prevails as the walls of the room dissolve (undermining one's conventional response to a naturalistic box-setting) to be replaced by the different dimension of film which reduces the actors to frozen silhouettes against the brightness of the screens, their humanity totally extinguished. Yet cinematic images in a theatre seem eerily out of place and insubstantial. There is a grotesque sense that if the fighting were happening outside their own walls, the members of the party would still be trying to decide an order of procedure, fixing a rota of speakers and asking for nominations for a chairman; protocol has become a disease within the group, beside which imaginative engagement with events in Paris fades into insignificance; indeed Paris is a situation they choose to keep at a necessary distance precisely because it tests the strength of their commitment. This effect is offset by one's sense of film as potentially a visual fiction which gives a kind of weight to the denunciation by the oldest member of the party of the motives of the French insurgents which he views as so much play-acting. One of the subsidiary themes of the play is to be the extent to which film and television have robbed man of the faculty for imaginative engagement with life in the process of history by wantonly confusing the boundary between fiction and fact. The very mode of setting the play, its surreal insubstantiality, activates moral, psychological and political resonances. (The mode is reminiscent of Genet's prescriptions for staging *The Balcony*, which similarly uses visual effects to *evoke* the condition of the modern, fragmented political consciousness which the action of the play then defines and explains.)

The party has been organised by Joe Shawcross, a television director of working class origins and somewhat fading Leftist inclinations; the house is his and he cherishes its ostentatious good taste as the proof of a successful career. Characteristically the debate is not his inspiration; the idea for the gathering together of a wide range of socialist opinion for a "frank exchange of views" originated with John Tagg, an ageing Scottish Trotskyist, who is seeking to revive interest in his political splinter group. Though a discussion has been envisaged, in the event the evening is dominated by two speakers — Tagg himself and Andrew Ford, a lecturer at L.S.E., a professional exponent of Marxist doctrine. Their evident distaste for each other generates a tension that culminates in a long statement of their individual positions which ends the first act.

Ford offers a resumé of the various revisions Marxist thought has undergone and outlines the historical reasons for them; the nucleus of his speech, for which this historical perspective is a subtle preparation, is the view that the force for social change has passed from Europe to the Third World to the exent that all that European socialists can now do is assist anti-capitalist movements amongst minority cultures abroad. It is the kind of speech which makes confusing play with ideas about "centres" and "epi-centres" of political activity; it is learned, beautifully structured but quite alienating to the uninformed in its reliance on jargon; it is less a contribution to a debate than an authoritative view insisting on respect, a performance (as played by Denis Quilley) by a professional who relies on sheer technique to win him approval. The manner is everything to the point where it has become empty mannerism. Quilley excels in roles where charm masks a total and often dangerous amorality (one recalls his Jamie in *Long Day's Journey Into Night* (New, 1971) and the relaxed bonhomie with which he encouraged his younger brother's imitation of his own degenerate ways). With Ford Quilley extended the type to include a degree of self-awareness; the charm had become a conscious part of the act, the last resort of a practised hand at appealing for sympathy to relieve him of the need to gain attention by genuinely stimulating thought, since such originality was patently quite beyond his intellectual powers. Repeatedly Ford resorts to convoluted language and sentence-structures to disguise what are essentially platitudes; and he openly delights in arguing himself out of the need for any immediate political activity regarding the Paris riots; he would like, he says, to talk about the French situation but perhaps there is a more pressing need to "tease out some basic agreement on terminology" first [p. 35]. The very language shows his retreat from any direct, *felt* involvement with what he is talking about:

The Marxian notion of a revolution carried by the majority of the exploited masses, culminating in the seizure of power and in the setting up of a proletarian dictatorship which initiates socialization, is overtaken by historical development. I would even argue that Marx himself would now see that that analysis pertains to a stage of capitalist productivity and organization which has been overtaken; it does not project the higher stage of capitalist productivity self-evidently achieved in the last half-century, including the productivity of destruction and the terrifying concentration of the instruments of annihilation and of indoctrination in the hands of the state or its class representatives. [pp. 38-39]

Like an old ham-actor, Quilley's Ford could make the specious sound meaningful by virtue of his technique. If he embarrassed his on-stage audience, it was at the disparity between his abstract, self-effacing language and the egotistical smugness of his tone of delivery. It was the proof of his lack of engagement with his audience that to the end he believed in the success of his manner to convince then. However bright he may formerly have been, Ford now verbalises to disguise his mediocrity and his lack of commitment, belief or vision. For Ford, as for Kabak, socialism is an occupation.

Tagg is quite different; he quickly puts his finger on Ford's weakness, that he is in a stage of intellectual inertia looking for scapegoats in repressed minorities as an excuse for not confronting his own frustration and misery:

You start from the presumption that only you are intelligent and sensitive enough to see how bad capitalist society is. Do you really think the young man who spends his whole life in monotonous and dehumanizing work doesn't see it too? And in a way more deeply, more woundingly? . . . Suddenly you lose contact . . . with the moral tap-roots of socialism. In an objective sense, you actually stop believing in a revolutionary perspective, in the possibility of a socialist society and the creation of socialist man. You see the difficulties, you see the complexities and contradictions, and you settle for those as a sort of game you can play with each other. Finally, you learn to enjoy your pain; to need it, so that you have nothing to offer your bourgeois peers but a sort of moral exhaustion. [p. 49]

The judgement is incisive, acute and phrased in beautifully measured prose. Olivier, embellishing the qualities intimated by such clear, dispassionate speech, played Tagg as the direct contrast to Ford: kindly, humane, shrewd, firm in his analysis, a man of real, though controlled feeling. Tagg is aware of the widespread disaffection in England and of its causes, and argues that the situation can only be remedied by a complete return to basic principles:

The party means discipline. It means self-scrutiny, criticism, responsibility, it means a great many things that run counter to the traditions and values of Western bourgeois intellectuals. It means being bound in and by a common purpose. But above all, it means deliberately severing yourself from the prior claims on your time and moral commitment of personal relationships, career, advancement, reputation and prestige. And from my limited acquaintance with the intellectual stratum in Britain, I'd say that was the greatest hurdle of all to cross. Imagine a life without the approval of your peers. Imagine a life without *success*. The intellectual's problem is not vision, it's commitment. You enjoy biting the hand that feeds you, but you'll never bite it off. So those brave and foolish youths in Paris now will hold their heads out for the baton and shout their crazy slogans for the night. But it won't stop them from graduating and taking up their positions in the centres of ruling class power and privilege later on. [pp. 52-53].

This drastic indictment of everyone else on stage and film ends Act One.

It is a challenging moment: Tagg seems to be voicing the long-suppressed conscience of the Left and to be offering a way of recovering socialist ideals. But what of his cynical dismissal of events in Paris? Is this all sound common sense and frank speaking, or something more? Olivier is a powerfully histrionic actor, a romantic whose control of an audience's emotions is superlative. The cool, unflamboyant (though highly musical) delivery, largely from a seated position, of this long aria of criticism obviously demanded considerable suppressions of his normal stage personality;[10] the tensions this set up he projected into his performance as Tagg in the form of a constant tightening of the already craggy lips and a nervous toying with a handkerchief regularly used to mop his brow. The voice remained calm, persuasive in its quietness, even when the criticism intensified, but these movements suggested that the apparent ease was an effort of will. Given the political crisis, the composure of the voice and of the reasoned attitudes seemed as strangely incongruous as Ford's hollow satisfaction. Olivier's voice was insidiously powerful in commanding assent; yet it did not leave one serene, but inwardly rebellious to a point of fury; one sensed one had been the dupe of a brilliant technique. Several of the visitors to Shawcross's party have previously warned him to be on his guard against Tagg. Hearing of Tagg's imminent arrival they have been openly hostile, yet they have each lapsed into deference or been tight-lipped on his appearance. Only Sloman, a playwright who uses his drunkenness as an excuse for abusing everyone's motives for being present, continues to be nasty to Tagg's face; but his resistence is childishly snide and petty — "Don't come your God the Father bit with me" [p. 42]. Tagg is unperturbed by Sloman's clowning, instead he speaks gently of the vision that once inspired Sloman's work but which is now lost:

"I can see the bright green . . . strip of grass beneath the wall and the clear blue sky above the wall, and sunlight everywhere. Life . . . is beautiful. Let the future generations cleanse it . . . of all evil . . . oppression, and violence, and enjoy it to the full." [p. 43]

Sloman is broken by this show of compassion. Tagg has unerringly pinpointed the weakness of everyone on stage but makes no attempt to redirect the emotions focussed in their guilt towards any more creative ends. His technique of gaining a hold over others by searching out their secret points of vulnerability renders them not malleable but impotent. And that in turn, as the second act shows, renders his own power impotent.

No one in the group has the intellectual stamina to oppose Tagg's analysis, and the second act opens with the group's dispersal, embittered and sullen — in itself a significant comment on his performance. Tagg, however, remains, anxious to establish contact by telephone with his sympathisers in Paris; Joe is astonished to observe Tagg's delight at knowing his French group have refused to join the fighting. Tagg's defence is that under the present circumstances, "insurrection is simply another term for suicide" [p. 59], since the proper revolutionary perspective does not obtain: the impulse for revolution must come from the working class, he argues, and if the French workers associate with the students, those "petty bourgeois anarchists" indulging in their *"folie de grandeur"*, then the true revolutionary spirit may well suffer an irreparable defeat. He tells how as a young man he met and was inspired by Trotsky — "a burning intelligence . . . refusing to be quenched, to be put out" [p. 61] — and bemoans the collapse of European socialism under the impact of Stalin's evil purges. Always the wrong man is leader and betrays the cause by the example he sets. Insistently he brings the conversation back to discuss this need for a leader and the ideal type he should be. The long first act discourse now emerges as an unstated appeal to Tagg's audience to recognise out of their own abject condition his superior intellectual and moral qualities that would make him the perfect, long-awaited Messiah of English socialism. The tense suppressions are seen now to be symptomatic of the man: he has steeled himself relentlessly to be a model of puritan virtues. Tagg's life has been one long self-denial, but for a cause that is at root personal and not altruistic. It is characteristic of the man that he should make no direct public reference to his ambition; only the tensions underlying his composure reveal his fear, given his powerful scruples, that he is guilty of the sin of pride in vaunting (if only by implication) his superior moral worth and of covetousness in desiring the leadership. As played by Olivier, Tagg became a study of the strengths and weaknesses of the puritan conscience. Tagg's whole performance in Act One emerges in retrospect as a highly subtle attempt at moral and emotional blackmail. His continuing failure to achieve the recognition he feels is his due is aggravated to despair at the thought of his age and the imminence of his death (he tells Joe with studied nonchalance that he is dying of cancer). His eloquence is motivated as much by self-pity nowadays as by ambition.

The extent of Tagg's desperation is revealed through the way he turns his story of meeting Trotsky into a far less subtle attempt to blackmail Joe into the position of disciple-elect: "We only die when we fail to take root in others" [p. 61]. If this is not an expression of his despair, it is a gross failure of perception and honesty with himself, for Joe, though the host of the party, has been the one character there whom everyone else has ignored. He is without zest or opinions; surrounded by good actors like Ford and Tagg, he has repeatedly muffed his lines and dissolved into incoherence; he is completely devoid of the charisma that allows them to "hug the stage" (to echo Groucho's telling remark from the prologue). The lack of theatrical stature, that Griffiths' handling of the role insists on, is an exact correlative for his lack of moral and political stature in the play's argument. Beside Tagg, as Joe all too readily admits, he has an "upper-second soul" [p. 46]. It is Tagg's fervent belief that no revolution will succeed that is not rooted in the working class. Joe and all the rest of Tagg's on-stage audience belong to the post-war generation of educated working-class children who have made it to the middle class and are too proud of their achievement to forgo their advantage. Tagg may talk of a brotherhood bound by a common purpose, but his audience is alienated from him and from each other by the guilt they feel at the wide gap in their lives between their principles and their practice. As the play progresses, they subside into drink, drugs, mind-blowing music, lose themselves in self-pity over the failure of their marriages or in frantic eroticism or talk of their desperate need for that new status-symbol of the middle classes — a psychiatrist. Joe is in agonies of indecision about whether to give his brother a fraction of his income to help set him up in his own business and finds bizarre excuses for never going North to visit his parents. Wealth has given them all access to the means to numb their guilt; but, becoming increasingly dependent on the means, they will never have the courage to purge the guilt. Joe, like Sloman, despises the work he is required to produce for television for its cultural poverty; though he clearly has standards in taste, he is too apathetic to make something creative of his disgust. Seeking to formulate some justification for himself and his peers and to express the grounds of his admiration for Tagg, Joe tells him: "I can find no trace of what my psychology tutor used to call 'the civilised worm' in you" [p. 60]. Tagg's reply — "I'm proletarian. I killed the worm before it turned. (*He takes in the room, piece by piece, then back to JOE.*) Mebbe you should've done the same" — admits to a difference between them which, insofar as it activates Joe's guilt, places him quite beyond the reach of Tagg's appeal for sympathy. It is the density of the psychological analysis working always behind and through the political discussion that gives Griffiths' play its richness of texture and shapes its dramatic excitements.

Though *The Party* takes apathy and isolation as its subject, it does contain one moment of real emotional contact in what is an original and daring piece of writing. When Tagg has left, Joe and Sloman start reminiscing about their childhood and adolescence in an urban slum in the North. The prevailing mood is one of nostalgia. Sloman chances to round off one of his stories with a quotation: " 'He that diggeth a pit shall fall into it.' Ecclesiastes." Joe suddenly takes it up as a challenge and, as the resulting sparring match gathers momentum, the two slough off their sentimentality:

JOE (*thinking*): 'Pride goeth before destruction, and an haughty spirit before a fall.' Proverbs.
SLOMAN: Good. Yes, Erm. 'They were as fed horses in the morning; everyone neighed after his neighbour's wife.' Jeremiah?
JOE: 'Saying peace, peace, when there is no peace.' Yes.
SLOMAN: 'Is there no balm in Gilead; is there no physician there?'
JOE: 'Write the vision, and make it plain upon tables, that he may run that readeth it.'
SLOMAN: Habukkuk! (*They both laugh*) Cunt! 'His head and his hairs were white like wool, as white as snow; and his eyes were something . . . as the flame of fire.'
JOE: 'His voice as the sound of many waters.'
SLOMAN: 'I am he that liveth and was dead.'
JOE: 'Be then faithful unto death, and I will give thee a crown of life.'
SLOMAN: 'But he shall rule thee with a rod of iron.'
JOE: 'And because thou art lukewarm, and neither cold nor hot, I will spue thee out of my mouth.'
SLOMAN: 'An behold, a pale horse, and his name that sat on him was Death.' [pp. 63-64]

Though they laugh it off ("There's nowt'll replace the formative intellectual matrices of a really well-run Sunday school"), it is a profoundly moving experience in the play because it is the one moment of pure, spontaneous joy. Albeit a travesty, another of the sophisticated games at the party, they both enter into it with exhilaration. The ancient poetic wisdom of the Bible provides some ironic glosses on the events and the personalities we have been watching, showing that its proverbial rhetoric still has not lost its relevance or its emotional bite. Interestingly the quotations have a lucidity, poetic richness and moral assurance that is unlike the quality of Tagg's speech. The game allows the men a point of genuine contact with each other in the shared recovery of a moment of childhood experience and with it the momentary recovery of a whole culture and its style of eloquence that, as Tagg implies, they have abandoned to their cost. The brevity and isolation of the moment within the play stresses the tragedy of that loss. That deep down such a culture still has its roots in their emotions is evident from the incident which foreshadowed this sequence, when Tagg reduced Sloman to helpless tears simply by reciting with quiet fervour a call for liberty phrased in the rhetoric of the Bible. If *The Party* examines the tragedy that lies in a generation's renouncing of its political heritage, the focus on language, speech-patterns and rhetoric as correlatives for different kinds of psychological evasion of reality shows that the political crisis is part of a larger cultural tragedy too — one which, since most of the characters are involved in education, theatre, television and the press, they are actively promoting with little sense of the consequences.

It is the merit of Griffiths' excellence as a dramatist that he does not allow the urgency of his themes to force him into statement; instead he trusts his audience to engage with his themes through the way they inform character and dialogue: Griffiths' ideas act as a principle of organisation behind a dramatic structure that ranges free of plot. One has only to compare *The Party* with David Mercer's *Cousin Vladimir* (Aldwych, 1978)[11] to see the force of this. It too is concerned with the moral bankruptcy of a particular well-heeled group, who in their state of near-perpetual drunkenness cannot distinguish cruelty from nastiness any longer in their dealings with each other. One of the group, Austin Proctor, introduces two Russian defectors to the circle, who resent their arrival, since it implies a new sense of political commitment in Austin that might jeopardise their chances of continuing to sponge on his wealth. After watching — for the most part silently — the drunken antics of Austin's friends, their petty betrayals, sexual infidelities, their misery, spite, boorishness and downright crudity, the Russians elect to return to Moscow. If Mercer's play appears shallow beside *The Party* it is because so much time is devoted to justifying in terms of plot (and none too plausibly at that) Katya and Vladimir's presence in the West, which is the essential premise of the play. Though the other characters self-consciously remark that they can hardly be considered as *representative* of English society, they are treated as such when the occasion demands it, as in Vladimir's final denunciation of the group for their want of courage, freedom and life. That statement of the play's intent in its closing moments affords no surprise: the abject condition of the English characters, made worse by their complete indifference to their state, has long been apparent and, even allowing for the fact that Vladimir's attack is couched in his halting English, as a dramatic climax the expression here touches the banal:

The moral struggle in the Soviet Union is one thing for us and another thing for you. Cousin Vladimir is not inspiring? How do you think you seem to Katya? . . . We had our so-called superfluous man in the nineteenth century — and quite enough of him thank you very much, . . . I only begin to truly love Katya since I see her watching you, Austin. . . . It is a matter for pain and remorse in my eyes that you are not in fact moved by her at all. . . . Forgive me, Austin, but your anguish suddenly seems trivial to me. [p. 86]

Moreover the play lacks texture and variety of pace; it was cruelly taxing even on fine actors like Julian Glover and George Baker to ask them to project nothing but deepening degrees of mental vacuity as their drink took its hold. The moral urgency of the idea behind *Cousin Vladimir* quite gets the better of its dramatic artistry: one felt in the last analysis that here was the material for a television play expanded to fill the requirements of a stage drama, risking obviousness and monotony as a result (how much more economically and realistically the television would render the characters' drunken decline through a rapid sequence of shots intimating the passage of time). Even so one would expect a more searching enquiry into the cause of the all-consuming and willed apathy of Austin and his circle than Mercer offers; instead the occasion for a subject is taken for the subject itself and the resulting play lacks depth. Despite the political possibilities of the situation, Mercer's area of reference remains exclusively moral and the prevailing tone one of distaste with the result that, wanting the range and delicacy of Griffiths' psychological insight, Mercer's subject never realises its tragic possibilities.

Where technically *Cousin Vladimir* has the edge over *The Party* is in Mercer's more accomplished deployment of a large cast: each of his "hard core" of drinkers has a firmly sketched life-history and the ensemble-work required of the actors does not prevent them sustaining individual characterisations. Griffiths brings a cast of eleven to his party but only four attract our interest; the remainder, especially the women, are largely cyphers required to improvise a background hubbub of party-chatter; even their response to the main speakers is collective, a barrage of sound in which different personal views make no impact. What impresses about Griffiths' development over the decade of the Seventies is the creative discipline evident in his recognition of technical difficulties and his perseverance in overcoming them. *Comedians* (Nottingham Playhouse and Old Vic, 1975)[12] is set in a night-school class of six students and their teacher; and the seven voices are graphically individualised as well as orchestrated as a group when they corporately engage in the exercises that teach them their chosen discipline. Once again it is the psychological and temperamental differences emerging between the various students and their tutor that foster the debate; every voice has a necessary contribution to make (as indeed have the three cameo roles of the examiner, the caretaker and the Indian visitor that make up the cast), which is important when much of the argument centres on the moral and political dangers of judging individuals as stereotypes.

What also impresses about Griffiths' work is the way that one play in a random detail will suddenly afford him the entire subject for another. At the end of *The Party* Sloman condemns the work he and Joe produce for television with withering sarcasm. They may congratulate themselves on creating socially-conscious drama but, he asserts: "This is a society that has matured on descriptions of its inequity and injustice" [p. 67]. Is it enough to make the liberal-minded *feel* good because their sympathies have been aroused? Should art, he argues, not aim to provoke a more active response than a wave of emotion of a kind that can quickly degenerate into self-satisfaction? Their predicament as artists extends the central discussion of the play: how can one effect a change in mentalities that have grown more than half in love with the easeful death of luxuriating in a sense of guilt? It is, as Griffiths shows, of the essence of apathy that it can absorb all experience and convert it to its own nature. An enquiry into this artistic dilemma forms the debate which creates the structure of *Comedians*.

The second act of the play is taken up with the performances in a Working Men's Club of a group of comedians who have just completed their training in the art of the stand-up comic. The various turns allow Griffiths the ideal outlet for his own versatile gift for jokes and for parodying unusual styles of speech, though the gifts are not indulged but disciplined to stimulate in his audience skilful and exacting discriminations, for what many might deem a low form of popular art is being shown to merit testing against the highest aesthetic standards. The art of the comedian is unusual in being an intimate form of public communication, the will and voice of one man exposed before the many. For success the comedian needs to create rapport with his audience so that they relax all the defences they normally adopt in public. To do this is to gain a power, a magical hold over them. What the comedian then does in and through this power is the subject that the play debates. Sam I in his play uses the audience's emotional involvement with him as an individual to make them question their own intellectualised responses to the class he represents: laughter at his parodies and mimicry of themselves becomes a way to enlightenment. How a comedian gains the sensitivity to direct his audience's sympathies in this manner provides the material for Griffiths' first act in his later play.

Here we watch the would-be professionals preparing for their performances and being given their final coaching by their teacher, Eddie Waters, a retired comedian who formerly had a considerable local reputation in the Manchester area. Through a series of limbering-up exercises we learn of the necessary disciplines such a performer must acquire — speed of verbal response; the quick, unexpected following line that augments an audience's laughter and possibly carries the original joke into a new dimension of experience; related to this, as a means to effect rapid transitions, is the power to invent spontaneous linguistic associations and puns; then there is accuracy of speech during fast delivery and the ability to adjust the timing and the pitch in tone of the patter so that punch-lines of jokes are expected yet take an audience by surprise. These are the disciplines that make for professionalism (the ones in fact that any actor must perfect): they must be mastered to a degree where they cease to require conscious effort and become a second nature, enabling the comedian both to concentrate his attention on the quality of the relationship he is establishing with the audience and to rely on his technique to adjust itself so that he can tune the atmosphere of his performance night by night to the pitch he requires.

One of Waters' pupils, McBrain, is fond of reiterating the maxim: "It's not the jokes but the way you tell them"; but Waters argues for more matter with less (overt) art. A display of proficiency for its own sake (and we recall Andrew Ford in *The Party*) is self-centred; it abuses an audience by teasing them with the promise of imaginative sustenance which is not subsequently provided and it exposes comedy to the accusation of being trivial. For Waters, technique, however brilliant, is not enough and he distrusts spontaneity. When another of the pupils, Price, excited by his own expertise, improvises a vulgar limerick, Waters quickly reveals the paucity of imagination that lies behind it, the inevitability that is established by the chosen rhyme-scheme which tantalises an audience over whether the speaker dare or dare not use a crude expression. The achievement of such a joke is negligible, childish in its delight in being merely naughty.

Provoked by the activities of the group into examining the principles governing the practice he is trying to instil in them,

Waters argues that comedy, to deserve the name, should aim at nothing less than catharsis, the liberating of the audience through laughter from fear, prejudices and crippling inhibitions:

It's not the jokes. It's not the jokes. It's what lies behind 'em. It's the attitude. A real comedian — that's a daring man. He *dares* to see what his listeners shy away from, fear to express. And what he sees is a sort of truth, about people, about their situation, about what hurts or terrifies them, about what's hard, above all, about what they *want*. A joke releases the tension, says the unsayable, any joke pretty well. But a true joke, a comedian's joke, has to do more than release tension, it has to *liberate* the will and the desire, it has to *change the situation*. [p. 20]

Comedy by this argument is necessary to man to help him to live and the duty of a comedian (note the pride with which Waters uses the word and how the repetition virtually invests it with the status of a title) is to search his own psyche and convert the truths he learns about himself into a humorous mould that will encourage others on the road to self-knowledge. It is fitting that Waters has become a teacher in his retirement from the stage since to be a comedian is clearly for him a vocation in the fullest sense of the term: it is to have the daring to reveal the frailties of the self in public to an audience so that they can learn to accept the realities of their existence. Comedy, as he views it, is a ritualised act of love involving intimacy and trust and reaching out towards a joyful confirmation of one's identity. To prove his point but without admitting his intention Waters asks the students to think severally of an experience that caught them where they are most painfully vulnerable; then he insists that each in turn talk about it. Ged, the first in line, tells of the birth of his child and of the almost paralysing fear he had that the baby would be in some way physically or mentally defective. The others chaff him at first, but he persists in the story making no appeal for their sympathy; the memory compels at first his and gradually their complete attention:

When I got to the ward, I couldn't go in. . . . . I thought, what if there's some'at wrong with it. (*Silence now, the story rivets.*) She were holding it in her arm. I saw it ten beds away. Black hair. Red face. Little fists banging away on wife's face. (*Pause.*) He were bloody perfect. He were bloody perfect. [p. 29]

The experience is commonplace enough, but that is precisely why it captures the imagination: the story realises a believable fear so that the release of that fear into wonder carries absolute conviction. Ged's innocence of the effect he is having also indirectly illuminates our appreciation of the *illusion* of innocence that many comedians cultivate to excite rapport and sympathy. If he were to tell the story again Ged would have to recover the air of innocence by technical expertise. That Waters' theories have won his students' assent is evident from McBrain's attitude to Ged's story. McBrain is the most thrusting of the group and he is next in line but his response is immediate: "I'm not following that, Mr. Waters". (This is an interesting reaction in view of later developments in the play and typical of Griffiths' attention to detail: he has proved his point and wishes to shift to a new subject but he selects McBrain to effect the transition here — a character who is subsequently to be shown as very deficient in artistic and moral honesty.)

That the students are more questioning than usual about Waters' instructions and methodology is indicative both of their growing nervousness as the time for their examination approaches and of an increasing tension amongst them provoked by Waters' openly confessed hostility to the man who is to examine them. Challenor exemplifies for Waters the danger of putting success before artistry, of trusting to technique and a familiar routine so that one's audiences rest content with stock responses. Implicit in Waters' argument has always been criticism of that alternative way. Challenor no sooner arrives than he generates a new atmosphere in the play by baiting Waters with undisguised satire. His quick, no-nonsense efficiency is in marked contrast to Waters' scruple; and Griffiths effortlessly matches the speech-patterns to Challenor's attitudes. His ideas, which patently he has never once questioned, have hardened into tight, staccato, jargon-phrases. There is no style to embellish thought, no energy behind the syntax that would suggest a process of reasoning. His every sentence amounts to an insistence on the one fundamental point:

Well. Nice meeting you. Good luck for tonight. (*He dwells, enjoying the attention.*) A couple of . . . hints. Don't try to be deep. Keep it simple. I'm not looking for philosophers, I'm looking for comics. I'm looking for someone who sees what the people want and knows how to give it them. It's the people pay the bills, remember, yours, mine . . . Mr. Waters's. We're servants, that's all. They demand, we supply. Any good comedian can lead an audience by the nose. But only in the direction they're going. And that direction is, quite simply . . . escape. We're not missionaries, we're suppliers of laughter. I'd like you to remember that. [p. 33]

Challenor's standards reach no higher than facility as a way to popular fame. Yet he is not the caricature he so easily could have been partly because, though he maintains this ingratiating, lickspittle attitude towards an audience, it is all a front: at heart he despises audiences deeply for their inability to be discerning; he offers them little and is disgusted when they rise gratefully to the bait; the excitement of performance for him clearly lies in watching the extent to which he can patronise an audience without them realising it. His creed is succinctly put: "all audiences are thick, collectively, but it's a bad comedian who lets 'em know it. . . . You don't have to love the people, but the people *have* to love you" [p. 60]. Challenor's way too requires a kind of daring; and he does not undervalue technique, though he sees it as no more than a mask behind which a performer laughs at his listeners' need for laughter. At all points Challenor's philosophy is a travesty of Waters'. If Griffiths successfully avoids making Challenor a caricature, it is because he never underestimates Challenor's power: as a talent scout, agent and union man, he can award an entry into the profession and his personality as a force to be reckoned with dominates the action long before he appears on stage, since he is the source of the mounting tension. Moreover, whatever *we* may feel about Challenor, given the moral framework of reference which Waters has set up to counterbalance that tension in his pupils, his brief appearance in the class before the examination is enough to make half the students decide radically to alter the acts they have prepared under Waters' supervision. Waters will not discover this until the acts are in progress but the sad-faced melancholy he sustained throughout the opening scene can be interpreted retrospectively to indicate his expectation that this will occur. It was particularly marked and disconcerting with Jimmy Jewel in the role that, though a great comedian himself, as Waters he neither smiled nor joked however much he was the stimulus to witty invention in the others. Why his care should be so anxious and fatalistic was not to be revealed until the final moments of the play.

Act Two is made up entirely of the performances by Waters' pupils at a Working Men's Club. Structuring the play as he has, Griffiths has given us a complex philosophical, aesthetic and moral frame of values with which to approach the five turns (one is a duo by Ged and his brother), which are brilliant parodies of the different styles of routines favoured by contemporary comedians. We are confronting the familiar but seeing it in a totally fresh light and Griffiths actually defies us to find some of the performances *funny*. This makes for a considerable unease of response: one constantly finds oneself seduced into laughter as a reflex action to cleverly timed techniques that intimate the comedian is expecting a guffaw at a given moment (the saucy look, the raised eyebrows, the uplift in the voice, the sudden pause), even at times when one may be embarrassed by jokes that are, as D. H. Lawrence would say, "doing dirt on life" — the jokes that confirm racial prejudices or sexual insecurity. What we sense now through our own mixed responses is the power of technique to compel assent to the performer's view of life, the mesmeric control over an audience that a comedian wields which makes a scrupulous appraisal of his material so necessary. Waters' standards may have seemed absurdly exacting, but experience makes us review that bid for integrity with profound respect.

Of the five acts, Mick Connor's which opens establishes Waters' ideal pattern. The humour is gentle: an Irishman, he speaks about the Irish with amused insight and pathos and with none of the derision implicit in the conventional 'Irish joke'; in fact the performance is a subtle criticism of that particular tradition in gags, as Connor steadily eases his audience through charm and affability towards a new awareness: "Next time you meet an Irishman, count to ten . . . and ask God to make you more inventive" [p. 40]. Samuels who follows attempts a similar line with the Jewish temperament but, remembering Challenor's comments and finding the audience unresponsive, he begins to improvise and play the Jewish stereotype: mean, obsequious, his humour always admitting that he expects to be the butt of other people's pettiness and spite. He debases himself to earn the patronage that is his audience's laughter and, feeling secure when he has it, he deflects their attention away from his own race by encouraging them to look contemptuously at West Indians, Women's Liberation and the Irish — "Smart, see. They published a book: 'The Wit and Wisdom of the Irish: Twenty Years of Social Security' " [p. 42]. That it requires considerable nerve and invention on Samuels' part to work tenaciously for rapport with his audience — however we may judge the nasty tone that finally prevails in his routine — is made clear when Phil Murray also begins to improvise for Challoner's benefit and Ged, loyal to Waters' teaching, leaves him to flounder. McBrain has a brilliant, smooth manner and he knows precisely how to touch an audience's reflexes to the extent that he can pare his material to an absolute minimum:

There's this coloured feller on his way to work. (*Stops.*) Don't you think that's funny? There's this very honest Jew. No favourites here. There's this very brilliant Irishman. From Dublin. I tried to get the wife to come. It gets harder, I dunnit though. [p. 46]

Here are all the techniques in versatility that were studied in Waters' class but McBrain's intention is just to keep his audience laughing at any cost. He sets up the reflex then lets it work quite mechanically, which quickly reduces an audience to a kind of mindless euphoria where they are happy to remain complacent while McBrain makes more and more daring inroads into the titillatory and finally into the downright obscene: "Listen, I've gotta go, I'm wife-swapping tonight. I gorra bloke's greyhound last week, made a change" [p. 49]. Sheer speed of delivery keeps his audience from questioning their complicity in all this. It is undeniably a virtuoso performance; but it is positively evil.

What the debate in Act One has not prepared us for is the last turn by Gethin Price, though, if we have been attentive to details in the classroom scene, it should come as no surprise. In all the exercises conducted by Waters, Gethin's proficiency is astounding: his projection and delivery are impeccable even at breakneck speeds; he can parody perfectly at will, assuming during the class a wide range of voices and speech patterns; his powers of observation are acute. If he excites Waters' approval more than the rest, it is because he has taken the trouble to learn the traditions and history of the comedian's art. Gethin speaks admiringly of Grock, of Frank Randle, even of Waters himself; and it is clearly out of no wish to curry favour but out of a serious belief in the integrity of their work which ensured that their invention was unique. And Price himself is an original amongst the group. Not only does he excel in vocal expertise, he has what the others lack — considerable physical prowess. He convinces in his impersonations because of the totality of his assumption of a persona, the stance and the movement as well as the verbal mannerisms. Price constantly rivets attention in the class by the grace of his acrobatic skills, finding in such displays an outlet for the exuberance he clearly feels at his technical mastery. The dynamism increasingly verges on the aggressive, the parody crossing the boundary into mimicry and burlesque, especially of Waters and his ideas. This starts covertly but becomes more subtle as it becomes more open. Though Ged's tale about his baby silences McBrain to Waters' evident satisfaction, Gethin immediately recalls in a dispassionate tone his first experience of knowing humiliation and of the cunning he then discovered in himself as a form of defence:

I went nutty once. . . . I thumped a teacher. . . . Were a woman. She called us a guttersnipe. In music. I clocked her one. It seemed the only thing I could do. She went white. Whiter than me even. Then she cried. Little tears. They sent me to a psychologist. Thirteen. Me I mean, *he* were a bit older. Though not much. We developed a sort of tolerant hatred of each other. He kept insisting on treating me as an equal, you know.

Patronizing me. The last time I saw him he gave me this long piece and he said, 'You see, Gethin, basically all any of us want is to be loved.' And I said, 'If you know so much, how come you wear a Crown Topper?' (*Pause.*) That's when I decided I'd be a comedian. [pp. 29-30]

Price couples Waters' idea of a vocation with motives quite different from love, showing in the psychiatrist how easily charity degenerates into sentimentality and patronage. This tale is not vindictive or even, curiously enough, hostile, just an assertion of a belief rooted in personal experience that care is not of itself a sign of integrity. Waters' favourite tongue-twister is "The traitor distrusts the truth"; Gethin has extemporised on it in the form of an emotional tirade. The implication of his story is that there are kinds of truths to which care may give one access but from which love alone offers no release.

Gethin's performance at the Club is a *tour de force*, a ritualised act not of love but of violent aggression. His appearance evokes both the clown and the contemporary 'bovver boy': over-sized boots; ill-fitting trousers; spangled denims; shaven head; a sickly white face that deadens all expression except for the eyes. "*The effect is calculatedly eerie, funny and chill*" [p. 49]. Throughout what follows (especially as performed by Jonathan Pryce) the grotesqueness is always offset by the beauty and exquisite control of the movement. The act is in fact predominantly a mime; when he does speak, it is less the precise words than the tone which compels attention. He begins with a recreation of Grock's act with the violin bow that has an obstreporously dangling thread but this soon takes an original turn as he sets it alight, then fails to douse the flame even when he tries to stifle it by putting the bow in his mouth. His lips shape a deep, silent scream; then, furious, he shatters his midget violin. The violence this introduces grows to a climax: "I wish I had a train. I feel like smashing a train up. On me own. I feel really strong. Wish I had a train. I could do with some exercise" [p. 50]. Till now Gethin has performed in studied isolation, as if unaware of an audience; but next he discovers on stage life-sized dolls of a beautifully dressed couple who become his audience. He tries to be chatty and amiable and, when that fails, servile. Jonathan Pryce's mime here seemed to give their indifference a palpable life as steely disdain. The one-sided conversation enters a manic phase as he wills them desperately to take some notice of his presence: the tone moves through insult, crude innuendo, obscenity to hysteria. The element of stylisation is never lost: this frenzy is evoked by a breathtaking display of acrobatics, terminating unexpectedly in a long-held pose suggesting formal politeness. Gethin breaks the silence to offer the woman a flower and *"with the greatest delicacy"* pins it to her dress: *"Silence. Nothing. Then a dark red stain, rapidly widening, begins to form behind the flower"* [p. 52]. With a babble of football and political slogans and accompanied by the strains of 'The Red Flag' played on a second tiny violin, Gethin begins to leave the stage; but he has one final comment on the situation he has created, which he looks back to address to the dolls:

I shoulda smashed him. They allus mek you feel sorry for 'em, out in the open. I suppose I shoulda just kicked him without looking at him. National Unity? Up yours, sunshine. [p. 53]

It is, as Waters says later, "brilliant", reaching back beyond the conventions of music hall performance to the roots of the comedian's art in circus and pantomime and the savage antics of the all-licensed fool. It is the proof of Gethin's dedication that he has seen fit to revive, perfect and include in his act so many traditional skills beside which the expertise of McBrain seems remarkably effete. It is crucial, however, if Act Three is not to appear an anticlimax that Waters' judgement "brilliant" is merited by Gethin's performance. When the production moved from Nottingham Playhouse and the National Theatre to the West End (Wyndham's, 1976), the role of Gethin was taken over by Kenneth Cranham. His account of the role was as B. A. Young put it, like the hammer after Jonathan Pryce's sickle.[13] Cranham went for the bullet-headed ferocity and missed the versatility the role demands and the icy detachment. Cranham's most impressive roles over the Seventies had been as the emotionally fraught and suicidal Don Parritt in *The Ice Man Cometh* (Aldwych, 1976) and as Shaw's Dubedat, (Mermaid, 1975) where the sustained husky timbre of his voice brought a tone of self-pity to the great speech in defence of art, making it the vision of a man who, dying, recognised his own inability to achieve so transcendent a goal.[14] There is no room for self-pity in Gethin and his conviction is absolute that his vision is realisable within his capabilities: he is quite impervious to Challenor's adverse criticism; he expected it; the examination set-up is meaningless beside his dedication to his art. There is too a moving humility before the fact of his own skill and genius (throughout Gethin's manner is assured not pig-headed), which the audience has to gauge through the sheer polish of everything he does. Cranham was adept in the part but one was conscious of the effort it took to surmount his customary stage personality and that left him little imaginative stamina to pursue the subtle discriminations in tone that the role requires. It was not in his power to establish by movement alone the mood at once grotesque and elegant that Griffiths evokes in his stage directions through such images as *"He's gone, out on an amazing tiptoe, like a dancer in a minefield"* [p. 35]. Jonathan Pryce, with the greater physical and vocal suppleness, seized on the implication of these images which Griffiths offers that Gethin constantly *stylises* his emotions, however intense his commitment. His Gethin was so complete an artist that we appreciated how for him a display of naked emotion risked offending an audience; he never relaxed his mesmeric control, never let Gethin cease to be the performer. Only in the final intimate discussion with Waters did Pryce's Gethin speak directly out of himself and then only because challenged to define what for him constitutes artistic honesty.

After Challenor has made his report and selected the talents he wishes to promote (Samuels and McBrain), Gethin stays when the others leave, feeling a need to explain to Waters why he did an act different from the one he had prepared. He is compelled to account for himself after the defection of Samuels, McBrain and Phil Murray: "I didn't sell you out, Eddie" [p. 63]. His action was an artistic necesssity, a wish to prove the value of what he had learned from Waters by showing him he could now range free of his influence and "be *me* talking out there" [p. 64]. The desire to be different is in its way a token of gratitude and, in asking Waters for his opinion, Gethin is not seeking praise any more than previously he curried Waters' favour; what he is after is the objective appraisal of a fellow artist. Waters admits it was "brilliant" but "ugly", not in its method but in its tone: "It was drowning in hate" [p. 65]. Lacking compassion it wanted truth; but Gethin retaliates that this is a failure of Waters' perception: questioning whether 'hate' and 'love' are appropriate terms to apply to the act of creativity, he tries to re-define the experience as a kind of self-destruction by either fire or ice, a ritualised, perhaps painful, depersonalising of the self as creator. Gethin has quested into the depths of his psyche to examine remorselessly his instincts for aggression and the behaviour that triggers them into activity (the story about his hitting the teacher gains a further relevance now). He knows in himself the humiliations that bring a 'bovver boy' into being; his artistic purpose is to bring that mental condition and *conditioning* to an audience's understanding. If there is no place for 'love', it is because the condition being defined is a totally loveless one; the pity is to be detected only in the rigorous objectivity of the portrayal, the refusal in any way to personalise the detail. Fidelity to life (Waters' concept of "Truth") demands of Gethin the complete stylisation of the experience; an overt expression of sympathy would be rhetorical and patronising. What Gethin is trying to do is encourage an audience to confront a social reality that to them is a source of embarrassment and more deeply of fear, because the very fact of its existence indicates a failure of liberal sympathy both in them and in the social system at large. If Gethin is to activate conscience and a proper awareness of responsibility in his audience, then he must seek a way to disarm their unease in facing up to the challenge that lies in the subject: the beauty of his art as a mime has to be sustained meticulously through the process of stylisation if the terror of the truth he conveys is not to be dismissed as repulsive, tasteless or obscene. His performance is a triumph of psychological and political insight and tact, where artistic discipline, the perfect wedding of method with matter, is a *moral* necessity.

Forced like this to justify himself, Gethin begins to question why, given his astute powers of analysis and his gift as a teacher for fostering discrimination in others, Waters has retired from the professional stage. He has pointedly refused to introduce his students at the Club; he chooses anonymity and he has never been seen to laugh. Impressed by Gethin's struggle to be honest, Waters tells how he came to devise his exercise about revealing one's most secret fear and inhibition. He describes a visit he made to a concentration camp in Germany during an ENSA tour after the war in which he was horrified to discover in himself erotic pleasure at the idea of mass punishment and torture. His imagination seized up with such knowledge: how could compassion confront this perversity in himself without appearing to condone it? To create out of so negative an emotion as abject disgust with himself defeated him. His courage and his discipline as an artist had found their limit; the anxiety that has throughout the early scenes of the play always accompanied his care is now seen to be a fear that his students should recognise that limit to his philosophy, his own inability to stand up, as few of his students can, to the most penetrating test he makes of their dedication. It is a mark of Gethin's intelligence that, as so many of his responses in the classroom reveal, he has sensed that failure of nerve in Waters; but he has too great a respect for him as a teacher to force him to a public confession. Throughout Act One his challenging of Waters' theories has been pitched at a level of communication that he knows Waters will understand but which will leave the other students merely guessing. To know one's own pain and not to communicate one's knowledge is to Gethin to acquiesce in the world's suffering: "I stand in no line. I refuse my consent" [p. 68]. Beside such sensitivity and perception 'hate' and 'aggression' are hopelessly inadequate definitions; yet beside such relentless, dispassionate probing, 'love' is inadequate too. With all the emotionalism and guilt between them admitted and burned away, a tone of pure calm ensues; with all the defences gone, their intimacy is direct, total and, above all, *felt*:

WATERS (*very quiet*): What do you do now then?
PRICE: I go back. I wait. I'm ready.
WATERS: Driving, you mean?
PRICE: Driving. It doesn't matter.
WATERS: Wait for what?
PRICE: Wait for it to happen.
WATERS (*very low*): Do you want help?
PRICE: No. I'm OK. Watch out for me.
WATERS: How's Margaret?
PRICE (*plain*): She left. Took the kiddie. Gone to her sister's in Bolton.
WATERS (*finally*): I'm sorry.
PRICE: It's nothing. I cope. (*Pause.*) What do you do then? Carry on with this?
WATERS: I don't know.
PRICE: You should. You do it well. [p. 68]

There is no questioning Gethin's absolute dedication to his art. And his insistence on the need to be exacting and carry Waters' precepts to their logical conclusion is productive. Left alone brooding on the night's developments, Waters is joined in the classroom by an Indian who has lost his way. Bemused by the idea of a school for "funny men", Mr. Patel shares an Indian joke with Waters:

A man has many children, wife, in the South. His crop fail, he have nothing, the skin shrivel on his children's ribs, his wife's milk dries. They lie outside the house starving. All around them, the sacred cows, ten, twenty, more, eating grass. One day he take sharp knife, mm? He creep up on a big white cow, just as he lift knife the cow see him and the cow say, Hey, aren't you knowing you not permitted to kill me? And the man say, What do you know, a talking horse. [p. 69]

Griffiths has conceived a moment of experience that brings all the issues he has been debating sharply into focus: the story tells of abject human desperation; it balances a respect for cultural pieties against a different code of values honouring man's personal dignity and wit. To a remarkable degree the joke actualises what it is to be Indian. Patel rocks with delighted laughter which Waters suddenly joins, determined despite Challenor to continue teaching ("Come on, I'll give you a lift. Listen, I'm starting another class in May, why don't you join it? You might enjoy it . . ."). The pain of being can be exorcised in creativity.

Comedians is nothing less than a triumphant defence of the necessity for theatre but of a kind that imposes on performer and audience alike the most taxing and discriminating of standards: standards which Griffiths' own art magnificently sustains.

CHAPTER SEVEN

THE HISTORY PLAY: EDWARD BOND

"All plays are metaphors," writes Pam Gems in a prefatory note to *Queen Christina* (Tricycle, 1982) and goes on to observe that "the dilemma of the real Christina . . . is perhaps not irrelevant today".[1] The implication is that what she is offering is not to be seen as simply 'costume drama' but a use of historical material to give a fresh perspective on a contemporary twentieth-century issue. The problem in dramatising historical subjects is to find a cogent and credible metaphorical dimension, an inner life for the play behind the rehearsal of known facts.

At the simplest level this takes the form of a fascination with an enigmatic personality or situation, for which the dramatist seeks to provide an ingenious explanation. Robert Bolt's *Vivat! Vivat Regina!* (Chichester and Piccadilly, 1970)[2] is a characteristic example of this: a bravura show-piece for two actresses of contrasting styles — one flamboyantly histrionic as Mary, Queen of Scots, (Sarah Miles) and one understated and tensely introverted as Elizabeth I (Eileen Atkins). Queen Elizabeth maintains her power by continually embracing abnegations in her private life, whereas Mary views rule as quintessentially the expression of self: "I am the Queen and more the Queen the *more* I am myself" [p. 9]; she is humbled finally to the point of despair when abnegation is forced on her in the form of total confinement at Fotheringham. Cecil observes: "I think our Queen sees Mary in the mirror" [p. 72]; and Bolt structures the dramatic climaxes of the play to amplify this image, showing Elizabeth in Act I reject Dudley as a suitor when he is implicated in his wife's mysterious death while in Act II Mary shamelessly weds Bothwell despite his obvious involvement in Lord Darnley's murder. Facing execution and bereft of everything, Mary appears clad in brilliant scarlet, the ultimate gesture of defiance at fate, and smiles patronisingly at the thought of Elizabeth, secure through having "avoided" life. This is a *simple* form because there is no attempt to reach beyond the study of a passionate and a cerebral personality in conflict together; the historical evidence is selected and shaped to elucidate this pattern of opposites; but the effect in performance is rather to suggest that Elizabeth's brilliant policy-making was, in Freudian terms, compensation for a repressed sexual identity and that Mary is little more than a wilful exhibitionist. The simple form tends to impose a simple view of events: Bolt in his introduction to the published text significantly asks whether he is drawn to historical subjects for plays because older times seem "more human" than the present [p. xxiv]. The process of simplification is easier the remoter the period under scrutiny, certainly. When he turned to recent history for *State of Revolution* (Lyttleton, 1977),[3] it was the inhumanity of the leaders of the Russian revolution that he chose to define, as Lenin, Trotsky and Stalin are repeatedly shown manipulating Marxist theory to justify the way they decide to determine events. "Big events aren't formed by people, people are formed by big events" is their cry but Bolt leaves us in no doubt that he sees this as hypocritical: "History is hard" Lenin claims; but Bolt asks whether it is so simply because it is the image of the man himself who is shaping Russia's destiny: Lenin is ultimately incapable of halting the rise to power of Stalin because he is the logical culmination of the process Lenin has set in motion. The Revolution is shown as an exercise of power used brutally and without caution — a view that is not presented in a fashion that allows an audience room for question or debate. Bolt prefaces the play as published with some notes on the characters of the main individuals involved, which intimate far more complex personalities than are actually presented in his text. They were men faced with intricate choices; but Bolt shows them only at times of taking decisions, so the motives for their seeming ruthlessness remain unexplored. There was more involved in the revolution than the naked will to power. In performance the director (Christopher Morahan) allowed the actors to invest their roles with a degree of their own personalities and some measure of dignity, which diffused the acerbity of Bolt's approach.[4] The *metaphors* of Bolt's plays tend to be, if not reductive, at least restrictive interpretations of history as the expression of powerful or quixotic personalities; they are not metaphors that, resonating with possibilities of interpretation, creatively disturb an audience's imagination.

Much the same holds true of Peter Shaffer whose brilliant theatrical sense often, as in *Amadeus* (Olivier, 1979)[5], masks an unwillingness to do more than pose a thesis in relation to the past. The play illustrates an idea rather than inhabiting it imaginatively. Shaffer is fond of the device of a commentator who presents the action in a way that exemplifies his own personal crisis of conscience, so that the audience views the world of the play largely through that character's perceptions. Salieri's account of his rivalry with Mozart allows him to voice his anguish at the waywardness of life: it endows a former child-prodigy in adulthood with both a prodigious genius and the enduring temperament of a child, while an upright, god-fearing individual like Salieri himself, altogether the proper man, is gifted merely with talent. (Schofield's innate fastidiousness and dignity were an asset here in playing Salieri; and Peter Hall was right to direct Simon Callow to carry off Mozart's moments of obscenity and horseplay with the unselfconscious grace of an infant and to make Felicity Kendal's Constanze vulgar to point the distinction.)[6] Envy undermines all Salieri's belief and his victimisation of Mozart becomes the expression of his rage against the injustice of God. Paradoxically the more Salieri destroys Mozart's social standing in Vienna, the more innovative and magnificently spiritual Mozart's art becomes. With an equally powerful irony, the more jealousy sharpens Salieri's critical faculties so that he recognises the brilliance of his rival's work compared with the conformist mediocrity of his own, the more his own art meets with financial reward. Success is his damnation and he knows it; Salieri searches relentlessly for a design behind what is increasingly revealed to him as a capricious and godforsaken world. He is trapped in an Absurdist nightmare, appalled at his own insignificance, his every gesture of defiance at the meaningless universe about him being rendered grotesque. Yet this is entirely a personal dilemma, the individual self rebelling against the accidents of nature, that has little to do with the process of history. The historical context allows Shaffer to use the music of an accepted genius as a yardstick against which to measure Salieri's failure; but beyond that *Amadeus* is fundamentally about the cruel ironies of chance rather than the way character is moulded by the pressures of the times. The circumstances that create the prodigy are to the last an inscrutable mystery. Despite the innovatory way music is used extensively in the play, the form of *Amadeus* is not experimental; middle-aged apologists for a failed life who preside as commentators over scenes illustrating their souls' undoing recur throughout the new drama of the Seventies: Christopher Hampton, Simon Gray, John Mortimer, Alan Bennett, Peter Nichols (to name but five writers) have each produced at least one play in that format. Shaffer is unusual in producing a historical example, but the soul-searching of Salieri's vast soliloquies has a peculiarly modern edge to it, which his repeated addressing of the audience as fellow mediocrities of a future age accentuates. It is not Salieri's historical distance but his psychological closeness that preoccupies

Shaffer. *Amadeus* is less a history play than a morality about the deadly sin of envy and covetousness.

Several plays recently have attempted to explore how the consciousness of the common man is affected by political upheaval. Storey's *Cromwell* (Royal Court, 1973)[7] imagines one farmer's struggle to preserve his integrity, if not his domestic security, amidst all the confusions and the rhetoric of the Civil War during the Protector's invasion of Ireland. Rhetoric is the subject too of Caryl Churchill's *Light Shining in Buckinghamshire* (Theatre Upstairs, 1976)[8], which juxtaposes documentary material from the time of the Civil War (*The Putney Debates* of 1647 and various pamphlets by Diggers or Levellers), passages from the Old Testament and imagined domestic dialogue to show how the apocalyptic language used to incite the common people to fight against the king and achieve a new Eden became a trap for rulers and ruled, once the king was overthrown and dead. For those who believed the rhetoric literally, the failure of a revolutionary utopia sharing a common wealth to manifest itself after Charles's execution was an outrage that genuinely undermined their faith. Churchill's play depicts kinds of innocence that grew through disillusionment into extreme forms of revolutionary zeal and anarchy in a desperate effort to will a more equitable world into being: one that could bring the poor some experience of ease. The production by Joint Stock was of the simplest — a minimum of furniture, basic costume suggestive of the period — so our constant focus was on language and the way its spoliation can convey much about the psychological, moral and social tenor of an age. A process of history was enacted in the way the poetic power of language was exploited and debased. "All men have stood for freedom" [p. 22] Winstanley utters from his *True Levellers' Standard Advanced*, yet finds that freedom is deemed not to be every man's birthright but a privilege for those with property and a right to vote. To advance the War the army commanders had to promise a new age of individualism, but then could not contain or combine the myriad expectations of the commonwealth when it occurred. "We fought as one man. But now we begin to be thousands of separate men" [p. 25] observes the officer Star trying to justify the ruthless curtailment of liberty, especially of speech, that Cromwell's faction begin to impose. Churchill's aim was to find a voice for "the thousands of men and women who tried to change their lives" at that time; she continues: "Though nobody now expects Christ to make heaven on earth, their voices are surprisingly close to us" [Authors's Note]. But she does not try to force parallels; she prefers to allow an audience's engagement with the issue of language and its debasement for political objectives to stimulate a width of possible reference.

Stephen Poliakoff's family in *Breaking the Silence* (The Pit, 1984)[9] respond to the upheaval of the Russian revolution largely by acting as if nothing has changed. Though they are required to live in the narrow confines of a former imperial railway carriage, Nikolai, the father, wills them to observe as much of the decorum of gracious living as circumstances permit. "Use your imagination. . . . transform the food," he advises his son, Sasha, when his gorge rises at the taste of dried millet: "Imagine the delicate flesh, fish . . . fresh baked with a touch of sorrel the way Liuba used to cook it for us, pink, with a little butter, and flaking . . ." [p. 13]. What lies behind Nikolai's will to ignore change is not a nostalgia for upper-class languor but a passion for experimental science; he is obsessed by the challenge of being the first to combine sound and image for the cinema and nothing must disturb the equanimity necessary to achieve that end. (An enlightened Commissar of Labour, Verkoff, recognising Nikolai's real talents, has given him the preposterous job of first Telephone Examiner of the Northern Railway to allow him the freedom to pursue his research and to save him from likely assassination given his aristocratic manner and appearance.) There is something both comic and frightening about the power of Nikolai's will as demonstrated in his ability to go on dining with serene composure at a table set with family silver while a battle rages outside the railway carriage and the rest of the family and the visiting Verkoff are hiding under the furniture for fear of shells. The will is here directed to good, to scientific goals that are themselves highly revolutionary, but in Nikolai's insistence on good form, his indifference to others and their feelings, and in the force of his character that compels obedience, one can see darker tendencies akin to those that provoked the social revolution. As Verkoff heatedly observes, Nikolai is absurd and infuriating "and he *flaunts* it" [p. 28]. (Daniel Massey's style is mannered in a way that can at times be obtrusive but his very *difference*, his cultured tone, his elegance of movement were perfectly matched to the significance of the role.) Nikolai must speak for many of his class when he confides to Verkoff of the recent changes: "There was a constant sensation of something pressing, pressing down on one like a weight on the walls — needless to say I was completely unaware of it until everything 'erupted' . . . then quite suddenly I realised it had been there all the time" [p. 26]. And that goes on being the quality of his response to the world about him, scarcely perceiving how his wife has ceased to be an idle beauty but has discovered in herself through the new freedoms offered to women a genuine skill in administration, or how much his son resents wearing clothes to school that make him conspicuous, or how their former servant, Polya, goes on living with them and assisting his work out of choice now not out of duty. As a consequence no one really can impress on Nikolai how precarious his position is: behind the comic portrayal of his eccentricities there is a growing tension that breaks with Lenin's death. A change of government policy and Verkoff's sudden demise send the family on a nightmare journey to the frontier and exile (and then only because Eugenia, the wife, has the bureaucratic skill to outwit the border guards). It is a potent image Poliakoff leaves us with of the family reasserting the loyalties that bind it together in the face of fear: they dread ever going back to a life where, as Eugenia finally admits, she was "festering underneath . . . beginning to cry and scream inside" [p. 49], because she had no consuming passion like Nikolai's to save her from herself; yet they are apprehensive of the unknown into which they are hurtling in increasing darkness in a carriage that is a tatty reminder of vanished imperial splendours. In *Breaking the Silence* the process of history is implicit in the rhythms of change that variously affect the characters' progress to self-awareness and in the tone of the many scenes that are exquisitely poised between the comic and the ominous. The characters are experienced as inhabiting historical time, though little historical fact is actually mentioned in the play. History is sensed here as a matter of nuance, sensibility, insight, effort of will.

Peter Barnes in *Laughter!* (Royal Court, 1978)[10] and C. P. Taylor with *Good* (Warehouse, 1981)[11] addressed themselves to the demanding task of imagining how the citizen of the Third Reich reacted to the fact of the concentration camps and Hitler's policy of a Final Solution. Barnes's "Auschwitz" is part of a larger play in which he questions whether, because humour is often a trick of the mind whereby it accommodates itself to outrageous, frightening or painful circumstance, laughter is exploited by the politically powerful as a subtle means of preserving the *status quo* they have established, however appalling it may be. Laughter, he postulates, may be an insidious form of propaganda. It is an interesting possibility but one that clearly requires extremely sensitive handling in the context of Nazism. Barnes shows us an office of civil servants, riven with petty rivalries for promotion, reeling off a nonsense language of bureaucratic jargon and statistics, and then suddenly reveals that the memoranda they bandy about relate to contracts for building the camps and the statistics to murdered Jews. Bureaucratic procedures had been a device to keep the staff in ignorance of what exactly they were dealing with; enlightened and fearful, they resort again to statistics and jargon to save themselves from the need to take a moral stance: ". . . it's all imagination and hard facts leave nothing to the imagination. We're trained to kill imagination before it kills us" [p. 66]. The idiom of the farce reasserts itself and Barnes defies us to laugh. It would be a better play if the black aspects of the farce were only gradually to impinge on an audience's awareness: that these office workers joke about Hitler and his government *because* they live in abject terror. Their awakening and the audience's is instead left to a crude bully whose motto is "bluff rudeness, stimulating abuse, is the true Aryan way, hard in the bone" [p. 37]. The use of a mime (with straw dummies simulating corpses) accompanied by an amplified realistic sound-track to illustrate Gottleb's account of the gas chambers was offensively crude in Charles Marowitz's slack production. The weakness of the dramatic structure and the poor production made the whole conception appear to be in very bad taste which, sadly, was to discredit a challenging premise about the relation of politics to comedy.[12]

C. P. Taylor's *Good* offers a potent image that takes us right to the heart of his play: Halder's mother, stricken with blindness in old age, cannot adjust to the need to *feel* her way now about her home; "use your imagination" Halder impatiently advises her [p. 41]. Halder is invariably impatient — with his wife, his friend Maurice, a Jewish psychiatrist, with anyone who asks him to spare a little consideration, to *imagine* anxieties other than his own. His response to his mother's growing senility is to write a novel out of his impatience making an imaginative case for euthanasia; all his encounters with people in his domestic life his mind spontaneously accompanies with imagined music, ironic and critical, played by bizarre combinations of instruments so that his detachment is ensured. The structure of the play follows the seemingly random flow of Halder's consciousness: new encounters break into or grow out of other exchanges imitating his mind's pattern of associations which implies more about him than he is personally aware of. It is an appropriate form for the study of a man who is totally self-obsessed; his mind can accommodate itself to any behaviour that will safeguard its own equanimity, because it is alarmingly divorced from feeling. Clever in a purely cerebral way, he cannot see how his ideas as a respectable academic are being used by the Nazi regime to give an air of reasonableness to their planned atrocities. An audience with hindsight can see more to Eichmann's conversations with Halder than praise for his published criticism of the "reactionary, individual-centred emphasis of the Jewish influence on Western literature" [p. 55]. Lured on by flattery Halder advances in the party hierarchy, the popular reputation he has secured by his novel making him an ideal person to report "objectively" to the German people on the humanity with which the camps are being planned. What Eichmann requires of him is "an evaluation of the recommendations for the processing of the diseased and the unfit . . . We're not monsters, for God's sake" [p. 64].

Good is a play about how one man out of self-interest connives at the debasement of language by his nation, even while joking to Maurice that Germany is in the grip of a collective nervous breakdown. There are no statistics, no overt accounts of atrocities; it is how quickly and unawares the callous becomes the casual in the characters' thinking, that is profoundly shocking: "I've got to burn down a few synagogues and arrest some Jews. I could be up all night" [p. 54]; "These books . . . When I think about them burning the books . . . I just say to myself: 'It's just a gesture. It doesn't mean anything. Most people. They're not even aware they exist' " [p. 50]. Till the last the 'imagined' music continues bizarrely to accompany the flow of Halder's memories — the mark of his self-satisfaction and his complete detachment emotionally from his experience. But while inspecting a camp for the first time he relaxes at the sound of a band playing Schubert only to become alarmingly aware that this band is of Jewish prisoners and it is *real*. The play ends as Halder is poised, horrified, on the brink of awareness.

Good traces from within the slow degeneration of a mind which embraces Nazism not through fear but complicity. It is the *ordinariness* of the life with its petty ambitions, guilt, frustrations that makes that complicity frightening to behold. Halder is indeed no monster, only a mediocrity with a middle-aged man's longing to be free of ties, responsibilities and the need to care. It is because he is so credible as a dramatic stereotype that his fool's progress is so chilling: an image in miniature of the historical process he lives through. *Good* observes a mind cheerfully conditioning itself to the tenor of the times.

Pam Gems deploys historical subjects the better to understand how the identity of women has been conditioned to serve specific social functions. Queen Christina, brought up on her father's instruction as if she were a man and used by statesmen in Sweden and the Vatican as a confederate against her own sex and against her own natural urges, finally rebels and asserts herself as *woman*: "What that is, heaven knows . . . the philosophy is yet to be written, there is a world to be explored" [p. 75]. Gems takes the popular dramatic structure for a history play, the character study of an enigmatic individual, places at its centre a woman — Queen Christina or Edith Piaf — who refuses to conform to type and whose fame rests in the fact of her difference, and then explores the pressures her chosen heroine had to resist to be uniquely herself. Christina, seen first as a silent waif clutching a doll, grows to have an astute political intelligence, physical prowess, the will to command and total shamelessness; she despises her mother for her feminine wiles, emotional blackmailing and a banality of mind that is the consequence of years of botched pregnancies, suffered through seeking to meet the demand for an heir. The carefully nurtured masculine intelligence in Christina begins to question the process of statecraft; she refuses to marry for purely dynastic purposes and abdicates the Swedish throne rather than submit to such a demeaning of the self. She turns to Rome and the Catholic Church in quest of greater spiritual and intellectual enlightenment only to find the prime demand is for obedience, self-restraint and submission to the will of the Pope, which again involves her commitment to his statecraft. A telling visual effect was achieved in the R.S.C. production (Other Place, 1977) by clever doubling of the roles so that, though the scenery and costumes changed appropriately from Sweden to Rome, the same masculine presences were in identical power-relations with Christina: the actor playing Chancellor Oxenstierna reappeared as the Pope, Prince Karl as Cardinal Azzolino and so on. Nowhere can Christina find her natural *place*. In the society of French bluestockings with their vindictive hatred of men and their chatter about their appearance and clothes she feels an imposter, for all their championship of her cause. No one recognises her need to express her whole self except to judge it as scandalous. As a character Christina is constantly subject to criticism and misprision as a means of stimulating the audience to sympathy. Pam Gems claims her play is a metaphor with a modern reference; the bold, blunt dialogue, which makes no pretensions to a literary style evocative of period, focuses one's attention directly on attitudes — of men towards women, of women about women — which reflect and in some measure satirize contemporary twentieth-century expressions of sexual stereo-typing. Christina is given a modern consciousness to explain why she was an 'outsider' in her time. Just as the visual effect of the doubling suggested that change of environment brought no fundamental change of situation for Christina, so the modernity of the dialogue implied that the passage of time had instituted no great change in that situation either. Within the individual consciousness the patterns of response remain predictably the same now as then; the revolutionary spirit is still rare and always at hazard. That is the play's challenge. Pam Gems's dramatic method is witty and subtly provocative.

Caryl Churchill believes in the possibility of change but questions whether freedom necessarily means fulfilment or contentment. More than Pam Gems she is conscious of the patterns of chance and choice that determine the individual life in time; to illuminate this theme she has a much freer way with history than any writer so far considered; she is altogether more experimental in her dramatic structures too. In *Cloud Nine* (Royal Court, 1979)[13] she observes a family group in Victorian times and then, more advanced in years, in a modern context; her method is satirical, stylised to the level of the cartoon to focus exclusively on the characters' sexual behaviour. In the Victorian past the characters are inhibited in their expression of feeling because their talk publicly is confined to an assertion of conventional mores; privately and surreptitiously they gratify their urges wherever they may lead; deviancy and promiscuity are the unacknowledged norm, while everyone pays lipservice to propriety and affects outrage if they catch someone else breaking the rules: "Harry, I cannot keep a secret like this", Clive assures his explorer friend who has just revealed his homosexual proclivities, "Rivers will be named after you, it's unthinkable" [p. 26]. In the modern age the freedom to experiment sexually is openly acknowledged and the characters discuss intimacy frankly; but the greater the freedoms they take, the greater their guilt lest they should be abusing a partner's freedom and curtailing his or her pursuit of fulfilment: "I feel apologetic for not being quite so subordinate as I was. I am more intelligent than him" [p. 40]; "I think I should warn you I'm enjoying this" [p. 43]; "Now stop it. I work very hard at not being like this, I could do with some credit" [p. 51]. The Victorian counterparts at least found pleasure in their secret liaisons. Caryl Churchill with a terse wit excels at rendering the traps people ensnare themselves in because they feel they must experience some degree of *angst* to prove to themselves that they are alive. Sexual liberation has brought the freedom to intellectualise about sex, to theorise about one's expectations at the cost of the experience. It is easy with history plays to make an audience feel superior to the past but in *Cloud Nine* Caryl Churchill holds past and present in a careful balance that prevents such arrogance.

These themes are more subtly handled in *Top Girls* (Royal Court, 1982)[14] where a historical dimension is again introduced to make us look at a modern situation from an unusual perspective. In an ingenious fantasy-opening Caryl Churchill brings Pope Joan (the only woman pontiff), Patient Griselda (the emblem of wifely patience and submission), Dull Gret, whom Brughel painted leading a troop of women to attack Hell, Lady Nijo (a Japanese imperial courtesan of the thirteenth century) and Isabella Bird (an intrepid Victorian explorer) to a dinner to celebrate Marlene's promotion to managing director. Each talks about her life and we are made aware of a deliberate clash of epochs, cultures, mores; none, even while speaking of hardships, regrets her past or envies opportunities available to others; the variety of experience is what engages our attention. Far from being subject to pressures to conform to types of womanhood, they severally responded to the accidents of birth in time and place and have shaped a lifestyle from the possibilities available to them. The larger part of the play is devoted to scenes from Marlene's life at the secretarial agency where she is about to become the Managing Director and with her sister. All the characters are women and all could at a first glance be seen as stereotypes: the pushy career-girl; the wife of the failed businessman whose life has been loyally devoted to his support; the stay-at-home sister who is the dowdy mouse; the teenager with the dreams of freedom who is destined to a life working behind the counter of a supermarket. The historical fantasy encourages us to look (or more pertinently with Caryl Churchill's plays *listen*) deeply and see the patterns of chance and, hopefully, choice that are shaping these lives. Marlene, with her successful career, is in one sense emancipated but she has abandoned a child to pursue her work and her political sympathies, tutored by her opportunism, are reactionary; her sister Joyce has stayed in their working-class background, living in Marlene's eyes the life of a drudge, but hardship has impressed on her the need for radical change. Which exactly is *liberated*? Marlene, given the demands of her work, is quick to judge character; she is prone to be superior, cutting, dismissive, especially of other women. The form of the play questions whether such shallow judgements are perhaps too easy, exemplary of too restrictive a feminist philosophy: Marlene's temperament is as much a product of chance and choice as any other woman's encountered in the play and choices throughout are seen to bring limited freedoms but at a cost. In Caryl Churchill's plays history illuminates the present to broaden our perception of ourselves; its presence excites discrimination.

What is notable about writers like Gems and Churchill is the extent to which, in conceiving forms of historical drama, they have broken away from Brechtian practice without losing touch with Brechtian principles. Brecht's great history plays, *Galileo* or *Mother Courage*, require an audience to engage actively with the past, not out of a curiosity about enigmatic personalities (though Courage and Galileo are both that beyond doubt), but out of his sense of their need to engage imaginatively and intellectually with the past in order to understand the present and by so doing choose to act decisively in shaping the future. In a pressing way his plays are about chance and choice as they determine human responsibility — his historical plays do not encourage an escape to the past but seek to foster an awareness of our debt to the future. Gems and Churchill seek to stimulate a like awareness but have devised ways (in the first case a mode of performance and in the second highly original dramatic structures) which achieve the necessary detachment of the audience from a sympathetic concern with personalities but which are quite different from Brecht's own battery of 'alienation effects'. Brecht, of course, never saw his own style as prescriptive, realising that imitation would make these effects over-familiar and so reduce their power to shock an audience into a critical relation to the play in performance. A *relaxed* audience was anathema to him and Brecht was all too conscious of how readily an audience will seize on the familiar because it permits apathy.

Interestingly this was the effect in production of one play in this period which most closely followed Brecht's own style: Paul Thompson's *The Lorenzaccio Story* (Other Place and Warehouse, 1977-8).[15] It was clearly conceived as an attack on *Romantic* theatre, being a re-writing of de Musset's tragedy of 1834 that aimed to shift the emphasis from personalities to politics. De Musset is fascinated by the mind of Lorenzo and what could induce him to lead a life of debauchery in order to cultivate the friendship of Duke Alessandro and so be surer of success in murdering him. Thompson is less interested in whether it is possible to lead a degenerate life, whatever the pretext, and keep the soul free of corruption than in exploring the social and political world in which Lorenzo conceived what proved a futile revolutionary gesture. He asks that his play be experienced as a *presented* action, a story, as his title indicates. Either through songs or through passages of soliloquised narrative, the characters repeatedly detach themselves from the situation to comment on their actions, as if with hindsight they were trying to justify what they did as the only possible choice available to them at the time:

Oh yes, in retrospect things are always more simple, one can see the choices that were available. But human affairs are in a state of perpetual movement, always either ascending or descending. It is never easy, at the time, to know what to do. [p. 12]

The cumulative effect of this is unfortunate: it is as if the characters are constantly apologising for their inactivity, their failure to read the tenor of the times rightly and understand Lorenzo's act as the cue for revolution that he intended. The only consequences of Alessandro's death are Lorenzo's assassination by a man hoping merely for reward and the establishment by the church and the military of another Medici despot in Florence. Lorenzo is shrewd enough to guess this will be the outcome — he knows too well that the self-interest of the merchant class and the stoicism of the elder patricians, like Strozzi, who perversely welcome the tyranny of Alessandro as a test of their fortitude and principles, will ensure a quick return of the *status quo* after a brief respite of anarchy following Alessandro's death. Knowing that, he still chooses to act because his own will demands it as proof that an otherwise negligible life has meaning. His idea of revolution is merely a private gesture against a world that offers him no other means of self-expression. The terms in which Lorenzo sums up his achievement are significant: "How could I live with the person I have become? [He will go out to meet his expected assassin.] I was a degenerate, I became a murderer, I am now an outlaw" [p. 56]. It is here that Thompson's motive with the play — its metaphorical dimension — becomes imprecise. One suspects he wishes this review of a historical event to resonate creatively in his audience's minds implying alternative possibilities for change, but the overwhelming image left by the play in performance was of futility. The Brechtian devices, instead of genuinely alienating an audience and provoking a critical response to the characters, seemed merely to endorse their self-pity; and this effect was augmented by Ron Daniels' chosen production-style which was slow, ritualised, dream-like and within a playing-space heaped with junk, clothes and a litter of props so that (in Thompson's own words) "the action unfolded as if it were a tale re-enacted by ghosts on the proverbial scrapheap of history" [p. viii]. That last image, if it is Thompson's central organising metaphor for his play, is one that comes perilously close to Lorenzo's world-view. Such a degree of identification is what Brecht's method was designed rigorously to combat. Simply to imitate his techniques is no guarantee that one will succeed in enhancing an audience's power of discrimination.

The futility of so much past history seems to obsess Charles Wood, but it goads him to a creative rage. He has a wonderful ability to devise stage pictures that are at once exhilarating and morally disturbing. The *tableau vivant* is a favourite device, never better used by him than in 'H' (Old Vic, 1969)[16], where his target is the conduct of the British Army under General Havelock during the Indian Mutiny. What emerges would be a farce, were it not for the lavish loss of lives that accompanies almost every scene. Repeatedly he creates visual images that convey his critical response: the evocation of the Field Hospital at Cawnpore, for example, in a tent of billowing white silk; the soldiers' uniforms, faces, exposed limbs are all faded to a dull yellow; the only colour is a single spurt of blood and the reddened arms of the surgeon as he proceeds about his tasks; intense silence alternates rhythmically with "passages of throat raw screaming and thrashing movement" [p. 96]. The execution of a captive Jemadar, who is shot from a cannon, is to be synchronised so that the flash and report is accompanied simultaneously by a black-out on stage, the illumination of the auditorium and a cascade of red petals over the audience. In Act Three Havelock's march to the relief of Lucknow is staged within a pyramid of corposes, flags, armaments like a vast funeral monument, a composition ostensibly celebrating military glory but in reality depicting squalor ('H' himself is dying of dysentry), ineptitude and confusion (because of a divided command, 'H' sharing authority with General Outram). Repeatedly out of the wreckage the characters drag tattered backdrops, on which are reproduced various celebrated paintings of the stages of Havelock's progress to Lucknow, and struggle to adopt the heroic gestures of their representations on canvas. The gap between the myth of history and the human reality is graphically defined and in a fashion that lives powerfully in the memory by making the spectacle and transformation-scene so popular in the Victorian theatre convey a trenchant anti-romantic vision.

The problem with Wood's technique is the difficulty it poses of sustaining a verbal artistry throughout of as powerful an intensity as his spectacle and his need within the sequence of tableaux to create a developing thematic interest. His attempt at a kind of prose-poetry for his dialogue works well in the passages of soliloquy but otherwise seems to be struggling for effects made more succinctly in visual terms. For theme Wood seems unsure which of several ideas to develop other than his outrage at the very fact of war. There is the insult to the Indian soldiers and their native culture contained in the order that they bite on a new style of cartridge that is greased with pig fat which provoked a mutiny when British officers chose to make the issue a test of their power to command obedience; secondly there is Havelock's personal mission in life to "reverse the Vile Falsehood that/it is never possible to be a/Soldier and a Christian at the/once" [p. 147] and his struggle to redeem his son, Harry, from atheism; thirdly Captain James Parry's greed for promotion and loot. These issues are stated, illustrated but not debated; and they pale in significance beside the images of the nightmare that is history when it is shaped by warfare and by an army whose objectives are confused and who fight simply as a demonstration of their discipline. Wood has a profligate imagination that risks over-reaching itself. 'H' needs a firm, thematic focus, the discipline of an inner dynamic that, in selecting and controlling incidents, would make more damning Wood's attack on the madness that lies behind the urge to make myths of the grandeur of military achievement. The play for all its excellences begins to pall; the tireless visual invention comes to seem like overstatement, because tact and intellectual rigour are damagingly absent. Sophisticated theatricality, however lavish, is not in itself ultimately enough.

Peter Barnes's work affords a useful comparison here. He too has a highly develped awareness of the visual possibilities of theatre and has shown himself similarly interested in adapting the techniques of black comedy to historical subjects. But Barnes is an authority on Renaissance theatre, especially Jonson and Marston,[17] and with a wit akin to the metaphysical poets can exploit the bizarre to reveal a sudden truth about human experience with peculiar immediacy. *The Bewitched* (Aldwych, 1974)[18] is a baroque fantasy about the life and reign of Carlos II of Spain. The prologue gives a fine sense of Barnes's style. The aged Philip IV is being prepared for bed with elaborate ceremonial; the Archbishop of Toledo urges on the king the need to beget an heir and blesses and sprinkles with holy water the royal member; the Queen appears in a grand procession headed by a litter bearing the skeleton of St. Isidore; the couple enter the giant bed amid much psalm-singing; as the curtains are closed about them, the *"sound of heavy machinery creaking into motion"* is heard [p. 8]; the Queen's orgasmic cries change to birth pangs; the skeleton jerks upright then collapses as the stage floor splits open to emit a monstrous foetus in a cawl; the Archbishop begins to intone the baptism service as the creature ascends the throne to its parents' feet; as the membrane splits open to reveal the mis-shapen Carlos, Philip, clutching his heart, reels over backwards into the darkness and the christening turns into a funeral. This scene not only demonstrates Barnes's creative freedom with historical fact, his ability to compress the passage of time into a series of images that powerfully evoke the quality of life in the Spanish court of the late seventeenth century, but it also succinctly introduces the real theme of the play: the obsession with getting an heir as essential to maintaining the *status quo*. (The politics of Carlos's life are wholly taken up with the matter of the succession after his death.)

Barnes argues that the privileged secure power to themselves by investing it in mystique, in ritual and ceremony; ritual is the rhetoric in which power displays itself to sustain its authority; to participate in the ceremony is a mark of submission to a pattern of rule. *The Bewitched* explores the absurdity of it all when the rituals of power are focussed on a man who is essentially a freak, when the rhetoric has to justify his right to his privilege and explain why he falls so far short of the ideal: for Carlos is a spastic, subject to impotence and epilepsy. His condition cannot be accepted as natural, a tragic genetic inheritance; it has to be explained as an evil perpetrated by an enemy to the State. Carlos, it is argued, is bewitched, so an elaborate *auto-de-fé* is organised to purge his person and the nation; when that fails, he is believed to be possessed and the entire court is subjected to torture by the Inquisition as a test of loyalty to the crown.

It is a gruesome piece of history made palatable by Barnes's dextrous handling of tone, his acute sense of the ridiculous as the court submits to any indignity rather than lose position: when Carlos cannot manage the elegance of the pavane, the aristocracy imitate his lurching skids, wobbles and flailing spins across the stage, utterly poker-faced, and congratulate themselves on mastering the difficult steps of "The Carlos"; they graciously deign to have their persons sniffed over by the royal laundress who is employed by the Inquisition to detect the "fungy stench" of Satan's witches; racked, bleeding and carrying the instruments of their torture, they still join Carlos in a hymn to their beneficent God; mutilated by the Inquisition, they have no difficulty now in imitating the king's wild antics that pass for dancing. The obsession with rank and good form is not confined to the clergy and the aristocracy: as the Inquisition hounds thousands in quest of a solution to the king's impotence, Alcala the state goaler bewails the evil times:

Every prison from here t' Seville's full o' suspect witches and more coming daily. We've jus' too much t' do. 'Tis no way t' run a torture chamber. (*He staggers accidentally against the Iron Maiden, the Prisoner inside gives a brief pierced cry as the lid slams shut.*) See, that wouldst not've happened if I wasn't so tired. . . . But what o' our reputation? T' tickle a true confession from a relapsed sinner takes time and patience, now we've t' gouge 't out, quick and bleeding. Standards're collapsing, Gomez. We're turning this house o' truth into a butcher's shop. I'll go brain-mad wi'out our integrity as craftsmen. [p. 125]

Barnes's Spain is a world facing ruin as a consequence of its unquestioning adherence to protocol. When in the epilogue Carlos's successor turns at his coronation to face the people he is seen to be a worse freak than his predecessor. A masterstroke in the play was Barnes's decision to make Carlos himself a sympathetic character: he is a sad figure who wants to live but who has to devote his thoughts relentlessly to the consequences of his death, and who has no private life except in the aftermath of his epileptic fits when, with startling lucidity, he perceives the extent to which he is the victim of preposterous circumstances, a puppet whose presence everyone needs but whose person no one loves or respects. There is genuine political insight, as he castigates "the basilisk", Authority:

> Twill make a desert o' this world
> Whilst there's still one man left t' gi' commands
> And another who'll obey 'em. [p. 138]

But no one hears this still, small voice of reason, when he appears to the world to be "touched".

Where Barnes succeeds over Charles Wood is in his dialogue which matches the visual power of his play with a strange, baroque idiom. Given his concern with the nature of ritual, he can exploit the language of ceremonial both to characterise individuals deftly with their private obsessions and to keep his over-riding theme dominant in our awareness.

VALLADARES: Ne'er fear, Sire, such difficulties act as a spur, t' the godly. I'll cauterize Spain's wounds. Mere words die i' the air, but the vision o' burnt and blistering flesh commands a lasting obedience. And wi'out obedience the Jews, Moors and Freemasons'd swarm free, f' heretics breed like maggots on the decaying carcass o' the Church. All'll be ready on the day, Sire, on that burning Day o' Judgement when the good taste the greatest joy in Paradise — watching the torments o' the damned below — whilst the wicked see the terror awaiting 'em in Hell. Thus a successful auto de fe's both joy and terror mixed. A mighty show t' dazzle eyes and purge the heart; till that radiant moment when the Christian faith's made real and the playing ends and the last fires're lit and women roast and men burn t'hot ash, smoke in the wind. Oh there's nothing so inspiring, as sinners burning at the stake. It's good t' see 'em roasting, it's fine t' see 'em bake. The Jews'll shout 'Ovai, Ovai!', the Moors'll start t' quake. But their souls go marching on . . . [p. 76]

Barnes achieves a feeling of period speech without resorting to heavy pastiche. The fact that ritual is at once the subject and the dramatic method of the play gives *The Bewitched* the kind of organisational metaphor that 'H' lacks, so that the stage images can be felt to be at once a presentation of historical facts and a criticism of them. If the criticism encourages us through laughter to keep that insane world in a proper perspective, it does not permit us to rest complacent: the use and abuse of ritual, pomp and circumstance for political objectives is an enduring fact of statecraft. It is uncomfortable laughter.

In *The Bewitched* Barnes takes his theme and argues his case more by amplification in the manner of Jonson and Marston than by debate and it might be argued that his technique of visual statement hardly allows for subtle discussion. *Red Noses* (Barbican, 1985)[19], his most recent play, proves such a supposition wrong. The subject is the Black Death and the efforts of authority, especially the Catholic Church, to preserve a degree of order and faith in the face of universal terror. It was a time of constant living with Last Things beside which the Church's rhetoric of power about sin and ensuing damnation quickly paled. Father Flote conceives the scheme to found an order of holy fools to bring joy to the dying in the hope that they will, as he does, find God in the sound of laughter. As the roughest of his disciples observes when he faces his own death: "Oh it's good to take smiles with us into that last darkness; they light the way" [p. 86]. His troupe devise a version of *Everyman* that makes Death the butt of all the jokes and horse-play till even God has to concede and grant Everyman a longer life for cheating Death so wittily and with such a dextrous hand at dice. The troupe's popularity and following excite the envy of others who hope to use the plague and the image of death as the Great Leveller to effect social change. Flote's serenity disarms them but cannot charm the Pope who, when the plague ends, seeks to reassert his command — "Go break the spine of the world" [p. 89] — and views as dangerous Flote's brotherhood preaching in its plays the equality of laughter; comedy is now to be the Great Leveller. Flote's portrayal of Herod's incompetence and evil in a Nativity Play does not amuse Clement and he orders the group to submit to being disbanded or to face death: "It's honest, God-driven men like you, Father Flote, I can't trust. You live by no rules except what's in your heart. Without rules and laws, every man becomes a law unto himself" [p. 100]. The irony is the Pope can see Flote is "God-driven" even as he condemns him to death.

It is a fascinating play that, like Griffiths' *Comedians*, uses an audience's experience of watching a comedy in performance to illuminate for them the nature of laughter or more particularly the possible ends to which laughter can be directed: to still an audience's fears; to make them accept their social condition; to make them question that condition. Flote argues for laughter that brings self-awareness; the Pope argues for laughter as propaganda, comedy that dulls the mind into acquiescence. The device several times repeated of the play-within-the play allows the inner theme about the relation of art to politics to be fully debated but always as a consequence of changes in the historical situation Barnes depicts: the many levels of the play — historical, theatrical, political, intellectual — are beautifully integrated.

Red Noses was not, however, served well by Terry Hands's production; it lacked clarity of definition. Anthony Sher caught Father Flote's magnetic innocence and encompassed the physical knockabout of the role superbly; but he is an actor who often asserts his acrobatic prowess at the expense of the intellectual demands of a role, his handling of speech being at times slapdash when it should be incisive. He seemed to have little feeling for the structure of Barnes's play or his crucial part in it as a man moving through spiritual vision to social awareness. He was not helped in this by the director who blurred the argument of the play by adding numerous gimmicky visual effects, not devised by Barnes, which distracted attention from the dialogue at crucial moments. The Pope and Archbishop Monselet soaring up and down in mid-air, apparently unsupported, like two battling angels was ingenious; but the text is a scene of cunning, political manoeuvres in which Clement decides to destroy Flote despite his private sympathies for the man. The tension was quite lost in performance and the complex portrait of the Pope trivialised. The weaknesses of the production emphasized in contrast with the text the extraordinary discipline controlling Barnes's invention, the scrupulous judging of detail so that effects advance both the action and the argument. He has a sure sense of the architecture of a play. Hands recognises this himself since he observed in interview that *Red Noses* marks a shift in Barnes's style from the Jonsonian to the Shakespearean;[20] his production, however, never seemed to find the play's shape or inner dynamic, partly because not enough distinction was made by him between the several kinds of performance Flote's troupe give, the different audiences they act for, and the varying receptions they get. Such detail is essential in furthering Barnes's debate about the nature of comedy. It was a flat production, in want of emphasis to stimulate necessary discriminations.

Dramatists must select material representative of their particular aims in treating historical subjects; as Gems observes, all plays are metaphors. From this survey of plays one can see that for some this involves isolating significant incidents that in their view explain the whole, while others prefer to reach beyond fact into fantasy that impressionistically conveys the spirit and tenor of the past. Whatever the dramatic method, two facts seem to intrude on the creative process — the decision whether or not to attempt a period idiom for the dialogue and, more crucially, the question of how to engage the audience intellectually as well as imaginatively in the play and to what end. Taylor, Gems, Churchill and Barnes devise unusual structures or styles of performance as strategies to excite in their audiences new perspectives of understanding about the relation of the individual to the process of history. While not being overtly didactic, they are conscious that the past is "a light to lesson [future] ages".[21] As Edward Bond asserts "we live in history"[22] and the best of the plays under discussion at once create and illuminate that awareness.

Bond himself has a unique voice in our theatre today; his finest works are history plays but of a special kind: whether his characters have a genuine historical past (Shakespeare, Jonson, Clare) or are borrowed or imitated from earlier styles of drama (Lear, Mrs. Rafi, Lord Are, Hecuba), his concern is with history as our cultural heritage. Literature and drama reflect the values of the age in which they were written and to accept them as our culture is in Bond's view to endorse these values and be shaped in turn by them. Bond's strategies are devised not simply to sharpen our discrimination about the present but to make us critically aware of *how* we respond to the past by challenging the assumptions of what might best be described as our cultural imagination. With *Lear* or *Restoration* Bond wishes us to keep a familiar play or style of comedy firmly in mind the better to perceive the differences in his treatment: he alerts us to what we accept as the conventions of a type of play, then begins critically to investigate what those conventions imply about the social values of the age in which that style of drama was conceived and found acceptable as an image of the times. Bond is not writing fantasy in order to come at an apprehension of the past so much as juxtaposing culture, as the image by which an age chooses to be remembered, with social history as the facts record it. Those plays, *Bingo* and *The Fool*, that take the life of a writer for subject explore the *angst* of the artist trapped between the apparently divided demands of art and history: myth-making and realism. Bond's is an art of discrimination, but of a most subtle kind: he asks an audience to observe their cultural allegiances as a reflection of their social attitudes now; how we choose to understand the past, he argues, shows us the condition of our own sensibility. What is remarkable about his best plays, given such a complex ambition, is their sheer economy of expression and of method. He pares down, stylises, minimalises to a degree where the austerity of what is left becomes richly allusive. His success in this depends much on the device of juxtaposition: he has developed a technique of double focus where scenes involve two centres of action played simultaneously in which the audience perceive patterns of irony, similarity and contrast which elude the characters involved. A subtle technique of juxtaposition has been apparent too in the clever casting of the London productions of Bond's plays (Gielgud as Shakespeare, Coral Browne as Mrs. Rafi, Simon Callow and Irene Handl as Lord Are and his mother), where an actor's personality and customary style aroused expectations as to the development of a role which the play then deliberately frustrated — an alienation effect that shocked audiences into an instant engagement with Bond's concern with the degree to which the cultured sensibility is apathetic, too lacking in critical rigour because too content to take our dramatic and literary heritage on trust.[23] History, for Bond, is a test of perception.

Bond achieved his characteristic pithy, terse style with celerity. *The Pope's Wedding* (Royal Court, 1962)[24] and *Saved* (Royal Court, 1965)[25] showed him in command of a blunt hard dialogue and a simplicity of staging which directed the audience's attention to unspoken moral dilemmas suffered by the characters that were of considerable intricacy. From the first Bond's drama has addressed itself to the difficulty of defining responsibility for evil in society, moved less by the instinct to assign blame and explore guilt than by a passion for justice. His remaining plays from the 1960s show him exploring ways of investing this clarity of design and bold expression with a power of allusion especially through the device of the double focus which makes the total impact of a scene for an alert audience more than the sum of its parts.

'*Early Morning*' (Royal Court, 1968),[26] his first history play, a phantasmagoria involving the chief figures of Queen Victoria's reign, traces the logical consequences of a society that pursues an ideology of self-help: it is a world in which dog eats dog, the characters' hunger for power in life becoming after their deaths simply a ravenous hunger satisfied in an endless round of cannibalistic feasts. As the play is a fantasy, meaning is conveyed largely through the plot; and the dialogue, though very funny, lacks much density of reference. It is something of an exception amongst Bond's plays in that it is to be enjoyed largely on the surface, though meaning is defined by very inventive episodes and graphic stage images: Prince Albert struggling to be a lively ghost despite the vast chains which keep pulling him back inside his tomb; Queen Victoria dressing Florence Nightingale as John Brown to avoid a scandal over her lesbian proclivities — "if they believe you're a man they think I'm just a normal lonely widow" [p. 71]. Even so, '*Early Morning*' places a considerable burden on a director over the question of focus: like *Saved*, the play shows one character — Prince Arthur — slowly developing a critical awareness that detaches him from his society as he hesitantly pursues a growing conviction that there could be alternative, better modes of living; at the end he will rise — literally — free of his savage contemporaries. Throughout, the director must control the playing of scenes so that the audience is conscious of both the total significance of the situation and of Arthur's response to it as a watchful, judging presence. Arthur acts largely as a guide for the audience's response.

Narrow Road to the Deep North (Royal Court, 1969)[27] uses two or more centres of action within a scene to challenge an audience with complex possibilities of moral choice. Shogo's first scene, for example, shows him moving to and fro between the interrogation of a prisoner about an attempt on his life and an audience with Basho to ascertain if he is indeed a wise man suitable to tutor the deposed Emperor's son (whom Shogo, despite his savage victory, is surprisingly keen to respect) and then turning to Kiro to solve the young priest's physical agony as he suffocates with his head trapped inside a sacred vessel. Shogo conducts three interviews simultaneously and resolves them all with a promptness that defines his no-nonsense efficiency as a ruler. But are his choices of action wise or impulsive? He shatters the pot to save Kiro but orders the prisoner's execution; a vicious action and a marked disrespect for sacred objects are offset by his honouring Kiro's life and his piety towards the Emperor's child. Are the values that govern his choices those of expediency or compassion, realism or superstition? There are no easy answers and the consequences of Shogo's choices in the ensuing action do not simplify the issue at all for the audience. Crucially throughout the play the choices are about life and death and the decisions made leave the audience pondering on the motive and troubled by the premise that the measures taken are never just ones, because always tinged in some degree with self-regard or self-pity.

Lear (Royal Court, 1971)[28] is the first of Bond's plays to give the issue of moral choice a cultural dimension, asking us to renew our engagement with Shakespeare's play, not as a tragic masterpiece of our heritage which is in large measure to patronise its achievement, but as a work profoundly concerned with the relation between private sanity and public, political responsibility. To impress on his audience the continuing urgency of Shakespeare's debate Bond makes some significant departures from his 'source', even as Shakespeare did from the old play of *King Leir*: Lear now suffers all Gloucester's humiliations and blinding as well as the destructive consequences of his own rash loss of his kingdom; and the Cordelia-figure, far from being a representative of love and trust, is a more efficient, ruthless tyrant than the daughters who depose Lear. Lear's moral dilemma becomes as a consequence the more all-embracing and the psychic journey he undergoes before he can see his way plain to an act which both absolves his guilt and emblematises the only sane future for his former kingdom is the more chaotic and spiritually daunting. The urge to self-pity is a long time dying in him, given the morass of horrors he must traverse.

The surprising factor about Bond's *Lear*, given its epic scope, is how few large-scale scenes there are — the vast number of roles can be accomplished through constant doubling by a relatively small cast. The effect of the way the scenes are written is to focus attention sharply on the divorce in the characters between their public and private selves. The mad scenes between Shakespeare's Lear, the Fool and poor Tom are frightening for the way that the three talk together, ostensibly wishing to share their several plights and find comfort in that, yet are too trapped in their individual thought-processes and private idioms ever to touch each other imaginatively. Three figures share the stage but under the guise of dialogue they separately soliloquise oblivious of the others. Long before Lear's mind breaks in Bond's play, this is the prevailing dramatic method. It is an insane world Lear inhabits because it is self-obsessed and has lost the ability to *care*. The wall Lear seeks to build around his kingdom is as much psychological as geographical; noticeably he does not abdicate but is usurped. When, exhausted, he is put on trial by Bodice and Fontanelle, the court is a farce; the officials are pawns embarrassed by their lack of genuine authority; the daughters have no moral grounds for sitting in judgement on their father, they are concerned only with a display of power; no one listens to Lear. When Bodice gives Lear her mirror ("Madmen are frightened of themselves"), he sees a caged, bleeding animal:

Who shut that animal in that cage? Let it out. Have you seen its face behind the bars? There's a poor animal with blood on its head and tears running down its face. Who did that to it? Is it a bird or a horse? It's lying in the dust and its wings are broken. Who broke its wings? Who cut off its hands so that it can't shake the bars? It's pressing its snout on the glass. Who shut that animal in a glass cage? O God, there's no pity in this world. You let it lick the blood from its hair in the corner of a cage with nowhere to hide from its tormentors. No shadow, no hole! Let that animal out of its cage! [p. 35]

Bodice seizes on the metaphor in the mistaken belief it emblematises Lear's fear and that she can use it to torment him. She replies apparently in the same idiom: "Yes! I've locked this animal in its cage and I will not let it out!" and Fontanelle is ecstatic at seeing tears in her father's eyes. That the trial has nothing to do with politics or justice but is pursued out of petty revenge is now abundantly clear. Though Bodice thinks she is sharing Lear's language, what she takes to be a metaphor is for Lear a reality; his tears are a sign not of abject humiliation but of pity. As Lear loses his sanity he begins to objectify his inner, emotional states (later the ghost of one of the victims of his refusal to care for others, the Gravedigger's Boy, will become a distinct presence in his prison cell). The caged creature and the ghost are embodiments of Lear's self-pity made real to his tortured perceptions. It is the fact that he can detach himself from his emotional state in this way that enables him to grow in self-awareness and see in time, as he comes to understand the past, that to experience guilt is not enough; nor (later in the play) is the desire to preach to his people of the need for social change in cunningly devised parables that elude Cordelia's censoring scrutiny. He must act to assuage the past and change the present and that in uncompromising terms which no one can misjudge. Knowing he will be shot, he takes a spade and begins to hack away the wall he devoted so much of his reign to building.

Lear has to find a way to *mean* something, to be a reality in his changed self to others.

The technique of the divided focus, of dialogue that repeatedly and deliberately fails to bridge the gap between people's experiences, is used by Bond for a variety of psychological effects. Lear in prison watches the autopsy Cordelia has ordered on Fontanelle's corpse: what to the doctor is biological fact — "You can see how she died. The bullet track goes through the lady's lungs" [p. 59] — is for Lear the substance of vision, of wonder at the *order* of the human form, the compact miracle of being; he suddenly knows the reality of Fontanelle quite detached from her childish temperament, and finds grounds on which he could now love her even at the moment she is utterly lost to him. When Bodice enters the cell, terrified that her assassination is imminent, Lear's attempt to share his newly won perception with her carries her to the edge of hysteria:

LEAR: That's your sister.
BODICE: No!
LEAR: I destroyed her.
BODICE: Destroyed? No, no! We admit nothing. We acted for the best. Did what we had to do.
LEAR: I destroyed her! I knew nothing, saw nothing, learned nothing! Fool! Fool! Worse than I knew! (*He puts his hands into Fontanelle and brings them out with organs and viscera. The soldiers react awkwardly and ineffectually.*) Look at my dead daughter!
BODICE: No! No!
LEAR: Look! I killed her! Her blood is on my hands! Destroyer! Murderer! And now I must begin again. I must walk through my life, step after step, I must walk in weariness and bitterness, I must become a child, hungry and stripped and shivering in blood, I must open my eyes and see! [p. 60]

Lear is reviewing his life, finding values by which to begin again; Bodice struggles to retain her political cunning and voice of command against the mounting realisation that she is to share Fontanelle's fate. Neither listens to the other. The possibility of joy Lear realises he might have known with Fontanelle, he could now share with Bodice; a reconciliation might calm her anguish; but the opportunity slips away. Lear is preoccupied with his guilt over Fontanelle, and Bodice is too concerned to preserve her dignity to see his fondling of her sister's viscera with any feeling but revulsion. It is a powerful moment that demands the actors concentrate the audience's attention on the play of the characters' minds and the tragic loss that occurs rather than the sensational element in the scene. If the audience shares Bodice's nausea, then the scene has lost touch with its inner dynamic.

It is here that one notes a potential weakness in the play: given the degree of concentration Bond exacts from his audience through his technique of the divided focus (one needs to follow the thought patterns of each of several persons in a scene), *Lear* does seem to lack structural balance (which is not true of his subsequent plays). It is partly Bond's concern to depict scrupulously the slow, tortuous progress of Lear's journey from blindness to moral insight that creates the difficulty. So many changes are partial or false steps in the process of awakening that Lear's final insight into what is his only right course of action lacks by contrast sufficient preparation and development. It risks seeming in performance an impulsive or, worse, a romantic gesture. Within three short scenes he travels from despair at his own futility — "I can do nothing, I am nothing" [p. 80] — to a clear perception of his life's worth:

I see my life, a black tree by a pool. The branches are covered with tears. The tears are shining with light. The mind blows the tears in the sky. And my tears fall down on me. [p. 86]

The change has been effected by an encounter with Cordelia, who wishes to place him yet again on trial; both of them recognise the absurdity of this, but she argues that their relative positions demand it. In seeing the extent to which Cordelia is letting herself become the prisoner of circumstance, Lear apprehends how he has freed his mind from bondage to what he believed to be necessity. His attack on the wall is a gesture celebrating that freedom, made to inspire others to follow his path. That image of the black tree of tears could sound like renewed self-pity were the moment not immediately preceded by the death of the Gravedigger's Boy's ghost who has always held out to him that temptation. The very clarity of his language now betokens an unashamed truth to self. Thereafter in the final scene Lear's tone is one of quiet self-command as he prepares to scale the wall, absolute for death. The psychological arc of these scenes is assured but it is conveyed in Bond's most allusive manner: all is implied through subtly changing nuances of tone, none of which is sustained beyond seconds of stage time. It requires a very gifted actor to communicate in performance the vast leap of imagination that Lear encompasses here and the great peace that comes to him once he sees his way forward. Bond has not taxed the creative stamina of his actors nor the imaginative engagement of his audience so formidably again. The narrative and psychological line of *The*

Woman which bears some resemblance to *Lear* is more closely integrated; but then it is a play less concerned than *Lear* to chart an individual's painstaking struggles through the miasmas of despair.

Lear is not strictly speaking a history play but it marks Bond's first attempt to galvanise an audience into a critical engagement with its cultural past. He makes it impossible to hold Shakespeare's tragedy at a comfortable distance by labelling it *Renaissance* drama, instead he asks us to go back to it with renewed vigour, conscious that its moral and political arguments still pose a challenge to us. If his treatment is harsher than Shakespeare's, it is to stress the urgency of our need to recognise the enduring truth of Shakespeare's perceptions about the nature of sanity. Subsequent history plays by Bond have not worked a pattern of variations upon a specific source but have used pastiche to intimate a style of drama and its conventions, which he wishes to subject to our scrutiny. Mrs. Rafi in *The Sea* (Royal Court, 1973)[29] is the first example of this technique. A gorgon with a voice of command, she keeps people in terror of her (consequently they are quick to respond to her every whim which, however bizarre, she can always justify with a rhetorical flourish); she will be the centre of any stage by sending rivals scuttling for the wings withering under her sarcasm; she can belittle others because she can scent their weak spots and use that insight to her advantage. The type of tyrannical dowager has a long stage-history but it is Wilde who gave the type *style*, a sense of deliberately playing a role to perfection; and it is this complex version of the stereotype that Bond chooses to imitate, catching exquisitely Lady Bracknell's epigrammatic idiom: "Jessica stop trying to sound like a woman with an interesting past. Nothing has ever happened to you. That is a tragedy. But it hardly qualifies you to give advice" [p. 18]. That Mrs. Tilehouse is a mouse is a tragedy but that is no excuse for Mrs. Rafi to treat the matter as a subject for abuse. She has a cruel accuracy of insight that never engages her sympathy.

In the closing moments of *The Importance of Being Earnest* Wilde gives us a sudden explanation of Lady Bracknell's excessive snobbery and her domineering tone:

I do not approve of mercenary marriages. When I married Lord Bracknell I had no fortune of any kind. But I never dreamed for a moment of allowing that to stand in my way.[30]

She is *nouveau riche*, not aristocratic to the manner born and so she has to *play* the manner to perfection to elude detection and gossip; she can never relax, must always assert her role, since the truth is too shaming, judged by her own values. Lady Bracknell is the lifelong victim of her own ambition; that knowledge does not, however, make her uncharitableness any the more appealing. Mrs. Rafi does relax her guard, once, with Willy and Rose, the young couple whom she is anxious should escape the small-minded rural community in which the play is set where, if they stay, they will be labelled, expected to fill predictable roles and offices, and never allowed to be themselves. She has coped herself by making it all a play in which she is invariably the star, but she knows the whole town waits for the moment they can take their revenge for the years of systematic bullying. Her past and present were determined; so too is her future; "old, ugly, whimpering, dirty, pushed about on wheels and threatened" [p. 57]. The insight is exact, but does not provoke sympathy because of the absurdity of the underlying assumption that it is all destined, *expected* of her (noticeably a favourite term), that it could not be different. As Rose observes afterwards: "she's such a coward" [p. 58], using her force of will to sustain a pattern in society which she wholeheartedly despises; she had the courage neither to go away and create a new life elsewhere nor to change the community for its good; as a consequence, "the town's full of her cripples" [p. 58]. Bond gives Mrs. Rafi a moment's self-knowledge only to show why, failing in responsibility to her considerable intelligence, she is a stereotype deserving our laughter and not an individual. Like Wilde, he detaches one from the convention so that one may understand both its nature the more completely and one's response to it.

It is a tightly-knit Edwardian community Mrs. Rafi presides over on the East Anglican coast but one far from idyllic. To give us a perspective on to the quality of life there, Bond turns not to Wilde but to Shakespeare and *The Tempest*: his final comedy that celebrates reconciliation, as intelligence in Prospero blossoms into sympathy and revenge gives place to compassion. Like Shakespeare, Bond opens his comedy in the full tumult of a storm as a young man, Willy, casts himself into the waters from a sinking ship; as he struggles to gain a foothold, two figures loom out of the mist from the beach: one drunkenly proffers a bottle and disappears, the other turns a torch on him and shouts vicious abuse, trying to force him back into the sea. The storm dies away but it is no place of "sounds and sweet airs, that give delight, and hurt not"[31] where Willy has landed: the turbulence continues in people's minds. In the dialogue of *Lear* one noted the disconnections between speakers; in *The Sea* the disconnections have become the feature of most characters' speech.

Like the sea, ideas ebb and flow in their minds, are traversed by cross-currents. Willy, for example, is advised to consult old Mr. Evens about where the body of his friend Colin who died in the wreck is likely to be washed ashore. Returning to the beach, he is overwhelmed with grief at the memory of what occurred. As he cries, Hatch, the man who abused him in the storm, reappears and begins to menace him. Evens is unperturbed:

We're into the spring tides now. He'll be washed up where the coast turns in. (*Points.*) You see? People are cruel and boring and obsessed. If he goes past that point you've lost him. He should come in. He's hanging round out there now. He could see us if he wasn't dead. My wife died in hospital. She had something quite minor. I sold up. They hate each other. Force. Make. Use. Push. Burn. Sell. For what? A heap of rubbish. Don't believe what they say: I don't understand the water. I know the main currents, but luck and chance come into it. It doesn't matter how clear the main currents are, you have to live through the details. It's always the details that make the tragedy. Not anything larger. They used to say tragedy purified, helped you to let go. Now it only embarrasses. They'll make a law against it. He should come out in the middle of next week. Don't count on it. There might be a flood. Then everything goes by the board. A man was drowned at sea and the next day a flood washed him miles inland and left him in his own garden hanging up in the apple tree. All the apples were washed off and went bobbing away in the water. His wife and children were stranded up on the roof watching him. They sat there three days. [pp. 13-14]

The speech is quixotic in its movement, proffering the information sought for and a gesture of understanding about Willy's tears, which aims to comfort; but beyond that there are intimations of a vision of the world as strange and inexplicable, prone to chance rather than sustained by order and design. The thought-processes of the other characters are as disconnected: Hatch the draper veers between the obsequious deference of the small trader and an increasingly frenzied assertion that the sea is being invaded by creatures from another planet which it is his duty as coastguard to destroy (Willy he deems one such); and Mrs. Rafi can yoke the most bizarre inconsequentialities together and insist on their relation by sheer force of rhetoric. When one of the cast in Mrs. Rafi's Amateur Dramatic Society objects to being cast as an animal yet again, she is quickly silenced: "You'll be a dog. You collect for your Save the Animals Fund every year and you never go away till we've given twice as much as we can afford. Now you have the chance to earn some more gratitude from your little friends" [p. 20]. The logic of this is preposterous; it cunningly moves from categorical insistence to personal criticism then concludes by being patronising, which leaves Mrs. Rafi's victim trapped between fear and flattery. The blackmail is subtle but it wins acquiescence at the cost of lingering resentment. Mrs. Rafi repeatedly urges others to remember who they are and respect their proper place in the community; yet in all the scenes of communal activity, it is not order that prevails but the anarchy of farce. The ceremony for scattering Colin's ashes, despite Mrs. Rafi's careful plans to keep the proceedings decorous and co-ordinated, quickly slides into mayhem: "Have you no respect for the dead?" she shrills at the townsfolk even while pelting them with the ashes in her rage [p. 53]. Disconnections abound, within speeches, between word and action; orderliness is as much a pretence as Mrs. Rafi's pose of authority. Farce relentlessly uncovers the social truth.

Hatch is the most wretched of Mrs Rafi's victims, goaded into laying out the entire capital on which his business rests to purchase some furnishing fabric for her, only to have her withdraw the contract because she feels he is failing in his duty as coastguard. She never realises her cruelty in this or his desperation; she asserts her sense of moral rectitude, blind to the fact that she is utterly breaking the man. His sanity disintegrates with the shock but he goes on hacking the material into three-yard lengths, his voice struggling to keep tears at bay by assuring her of his proficiency and his sense of the dignity of his trade: "You see I cut it all myself. You have to know cloth. There's an art to this. . . . Look at that edge. . . . These shears are part of my hand. Watch how the cloth leads them. That's the gesture of my soul, Mrs. Rafi, there's a whole way of life in that . . ." [p. 36]. Mrs. Rafi's sense of order depends on a refusal to imagine the condition of others; she cultivates detachment and insists she be the arbiter of what is best for people. Coolly she provokes this scene as a moral lesson to Hatch and unleashes on the town a maddened individual, who reduces the dignity of her remaining appearances in the play to farce. It is Bond's comic method in *The Sea* to show us complex individuals like Hatch and Evens where Mrs. Rafi sees only types, and show her to be a type when she prides herself on being a developed personality.

The technique of the divided focus of action grows naturally out of the many disconnections that make up the fabric of the play. Bond uses the device chiefly to isolate Willy and Rose, who are moved by Colin's death not to indulge in rituals of mourning like Mrs. Rafi but to review their lives against the farcical world they might be expected to inhabit till they recognise a shared need to find some alternative. Beside the townsfolk, Willy does seem, as Hatch supposes him to be, a creature from another world; only Evens realises that that is Willy's strength, that the psychic shock of the storm has set him on the path of inner peace. In the turbulent farce his is a figure of contained stillness that magnetically draws Rose to him in search of security. The most impressive effect of this counterpointing of movement and stillness occurs in a scene on the beach, where Willy crouches downstage while Hatch at the rear discovers Colin's body newly washed ashore and believes it to be a sleeping Willy, his enemy from the dreaded beyond. Hatch stabs the corpse more and more savagely, as to his amazement it emits water not blood and seemingly refuses to die. Throughout Willy has his back turned to Hatch; he is fearless even while imagining accurately what is going on: "Hit it. That's an innocent murder"[p. 45]. There is no outrage, no judgement in that, but an exact understanding of Hatch and the incident. Willy has no knowledge, as the audience has, of the train of events that have led to this bizarre attack, but he accurately gauges Hatch's total desperation, his need for violent release. Willy is neither amused nor superior. When Rose sees the mutilated corpse, she reiterates "How terrible. How terrible." But Willy questions why: "I don't see it. What does it matter? You can't hurt the dead. How can you desecrate dust? . . . He's just dead bait for a mad man"[p. 46]. This is not callous, but a refusal to pretend to a piety he does not feel; and the remark does not offend Rose's sensibility, instead it calms her outburst. His matter-of-fact tone intimates that he speaks out of a truth to feeling, not out of how he supposes he should behave. It is his freshness of response, his careful objectivity, that defines Willy's moral stature.

Bond's tempest precipitates us not into a fantasy world where magic can effect ideal solutions to human error, deceit and injury but into a world that declines into a savage farce despite Mrs. Rafi's efforts to maintain the decorum of a comedy of manners. *Style* in her is usually an excuse for callous insensitivity to others; she knows this but perseveres with unabashed cynicism. Where Prospero seeks to use his intelligence creatively for a common good, she betrays hers in using it to belittle everyone about her. It is appropriate that throughout the play she is obsessed with rituals of death and mourning for there is nothing life-enhancing in her temperament. Brilliantly Bond juxtaposes several styles of comedy in *The Sea* to encourage us to perceive the *social* evil in the type she represents. Her wit is heartless and the play is designed to show us the full consequences of that. Bond has renewed our appreciation of the satirical impulse that went to the creating of the comic stereotype in the first place and by so doing has enlarged our cultural perception.

"Bells love silence"[p. 16], Shakespeare observes in *Bingo*

(Royal Court, 1974)[32]. As he says it, he signs a document that compromises his finely tuned moral scruple: it is an agreement with Combe, a landowner, not to interfere with his efforts to enclose the common lands of Stratford; Shakespeare is guaranteed in return the equivalent of any rents he might stand to lose. (The authentic document survives.) He is acting out of fear lest, like his father before him, he lose in old age the security he has worked for, represented on stage by the great sheltering yew hedges of his secluded garden. The remark about the bells might seem a chance poetic effusion, were it not clearly tinged with envy. The mind might also be said to love silence, but the voice of conscience constantly intrudes.

Willy was a character who grew in stature largely in silence, a watchful presence whose few remarks were incisive and exact. With Shakespeare the silence is more complex, tense: his insight, like Willy's, is penetrating but it brings repeatedly a judgement on himself. His writing has developed his moral sensibility to a degree where his understanding of others brings a deepening awareness of his failure in responsibility to them. He worked to know an idyllic silence, retired to his garden in old age; but pure silence eludes him. The dramatist's final Romances evoke an ineffable peace through the reconciliation of families who were lost to each other, who pass through suffering to learn how to care and cherish. That knowledge adds to our sense of painful irony as we watch Bond's Shakespeare struggling to control his revulsion from his daughter, Judith, whom he finds banal, insensitive, obsessed with duties, chores, money. Bond does not stress the parallel but leaves us with our inheritance of Shakespeare's plays to infer it. Family, neighbours, townsfolk, a fellow-poet (Jonson on his way North to sponge on a credulous Scot), all excite a sense of having betrayed them and himself, because he cannot get involved in their lives and use his moral scruple creatively. What is an anguished impotence, they jeer at as mandarin indifference, serenity. (It is a considerable challenge to the actor playing Shakespeare to shape his silence to convey that distinction — Shakespeare is throughout the action engaged, thinking, tortured by the fact of the silence; he is not withdrawn intellectually or emotionally; his few substantial speeches in the play are all the product of pent-in thoughts and feelings exploding to find release.)

The one character who can calm him is the Old Woman. Like the many compassionate servants in Shakespeare's plays, she is gifted with intuition because she has learned to live with suffering as a habitual condition and so can speak to the pain in others: "Yo' yont named for cruelty. They say yo'm a generous man. Yo' looked arter me an' father. Give us one a your houses t' live in .... If yo' yont allow yo'self t' be helped, what shall us do?" [p. 27]. Her husband's brain has been damaged by an accident; he now has the mind of a child and is utterly dependent on her. She does not *talk* about responsibility, as Judith does, but her account of her husband demonstrates what responsibility is: "He's a boy that remember what's like t'be a man. He still hev a proper feelin' for his pride, that yont gone. Hard, that is — like bein' tied up to a clown" [p. 11]. There is no shrinking here from imaginative sympathy; the Old Woman can always find grounds for respecting the dignity of another individual. This enables her to bring a measure of comfort to Shakespeare but it is not ultimately enough: Shakespeare may relax at her mothering tone, but she cannot touch or assuage his particular guilt because she never thinks of him as an artist whose work is a continual challenge to him as a man: "Every writer writes in other men's blood. The trivial, and the real. There's nothing else to write in. But only a god or a devil can write in other men's blood and not ask why they spilt it and what it cost. Not this hand, that's always melted snow . . ." [p. 42]. The very integrity of his art makes him doubt his humanity; his essential genius renders it impossible for him to forgive his failure as a man; and ultimately he takes his own life as the one possible atone-ment.

It is a mark of creative tact on Bond's part to expect an audience to bring their knowledge of Shakespeare's artistry to articulate the silences in the play as the balance, always present to his consciousness, in which Shakespeare weighs himself relentlessly and recognises how much he is wanting. This also allows Bond to conduct an intricate moral debate with astonishing economy: how much he asks is what in *personal* terms is Shakespeare's final moral triumph in *social* terms a defeat? The device of the double focus of action is at a premium here. Scene Four in the inn is a good example. Shakespeare is drinking with Jonson, who keeps turning the gossip about London round to theatre business in the hope his old rival will let slip some information about his current work. Jonson takes Shakespeare's silence to be a sly playing of the cards close to his chest; he cannot believe that Shakespeare is really doing *nothing*. Jonson's beery amity soon reveals itself as a pose with a purpose: he wants a loan but, embarrassed at his need, he proceeds to bite at the hand he wants to feed him. (Shakespeare's silence has an unerring ability to bring out the worst in others.) Jonson speaks of his great hatred for his fellow dramatist but it seems a petty response confined to sniping at Shakespeare's "lack of education or as I put it genuine ignorance" [p. 33], his thrift — "I had to borrow to bury my little boy. I still owe on the grave. I suppose you buried your boy in best oak" [p. 38], his maddening apartness — "Can't imagine you walking to Scotland. That sort of research is too real" [p. 30]. He tries to find a raw nerve to probe, but Shakespeare cherishes no sense of prestige that might allow Jonson to rile him. His very simplicity offsets Jonson's self-importance, small mindedness and bile and all quite unwittingly, which doubles the humour. It is Jonson's repeated gibe that Shakespeare has successfully avoided contact with the sordid, vicious aspects of Jacobean London, the prisons, the maimings, the law. But the weight of the play turns that judgement againt Jonson: there are degrees of knowing; experience is not necessarily the same thing as engagement or understanding. A sentence for murder is hardly a matter to crow about; nor is it proof of one's artistic integrity, as Jonson tries to imply: "Fellow writer. Only way to end a literary quarrel. Put my sword in him. Like a new pen. The blood flowed as if inspired" [p. 31]. Jonson accuses Shakespeare of indifference, but what greater moral indifference can be imagined than these clipped phrases?

The scene opens out suddenly with the arrival of a group of townsfolk who have been digging in ditches under cover of night in an effort to halt Combe's enclosure schemes. They are tense, frightened, unsure of what Shakespeare and Jonson might overhear or suspect. If caught, they are likely to be imprisoned; they feel they are in the right but know it is the nature of the law to back the powerful not the poor, and so, to reassure themselves, they repeat their motives: "That's us land. Shall us sit down an' let 'em rob it? How I live then? How I feed my wife an' little uns?" [p. 34]. Jonson throughout this expatiates on hate, especially hate for Shakespeare "because you smile. Right up *under* your eyes" [p. 34]; Shakespeare collapses in a drunken stupor. Combe enters and begins to threaten the other party while Jonson drunkenly extols the bucolic life; hearing mention of digging as he lurches out to replenish his drink, he returns planning to write a "sound practical manual in a good, simple, craftman's style" on the spade [p. 36]. Experience with Jonson amounts to no more than aesthetic gestures. Shakespeare is in an altogether finer mould, yet his presence in this scene is disturbing as he submits to Jonson's pressure to drink till he is insensible. Through the device of the double focus Bond is asking us to adopt two perspectives on the action.

His purpose clarifies in the final scene. In the closing moments of *Bingo* Shakespeare dies (writhing on the floor of his room), poisoned by his own hand; his last words are the question "Was anything done?" [p. 50]. Judith is tearing his bed apart in quest of a codicil to his will, but her efforts are in vain and she mutters to herself in desperation again and again "Nothing!" We are left with the choice of how closely we relate the two centres of action. The moment comes at the climax of a series of episodes which make that choice a matter of pressing urgency yet peculiarly difficult. The scene opens with Shakespeare in bed being tended by the Old Woman; she is preoccupied with grief at the strange death of her husband, shot in the fields the previous evening apparently by accident. Shakespeare asks twice "Was anything done?" and she cannot calm him: he has found the root of his pain but it is beyond the scope of her imagining and one becomes conscious of the extent to which she never grasped his true need. Her past reassurances were really an inducement to be self-pitying. Judith and her mother suddenly arrive outside the door but it is locked against them. They abase themselves abjectly: the wife stages a hysterical fit, scratching at the door, while Judith kicks it and threatens suicide. That it is all calculated, emotional blackmail is apparent from the calm that ensues the instant Shakespeare pushes his will under the door to them. The Old Woman's son comes next and is admitted; he has led the digging party against Combe's enclosures, carried a gun, and quite likely was responsible for his father's death. He has come to confess to the murder once Shakespeare and he are alone. It is as if the dramatist is being visited by one of the characters from his earliest play about civil war, the Son Who Has Killed His Father. This son wishes not to mourn his fate, like his prototype in *Henry VI*; he comes to justify himself: "I yont give meself up. Us'll foight for us land. Outside a me they'd give in. I'll go off later. When mother's settled. T'ent easy t'be with her now. T'ent decent" [p. 48]. Combe appears in his role as magistrate, knowing Shakespeare was in the fields the previous night, to ask if he saw anything of the murder. Shakespeare asks Combe to pass him some pills, that we know are poison, but honours the Son's trust and says nothing about his admission. Combe goes, trying to salve his own conscience about the enclosures by admitting one of his men might have ignored instructions to take only sticks and have armed himself with a gun. Left to themselves, Shakespeare swallows the pills, while the Son seizes on Combe's remark to slide out of the moral courage he just showed by deft equivocation: "I fire a gun — I yont hide no truth. That yont mean I shot him. Someone else'n moight a fired. Death on an unarmed man — that's more loike the sort a think Combe'd get up to" [p. 50]. He goes; Shakespeare falls to the floor; Judith enters to savage the room.

The progress of the scene has a stark simplicity yet the cumulative effect defies easy analysis. Shakespeare, though addressed by the other characters, is wholly intent on dying, his only direct communication is with the Son in his moment of strength: "A murderer telling a dead man the truth? Are we the only people who can afford the truth?" [p. 48]. What the different encounters seem designed to show are the possible motives we should discount in responding to Shakespeare's suicide: it is not done out of self-pity, or staged as emotional blackmail, nor is it a subtle evasion. It is an act of judgement on his life when weighed against the absolute values of his work, without which those values would have been betrayed and nothing done. Artistic scruple and objectivity have refined Shakespeare's conscience. His death in consequence is a personal moral triumph. But we are conscious of the pain in other lives which is left unappeased by his death and for which he is in varying degrees responsible, within his family and within the town over the issue of the enclosures. None of those left to suffer has expressed any recognition of the value of his art so will not see his death in other terms than suicide. It is in every sense a lonely death. The dramatic method of the play activates two sets of values, private conscience and social justice, and leaves us with the problem of choice. How we judge, how we answer Shakespeare's dying question — "Was anything done" — reflects on our cultural awareness. Shakespeare's dilemma in *Bingo* is shown progressively to be ours.

Where Shakespeare's tragic suffering in *Bingo* springs from his idealism, Clare's in *The Fool* (Royal Court, 1975)[33] derives from the realism of his art, his refusal to be a poet of "charm" and "true melody" with a "fine love of English landscape" [p. 41]. 'Landscape' captures Clare's difficulty exactly — it implies what his wealthy patrons require: aesthetic distance, the ability to view nature in a way that flatters one's own heightened sensibility. Imaginative engagement with the countryside as Clare experiences it, as his home, his means of sustenance, a place of hardship and deprivation as well as pleasure, they condemn as "mawkish" [p. 41]. When Admiral Lord Radstock and Mrs. Emmerson try to censor Clare's poems, they are attempting to divorce cultural expression from social and moral awareness; but that is to take the life-blood and the sanity out of Clare's art. They are asking him not only to compromise his integrity as an artist but to limit his vision and understanding as a man. The rhythm of their dialogue is inexorable; it is a calculated attack, the nastier for the tone of anxious solicitude for Clare's welfare:

ADMIRAL: I have one reservation. Not serious. The fault of a narrow horizon. Those remarks in — poem named after your village —
MRS. EMMERSON: Helpstone.
ADMIRAL: (You see we've discussed it) — which criticizes the landowning classes — smack of radicalism.
MRS. EMMERSON: (*reciting*) Accursed Wealth! —
ADMIRAL: That bit.
MRS. EMMERSON: O'er bounding human laws
        Of every evil then remainst the cause.
ADMIRAL: And so on.
MRS. EMMERSON: Including lines from 'Winter'.
  (*Reciting*.) What thousands now half pined and bare
        Are forced to stand thy —
  (*Explains*) That is, Winters —
  (*Reciting*.)   — piercing air.
ADMIRAL: Now, now sir.
MRS. EMMERSON: All day near numbed to death with cold.
        Some petty gentry —
ADMIRAL (*shaking his head*) At it again.
MRS. EMMERSON: — to uphold.
ADMIRAL: Tut tut!

                               [p. 42]

This is asking Clare to be a hack. Patronage has two meanings and here the evil of condescension is masquerading behind seeming encouragement.

The Fool charts the shaping of the romantic spirit in Clare, whom circumstances make a radical individualist so that, paradoxically, he can speak for his people, voice for them emotions they experience but cannot themselves articulate. His patrons wish him to forsake his roots and his truth to self to become one of the tribe of *literati*, mouthing effusions remarkable only for their inanity. The dramatic method of the play is exciting in the way that Clare's is hardly distinguished as the central role for much of the first act. He is but one of a party of Mummers performing the Play of St. George for Lord Milton's houseguests in the opening scene, and he is noticeably silent when some of the men try to express their sense of grievance at their hard lot; he is then seen briefly being pursued by Patty, his friend Darkie's sister, and himself pursuing the wild Mary; when the villagers, starved into desperation, riot against the gentry, Clare is absent; he accompanies Patty when she visits Darkie and the men who are in prison over the thefts and it is there that he is suddenly distinguished from the group and, eerily so, by a bout of prolonged laughter. Clare spent much of his life gaoled in a mental asylum, judged mad by his contemporaries. Bond asks us in *The Fool* to question the standards by which we assess madness; he sees Clare as possessing a heightened moral sensitivity, a perception that disturbs others because of its essential difference.

The laughter is an unnerving experience for the audience. Patty and Clare have found Darkie and his friends in profound gloom, expecting to be sentenced to hang. Patty can only express her concern for her brother through anger and irritation — "O boy *I* don't know what to say. Thass a fact" [p. 28]; she has brought his best coat — "On't goo like a tramp an' disgrace the family" [p. 27]. Their tension together, constricted by feelings they cannot utter, is disrupted by wild laughter from adjacent cells as the news slowly filters through that most of the prisoners are to be reprieved and transported. Darkie's name is not on the Governor's list; he is to be made an example. The great surge of hope in the cell is damped down as his friends, struggling out of deference to suppress their elation, are removed to different quarters. Darkie rejects the Parson's sanctimonious rhetoric and on impulse gives Clare the decent coat: "On't waste it on show. Kep' us in rags, on't dress up for 'em when I die. On't their circus" [p.32]. It is a gesture to save his integrity and it has in performance a compelling dignity, like a ritual handing on of trust. Patty has told Darkie of Clare's growing name as a poet "Scribblin' come t'summat. Gen'man bin. Talk 'bout a book" [p. 28]; it is as if Darkie is now investing Clare with his sense of deep social protest; and Clare's response is laughter, extensive, all-consuming, irrepressible. It wells forth in the silence, shocking Patty: "On't right. Ought a think a Darkie. Not allus self" [p. 34]. Though it pains him, it goes on inexorably. Darkie noticeably is not critical. It takes the whole play to define the tone of that laughter as an awakening to the terrible injustice and inequalities of the world Clare inhabits, a chilling perception of the extent to which the enormity of the social situation renders any response inadequate. Darkie is a victim of the processes of the law, but can that process be described as justice? (Bond is marvellously perceptive of the way emotion in unsophisticated or inarticulate people is often an index of moral scruple — in the preceding scene, where the rioters strip the Parson of his clothes, silver buckles and diamond studs, they weep when they see him naked, not out of guilt but out of shame that penury and degradation should compel them to such an act to make their suffering *known*.) Clare's laughter is not as it might seem manic, but the mark of a profound engagement, an awareness of the full demands upon him as man and poet. His patrons will seek to trivialize that awareness and, when he resists, will interpret it as a sign of madness. Bond defies us to judge that laughter insane.

The rioters' tears and Clare's laughter are a recognition of the extent to which circumstances brutalize their natures. The central scene of the play exploits a divided focus of action to render this perception more immediately for us. While Clare, sporting Darkie's coat, strolls with Mrs. Emmerson and the Admiral in Hyde Park and they dictate what is acceptable in poetry, a boxing match is played out upstage of them: a Negro and an Irishman are set against each other as sport; bets have been laid on the outcome. For much of the scene there is no contact between the two areas of interest except to deepen our sense of the offensive cruelty of Mrs. Emmerson's efforts to tutor Clare's genius; a poet, she informs Charles Lamb, has "no call to go round putting ideas in people's heads" [p. 39]. The random shouts from the fight carry ironic reference to the aesthetic debate: "He'll come like a well-trained puppy now and stand to be whipped. Don't thrash him too soon" [p. 41]; "Bang him and keep him raw" [p. 41]; "I invested in you Jackson. . . . Just behave" [p. 41]; "Put the fella down now Porter" [p. 43]. The Admiral's phrases are cultivated but his injunctions to Clare are essentially the same; the physical pain of the one drubbing is a visual metaphor for the psychological wounding of the other. When the literary party does take note of the boxers, the Admiral and Mrs. Emmerson cheer the victor whereas Clare is drawn instinctively to the loser, fascinated as to why he "kep comin' back"[p. 47]. The failing but resilient boxer provides him with an image that helps him maintain his integrity throughout the cruel scenes that follow in which he is imprisoned by his *friends* as mad. The device of the divided focus of action adds a complex metaphorical dimension to the play that shows the brutalising process in action and Clare searching to find the power within himself to resist its impact, when the painful cost of resisting is becoming dreadfully clear to him.

"The people you criticize", says the Admiral, "are the only ones who can afford books." And adds as his trump card: "The only ones who can read!" [p. 43]. It is a shocking comment on contemporary culture and taste but ominously true as the next scene shows, where Clare sits marble-faced as the stage is filled by his patron-friends with parcels of his unsold works. How slight their faith in him was is evident from the care with which they connive at certifying him insane, as if it is necessary so to satisfy their consciences for having, as they suppose, misprized his talent. Again we have a double focus: Clare sits silent in his garden, incapable of writing or working; Patty, now his wife, moves in and out of their cottage but is largely heard urging him to go labouring or at least help her with her chores. Her voice is bitter with the struggle of surviving, devastating in its attack on his manhood as she dismisses his "scribbling" as selfish and threatens to "shame" him, being "sick t'death a the whole bloody thing" [p. 50]. She seems wantonly callous and unloving, the more so when we realise later that she has been questioned at the Parson's and knows that Clare is about to be certified. But Bond is not content with easy judgements. We remember how Patty's anxiety for Darkie showed itself in sharp snubbing retorts and this is a similarly complex moment: brutalised by sheer basic human need, she has nothing but that brutal condition through which to voice her care. His refusal to be galvanised into making efforts for the family's subsistence seems to prove to her what the gentry have warned her is Clare's state; and she has no values by which to challenge their opinion. The very roughness of her tongue is the mark of her sense of helplessness and concern; Patty embodies the grim reality of country life that Clare's art sought to express in its refusal to be conventional, self-consciously literary and escapist. The fact that she is how she is is precisely why he must not recant and become 'acceptable'. In a strange dream-like sequence Clare, escaping the asylum, meets Darkie transformed into a boxer; the effect is to confirm for us the two men's identity of purpose: that Clare's martyrdom in the madhouse is his gesture of social protest, a refusal to compromise with his vision and prostitute his art. In the concluding scene Clare, back in the asylum, is a wordless, "shrivelled puppet", his face white and nodding like a doll's. Milton brings Patty on a final visit; it is twenty-three years since they last met. Bond has set two modes of judgement resonating in our minds: we register the horror and the pathos of the stage-picture before us, but reach beyond these simple responses to wonder at the strength of the man's truth to self. Lamb, when he observed Clare walking with Mrs. Emmerson in Hyde Park, remarked darkly that the Greeks represented the wisdom of the goddess Athena as an owl, a bird of prey, but "fools have hunted *her* and put her in a cage" [p. 39]. Patty grown mellow in old age cannot at first face meeting Clare, but the act of forcing herself to stay gives her confidence and she relaxes into a greater intimacy with him than she has ever before shown in the play; her sudden gesture of affection is less motivated by pity than a dim apprehension that his fate had a willed purpose:

Sorry you on't had a proper life. Us hev t'make the most what there is. On't us, boy? No use lettin' goo. (*Pats his arm.*) Learn some way t'stay on top.

I'd be a fool t'cry now. [p. 71]

Here is not a scene for tears.

The fool of tradition took on himself the ills of society, saw through the pretensions of the times and was their scourge. So too does Bond's Clare as rebel and martyr. Through eight sharply etched scenes he refocusses our perception about Clare's life, asking us to revalue his madness if we are to honour fully the quality and value of his art as poetry whose very clarity cost him a dear sacrifice. The bitter nature of Clare's genius was that of necessity it isolated him increasingly from the class whose interests it aimed to serve. That Clare accepted that necessity was the mark of his moral courage: he never betrayed his belief in the sanity of his perceptions. The power of the play lies in Bond's handling of dramatic structure to make us see both why his age chose to judge Clare as it did and why as a mark of cultural faith we must judge differently. For Bond, the history play is our means of reclaiming the past.

The difficulty for actors with Bond's plays is the temptation to explain a character rather than evoke it; to do so risks destroying much of the challenge of the play for the audience, which lies in their growing perception of the complexities of moral choice confronting both the characters and themselves. This point has been illustrated by Simon Callow's observations on the trouble he had rehearsing Lord Are in *Restoration* (Royal Court, 1981).[34] Are is a cynical aristocrat who kills his wife and contrives that one of his servants, Bob Hedges, should hang for it. Callow saw Are as the villain of the play, "a machiavel, a devil, a daemonic, Olivierian figure": he practised a repertoire of sneers and grimaces and, in Stanislavski-fashion, imagined the characters "private life in the Hell-Fire Club". Bond, directing, criticised it all as "too 'emotional', too 'sinister' ".[35] It was a complete misconception of the role that crucially missed the humour. Lord Are, like Mrs. Rafi, is a brilliant recreation of a theatrical type: the fop of Restoration comedy, obsessed with his clothes, his reputation, his wit, his breakfast: "I intend to bequeath posterity the memorial of my life not some snot-nosed brat! If I have a boot or cape named after me — as I hope to have a hat — I shall be content" [p. 12]. The tone is a careful pastiche of that specific dramatic style — "I hate the gross odours the country gives off. 'Tis always in a sweat" [p. 5] — and Callow was playing instead in the manner of nineteenth-century melodrama. Inevitably the result was leaden, because he was simplifying, acting his *judgement* of the character as a dastard.

The villain of melodrama is consciously wicked and relishes the fact; Restoration cynics like Horner in *The Country Wife* and men of mode like Etherege's Dorimant have no moral sense: their conduct is determined entirely by what they deem the privileges of their position in society. Callow finally broke through to Bond's conception of Are when the dramatist observed: "Don't you see, when he talks to the audience, he's talking to his friends. He expects them to agree with him". Callow adds: "It all came in a great rush. The essential sunniness of the man's temperament became clear. His whole life is played out in the confidence of his friends' approval; and what else matters to a gentleman?"[36] Nothing must disturb Are's pose of easy indifference, his level tone, his absorption in himself — not even murder.

Bond's strategy with the character is clearly apparent from this. In a long opening soliloquy Are introduces himself. 'Soliloquy' is interestingly Callow's term for the scene; there is in fact a servant present, helping the Lord to arrange himself picturesquely against a tree where Are chooses to be seen first by his intended bride as the acme of fashion in matters of courtship. Are has a sketch to hand of the ideal pose for a love-sick gallant and it is the servant's duty to ensure Are's success in copying the image to the last detail. Frank, the valet, speaks only to flatter Are's self-image; he has no independent opinion; the scene *is*, perversely, a soliloquy. The audience laughs at a recognisable type, encouraged to do so by his blissful conceit; the assumption always is that this is how one ought to behave. Are is joined by ironmaster Hardache and his daughter Ann to arrange a marriage that provides the Lord with some convenient cash to defray his debts and the wife-to-be with a convenient title to satisfy her aspirations. The staple themes of Restoration drama — marriage and money — are the focus but motives and appetites are treated with a forthright nakedness uncharacteristic of the prototype: 'Must have' is the recurrent verb throughout the scene. Are's apparent vigour affords Ann no lubricious thoughts; she sees it as a sign that her father is failing in his proper duty to his daughter in not giving her easy access to a prosperous widowhood: "Can't you find one in a wheel-chair or at least on a crutch so a body might hope? Did you enquire if the family die young? No — you are a thoughtless man father" [p. 7]. It is not lust for physical satisfactions that drives these characters on, but desire for the privileges of wealth; and these are rapidly being defined as the chance to be free of moral concerns. In one swift scene, the wit, the tone, the heartless cynicism and the subject matter of Restoration comedy are deftly evoked; so too is the conventional displacement of the servants in such drama to the periphery of the action.

The servants become, however, Bond's chief concern, more particularly the attitude of mind that keeps them in a state of subservience. They have no illusions about Are and his new Lady but they will suffer any treatment at their hands rather than jeopardise their own security: "Ont git another job with a bad name" [p. 15]. When Frank is discovered by Bob and his mother, the housekeeper Mrs. Hedges, to have stolen some silver, they find it necessary to salve their own consciences, even though he hands it back, to make him a prisoner in the kitchen and report his theft: "I lose my silver I lose my job" [p. 15]. *Security* means being in his Lordship's favour. Rose, Lady Are's fashionable "little black maid", is a slave's child from the West Indies; taught by her mother a slave's cunning, she is astonished by the servants' lack of anger, by their acceptance of the pattern of their lives in gratitude. Rage is the source in her of energy and intelligence. When Bob becomes the scapegoat for Are's crime, Rose tries to awaken him to distrust Are's promises of securing a pardon. When that fails, she tries to set Hardache against his son-in-law but miscalculates the depth of the ironmaster's greed: were Are hanged his land would be confiscated; Hardache knows that under the estate there is a coalfield; it is in both their interests that Bob should swing. Rose turns next to Are's mother, trying to excite her hatred of her son into effecting his disgrace or, failing that, to discompose him by using her position as the king's former mistress to achieve Bob's pardon. She uses Are's own standards and practices to frustrate his intentions (rage in her is a controlled impulse of the mind not the emotions), and almost succeeds. But, instead of a last-minute reprieve from the gallows in the manner of *The Beggar's Opera*, Are triumphs and the play concludes with a scene of grim social realism in which Bob is rendered insensible through drink by Rose and the gaoler's wife so that he will not know the full horror of a public hanging.

In the manner of eighteen-century ballad operas like Gay's, Bond frequently disrupts the action with songs. Far from being period pastiche, in his own production the music was aggressively modern and the lyrics were delivered in a forthright manner like the songs in Brecht. The theme is continually judgement:

> The house is on fire
> Dark figures wave from the roof!
> Shall we fetch a ladder

Or light brands to burn down the rest of the street?
    You to whom the answer is easy
    Do not live in our time
    You have not visited our city
    You weep before you know who to pity
    Here a good deed may be a crime
    And a wrong be right
    To you who go in darkness we say
    It's not easy to know the light

                                      [pp. 18-19]

The tone is, like Rose's, one of rage; the effect in performance is to detach one completely from one's experience of the comedy, to see with what, if one laughs along wih Are, one is sharing complicity. We begin to detect behind his pose a steely intelligence (no simple fop, this); his resilience in eluding justice is the measure of how vicious his effrontery is. Bond's control of tone is masterly: Are's witty pose never slips yet he can manipulate events, create scenes, turn seemingly adverse circumstances into his favour with consummate skill. By preserving the level of farce throughout Are's scenes, Bond has us plumb the depths of callousness in the man. Are stabs his wife with a rapier when she comes to him at breakfast dressed like the family ghost (she is trying to frighten him into taking her back to London). His response, typically casual, is to bemoan his reputation now jeopardised and his breakfast now ruined.

    He next summons Bob (Boob as he privately calls him), knowing he can easily exploit the servant's absolute dependence on him; gets him hysterical at the sight of the 'ghost', which Are manipulates like a puppet; encourages him to hold the rapier as a cross to protect himself and, when Bob holds the weapon out blindly at arm's length, sees his advantage and impales Ann afresh. The ever-gullible Bob accepts Are's interpretation of events:

I see it now. A practical joke, a jape. Her ladyship ennuied by rural life — which must be said in her favour — tried thus to brighten our morning. But Bob you have no sense of humour.... This morning you were overzealous. [p. 21]

It is rare that farce carries such a wealth of social and psychological insight. It would be wrong for an actor to act his judgement of the character of Are, for it would prevent an audience experiencing how the man actually sees himself as a product of a specific social milieu. That is to know the real evil of the man and the theatrical type he influenced. His cultivation of *ennui* —

boredom as a principle of being — is seen to be an infinitely subtle means of preserving the *status quo*, to inhabit society as one of its figureheads while observing none of its fundamental obligations. Are's nonchalance continues unabashed: a reprieve is in fact forthcoming through the intrigues of Are's mother but he tricks the officer into letting him deliver the warrant himself, then gives it to the illiterate Mrs Hedges to light the fire with and throws a tantrum with her because she has not laid out a decent suit for him to wear to the hanging. 'The style is the man' was a popular quip of the eighteenth-century; Are's terse, epigrammatic mode of speech, which he himself calls wit since it amuses him vastly, is a way of skimming elegantly over the surface of experience; it never encompasses imaginative engagement with a subject, which is where true sensitivity resides. In his own eyes Are is the epitome of human excellence but by now we know him to be the mere husk of a man and so an obscene outrage as a representative of power and social order.

One can the better appreciate the richness of Bond's achievement if one compares *Restoration* with two other recent history plays about this period. Howard Barker's *Victory* (Royal Court, 1983)[37] examines the consequences of the return of the monarchy through the plight of the puritan Mrs. Bradshaw, widow of one of Charles I's judges, as she tries to recover her husband's skeleton for burial after it is dug up, dismembered and publicly desecrated by the newly triumphant Cavalier faction. Partly the play is concerned to depict the roistering crudity of aristocratic values, which are cavalier in the worst sense of the word: the obsession with sex and with the money that might procure it. The explicitness and obscenity pall because shock is not a response that readily activates imaginative or intellectual discrimination. The power of the play resides in the portrayal of Widow Bradshaw suffering every outrage to her person with a stark dignity, an inner strength, that comes from her determination to honour her husband's corpse. In a world of frenetic sexuality, she alone knows a sense of obligation to another: for all the coarseness of manner she has outwardly to adopt to survive, her essential being is nourished by love. History provides a context for Barker but little more: *Victory* is fundamentally a study of how an individual sustains a private integrity in the face of seemingly overwhelming odds; it is about the astonishing subterfuges necessary to keep alight the spirit in an age of darkness. Other historical periods could have afforded analogous contexts.

This is not true of Timberlake Wertenbaker's *The Grace of Mary*

Traverse (Royal Court, 1985)[38] which makes deliberate use of period idiom and cultural patterns in ways similar to Bond's. She takes the Hogarthian and Fielding-inspired model of the Good and Bad Person's moral progress, the demise of the rake and the rise of the virtuous apprentice; her structure is that of many an eighteenth-century picaresque novel. The difference is that she places a woman at the centre of the action, one who renounces the sheltered life of her sex and class and goes in quest of what she deems a larger reality, which she equates with a man's social freedom. She chooses to live as a man (though in her own person not in disguise) the better to know herself as woman; she seeks a freedom from mental as much as physical and social constraints; refusing to conform to a type, she yearns for individuality. Gambling, sex, business-scheming, the politics of anarchy cannot satisfy her lust for identity; however successfully she assumes masculine attitudes, men can still trick her into an inferior position; she is invariably there for their use. At the last she recognises that to be herself she must work from within, follow no one else's pattern. Much is gained in the play from its exploitation of a recognisable literary and cultural structure and from the final decision to reject that pattern, but the usage is wholly satirical. The play does not (as Bond's *Restoration* does) explore a literary convention or prototype from within, to show how it came into being, what the moral and social values are that it enshrines, and to question how we in a different age ought to relate to it. There is nothing in *The Grace of Mary Traverse* that matches Bond's pressing awareness of how our cultural inheritance can condition our contemporary values. The world of Defoe or Fielding's novels is for Timberlake Wertenbaker a metaphor through which she can satirise what seem to her inadequate, unimaginative Feminist values; the past affords a witty illustration of certain current *mores*. *The Grace of Mary Traverse* stops short of inviting an audience, as *Restoration* does, to live through the process by which a cultural inheritance comes into being.

Bond's most ambitious and indeed his finest play to date is *The Woman* (Olivier, 1978).[39] It differs somewhat from the preceding plays under discussion in being an exploration of the roots of the whole European, rather than specifically English, cultural heritage in Greek drama. It might be argued that the play is more about myth than history and yet at its heart it is debating how much we have kept faith with our cultural past, whether that past works *creatively* in the present, and whether we truly learn from what we designate masterpieces of art. The dominant influences on the conception of *The Woman* are Euripides and Aristophanes, those great questioners of masculine pretension, sophistry and belligerence, who cast such scathing criticism on all apologists for war. Bond like Euripides finds a focus for his compassion in the suffering of certain clear-sighted women trapped by a political process whose augmenting viciousness their male opponents seek to justify on the grounds of necessity. Both dramatists turn for their subject matter to Homer and the Trojan War.

The Woman begins at the moment of Priam's death. The Greek commanders meet to revise their campaign and imagine life inside Troy. Bond originally conceived here an inserted scene for Hecuba and her family haggling for power over Priam's corpse. In rehearsal the lines were re-allocated to the Greeks so that, as it was performed, the scene beccame a vicious parody with Hecuba's grief exposed to her enemies' derision [pp. 16-17]. With squeaking falsetto, bent arms simulating pendulous dugs, old Nestor travesties the Queen as a whore whose histrionics are shrewdly calculated political moves to oust her son from inheriting crown and power. This image of a woman is a compound of fear, hate and malice, the essence of propaganda. The change in production was a masterstroke welding narrative compactly with thematic intent. Bond's Trojan War is a struggle to possess not Helen of Sparta but a statue of the Goddess of Fortune, an ancient talisman believed to ensure fertility and concord. Greeks and Trojans worship a feminine principle as controlling the universe and human destiny, yet in the issue of the war deny the very demands of that ideal preferring the easier masculine code of political necessity, which is an excuse rather than a justification not only for warfare but for any form of anarchy. The double-thinking is ingrained. In scene after scene the different working of male and female minds is exactly rendered: in a private moment, for example, Ismene, wife of Heros the Greek commander, shares her reverie with her husband:

ISMENE: I wonder what she'll look like.
HEROS: You won't see for paint. Her husband married her [Hecuba] when he was old. That's the most ruttish sort of infatuation. My father met her. He understood Priam. All that old man's excesses lie at her door. She pushed him.
ISMENE: I meant the statue.
HEROS: Ah. When I was a child people still called Troy the fabulous city of the East. We played sacking Troy. [p. 20].

It is convenient for men to see themselves as victims of the power they wield, as subject to the will and needs of the country they claim they rule; it saves them from the need to be truly courageous and act creatively, be original. The war is at a stalemate because each side knows the other will move along set ways.

With a woman in power in Troy there is a chance of change and Ismene is sent with the next Greek embassy to the city. She and Hecuba unite to try and end the senseless massacre: the Trojans will give the Greeks the statue but keep Ismene as hostage to guarantee they return to Athens without pillaging the city; she will be an emblem of the Greeks' keeping faith, a symbol of trust, and will be returned to her husband when his army has left in peace. It is a superb move, a feat of imaginative daring. The women are defeated by the forces of superstition and bloodlust motivating soldiers and Trojan populace alike. Desperation triumphs not insight: Troy is sacked; Heros celebrates recovering the statue of Fortune with unstinting atrocity; Ismene is immured alive for her treachery; the wealth of suffering about her dehumanizes Hecuba, who blinds herself rather than watch her grandson's execution. The woman once worshipped as the Queen of Asia crawls in her own blood to a chorus of Greeks catcalling — "Bitch!" — the insult that most desecrates a woman's essential self, her fertility and intelligence [p.61]. Amidst the smoking ruins Nestor revels, drunk with looting, lauding his virility — himself a caricature now: senile, degenerate.

Bold, clear, visual images throughout advance the narrative and crystalise memorably the deeper intricate resonances of the dialogue which define Bond's argument. The terse, pithy sentences are a fine stimulus to the imagination. Bond does not strive after the poetic but, being keenly responsive to the fluctuations of the characters' moods, his pared style is rapidly invested with a dense texture of implication, ironies and witty nuance. The first encounter of Hecuba and Ismene has an exemplary brilliance. With a cool politeness edged about with insults each tests the other's will, searching for a weakness, an exposed nerve through which to shake the other's pose of confidence:

ISMENE: You've been misjudged. But what can I do? Return the statue — then we can leave you in peace.
HECUBA: One good reason?
ISMENE: The plague! Set us free — all of us — and I'll kiss your hand when we go!
HECUBA: Why should I trust your husband?
ISMENE: The Greeks. Athens is a republic.
HECUBA: Your husband.

ISMENE: He's not only handsome — *he's* a born leader. He makes good decisions.

HECUBA: He married you. Though I ask myself why. I ask for the sake of my people. I must understand him. You're not the most beautiful woman in the world.

ISMENE: No. Now let's talk about what we —

HECUBA: Perhaps you're the wisest? Or the best?

ISMENE: No.

HECUBA: What a pity. At your age I was sensational. A great beauty! I wish you'd seen me. They called me the Venus of Asia. Of course you know that. I can still see it in the glass. [p. 30]

Almost despite themselves, however, they begin to speak the truth, sensing a shared misery and outrage at their political impotence. Hesitantly, all but unconsciously under the waspish banter, they have pledged a trust which gives Ismene the courage to volunteer herself as hostage. Emotional intricacies here are conveyed with astonishing clarity. How perfectly timed and judged is the intrusion of the child, Astyanax, into the scene, his innocence — "I can make houses out of paper. . . . (*to Ismene*) You're a sad lady . . . Are you sad because you'll lose the war? When you're in prison I'll come and show you how to make houses out of paper. Can I grandma?" — offsetting the delicate political manoeuvring and the sharpened sensibilities of the two women. Ismene's sadness here is in part a reflection on her own childless condition. The pathos of this impressed one because of the way Bond as director staged the earlier scene of intimacy between Ismene and Heros. She is preparing for bed; he writes a report for Athens. The tone is one of shared confidences yet, as we have seen, their musings are along quite separate paths: he as always trying to justify himself to himself, as if dimly aware of his constant betrayal of his humanity. And there is no physical contact between them that might bridge the divide and heal Heros's torn psyche. The setting was of the simplest: an arrangement of white sheets on the floor in which Ismene lay waiting for Heros to join her. As his mind moved from his report to the need to inspect the sentries, give commands, she slowly wound the sheets around her till, when he suddenly left, she lay enshrouded like a corpse, emblem of the spiritual reality of their marriage. (Later at her trial for treason, he will accuse her of being an unyielding virgin, forever taking but incapable of giving.) It was by such directorial images that Bond invested the dialogue with its wealth of unstated implication. How painful at the conclusion of that scene was Heros's observation that his fingers in the moonlight looked like five white towers [p. 21]; the hand as emblem of power, not a sentient reality shaped to caress!

The nightmare world of war and diplomacy gives place in Act Two to an open seascape. Years have passed; Hecuba, while being carried to Greece, has been shipwrecked on an island; she guards its shrine and protects Ismene (saved from death by looting soldiers but left a mindless child). Her mothering of Ismene is the one human consideration that disturbs the elemental calm that Hecuba has discovered beyond heartbreak and desperation. Care alone humanizes her as she sits in her rags like a primitive stone carving amongst the rocks on the shore. It was another fine directorial image that Hecuba came increasingly to look like the statue of the goddess, seen fleetingly in the sacking of Troy: mutilated, a wasted skeleton, yet a prodigious force of mind. Heros reappears; Athens is rebuilt, wealthy, a monument of male design, power and rationality. Yet Heros needs Hecuba in Athens to settle his private guilt and Athens needs the statue of Fortune to perfect its security. Irrationality and superstition still bedevil the grand design. To experience Hecuba's inner strength, as Bond encourages us to do, is to realise the degree to which Heros's victory was Pyrrhic, as he has in chagrin to admit. He only respects power and power now resides with Hecuba:

Your're strong. You have nothing and want nothing, so you have nothing to lose. Yet you have what I want. No power on earth can move you. I'm in your power. I've never been in this situation before. [p. 81]

It is Hecuba's mind refined by pain that is the source of her power, as Heros intuitively perceives (perhaps that ironically is the secret of Fortune), but he rationalises that awareness, explains it as an enemy's cunning revenge, because he suspects she knows the whereabouts of the statue lost in the sea during the same shipwreck that stranded her on the island. Nothing that Hecuba can do can arrest that suspicion, that she is lying to him in denying any such knowledge in order to glory in his humiliation. Judging, he stands judged, relentlessly. This point was again imaginatively amplified in production by a remarkable sequence of gestures. Heros was fascinated by Hecuba's eyes; only one was completely savaged in her grief, the other was partially damaged and is covered now for protection from the light. As they talked, Heros repeatedly put his arm about Hecuba turning her towards him; from him it seemed a surprising gesture of amity, till one realised he was trying to position her so that he could see her eye behind its veil and confirm his belief that she is telling him lies. Sensing his intent, Hecuba sank

to the ground keeping her face covered, unresponsive to his
cajoling tones which she clearly recognised as deceit, a strategy to
test her guard; and he, behind her, wiped his hand on his uniform
as if nauseated at touching filth. Then he asked nakedly to see her
eye, still unwilling to show or recognise trust.

Heros decides that, as the statue was lost in the shipwreck, the
Greeks will compel the islanders to dredge the sea till it is found.
Hecuba watches Heros's mania grow, knowing that he can never
accept failure and that if the statue is not found he will destroy the
islanders out of duty to Athens. Cleverly she traps Heros,
unsuspecting, in the web of his own obsessions and brings about
his death, inventing a scenario for his demise in which he appears
to be the victim of that very Fortune he claims all along controls
men's lives. Her private revenge is exacted but she works only to
safeguard the freedom of the islanders from Greek exploitation and
preserve their life of unsophisticated pieties. It is the presentation
of this people uncontaminated by political sophistry as the
background to Hecuba's psychological combat with Heros that
communicates a potent sense of the nature of invasion. The
islanders' life in time is entirely suffused with ritual; work and play
are an expression of faith. When Nestor applauds some girls
dancing and, clapping his hands, attempts to instigate a repeat
performance, he is courteously but firmly informed that he is not
being entertained: "The dance is over for the year. We can't dance
it twice. . . . If we danced something else we wouldn't catch fish!"
[p. 102]. Everything in the islanders' experience has a like sacred
decorum; but their simplicity does not make them seem naive,
rather by contrast, it renders Nestor gross. As Heros is transformed
by his encroaching madness, so his former wife Ismene is
transformed by joy. She finds on the island a dark man, a nameless
slave, his body crippled and stained by years of labouring in the
Greek silver mines, from which he has escaped. The child-woman
and the mis-shapen dwarf make an ill-assorted couple yet their
strengths and limitations are complementary and they grow into a
mutual dependence; it is a depiction of the power of love to heal
that is quite free of sentimentality. One of Bond's most
courageously daring scenes in a play of such tragic import involves
a game of tickling between the couple in which they include
Hecuba, where all three wholly abandon themselves to the pleasure
of laughter, spontaneous, rich, unselfconscious. This is true
freedom, joy in the reaches of the soul, not Heros's *pax Athenaea*.
It is this honesty, this trust (so innate a part of daily life on the
island that the inhabitants are oblivious of the real value of such

qualities) that Hecuba risks everything to protect: she, the most astute political intelligence in the play, has come through tides of suffering to *know* their worth as essential to a proper humanity. And she knows Heros better than he knows himself, how he pollutes and perverts the lives of people wherever he goes with his unending suspicion of their motives and his double-thinking: "It's not to protect the city. Or make me famous," he says of his inexorable quest for the statue, "It's a millstone round my neck. God rot it. I must close the past! Say: finished, complete" [p. 86]. He is a death-bringer and the only freedom he will ever find from his torment is in death. Hecuba accepts that it is she alone who can complete the pattern of events.

The Woman marked Bond's debut as a director and a most thrilling experience it proved for audiences. His plays demand scrupulous attention to their inner dynamics, their subtle strategies of tonal balance, contrast, varied points of focus; though a challenging didactic writer, he is never (at his best) explicit, dogmatic. But for the experience of his plays to be exploratory for an audience, a director must find ways of allowing the dense texture of implication in Bond's writing to register fully. His language is compelling when actors do not *point* it in a manner that explains its significance and so limits the range of reference. Disciplined restraint was the hallmark of his production. Each of the numerous scenes was remarkable for a quality of stillness that was not posed like a tableau but alive with energy. Bond's policy seemed to be one of richness through austerity which made for a particularly bold handling of the epic dimensions of the Olivier stage, backed simply in Hayden Griffin's design by great steel shutters that at first represented the walls of Troy then, lit horizontally with slowly undulating lights, evoked an endless vista of sea. There were powerful full-stage effects: the plague-women let out of Troy and swaying, black-veiled, towards the Greek army like vultures on the wind of prey; Ismene, floodlit, addressing the Greek camp from the walls of Troy while in silhouette the soldiers clattered swords on shields to drown her appeal; the poor of Troy swarming from every corner of the stage into the temple to seize the statue; the final race and sacrifical murder of Heros: his naked white body and spurting blood caught for a moment as if transfixed in time, vulnerable, isolated against a cast and setting uniformly grey and silver. But it was the attention to language, the tones that allowed every nuance of meaning, every least resonance its full weight, that most captured the imagination. Poetic drama with this magnitude of scope requires tense concentration from an audience if the relation of detail to larger structural patterning is to be appreciated; by refining detail to the absolutely essential in each scene Bond ensured our rapt engagement with the psychological strategies of his characters out of which the play's narrative structure grows. His characters shape events out of the depths of self. At the point at which *The Woman* was staged in the Olivier, Greek tragedy had been conspicuous for its absence from the National's repertoire. The explanation offered was that the company were searching for a suitable style. Appropriately in rediscovering through *The Woman* the grounds on which we should respect Greek tragedy, Bond, as director, found a style that was ideal for staging the prototype, for it too refines in order to intensify.[40] *The Woman* as text and as performance was a brave act of cultural reclamation.

Since *The Woman* and *Restoration* Bond has written only one further historical play, *Summer (Cottesloe, 1982)*,[41] about the consequences in everyday lives of the last World War and the effects in the present of choices made then about whether to resist or be compliant with Nazism. Xenia used her father's 'friendship' with the Germans to free Marthe, their servant, when she was arrested as a hostage:

You were standing beside an officer. You held the strap of your patent leather handbag in both hands. The soldier saluted. You nodded. . . .The officer clicked and saluted you. I followed you to the landing place and on to the military boat. . . . I spent the next day in my room. I heard the shooting from there. [p. 26]

Xenia is proud of that moment, her tone continually affirms it years after the event. Their fortunes have changed: Xenia, married, lives these days in another country; Marthe, as a consequence of a new political regime, now owns by right the house which she entered as a servant; if Xenia visits, she comes as Marthe's guest. Yet, whatever the social changes effected by time, Xenia always sees Marthe as subservient: it is intimated in her every tone. Marthe is dying; it will be their last time together; Marthe summons her failing strength to insult Xenia, to spit in her face with a passionate hatred; her gesture, she explains, is on behalf of the hundreds of her countrywomen who, trapped as hostages, were not saved, which is cause for a profound humility.

Hecuba, when she re-meets Nestor years after the sacking of Troy, affirms: "The past gives nothing back, so why should I let it manage my life now?" Hecuba does not brood in rancour on the past but it informs creatively every second of her life in the present.

Similarly Marthe: her anger is not all-consuming; she can welcome her son's love for Xenia's daughter and as a token of keeping faith with their future prepare them a breakfast table with such loving care that it seems an age-old ritual celebrating the essential pieties of the home. In the pain of death, she honours life. It was a mesmeric moment in performance, when Yvonne Bryceland as Marthe arranged the objects like a still-life:

Pour the milk in a jug. A jug to make the table beautiful. . . . It will be beautiful. You'll think of me with fondness. Put a chair in front of each place. [p. 48]

A fragile emblem, perhaps, to shore against the ruin and waste of war, but an enduring and timeless image of peace and hope. If *Summer* for all its excellence seems a chamber play beside *The Woman* (to the second act of which it relates as a kind of thematic commentary) that is less because its focus is limited to only five characters than because it lacks that dimension where Bond examines art and culture as the long-term repository of our historical awareness, the medium through which history can and should most directly impinge on our contemporary experience. Since *Summer* Bond has conceived plays as parables showing through imagined futures the possible consequences of current social values. He invites us, in works like *The War Plays* (The Pit, 1985)[42], to project ourselves forward in time and conceive *now* as history. To know the present, he would seem to argue, we must engage imaginatively with the past as our inheritance and with the future as within our gift. His is a profoundly healthful vision. It is Bond's firm rejection of the belief that time is the determiner of human destiny that makes his history plays passionate, poetic conceits of infinitely complex reference. *The Sea, Bingo, The Fool, Restoration* and, above all, *The Woman* are theatre-poetry of the highest order.

NOTES

(Full bibliographical details of plays discussed in this study are given in these notes. Page-references included after quotations in the body of the text are to the editions cited here.)

Chapter One: HAROLD PINTER

1. Harold Pinter: *Landscape and Silence*, (Methuen), London, 1969.
2. Peter Hall: "Is The Beginning The Word", *Theatre Quarterly*, Vol. II, No. 7, July-Sept., 1972, p. 10.
3. Harold Pinter: *Old Times*, (Methuen), London, 1971.
4. This is another point of resemblance between *Old Times* and Strindberg's late works, such as *Dream Play*, *To Damascus* and the chamber plays, which often require the settings to appear to change while remaining in essence the same. The implication being that however much the characters wish to change their environment, they are always trapped in a void: spiritually they can effect no change in their condition.
5. Caryl Churchill: *Traps*, (Pluto Plays), London, 1978.
6. E. A. Whitehead: *Old Flames*, (Faber), London, 1976.
7. E. A. Whitehead: *Alpha Beta*, (Faber), London, 1972.
8. Harold Pinter: *The Proust Screenplay*, (Methuen with Chatto and Windus), London, 1978.
9. Harold Pinter: *No Man's Land*, (Methuen), London, 1975. The play was first published in *The New Review*, Vol. 2, No. 13, April, 1975, pp. 3-18. Page-references are to the more accessible Methuen text.
10. The phrase is Villiers de l'Isle Adam's ("As for living, our servants will do that for us"). It was a popular pose in *fin de siècle* artistic circles in the Eighteen Nineties.
11. See pp. 155-164.
12. Kenneth Tynan: *Show People*, (Weidenfeld and Nicolson), London, 1980, p. 30.
13. Harold Pinter: *The Hothouse*, (Methuen), London, 1980.
14. Harold Pinter: *Betrayal*, (Methuen), London, 1978.
15. David Mercer: *No Limits to Love*, (Methuen), London, 1980.
16. Harold Pinter: *Other Places: Three Plays*, (Methuen), London, 1982. *Family Voices* had previously been published as a "play for radio" by Next Editions in 1981, where the text was illustrated with seven paintings by Guy Vaesen. This play was also broadcast and given as

a platform performance in the Lyttleton before the collection of three plays was staged by Peter Hall in the Cottesloe in 1982.

17. In tragic situations this can endow Judi Dench's performance with a vulnerability and pathos that are the more poignant for being incidental rather than sought for or forced. One recalls her utterly self-less commitment to her husband's cause as Lady Macbeth (1976-78), unfliching till her very will and stamina broke down. The complex transitions involved in playing this character were lucidly structured, the nightmares of the sleepwalking scene being foreshadowed in her departure from the banquet, dragged away like a lifeless doll on Macbeth's arm, her every physical and mental resource drained away by her prodigious efforts at shielding his honour and reputation; her ambition was solely to realise his desires, her actions were constant proof of her unstinting devotion.

18. On this occasion *A Kind of Alaska* was played with *Victoria Station* and *One For The Road*. The director was Kenneth Ives.

19. Harold Pinter: *One For The Road*, (Methuen New Theatrescripts), London, 1984.

20. The television production of the play lost much of the subtlety of Bates's conception by continually photographing him from unusual, generally low-positioned camera-angles that distorted his features and made him look a real brute. This gave the spectator an immediate judgement of the character so that the play became a demonstration of evil rather than an imaginative discovery, which was the effect of Bates's performance in the theatre.

21. The words are Bosola's, explaining his motives in torturing the Duchess of Malfi with a series of psychological horrors. See John Webster: *The Duchess of Malfi*, IV. ii. 177.

Chapter Two: NEW FORMS OF COMEDY: AYCKBOURN AND STOPPARD

1. Joe Orton: *What The Butler Saw*, (Methuen), London, 1969.
2. See Katharine J. Worth's witty account of the play in *Revolutions in Modern English Drama*, (Bell), London, 1973, pp. 150-156.
3. Alan Bennett: *Habeas Corpus*, (Faber), London, 1973.
4. At the end of the play the characters quite literally climb out of the farce setting, which has become an intricate trap sprung about them all, into a blinding light. They are naked, bruised, blood-stained but unbowed and beyond shame.
5. *The Guardian*, May 11, 1973.
6. Alan Bennett: *Forty Years On*, (Faber), London, 1969.
7. Alan Bennett: *Getting On*, (Faber), London, 1972.
8 Alan Bennett: *The Old Country*, (Faber), London, 1978.
9. Peter Nichols: *The National Health*, (Faber), London, 1970.
10. Peter Nichols: *Privates on Parade*, (Faber), London 1977.

11. Peter Nichols: *Poppy*, (Methuen), London, 1982.
12. Peter Nichols: *Chez Nous*, (Faber), London, 1974.
13. Peter Nichols: *Passion Play*, (Methuen), London, 1981.
14. Michael Frayn: *Alphabetical Order and Donkeys' Years*, (Methuen), London, 1977.
15. Michael Frayn: *Clouds*, (Samuel French), London, 1977.
16. Michael Frayn: *Noises Off*, (Methuen), London, 1982.
17. Michael Coveney. "Scarborough Fare: An Interview with Alan Ayckbourn", *Plays and Players*, Vol. 22, No. 12, September, 1975, p. 16.
18. Alan Ayckbourn: *Living Together* from the trilogy, *The Norman Conquests*, (Penguin), Harmondsworth, 1983, p. 109.
19. Alan Ayckbourn: *Absurd Person Singular* in *Three Plays*, (Penguin), Harmondsworth, 1979. *Bedroom Farce* and *Absent Friends* are included in this edition.
20. Alan Ayckbourn: *Three Plays*.
21. Alan Ayckbourn: *Joking Apart and Other Plays* (*Just Between Ourselves*, *Ten Times Table* and *Sisterly Feelings*), (Penguin), Harmondsworth, 1982.
22. Ibid.
23. *Three Plays*, Preface, p. 9.
24. Alan Ayckbourn: *Way Upstream*, (Samuel French), London, 1983.
25. Alan Ayckbourn: *Joking Apart and Other Plays*.
26. Alan Ayckbourn: *A Chorus of Disapproval*, (Faber), London, 1986.
27. Tom Stoppard: "Ambushes for the Audience: Towards a High Comedy of Ideas", *Theatre Quarterly*, IV, No. 14 (May-June 1974), p. 8.
28. Tom Stoppard: *Rosencrantz and Guildenstern Are Dead*, (Faber), London, 1967.
29. Tom Stoppard: *Jumpers*, (Faber), London, 1973. The text of the play has several times been revised while revivals were in rehearsal.
30. Tom Stoppard: *Every Good Boy Deserves Favour* and *Professional Foul*, (Faber), London, 1978.
31. Tom Stoppard: *Dogg's Hamlet, Cahoot's Macbeth*, (Faber), London, 1980.
32. Tom Stoppard: *Dirty Linen* and *New-Found-Land*, (An Ambiance/Almost Free Playscript), London, 1976.
33. Tom Stoppard: *Night and Day*, (Faber), London, 1978.
34. Tom Stoppard: *Rough Crossing*, (Faber). London, 1985.
35. Tom Stoppard: *The Real Thing*, (Faber), London, 1982.
36. Both Paul Shelley and Michael Pennington essayed the role before the end of the London run. The key to Roger Rees's success has been wittily defined by the actor himself in an essay he has written about creating the role of Posthumus in Shakespeare's *Cymbeline*: "I can readily understand why as an actor I was attracted to the character's plainness and lack of sparkle; for some time I'd been cornering the market in chaps unheroic, blokes like Roderigo in *Othello* . . . Gratiano in *The Merchant of Venice* . . . Aguecheek in *Twelfth Night*

. . . and . . . Baron Tusenbach in Tchekov's *Three Sisters*. . . . All these characters fail, either in life or as personalities. But I was attracted to them as men who are lucky enough to glimpse, each of them, one small inch of mastery in their lives; all find a tiny moment of decorum and dignity that they never expected they were capable of" (*Players of Shakespeare*, edited by Philip Brockbank, Cambridge University Press, Cambridge and London, 1985, p. 142). The role of Henry in *The Real Thing* certainly has sparkle, but the character's central dilemma is how to face cuckoldom and retain a degree of dignity, how to be faithful in a world where most individuals are quietly or flagrantly promiscuous, and not appear a sentimental fool. Rees contrived to make Henry the moral centre of the play while being exuberant, warm and convincingly tender.

37. Tom Stoppard: *Travesties*, (Faber), London, 1975.
38. See Act One of Wilde's comedy and *Ulysses*, (Penguin Modern Classics), Harmondsworth, 1969, pp. 586-658.
39. *Ulysses*, pp. 254-6.
40. Several other plays in the period have used a comic structure as a base from which to conduct debates about aspects of twentieth-century cultural history but none of these achieves the richness and density of Stoppard's *Travesties*. David Pownall's *Master Class* (Old Vic and Wyndham's, 1984) looked at the impact of Stalin and Zhdanov's cultural 'reforms' though their brow-beating and demoralising of Prokofiev and Shostakovich; the structure deployed was that of the traditional, realist, well-made play and this was wittily appropriate since Stalin's ambition is to make all artists conform to a style of social realism. The mental anguish of the two composers has to be conveyed entirely by implication. Christopher Hampton's *Tales from Hollywood* (Olivier, 1983) employs a fantasy structure, imagining that von Horvath escaped the Nazis and joined the many Germans who sought exile in California and an income from working in the cinema industry. Essentially Hampton's chosen structure allows him to explore how a number of artists coped with the fact of exile and with the eccentric life-style of Hollywood. Horvath is a sad-eyed, world-weary ghost viewing the proceedings and linking the scenes together in the manner of a commentator/compère. A conflict of ideals and principles about art is presented through the figures of Brecht and the two Mann brothers, Thomas and Heinrich; but it remains at the level of conflict and never becomes as in *Travesties* a debate; and the element of fantasy never becomes more than a structural device. In *Travesties* fantasy becomes the means of introducing the debate and it provides a measure against which that debate about art and the nature of the human mind can be tested. Dusty Hughes's *The Futurists* (Cottesloe 1986) for all its elements of theatrical spectacle largely took the form of a documentary history about the situation of artists in Russia immediately after the Revolution. As such, it offered an interesting

commentary on the sections of *Travesties* devoted to Lenin and Tzara.

Chapter Three: MONOLOGUES AND SOLILOQUIES: SAMUEL BECKETT

1. St. Luke. VI. 37. This is a recurrent concern of contemporary drama: see pp. 207 ff.
2. Peter Nichols: *Forget-Me-Not Lane*, (Faber), London, 1971.
3. Peter Nichols: *Born in the Gardens*, (Faber), London, 1979.
4. Michael Frayn: *Benefactors*, (Methuen), London, 1984.
5. John Osborne: *The End of Me Old Cigar and Jack and Jill*, (Faber), London, 1975.
6. Arnold Wesker, *The Old Ones*, (Cape), London, 1973.
7. Barry Collins: *Judgement*, (Faber), London, 1974.
8. See pp. 12-13.
9. All page references to Beckett's plays given in the remainder of this chapter relate to *Collected Shorter Plays of Samuel Beckett*, (Faber), London, 1984. The recent plays were also published separately by Faber usually to coincide with their first performances.
10. Magee played Hamm in a revival of *Endgame* at the Royal Court in 1976.
11. Beckett's plays bear a marked resemblance to Yeats's but this is one aspect where they differ: in Yeatsian drama the reverie is always "excited", and the voices ring full with an immediacy of feeling.
12. The musical terminology seems apt, since Billie Whitelaw has in her recent revival of the play (Riverside Studios, 1986) begun consciously to 'place' the voice melodically even more than in the initial production; she now sings or intones through words, giving the effect of a sung requiem for the relationship that the play explores. It is as if the voice is dragged out of a well of sleep and pain.
13. The phrase is Yeats's from "At The Hawk's Well" in *Collected Plays*, (Macmillan), London, 1969, p. 208.
14. "A condition of complete simplicity/(Costing not less than everything)". See T. S. Eliot: "Burnt Norton", *Four Quartets*, (Faber), London, 1944, p. 59.
15. Just how important a rigorous observation of that discipline is was evident from the recent revival of *Footfalls* at the Riverside Studios: the lighting here was not, as in Beckett's original production, a thin path at May's feet but a great slab of light like a grave-stone which she paced along. This held some of the right connotations but became in time restrictive. Also the light was focused from immediately above the actress so that inevitably her head and shoulders were more pronouncedly lit than was the case when the light suffused upwards from the ground. The final 'mirage' effect, that was so moving a conclusion to Beckett's production, was quite lost. Also the lighting designer chose to add a further strip of vertical light to stage left of the

pacing figure; this was immensely intrusive, serving no symbolic function whatever; and it distracted attention from Billie Whitelaw, as one had consciously to turn one's head away from the glare. Beckett's prescriptions for the staging of his plays have to be followed meticulously.

Chapter Four: POETIC NATURALISM: DAVID STOREY

1. "The Theatre of Life: David Storey in interview with Peter Ansorge", *Plays and Players*, Vol. 20, No. 12, September, 1973, p. 32.
2. David Storey: *Early Days, Sisters* and *Life Class*, (Penguin), Harmondsworth, 1980.
3. "The Theatre of Life", p. 32.
4. David Storey: *The Restoration of Arnold Middleton*, (Samuel French), London, 1967.
5. David Storey: *In Celebration* and *The Contractor*, (Penguin), Harmondsworth, 1971.
6. Both roles were originally performed by Alan Bates. Throughout the period under discussion he has established a reputation as a stage-actor as distinct from his career in films in a range of roles that have required him to play the part of a witty but lethal stage-manager of crises in other people's lives, the most recent being the title role in Peter Shaffer's *Yonadab* (Olivier, 1985).
7. Henry James: "Guy de Maupassant", *The House of Fiction*, edited by Leon Edel, 1957, p. 161.
8. *The Contractor* was initially printed in *Plays and Players* in December, 1969. I have used the text printed with *In Celebration* by Penguin Plays, which is cited above in note 5.
9. David Storey: *Home, The Changing Room* and *Mother's Day*, (Penguin), Harmondsworth, 1978.
10. *The Financial Times*, September 23, 1976.
11. *Sisters* has been published by Penguin Plays along with *Early Days* and *Life Class* in the edition cited above in note 2.
12. David Storey: *The Farm*, (Cape), London, 1973.
13. David Storey: *The Changing Room*, (Cape), London, 1972.
14. David Storey: *Cromwell*, (Cape), London, 1973.
15. The words are Matthew Arnold's from the conclusion to his poem, "Dover Beach".
16. David Storey: *Home*, (Penguin), Harmondsworth, 1972. The play was originally published in *Plays and Players* for August, 1970.
17. "The purely literal level has to work first. . . . Leave the audience to fathom the symbolic level." See "The Theatre of Life", p. 35.
18. I have used the text of *Early Days* printed by Penguin Plays with *Sisters* and *Life Class* cited above in note 2.
19. Peter Gill: *The Sleepers Den* and *Over Gardens Out*, (Calder: Playscript 44), London, 1970.
20. Peter Gill: *Small Change*, (Samuel French), London, 1976. The play

was initially published in *Plays and Players* (Act One in Vol. 23, No. 11, August, 1976 and Act Two in Vol. 23, No. 12, September, 1976).

21. "When Peter Gill's production opened at the Royal Court it was played on a 24-foot square, steeply raked stage in which the gradient was 1:8. The stage was constructed of plywood shattering board which came from a building site and was cantilevered so that, when lit, it appeared to be floating. In order to avoid being overly austere the surface of the floor was painted with a collage of images suggestive of the atmosphere of the play." Production Note, *Small Change*, p. 4.

22. ". . . a neat instance of Storey's preference for this pragmatism of the theatre [is] shown in his constant admiration for people who complete a particular action or job on stage — the erection of a tent, the playing of a good day's rugby, the ferryman who knows his boat . . . [Storey:] 'I think that this kind of activity unifies people in a way that perhaps they don't get unified anywhere else. Personal relationships are constantly breaking down. So the only unifying element is work itself. It's not just a personal thing but demands an impersonal contribution. You subject your responses to a more impersonal thing. It gives a structure and a dignity to life — a unity which otherwise may not be there.' " See "The Theatre of Life", p. 35.

Chapter Five: POLITICAL DRAMA AND DAVID HARE

1. John Bull: *New British Political Dramatists*, (Macmillan Modern Dramatists), London and Basingstoke, 1984.

2. Catherine Itzin: *Stages in the Revolution: Political Theatre in Britain since 1968*, (Methuen), London, 1980.

3. *A Short, Sharp Shock for the Government* was the title of a savage satire on new-style Conservatism written by Howard Brenton and Tony Howard in 1980. It was staged at the Theatre Royal, Stratford East in 1980 and published with Brenton's *Thirteenth Night* (Methuen New Theatrescripts), London, 1981.

4. Howard Barker: *No End of Blame*, (Calder: Playscript 99), London, 1981.

5. Howard Barker: *Crimes in Hot Countries*, (Calder: Playscript 107), London, 1984.

6. Howard Barker: *The Castle* and *Scenes From An Execution*, (Calder: Playscript 110), London, 1985.

7. Stephen Poliakoff: *City Sugar*, (Samuel French), London, 1976.

8. Stephen Poliakoff: *Strawberry Fields*, (Methuen New Theatrescripts), London, 1977.

9. Stephen Poliakoff: *Shout Across the River*, (Methuen New Theatrescripts), London, 1979.

10. David Edgar: *Mary Barnes*, (Methuen New Theatrescripts), London, 1984.

11. David Edgar: *Destiny*, (Methuen New Theatrescripts), London, 1976.
12. David Edgar: *Maydays*, (Methuen New Theatrescripts), London, 1983.
13. Howard Brenton: *Christie in Love and Other Plays*, (Methuen Playscripts), London, 1970.
14. Howard Brenton: *Magnificence*, (Methuen Playscripts), London, 1973. The play was first performed at the Royal Court in that same year.
15. "I think one of the glories we've lost in the arsenal of the playwright is to use different styles completely" (Howard Brenton: "Petrol Bombs Through the Proscenium Arch", *Theatre Quarterly*, Vol. V, No. 17, 1975, p. 13).
16. Howard Brenton and David Hare: *Brassneck*, (Methuen), London, 1974.
17. Howard Brenton: *The Churchill Play*, (Methuen), London, 1974. The play was revived at the Other Place and the Warehouse, 1978–9.
18. Howard Brenton: *Weapons of Happiness*, (Methuen), London, 1976.
19. Howard Brenton: *The Romans in Britain*, (Methuen), London, 1980.
20. *The Genius* (Royal Court, 1983) begins with a wonderful premise about a brilliant mathematician who discovers a 'beautiful' equation that, if applied in nuclear physics, would mean the end of the universe. The play explores Lehrer's attempts to flee from his own mind and its creations; but Brenton shies away from examining the full implications of this (he claims he dislikes psychology in the theatre) and the plot loses its initial impetus in a welter of implausible fantasies about a girl-student who discovers the same equation and the attempts of the two mathematical geniuses to elude intelligence agents and political spies who masquerade as students and university personnel. *Bloody Poetry* (Hampstead, 1984) looks at the Byron-Shelley circle and poses any number of interesting questions about the nature of the revolutionary spirit, about the relation of art to politics, and of ideals of free love to physical realities. All are touched on as potentially viable themes for a play but none is extensively developed, so the structure of *Bloody Poetry* is dictated by historical fact; it does not evolve as a consequence of some inner debate and so lacks momentum.
21. Howard Brenton and David Hare: *Pravda: A Fleet Street Comedy*, (Methuen), London, 1985.
22. David Hare: *Knuckle*, (Faber), London, 1974.
23. David Hare: *Fanshen*, (Faber), London, 1976.
24. David Hare: "A Lecture", published with *Licking Hitler*, (Faber), London, 1978, p. 70.
25. David Hare: *Teeth 'n' Smiles*, (Faber), London, 1975.
26. The words are Yeats's from "The Gyres", *Collected Poems*, (Macmillan), London, 1961, p. 337.
27. Barry Keefe: *Bastard Angel*, (Methuen New Theatrescripts), London, 1980.

28. David Hare: *Plenty*, (Faber), London, 1978.
29. There is much here, as in *A Map of the World*, that suggests Pirandello's influence on David Hare. Early in his career Hare translated and adapted Pirandello's *The Rules of the Game* for the National Theatre (New, 1971).
30. John Osborne: *West of Suez*, (Faber), London, 1971.
31. Katharine J. Worth: *Revolutions in Modern English Drama*, (Bell), London, 1973, p. 72.
32. David Hare: *A Map of the World*, (Faber), London, 1982.
33. There are analogies here with the opening sequences of Howard Brenton's *The Churchill Play* (see p. 181). *A Map of the World* similarly exploits a technique of disjunctions but Hare uses a structural device to develop a far more complex debate than Brenton attempts.
34. St. Luke. VI. 37. See too the discussion of this theme in Chapter Three.

Chapter Six: TREVOR GRIFFITHS

1. "A Play Postscript: Trevor Griffiths talks to Nigel Andrews", *Plays and Players*, Vol. 19, No. 7, April, 1972, p. 83.
2. Ibid. p. 82.
3. Trevor Griffiths: *Sam, Sam*, in *Plays and Players*, op. cit., pp. 65-79.
4. *The Times*, February 10, 1972.
5. Trevor Griffiths: *Occupations* and *The Big House*, (Calder: Playscript 62), London, 1972.
6. "A Play Postscript", p. 82.
7. *The Times*, October 14, 1971.
8. The dates of Kingsley's performances referred to are: Hamlet (Other Place and Roundhouse, 1975-76); Baal (Other Place and Warehouse, 1979-80); Mosca (Olivier, 1977); Ford (Stratford and Aldwych, 1979-80); Brutus (Stratford, 1979).
9. Trevor Griffiths: *The Party*, (Faber), London, 1974.
10. Interestingly exactly the same effect was achieved in the recent revival of *The Party* by the R.S.C. (Other Place and Pit, 1985), where the part of Tagg was played by Ian McDiarmid, another actor with customarily a flamboyant, histrionic stage persona.
11. David Mercer: *Cousin Vladimir* and *Shooting the Chandelier*, (Methuen), London, 1978.
12. Trevor Griffiths: *Comedians*, (Faber), London, 1976.
13. *The Financial Times*, January 29, 1976. Irving Wardle wrote of Cranham's performance in comparison with Pryce's that he "converts it from the grotesque to the directly rebellious. Shaven and bullet-headed, Mr. Cranham comes over as a straight urban guerilla performing his routines with ferocious expertise but less than believable as a would-be comedian" (*The Times*, January 21, 1976).

14. One of Cranham's finest performances in the period was in Stephen Lowe's *Tibetan Inroads* (Royal Court, 1981), which tells of a young man who suffers castration, the traditional Tibetan punishment for committing adultery, but who steadily rises above self-pity, channelling his creative energies into building a new society after the Chinese invasion.

Chapter Seven: THE HISTORY PLAY: EDWARD BOND

1. Pam Gems: *Queen Christina*, (St. Luke's Press), London, 1982, n.p.. It was first performed at the Other Place in 1977.
2. Robert Bolt: *Vivat! Vivat, Regina!* (Heinemann), London, 1971.
3. Robert Bolt: *State of Revolution*, (Heinemann: National Theatre Plays), London, 1977.
4. Peter Hall felt this was a mistake on the director's part: "What I read was an anti-Marxist play. Yet in performance it seems to be too soft, too fair, too reasonable, too liberal in its understanding of the extremists' point of view". See *Peter Hall's Diaries*, edited by John Goodwin, (Hamish Hamilton), London, 1983, p. 295.
5. Peter Shaffer: *Amadeus*, (Penguin Plays), Harmondsworth, 1984.
6. "I must be careful that Simon [Callow] does not act Mozart too coarsely, despite the oafishness in the part. Mozart admired grace and precision in everything."
   "As far as Felicity Kendal and Simon are concerned, I almost want them to change roles. I want Felicity to be coarse and common as Constanze, Simon to be refined." *Peter Hall's Diaries*, pp. 462 and 463.
7. For a detailed discussion of this play see pp. 151-155.
8. Caryl Churchill: *Light Shining in Buckinghamshire*, (Pluto Plays), London, 1978.
9. Stephen Poliakoff: *Breaking the Silence*, (Methuen), London, 1984.
10. Peter Barnes: *Laughter!*, (Heinemann), London, 1978.
11. C. P. Taylor: *Good*, (Methuen), London, 1982.
12. Barnes was to return to this theme in *Red Noses*, where it is explored with considerable wit, invention and intellectual discipline. See pp. 266-268.
13. Caryl Churchill: *Cloud Nine*, (Pluto Plays), London, 1979.
14. Caryl Churchill: *Top Girls*, (Methuen: Royal Court Writers Series), London, 1982.
15. Paul Thompson: *The Lorenzaccio Story*, (Pluto Plays), London, 1978.
16. Charles Wood: *'H': or Monologues at Front of Burning Cities*, (Methuen), London, 1970.
17. Barnes has adapted Jonson's *The Devil Is An Ass* and Marston's *Antonio and Mellida* and *Antonio's Revenge* for performance at Nottingham Playhouse.

18. Peter Barnes: *The Bewitched*, (Heinemann), London, 1974.

19. Peter Barnes: *Red Noses*, (Faber), London, 1985.

20. *"Red Noses* at the Barbican: Terry Hands in Interview" in *Plays International*, Vol. 1, No. 1, August, 1985, p. 16.

21. The words are taken from the conclusion to Byron's historical tragedy, *Sardanapalus*; the hero has been defeated in his attempt to institute a new pacifist philosophy throughout his kingdom and end decades of militaristic thinking and values; he believes in man's need to cultivate the life of the mind and of the senses. Rather than submit to capture, imprisonment and execution, he builds a vast funeral pyre and leaps to his death in the flames, voicing the hope that his beliefs and example might profit future ages.

22. From the poem "Summer" which prefaces Bond's play of that same title, published by Methuen, London, in 1982.

23. For much of *Bingo* Shakespeare is a silent, watching presence. With Gielgud in the role the audience were deliberately frustrated in their expectations of hearing his famous, musical voice. It was a potent image for the way the creative impulse is now stifled in Shakespeare and incapable of expression. The casting of Harry Andrews as Lear was nicely judged too: he has made countless appearances on stage, television and film in the role of commanding officer, general, brigadeer, his bearing and clipped delivery making him the ideal embodiment of military values and discipline. As Lear he had to grow out of that image which has almost become a stereotype for him and discover a new, poetic, mystical authority. The choice of actor added immensely to the significance of the play. So too with Coral Browne and Simon Callow: both have a distinctive stage personality: she excels in the role of *grande dame*; he is a wild, untutored actor, needing firm direction to prevent him grabbing an audience's attention at the expense of the rest of a cast; both create a powerfully focussed but slightly uneasy relation with an audience. It is the implications of just such a commanding hauteur that Bond seeks to investigate in Mrs. Rafi and Lord Are. Bond in each of these cases was asking the actor to have the courage to scrutinize his or her own preferred technique and style of playing.

24. Edward Bond: *The Pope's Wedding*, (Methuen), London, 1971.

25. Edward Bond: *Saved*, (Methuen), London, 1971.

26. Edward Bond: *'Early Morning'*, (Calder and Boyars, Playscript 18), London, 1968.

27. Edward Bond: *Narrow Road to the Deep North*, (Methuen), London, 1968.

28. Edward Bond: *Lear*, (Methuen), London, 1972.

29. Edward Bond: *The Sea*, (Methuen), London, 1973.

30. Oscar Wilde: *Plays*, (Penguin), Harmondsworth, 1979, p. 305.

31. William Shakespeare: *The Tempest*, III. ii. 148, *Complete Works*, (Oxford Standard Authors), London, 1954.

32. Edward Bond: *Bingo*, (Methuen), London, 1974.

33. Edward Bond: *The Fool* and *We Come To The River*, (Methuen), London, 1976.
34. Edward Bond: *Restoration*, (Methuen: Royal Court Writers Series), London, 1981.
35. Simon Callow: *Being An Actor*, (Penguin), Harmondsworth, 1984, p. 165.
36. *Ibid.*, p. 134.
37. Howard Barker: *Victory: Choices in Reaction*, (Calder: Playscript 104), London, 1983.
38. Timberlake Wertenbaker: *The Grace of Mary Traverse*, (Faber), London, 1985.
39. Edward Bond: *The Woman*, (Methuen), London, 1979.
40. When Peter Hall finally staged *The Oresteia* at the National Theatre, his production, designed by Jocelyn Herbert, used the great expanse of the Olivier stage in an unadorned fashion very reminiscent of Bond's staging of *The Woman*. Hall similarly deployed as background to his settings the massive steel doors which are a permanent architectual provision in that theatre. Hall's *Diaries*, recording his impressions on visiting rehearsals for Bond's production, immediately comment on the staging: "The big and pleasurable surprise is that it is magnificently staged. The use Bond has made of the Olivier is exemplary, and the visual emblems are superb" [p. 365].
41. Edward Bond: *Summer and Fables*, (Methuen), London, 1982.
42. Edward Bond: *The War Plays*, (Methuen New Theatrescripts), Two Volumes, London, 1985.

Bibliography

(Full bibliographical details of all plays discussed in this study are provided in the Notes after the first mention of the play in the text. What follows is a select, working bibliography of the most valuable background material I have consulted in the form of drama criticism and theatre history.)

Michael ANDERSON: *Anger and Detachment: A study of Arden, Osborne and Pinter*, (Pitman: Theatre Today), London, 1976.

Peter ANSORGE: *Disrupting the Spectacle*, (Pitman: Theatre Today), London, 1975.

John ARDEN: *To Present the Pretence: Essays on the Theatre and its Public*, (Methuen), London, 1977.

C. W. BIGSBY (editor): *Contemporary English Drama*, (Arnold: Stratford-upon-Avon Studies 19), London, 1981.

Michael BILLINGTON: *The Modern Actor*, (Hamish Hamilton), London, 1973.

Peter BROOK: *The Empty Space*, (MacGibbon and Kee), London, 1968.

John Russell BROWN: *Theatre Language: A study of Arden, Osborne, Pinter and Wesker*, (Allen Lane), London, 1972.

Terry BROWNE: *Playwrights' Theatre*, (Pitman: Theatre Today), London, 1975.

John BULL: *New British Political Dramatists*, (Macmillan: Modern Dramatists Series), London, 1984.

Colin CHAMBERS: *Other Spaces: New Theatre and the RSC*, (Methuen Theatrefile), London, 1980.

Tony COULT: *The Plays of Edward Bond*, (Methuen Theatrefile), Revised edition, London, 1979.

Sandy CRAIG: *Dreams and Deconstructions: Alternative Theatre in Britain*, (Amber Lane), London, 1980.

Keir ELAM: *The Semiotics of Theatre and Drama*, (Methuen), London, 1980.

John ELSOM: *Post-War British Theatre*, Revised edition, (Routledge and Kegan Paul), London, 1979.

Peter HALL: *Peter Hall's Diaries*, edited by John Goodwin, (Hamish Hamilton), London, 1983.

Malcolm HAY and Philip ROBERTS: *Bond — a study of his plays*, (Methuen), London, 1980.

Ronald HAYMAN: *The Set-Up: An Anatomy of the English Theatre Today*, (Methuen), London, 1973.

— *The British Theatre Since 1955: A Reassessment*, (Oxford University Press), Oxford and London, 1979.

John HAYNES: *Taking the Stage*, (Thames and Hudson), London, 1986.

Catherine ITZIN: *Stages in the Revolution: Political Theatre in Britain Since 1968*, (Methuen), London, 1980.

Andrew KENNEDY: *Six Dramatists In Search of a Language*, (Cambridge University Press), Cambridge and London, 1975.

Oleg KERENSKY: *The New British Drama*, (Hamish Hamilton), London, 1977.

John McGRATH: *A Good Night Out: Popular Theatre: Audience, Class and Form*, (Methuen), London, 1981.

Rob RITCHIE (editor): *The Joint Stock Book*, (Methuen), London, 1987.

John Russell TAYLOR: *Anger and After*, (Methuen), London, 1969.

— *The Second Wave: British Drama in the Seventies*, (Methuen), London, 1971.

Kenneth TYNAN: *Show People: Profiles in Entertainment*, (Weidenfeld and Nicolson), London, 1980.

Irving WARDLE: *The Theatres of George Devine*, (Cape), London, 1978.

Katharine J. WORTH: *Revolutions in Modern English Drama*, (Bell), London, 1973.

— *Beckett the Shapechanger*, edited by Katharine J. Worth, (Routledge and Kegan Paul), London, 1975.

— *The Irish Drama of Europe from Yeats to Beckett*, (Athlone), London, 1978.

Also of value in the study of the drama of this period are the following magazines and journals: *London Theatre Record* (Ian Herbert), 1981 to the present; *Plays and Players*, (Hansom Books), 1953 to June, 1980; *Plays and Players*, (Brevet Publishing), October, 1981 to the present; *Theatre Quarterly* (British Centre of the International Theatre Institute), 1971 to 1981; *New Theatre Quarterly* (Cambridge University Press), February, 1985 to the present. *Macmillan Modern Dramatists Series* edited by Bruce and Adele King also offers some excellent titles on dramatists of the contemporary British stage: Ayckbourn, Orton, Pinter, Arden, Beckett, Stoppard and Bond.

Index

317